Acclaim for Ann Dou
Previous Books in th

The Mother of All Pregnancy Books

"A book that lives up to its name.... Incredibly comprehensive yet easy to follow."
—*Chicago Tribune*

"The must-read pregnancy book! Ann Douglas has created the most comprehensive guide to pregnancy we've ever seen."
—Denise and Alan Fields, authors, *Baby Bargains*

"At long last, a new pregnancy bible for women of my generation and younger has emerged in the form of *The Mother of All Pregnancy Books*. With humor, sensitivity, an easy, no-jargon style, and a million 'extras' that the leading pregnancy books don't cover, Ann Douglas holds nothing back. Not only do I love this book, but I will use it as a valuable tool in my own work as a women's health author."
—M. Sara Rosenthal, author of *The Pregnancy Sourcebook* and
The Breastfeeding Sourcebook, and founder of www.sarahealth.com

"Start reading this treasure trove even before you get pregnant so you can make it through every jam-packed page before your baby arrives."
—Paula Spencer, "The Mom Next Door" columnist, *Woman's Day*
Magazine; author of *Everything ELSE You Need to Know When You're Expecting*

"Finally, a pregnancy book that includes essential pre-pregnancy concerns, such as planning and physical and emotional preparation! Ann Douglas has written her masterwork *The Mother of All Pregnancy Books* in the same unpretentious, concise style as her Unofficial Guide. She also stays true to her goal of informing parents and prospective parents as completely as possible, so they will be well equipped to sort through the pros and cons of their own life choices as they see them. Not one to forgo difficult issues, her chapter entitled 'When Pregnancy Isn't Perfect' is one of the best I've read, both for its sensitivity and for its emphasis on coping and prevention. This is a book that will serve women and their families well."
—A. Christine Harris, Ph.D., author of *The Pregnancy Journal*

"This is truly 'the mother of all pregnancy books'—an intelligent resource that covers every pregnancy-related topic imaginable in a fun, reassuring way. Ann Douglas has done an exceptional job of arming parents-to-be with the facts they need to make the healthiest possible choices from preconception through postpartum. A must-have!"
—Susan Newman, Ph.D., author of *Parenting An Only Child: The*
Joys and Challenges of Raising Your One and Only

"*The Mother of All Pregnancy Books* is a comprehensive and incredibly informative resource about pregnancy (and what comes before and after!). Ann Douglas tells all in her witty style, entertaining readers along the way. Unlike other pregnancy books, Douglas combines thorough research and reporting with the human touch, offering her own experiences and insight while educating her readers at one of the most important times in their lives. This book is not to be missed!"

—Elisa Ast All, Editor-in-Chief, *Pregnancy Magazine,*
Baby Years Magazine, and iParenting.com

"If you're looking for an all-in-one 'Tell me everything, and tell it like it is' book for your pregnancy, *The Mother of all Pregnancy Books* is it. Not only is this hefty volume filled with facts about fertility, pregnancy and birth, it also contains hundreds of anecdotes from moms who lived—and maybe even loved—pregnancy. Author Ann Douglas knows her stuff, and is wise but not preachy, friendly but not overbearing. Keep this book close at hand for instant guidance through the highs and the lows of this extraordinary time!"

—Nancy Price, ePregnancy.com

"Here's a book that's packed with up-to-date information and practical advice on almost every aspect of pregnancy—from prenatal testing to proper nutrition, from infertility procedures to financial planning, from bedrest to breastfeeding. Yet despite its breadth and depth, the text is not dry or dull. Instead, Ann Douglas's reassuring style and insightful anecdotes make readers feel like they're chatting with a savvy, smart, sympathetic friend."

—Tamara Eberlein, coauthor of *When You're Expecting Twins, Triplets,*
or Quads and *Program Your Baby's Health*

The Mother of All Baby Books

"Indispensable! Every mom and dad should be issued a copy of this book at the hospital!"

—Denise and Alan Fields, authors, *Baby Bargains*

"With humor, sensitivity, an easy, no-jargon style, and a million 'extras' that the leading baby books on the shelves don't cover, Ann Douglas holds nothing back. Finally, a baby book written for women of my generation!"

—M. Sara Rosenthal, author of *The Breastfeeding Sourcebook,* and
founder of www.sarahealth.com

"Down-to-earth, informative, empowering and entertaining, this book holds your hand when you're uncertain, hugs you when you're discouraged, makes you laugh when you're aggravated, and inspires you when you're pushed to your limits. Also, this book doesn't shy away from looking at the issues around childbearing losses. So if you're a mother with special circumstances, you can pick up this book with ease, knowing that your experiences are reflected and gently acknowledged."

—Deborah L. Davis, Ph.D., co-author of *The Emotional Journey of Parenting Your Premature Baby: A Book of Hope and Healing*

"*The Mother of All Baby Books* is an amazing resource that all new mothers will love. Brilliantly presented, the book is both practical and inspirational, and no topic is left unexplored. Ann Douglas is the kind of savvy and reassuring guide that you'll want by your side as you embark on the monumental journey into motherhood."

—Cecelia A. Cancellaro, author of *Pregnancy Stories: Real Women Share the Joys, Fears, Thrills, and Anxieties of Pregnancy from Conception to Birth*

"*The Mother of all Baby Books* provides excellent advice for topics that are easily overlooked during the pregnancy/baby adventure. The real life examples do a superb job supporting these topics in addition to giving you creative ideas on how you can implement these helpful suggestions into your life."

—Sandra Gookin, co-author of *Parenting For Dummies,* and *Parenting For Dummies, 2nd Edition*

"There's nothing like another 'Mother' to help you navigate the amazing first year with a new baby. *The Mother of All Baby Books* has advice for almost everything you'll encounter."

—Paula Spencer, "The Mom Next Door" columnist, *Woman's Day Magazine;* author of *Everything ELSE You Need to Know When You're Expecting*

"A major thumbs-up goes to *The Mother of All Baby Books*—a fabulously written, comprehensive guide to baby care that is definitely a must-read for any parent or caregiver. Full of real-life experiences and wonderful tips, this book answers all those nagging little questions that plague parents, as well as providing scads of valuable ideas on how to do a bang-up job of baby care. It covers the whole spectrum-everything from getting prepped for the magical moments (meeting/greeting your brand-new baby), to brass-tack practicalities, such as choosing a baby carrier. (I'll definitely keep this book close at hand for my own new-baby questions this year!)"

—Jennifer Shoquist, M.D., author of *Potty Training For Dummies*

"Ann Douglas has done it again! Like her pregnancy books, this new baby-rearing guide is comprehensive yet easy to read. Parents will find answers to all their questions, from big decisions ('How do we choose a pediatrician?') to minor matters ('Which wallpaper for the nursery?'), from age-old anxieties ('Is my baby eating enough?') to contemporary concerns ('Should we bank the umbilical cord blood?'). Plus, the book is reader-friendly and fun, with its practical suggestions reinforced by lively anecdotes from savvy, experienced parents."

—Tamara Eberlein, coauthor of *When You're Expecting Twins, Triplets, or Quads and Program Your Baby's Health*

"As the old saying goes, 'Babies don't come with instruction manuals.' Well, Ann Douglas' *The Mother of All Baby Books* is really the next best thing! Covering everything imaginable—from newborn care to bathing basics, babyproofing your home to coping with sleepless nights—you will find ways to nurture this amazing new little person in your life while still keeping your sanity. Ann's wise ideas, researched information and real-life tips will help you make this time even more magical and memorable."

—Nancy Price, Editor, GeoParent.com, ePregnancy.com and ePregnancy Magazine

The Mother of All Parenting Books

"I found this book to be unusually insightful on psychologist issues, whether how to deal with your preschooler's bossiness or an older child's 'attitude' problem. Douglas also offers sane advice on how to maintain those loving feelings for your mate even when you're being torn in too many directions by the early years of childrearing. Her coverage is comprehensive without being stuffy, easy-to-digest without slipping into simplistic solutions. Sure to become a cherished reference."

—Susan K. Perry, Ph.D., author of *Playing Smart: The Family Guide to Enriching, Offbeat Learning Activities for Ages 4-14*, and Fun & Games Expert, ParentCenter.com [and Love Advice columnist for AOL's Netscape.com]

This book has *all* the answers that are missing from other parenting books! It's honest, complete, well researched . . . and not preachy. Finally, a book I can hand to parents with confidence that they will not end up feeling guilty.

—Dr. Cathryn Tobin, author of *The Parent's Problem Solver*

"Expert advice is good. Firsthand knowledge is even better. And the best is Ann Douglas, my favorite fellow-mother-of-four parenting writer, who puts experts and expertise together to help you answer the questions you'll ask yourself again and again between the preschool and preteen years: "Who ARE these people living in my house?" and "Now what do I do?"

—Paula Spencer, "The Mom Next Door" columnist, *Woman's Day*, and contributing editor, *Parenting*

A comprehensive book covering all the basics in which Ann Douglas is engaging, funny and direct. Most importantly, she offers solid, practical parenting advice based on a wealth of research and personal experience. And she doesn't shy away from tackling the more difficult issues, approaching them with a refreshing sensitivity and honesty.

—Stacy DeBroff, author of *The Mom Book, 4,278 Tips for Moms!* and founder of www.momcentral.com

The Mother of All Parenting Books is a comprehensive guidebook designed to help moms and dads cope with the day-to-day demands of parenting. Because this very practical book is written in an easy-to-read, parent-friendly style, it is the kind of book parents can turn to again and again.

—Nancy Samalin, best-selling author of four parenting books including *Loving Your Child is Not Enough* and *Loving Without Spoiling*

Whether you are parenting toddlers or preteens, Ann Douglas turns parents into confident experts. She performs amazing feats of imparting her vast wealth of knowledge in a casual, yet oh, so comprehensive way. *The Mother of All Parenting Books* is for parents who want to be secure and sure of themselves in all aspects of raising their children — from how they feel about being parents to techniques for disciplining and keeping lines of communication open. If you have questions, Douglas's book has the answers.

—Susan Newman, Ph.D., author of *Parenting an Only Child: The Joys and Challenges of Raising Your One and Only*

the
mother
of all
parenting
books

the
mother

The Ultimate Guide
to Raising a Happy,
Healthy Child from
Preschool through
the Preteens

of all

parenting
books

ANN DOUGLAS

WILEY

John Wiley & Sons, Inc.

*To my parents Rod Bolton and the late
Barbara Bolton, for taking on the Mother
of All Parenting challenges—raising me!*

*Dad: you will always be my role model and hero.
Thank you for being my Dad.*

*Mom: You were very much with me during the writing
of this book, even though you are no longer here on
Earth. Thank you for being my Mom.*

Acknowledgments

It's impossible to write a book of this magnitude without tons of behind-the-scenes help from a whole lot of people. So you may want to pour yourself a cup of coffee while I go through my usual round of thank yous. (Those of you who've read my books in the past know that my meaty list of acknowledgements is at least partially to blame for the thickness of my books!)

First of all, I'd like to thank the parents who agreed to serve on the parent advisory panel for this book. Your insights and anecdotes really helped to bring the book to life. Thank you for sharing so much of your parenting wisdom with me: Karen Amyotte, Rita Arsenault, Karen Babichuk, Aubyn Baker, Nicole Barker, Christina Barnes, Jennifer Beauchamp, Shelly Blizzard-Jones, Catherine Blundon, Ed Boose, Susan Borkowsky, Shelley Borle, Vicky Boudreau, Lanny Boutin, Mandy Bridgman, Carol-Anne Brockington, Cindy Buckle, Deidre Byberg, Janice Byer, Rina Carali, Jo-Anne Carmichael, Karen Chamberlain, Jill Chongva, Victoria Coates, Shannon Comire, Michelle Cordeiro, Stacey Couturier, Mary Cragg, Brenda Davie, Tracie DeCecco, Chonee Dennis, Sara Dimerman, Olivia Dirven, Kara Doerksen, Judy Dubois, Julie Dufresne, Paula Edwards, Don Estabrook, Stephanie Estabrook, Maria Ferguson, Natalie Forbes, Anne Gallant, Kristina Garswood, Danielle Gebeyehu, Dale D. Genge, Rhiannon Gibbons, Patti Giroux, Debbie Green, Sandra Grocock, Mary Grzeskowiak, Sue Guebert, Bonnie Hancock-Moore, M.T. Hare, Wendy Hawthorne, Jennifer Henderson, Samantha Howard-Jackman, Tracy Jackson, Angela Hoyt, Tara Bethany Huestis, Lisa Ivaldi, Cathy Kerr, Anne King, Karen Kozma, Cindy Legare, Ellen Limburg, Sheri Lockyer, Sharon Louie, Colleen MacCuaig, Jennifer MacDonald, Stephanie MacDonald, Joan MacNeil, Catherine Marion, Denise Martin, Kathy Matts, Jennie Maynard, Julie McDermott, Sherri McKenna, Melanie McLeod, Charlotte Millington, Rhonda Moffatt, Eve Morgan-Langille, Jacqueline Mosco, Diane Munro, Lisa Murphy, Karen-Anne O'Halloran, Kevin O'Shea, Lusanna O'Shea, Tami M. Overbeck, Kerri Paquette, Anita Paradis, Lana Parsons, Kshama Patel, Leanne Paty,

Diane Pepin, Tina Phelps, Maria Phillips, Marjory Phillips, Merna Prete, Megan Reed, Caroline Rosenbloom, Lisa Rouleau, Lynn Rozon, Shelah Rymill, Jeannine St. Amand, Donna Sanders, Russ Sanders, Denice Schneider, Elouise Simms, Janice Smith, Janie Smith, Christine Latter Stratton, Charlie ten Brinke, Melinda Tuck, Pam Vanderbraak, Kristina Vienneau, Kelly Wall, Amanda Warcholyk, Kathryn Watcham, Tanya Weiner, Cindy White, Judy White, Tammy Whitehouse, Cindy Wilkins, Dorothy Williamson, Joanne Wilson, Lillian Wilson, Lee Ann Xerri, Jodi Yokubowski, and Susan Yusishen.

I'd also like to thank the book's technical reviewers for the many hours and painstaking effort they put into reviewing the manuscript for this book:

- Richard Whatley, M.D., a wise and caring family physician and father of four who is famous for his commonsense approach to family medicine;

- Laura Devine, R.N., a caring and committed nurse and family educator who is one of the most "together" parents I've ever known;

- Cathy L. Kerr, M.A., an early childhood consultant and mother of two and a lifelong friend.

As always, I am grateful to my family and friends for everything they did to keep the rest of my life on track while I was busy writing this book. I owe a particularly enormous debt of gratitude (and a few months' worth of home-cooked meals) to my husband, Neil, whose willingness to pitch in with every conceivable household chore and to whisk all four kids away for days at a time so that I could write in peace is nothing short of heroic.

Last but not least, I'd also like to thank my research assistants Lisa Clarke and Suzanne Boles; the editorial "dream team" at Wiley Publishing Inc., who worked with me on the U.S. edition of this book (take a bow Suzanne Snyder, Roxane Cerda, and Cindy Kitchel); early childhood specialist Doreen Weinschrott, pediatrician Louise Tetrick M.D., and my Canadian editors Michael Kelly and Joan Whitman. I'd also like to thank the countless unsung heroes in the production, sales, and marketing departments who have worked so hard to make "The Mother of All Books" series so successful. I know that when I look back on my publishing career, this series will stand out as one of those once-in-a-lifetime opportunities. Thanks to everyone who has helped to make that possible.

Table of Contents

CHAPTER 10
The Health Department 357

Introduction

Congratulations! You've managed to make it through the first leg of the most grueling marathon known to man: that (at least) 18-year-long endurance test known as parenthood. Now that you've completed the baby and toddler portions of the event, it's time to get psyched for whatever challenges may await you over the next hill or around the next bend.

After all, if there's one thing you can count on when it comes to parenting, it's this: some new challenge is always waiting for you, even if you can't actually see it from where you're standing right now. In fact, if you think about it, raising a child is not unlike running a marathon fully blindfolded: you never have any idea when you're going to step into the next patch of boggy swampland or hit the next patch of rocky terrain.

The Ultimate Personal Growth Experience

As any seasoned parent can tell you, raising a child is the ultimate personal growth experience—an endless opportunity to stretch yourself in all kinds of new and unforeseen directions (and, no, I'm not talking stretch marks here). Just when you think you're getting the hang of caring for a baby, your child morphs into a toddler, giving you the opportunity to hone your patience skills to such a degree that you figure you should pretty much be a shoo-in for sainthood. Then your toddler drags you kicking and screaming into the preschool years, forcing you to switch gears and work on your debating skills instead (those debating skills, of course, being your only hope of being able to hold your own in conversations with your increasingly verbal three-year-old). So it goes from one stage to the next: you no sooner master one set of skills when you're sent back to Parenthood U for another round of quick crash courses. That's what makes this parenting thing so interesting and so much fun: you never have the chance to get stuck in a rut.

Of course, parenthood can be exhausting, too. In fact, mind-numbingly exhausting. You may have days when you feel as if you've been conned into appearing as a contestant on the most grueling reality television show yet: Parent TV! On bad days, parenthood can do a real number on your self-esteem. (If you're tempted to borrow a line from *Saturday Night Live*'s Dana Carvey and go around the house muttering "I am not worthy. I am not worthy," you can pretty much assume you're having a low self-esteem kind of day.)

A Book for (Gloriously) Imperfect Parents

While I'm researching my books or conducting my parenting workshops, the parents that I encounter tell me that they're feeling frustrated, exhausted, and overwhelmed by the day-to-day demands of parenting and that they're desperately looking for information and advice about what it takes to raise healthy, happy kids. They also tell me that they're sick of being preached to by "experts" who pretend to have all the answers or who package themselves as perfect parents. "What I'm after is the real story—not a book written by a Martha Stewart cut-out of the perfect parent, but a book about real-life struggles: real-life stories of mistakes parents have made and are willing to admit for the sake of saving other parents from experiencing the same heartache," stated one parent.

What parents today are looking for is nitty-gritty, from-the-trenches advice from other parents—the only people on the planet who really and truly understand what it's like to be a gloriously imperfect parent raising gloriously imperfect children. There's a growing backlash against advice givers who have lost touch with the needs of real families: so-called parenting experts who offer highly simplistic, formulaic solutions that don't take into account the countless messy variables that are the very essence of family life and who refuse to accept the fact that one-size-fits-all parenting solutions fit most kids as well as one-size-fits-all jeans.

That is the kind of book I've attempted to write here: a book that believes that pooled knowledge and shared experience beat formulaic solutions hands down every time.

A One-of-a-Kind Parenting Book

There's something else that makes this book stand out from the crowd: the breadth of the subject matter it attempts to address.

As you may have noticed, most parenting books tend to zero in on a single topic. That's why you'll find separate titles devoted to behavior, discipline, health, nutrition, education, and the gazillion and one other topics that typically fit under the parenting umbrella.

The parents that I consulted while I was writing this book encouraged me to steer clear from the one-topic trap and to write a book that was much more comprehensive and far-reaching than your typical run-of-the-mill parenting book. The mission that they set out for me was actually more than a little daunting: they asked me to concisely summarize the most useful and up-to-date information on the key issues involved in raising kids—in other words, to write a book that was truly deserving of the title *The Mother of All Parenting Books.*

If you take a quick flip through this book, you'll see that I've certainly tried to deliver on that request. I've made an effort to shoehorn in as much genuinely useful information as possible without turning the book into an encyclopedia-like tome. After all, if there's one thing that's in chronic short supply in the life of an average parent, it's an abundance of leisure time for reading!

Here's a quick snapshot of what you'll find as you make your way through the book:

- a frank discussion about why it's so tough to be a parent and why even good parents have bad days

- practical strategies for avoiding parent burnout

- tips on teaching kids morals and values

- advice on passing along the skills and personality traits that tend to lead to happiness and success

- the facts on discipline—what works, what doesn't, and how your discipline methods need to evolve as your child grows older

- from-the-trenches advice on managing mother (and father) guilt and sidestepping the indulgence trap

- parent-proven techniques for short-circuiting power struggles

- important information about differentiating between routine and serious behavioral problems

- tips on promoting healthy communication between parent and child and weathering the tough stuff as a family

- the inside scoop on the important role you have to play in encouraging your child's academic success

- tried-and-true methods for helping your child cope with rejection, teasing, and other friendship rites of passage

- an update on the latest research on bullying and what it means for parents and kids

- answers to your top 20 pediatric health questions

- immunization schedules

- advice on dealing with sleepwalking, nightmares, middle-of-the-night visitors, and other sleep issues

- the lowdown on what it takes to keep kids safe today without smothering them

- the facts on fitness, nutrition, and body image, and the important role that parents have to play in modeling healthy living for the next generation

- tips on coping with the roller-coaster ride that is the pre-teen years

- a detailed glossary of key pediatric health and child development terms

- a directory of organizations of interest to parents

- a directory of Internet resources of interest to parents.

Of course, what makes *The Mother of All Parenting Books* really stand out from the other parenting books on the shelf are the advice and anecdotes of the more than 100 parents who agreed to be interviewed for the book. They passed along their best advice on dealing with preschool food fights, preteen clothing battles, and everything in-between. It's their from-the-trenches advice that really brings the book to life. After all, who better to turn to for tips on dealing with a child who knows more swear words than you do, than another parent who has found herself struck speechless by her child's new-found vocabulary!

You'll also find a few other bells and whistles as you make your way through the book:

 Mom's the Word: Insights and advice from other parents.

 Mother Wisdom: Bright ideas, practical tips, pop culture tidbits, and more.

 No Kidding!: Surprising facts and statistics related to parenting.

 Fridge Notes: Leads on resources that are definitely worth checking out.

As you've no doubt gathered by now, *The Mother of All Parenting Books* is quite unlike any other parenting book you've ever encountered. It's comprehensive, it's fun to read, and—best of all—it's based on from-the-trenches advice from other moms and dads, the true experts when it comes to the sometimes wild but always wonderful adventure of raising kids.

I hope you enjoy the book.

Ann Douglas

P.S. My editors and I are determined to make *The Mother of All Parenting Books* the best parenting book available, so if you have any comments to pass along—good, bad, or ugly—we would love to hear from you. You can contact me via my publisher: Wiley Publishing, Inc., 111 River St., Hoboken, NJ 07030, www.wiley.com.

CHAPTER 1

The Truth About Parenting

"I think parenting needs to come out of the closet as the messy,
wonderful, scary, daring occupation that it is."
—*Natalie, 32, mother of two*

"I used to think parents who told me that my whole life would
change when I had kids were either bad parents or crazy.
How could it be that hard? Then I had Olivia!"
—*Mary, 37, mother of one*

Back when my first three kids were all under five and still small enough to fit in the bathtub at the same time, we had this crazy bath-time ritual. I would put everyone in the tub, pop my favorite CD into the portable stereo, and crank the tunes up loudly enough that the floor would begin to vibrate. (Hey, where is it written that mothers can't be party animals?)

Anyway, the CD in question was Momnipotent singer/ songwriter Nancy White's ode to motherhood. Although the CD is mainly filled with songs that speak to how frustrating and exhausting it is to be a mother, one song on the CD touched my heart like no other song about motherhood ever has. The song in question, "Mammas Have a Secret," talks about the powerful bond between parent and child—and why it's impossible to explain that bond to anyone who is not a parent.

Here's how the song starts out:

Mammas have a secret
Daddies have, too
it's a little secret they'll never tell you
'cause if you don't have a child so naughty and sweet
they don't want you to feel that your life is incomplete
and if you have a child there's nothing to say
because you know the secret anyway.

I think what's inspired me to write (literally) millions of words about pregnancy and parenting over the years is a passionate desire to capture some of the magic of that parent-child bond on paper. The more I try to write about it, however, the more obvious it becomes to me that a lot of what happens between parent and child simply defies description. It can be a kind of humbling experience if, like me, you're someone who makes her living working with words!

As you've no doubt gathered by now, the focus of this chapter is on what it's like to be a parent today—the good, the bad, and the ugly (let's just say I'm big on full disclosure). I start out by talking about why no one can tell you how tough it is to be a parent; like riding a bicycle, it's one of those things you have to learn by doing. Then I share with you what no one ever seems to mention (at least until you become a parent) but that you definitely need to know—my attempt to put down on paper some of the things I've learned over the course of my parenting career. Next, I discuss what's involved in mastering the fine art of coparenting— sharing parenting responsibilities with another human being. Then, I focus on the importance of investing in your relationship with your child's other parent—assuming that you still have a relationship with this person—even including how you can keep the sizzle in your sex life after you have kids. (Bet you didn't realize that this was going to turn out to be such a steamy read! To think my publisher slapped such a respectable-looking cover on the book!) Finally, I wrap up the chapter by talking about why it's so important to ensure that you meet your own needs while you're raising a family. As they like to say on airplanes, "Put on your own oxygen mask first."

Why No One Tells You How Tough It Is to Be a Parent

So, what is it that makes it so difficult for us to talk about the experience of being a parent—particularly the low points? (The high points, after all, inevitably find their way into Hallmark cards, long-distance phone company commercials, and other pop-culture outtakes. It's the low points that we seem to want to kick under the carpet.)

I think a couple of things discourage us from being forth-coming about what parenthood is all about. For one thing, we all tend to suffer from parental amnesia: a condition that sets in as whatever childrearing crisis you were dealing with last month or last year recedes farther and farther into the parenting fog. I also think that our society fosters a well-meaning desire to save other parents some unnecessary worry. (Who knows? They may luck out and end up with the world's first truly trouble-free adolescent, so why should you burden them with all the hair-raising tales of the latest exploits of your little darling?) And then, there's a slightly more selfish reason for holding our parenting cards close to our chests: We don't want to admit that we haven't quite got our act together on the parenting front.

You see, although most of us are happy to admit that dishes sit unwashed in the kitchen sink or that we had to forage around inside the clothes dryer in order to find a clean bra to put on this morning, we're reluctant to turn to others in our lives for support if our nine-year-old is acting like a bully at school or our sixteen-year-old is experimenting with sex and drugs. The June Cleavers of the world may have managed to escape from the kitchen and allow themselves to break free from the pressure to play the role of "the perfect housewife," but it may be another few decades before we learn how to let go of the pressure to be "the perfect mother"—the most impossible role of all.

What no one ever tells you until you become a parent

If Leo Tolstoy were a modern-day self-help book writer, he no doubt would have rewritten the opening line of *Anna Karenina* like this: "Every family is dysfunctional in its own way."

That may be true, but we can still learn a lot from the experiences of other parents. There have been countless times in my life when I have thought to myself, "I wish someone had told me it would be like this"—most notably during the extreme culture shock associated with becoming a parent for the first time and upon becoming the parent of an adolescent for the first time. (For those of you who haven't experienced the latter yet, let me give you a quick heads up—it's kind of like postpartum times 10,000.)

Although I don't pretend to have all the answers (please see my repeated disclaimers in the introduction and elsewhere in this chapter!), I feel that I owe it to the universe to put down on paper the few things I have managed to learn about parenting as a result of raising four children over the course of the past 15 years. (Just think of the number of "parent hours" I've clocked during that time!)

I'm not promising that these are the most profound things you're ever going to read on the subject of parenting. In fact, I can pretty much guarantee that they're not! But, I hope that you'll gain at least a few insights from reading my thoughts on the subject.

Anyway, here are 10 things that no one ever tells you about becoming a parent, but that you definitely need to know:

1. **There's no job description for the job of parent.** Can you imagine agreeing to take on a job for which there was no job description, no orientation program, no training program, no performance review process—in other words, none of the usual bells and whistles that we have come to expect in a typical employment situation? That's what parenting is like. It's the ultimate fly-by-the-seat-of-your-pants experience. Until you're on the job, you have no idea what the job involves or how difficult it really is, which explains, I suppose, why so many of us end up applying for the job in the first place!

2. **There's no such thing as "the perfect age."** You often hear parents talk about how much they are looking forward to their kids reaching such-and-such an age because it's "the perfect age." Well, I hate to be the bearer of bad news, but there is no such thing. Every age comes with its own unique mix of joys and challenges. Cathy, a 37-year-old mother of two, agrees with me on this point: "I used to wish that my kids were older, thinking that it would get easier once they reached a different stage. I've stopped doing that because I now realize that it's all challenging, and you've just got to concentrate on whatever stage you're dealing with right now. This too shall pass, and then another complicated stage will kick in!"

3. **Nothing about parenting happens in a predictable, linear fashion.** If there's a Murphy's Law of Parenthood, it goes something like this: The more convinced you are that you've finally gotten through a rough stage with your child, the greater the likelihood that your child will immediately take three steps backwards. (Ah, how much easier life would be if children were programmed to make constant

movement forward, like little wind-up robots. Never mind the fact it would be supremely boring, of course; we're talking about efficiency here, ladies and gentlemen!) As any veteran parent can tell you, it's a case of two steps forward and one step back whenever a child is attempting to master a new skill. I've also noticed that certain behaviors can return years after the fact. The whining and temper tantrums that were so common during the toddler years can make themselves felt again during the preteen years. There are days when I swear my daughter's infant colic has come back to haunt us again, some 15 years after the fact!

4. **The experts don't have all the answers.** Now that may sound like blasphemy coming from the lips of a parenting book author, but I've hung out with enough emperors to know that a lot of them don't own any clothes. (Just in case you're wondering, I certainly don't pretend to have a particularly extensive wardrobe myself!) Part of the problem, of course, is that the parenting experts rarely agree about anything. Put an attachment-parenting guru next to an advocate of tough love on a TV talk show, and you're likely to see a fist fight break out during commercial breaks! The net result for parents, unfortunately, is information overload and an unwillingness to trust our own parenting instincts.

5. **Parenting in the real world is a whole lot messier than parenting on TV.** (Unless, of course, you happen to tune into *Malcolm in the Middle*.) "The media paints a much rosier picture of what parenting is all about," says Stephanie, a 30-year-old mother of one. "Take sitcoms that revolve around families, for example. The issues that they deal with are always watered down, and the solutions always come so easily. The parents' reactions are always terribly politically correct and usually nothing even close to reality." The fact that the parenting issue of the day can be solved in 30 minutes or less only adds insult to injury.

Unless you happen to be raising a tribe of Walton or Cosby clones, you're unlikely to be able to pull that off in the real world!

6. **Parenthood is a long-term project.** You have to wait for the final payoff. The ultimate reward for any parent—successfully raising a happy, healthy child to adulthood—is many years in the making. What's required in the meantime is a huge leap of faith that things will turn out as they should. "It would be great to be able to look inside a crystal ball and know that everything you are doing as a parent will work out in the end," says Cindy, a 32-year-old mother of three. "It can be difficult to make decisions for your children now without knowing what the future may hold."

7. **Parenting can be hell on your self-esteem.** "My confidence in my parenting abilities definitely ebbs and flows," confesses Tracie, a 27-year-old mother of two. "Some days I wonder how anyone can let me be a parent: My house is a disaster, my child is not listening and is being cranky, and I'm yelling. And then, other days, we have a really good time doing something together, and I am really amazed at just how much my son knows and is learning, and I take a moment to pat myself on the back for the part I have had to play in that. Knowing that he is happy, confident, and secure makes me realize that I must be doing something right. Still, I would have to say that parenting can be hell on your self-esteem!"

8. **Kids force you to confront any "stuff" that you may have tried to bury underneath the carpet.** If you try to ignore the stuff that's hidden under the carpet, you're likely to trip over it and fall flat on your face. "Kids will make you love them in a way you never thought possible," writes Harriet Lerner in *The Mother Dance: How Children Change Your Life*. "They will also confront you with all the painful

and unsavory emotions that humans put so much energy into trying to avoid. Children will teach you about yourself and what it's like not to be up to the most important responsibility you'll ever have. They'll teach you that you are capable of deep compassion and also that you are definitely not the nice, calm, competent, clear-thinking, highly evolved person you fancied yourself to be before you became a mother."

 MOM'S THE WORD

"I continually second-guess myself regarding my parenting abilities. I hate being the mean dad. I hate having to uphold the rules. I have a habit of asking the girls the same set of questions at the end of every weekend I have them: 'Did you enjoy yourself?' 'What did you like most about the weekend?' 'What did you like least?' and 'If you could have done something different, what would it have been?' The girls, who are 10 and 8, look at me like I have two heads, like, 'Come on, Dad, we are just kids. We played and had fun. Let it go. Don't psychoanalyze us!' I feel that I am stressing them out at times. Other times, they will come up and give me a hug for no reason at all, and I feel like I am king of the world."

—*Ed, 36, father of two*

 MOTHER WISDOM

"Motherhood [is] like some kind of delicate juggling act where sometimes you have all the balls in the air and can do cartwheels without missing a toss. Then the next moment everything comes crashing down around you, and it turns out you were juggling eggs and one has landed on your head and the rest are splattered all over the floor. . . . There are good mommy moments and bad mommy moments. And, if you're lucky, your child's college tuition will still cost more than his therapy bills."

—*Celina Ottaway, "Bad mommy days can pack quite a punch,"* The Times Union *of Albany, New York, September 15, 2002*

9. **Nothing can prepare you for the depth of the love you will feel for your child.** Now we come to the final truth about parenting: Life doesn't get any better than this. "No matter how much other people, even those you trust, tell you about parenting, I don't think anything can fully prepare you for the love you will feel for your child," says Stephanie, a 30-year-old mother of one. "The emotions are so strong and so intense that you cannot imagine them until you experience them for yourself."

10. **The physical demands of parenting are the easy part. It's the emotional demands that practically sink you.** A dear friend of mine is due to give birth to her first child any day now. I haven't had the heart to tell her that the aches and pains of pregnancy and childbirth are just the beginning of the pain that she can expect to experience during the next 18 years and beyond. (What can I say? I just can't stand to make a pregnant woman cry!) It's watching your child experience the emotional bumps and bruises of life that really hurts, insists Chonee, a 38-year-old mother of three: "The most challenging thing about being a parent is not being able to make every hurt go away. Not being able to protect them from the cruelty of society. Having to explain what 'war' means and why they are hearing about it—and why some person would fly a plane into a building. Not being able to protect them from mean kids who use foul language. Not being able to explain why some foolish parent thought it would be okay to invite only half the boys in the class to a birthday party—and having to watch the other four boys with tears in their eyes. Not being able to hold my kids when they fall down at school or protect them when they get yelled at by some angry adult. I could go on and on. But, I think I find it most difficult to watch my children's innocence being watered down by society. The earaches, stomachaches, and cutting teeth I can handle."

MOTHER WISDOM

Sociologists feel that part of what's fuelling the current outbreak of parenting angst is the fact that we are having fewer children than ever before—something that leaves us all too aware that we only have one or two kicks at the proverbial parenting can. While back in the 1800s, a typical American woman could expect to give birth to seven children over the course of her lifetime, by mid-2002, that number had declined to just 2.1 children.

That was then, this is now

Don't expect to be able to pick up the same well-worn copy of *Dr. Spock's Baby and Child Care* that served your parents well during the 1960s. The world that you're raising your kids in today is very different than the world you grew up in just a generation ago. Here's a quick snapshot of how the world of parenting has changed over the course of the past generation, for better and for worse:

- **Our ideas about what it means to be a good parent have evolved considerably.** The current generation of parents is playing a more active role in their children's lives than previous generations of parents had the time or the inclination to do. All that quality time spent at the dinner table and in front of the basketball hoop seems to be paying off. A survey conducted by *Parenting* magazine in 2002 found that 95 percent of parents believe that their kids feel at least as loved or more loved than they themselves did during their own growing-up years; while 57 percent of parents report that they are more affectionate and involved than their own parents were when they were children.

    Unfortunately, there's a downside to all this (hyper)involvement and navel-gazing: we've massively raised the bar when it comes to defining what it means to be a good parent. It's no longer enough to keep your children healthy and safe and to feed them reasonably nutritious food; now you're expected to read up on all aspects of child development so that you can ensure that your child is exposed to the appropriate stimuli during the key developmental periods, to arrange for your child to participate in a playgroup from birth onwards so that her social skills don't lag behind those of her peers, to ensure that your child's evenings and weekends are programmed with activities designed to promote cultural and/or scientific literacy, and, of course, to compete in the mommy world's equivalent of the Olympic Trials each October by designing the ultimate hand-sewn Halloween costume. Frankly, it's enough to make even Supermom want to wave the white flag!

- **Our discipline techniques have become much more child-friendly.** In general, our ideas about discipline have evolved right along with our parenting philosophies. Gone are the days when the primary discipline tool a frustrated mother had at her disposal was a veiled threat to "just wait until your father gets home!" For the most part, parents these days are trying to motivate their children with love, not fear. Although beating children in the name of discipline was never a good thing for parents or kids (despite what some members of the older generation may have you believe!), such great shifts in parenting philosophies inevitably result in a few growing pains. Like it or not, we're guinea pigs when it comes to disciplining our kids. Now that the previous discipline playbook has been yanked from the game (you know, the playbook that said "hit first, ask questions later"), we're having to come up with a whole new discipline playbook. I predict that the next generation of parents (our kids) will benefit hugely by analyzing the mistakes our generation of parents has made when it comes to disciplining, or not disciplining, our kids. Just think of the great material that sitcom writers will have to draw upon when they choose to put the current generation of parents under the microscope in 2020. (Talk about 2020 hindsight. . . .)

- **Parents are facing a chronic time crunch.** According to an article in the *Journal of the American Medical Association*, parents today spend 10 to 12 hours less per week with their children than parents did a generation ago. What's more, according to Richard Judy and Carol D'Amico, authors of *Workforce 2000: Work and Workers in the 21st Century*, only half of women believe that they can do an adequate job of parenting while working full-time. Barbara Kantrowitz and Pat Wingert were even more pointed in a recent article in *Newsweek* when they described the time crunch that parents face today: "Raising kids today is like competing in a triathlon with no finish line in sight."

 NO KIDDING!

A study conducted in 2002 by the nonprofit think tank Public Agenda revealed that 76 percent of American parents feel that being a parent today is a lot tougher than it was a generation ago.

- **The dual income family has become the new norm.** According to the Bureau of Labor Statistics, by 1997, nearly 60 percent of American women were working outside the home, as compared to just 33 percent in 1950. This represents a seismic shift over the course of a single generation and goes a long way toward explaining why we're still experiencing some sizable aftershocks.

- **Working nonstandard hours is becoming much more common.** A recent article in the *Journal of Marriage and the Family* states that in 31.1 percent of families with children under the age of 14, at least one parent works evening, night, or rotating shifts, and in 46.8 percent of families with children under the age of 14, at least one parent works weekend shifts. Although working opposite shifts can eliminate childcare headaches for some working couples, it can make it difficult for couples to discuss parenting concerns, to parent as a team (as opposed to operating as two solo acts), and to stay connected.

- **A significant number of American children are growing up in households headed by a single parent.** According to the Census Bureau, there are 11.9 million single parents in America, one-sixth of whom are men.

- **The world today seems like a scarier place than the world in which we grew up.** More than 80 percent of parents surveyed by *Today's Parent* magazine in 2002 believe that there are a lot more dangers for kids today than there were when they were kids. They don't feel confident allowing their kids to roam the neighborhood as freely as they did during their own growing-up years. "The world is very different than the one that I grew up in, and I'm not that old," says Jennifer, a 29-year-old mother of three. "I find it very sad that my children will never be able to experience some of the carefree experiences that I did, just because of the kind of world they will grow up in." The net result, according to many child development experts, is that children today have fewer opportunities for unstructured outdoor play—the very stuff of which our own childhoods were made. Although it's only natural to want to protect your child from unnecessary harm, it's easy to fall into the trap of being an overprotective parent—to become an "über parent" or "smother mother" (to pick up on some of the current lingo). If all your parenting decisions are made on a worst-case scenario basis and you're constantly attempting to quarantine your child against danger, it could be that you're approaching this parenting thing with more paranoia than prudence. (Note: In Chapter 12, I discuss strategies for balancing your need to keep your child safe against your desire to allow your child to enjoy a certain degree of freedom.)

- **Parents feel like they are constantly trying to ward off the negative influences of popular culture.** A 2002 study conducted by the nonprofit think tank Public Agenda revealed that 47 percent of American parents are concerned about the negative effects of popular culture on their children. ("Soon they'll be killing people on the cooking channel," said one of the fathers interviewed for the study.) Of course, it's not just television that's got parents up in arms: Studies have shown that video games, DVDs, music videos, and the Internet are all doing their part to cause sex, violence, and other inappropriate material to show up on the radar screens of increasingly younger children. (Note: In Chapter 2, I take a look at some strategies for fighting back against the negative influences of popular culture.)

- **Kids aren't leaving home the way they used to—or sometimes even at all.** If you're thinking of parenting as an 18-year commitment, you may want to rethink your timeline. Kids aren't exiting the family nest in quite the same way that they used to—and, even when they do leave home, the odds are pretty good that they'll make like migratory birds and return to their traditional nesting ground. According to the Census Bureau, in 2002, 8 percent of young women and 14 percent of young men between the ages of 25 and 34 were living with their parents—a noteworthy increase over the 7 percent of young women and 11 percent of young men in the same age group who were living at home in 1981. This means that your parenting "career" may not necessarily end the day your children head off to college or university or move out to take that first job. You may have to psych yourself up for a second or subsequent wave of parenting challenges. (This parenting marathon is starting to sound more like an Ironman distance triathlon, now isn't it?!)

MOM'S THE WORD

"The world has become such a dangerous place. It seems that there is so much more to be afraid of than when we were kids. Finding the balance between vigilance and overprotectiveness has been very difficult, but I try to give my children as much space and freedom as I can because I want them to be able to live their lives fully. I don't want them to grow up to be adults who are fearful of what the world has to offer."

—*Karen, 34, mother of three*

You would think, given all the challenges that modern-day parents can expect to face, that prospective parents would be stampeding to the doctor's office in search of fail-safe birth control. Well, either hope springs eternal, or we're gluttons for punishment: a 1997 *Time*/CNN survey of graduating high school seniors found that 93 percent intended to have at least one child. Oh, baby!

United We Stand, Divided We Fall

Divide and conquer is a proven military strategy. It also works well in the world of business—in any negotiating situation, in fact. So, if you share parenting duties with someone else, don't leave yourself vulnerable to the old divide-and-conquer ploy. Otherwise, you stand to lose big the next time your kid decides to play hardball. Here are some tips to keep in mind when it comes to mastering the fine art of coparenting:

- **Accept the inevitability of parenting disagreements.** You and your partner are unlikely to see eye-to-eye on every conceivable parenting issue. After all, you're two entirely different people. Although you'll probably find that most of your parenting conflicts are relatively easy to resolve—for example, for the sheer sake of marital harmony, you may be able to live with the fact that your partner lets the kids eat chocolate chip cookies for breakfast occasionally—other conflicts may be a bit trickier to resolve, particularly if those differences come down to a fundamental difference in parenting styles. In this case, some heavy-duty backroom negotiations may be in order so that you can present a united front to the kids.

MOM'S THE WORD

"Always back each other up in front of the kids. Present a united front even if you disagree with your partner on a particular issue; you can discuss it at a later time when the other kids aren't around. If they think they can play one parent off against the other, your battleship is sunk! And, *it is* a battle—a battle of wits. But we can win if we stick together."

—*Mary, 36, mother of three*

- **Keep it private.** If you and your partner have some fundamental differences of opinion on how certain types of parenting situations should be handled, try to work out those differences in private. If you find that you disagree more than you agree, you may want to consider taking a parenting course together or working with a marriage and family counselor to try to identify some parenting common ground and to find out if some unrelated issues may be causing problems in your marital relationship. Remember to treat your partner with respect as you attempt to work through these difficulties. It's important not to allow any marital problems the two of you may be experiencing to affect the quality of your parenting decisions.

- **Don't let your kids get away with playing one parent against the other.** If your six-year-old daughter tries to tell you that her father told her she could have ice cream for breakfast, attempt to verify that claim. If your partner is unavailable, you get to make the call on this particular nutrition issue. If she happens to do such a great acting job that you buy her story, hook, line, and sinker, then you'll definitely want to call her on her deception and ensure that there's some sort of consequence for her actions (for example, you may decide to implement a rule that says that if you can't check out any future stories with her father, she will have to wait until he gets home so that her claims can be verified).

 MOM'S THE WORD

"Children have built-in radar. (Just ask any parent who has ever tried to enjoy an intimate moment alone!) They can and will attempt to divide and conquer if they sense a division within the parenting ranks. This is why you have to discuss any and all parenting conflicts privately with your partner."

—*Karen, 34, mother of three*

 MOM'S THE WORD

"As silly as it sounds, my husband and I have become quite fluent in speaking Pig Latin, so if we have to have a conversation about a parenting issue when the kids are present—in the car, for example—then we can speak without having to worry about them knowing what we are saying. It has worked out great for us and will until they learn how to speak it!"

—*Sandi, 32, mother of two*

- **Identify your areas of strength and divvy up the parenting duties accordingly.** If your partner has a real knack for getting the kids to settle down at bedtime, you may want to put him on permanent pajama duty. Likewise, if your partner is totally hopeless at getting the kids to clean their rooms—largely, you suspect, because he never actually learned how to clean his own!—you may want to assume responsibility for conducting room inspection. Just make sure that you balance out the fun jobs and not-so-fun jobs. This is one situation where the "good cop, bad cop" routine doesn't play out well at all.

- **Know when it is—and isn't—okay to encroach on the other parent's turf.** It's not fair for one parent to barge into a parent-child conflict and side with the child, nor is it acceptable for a parent to override the other parent's rules just because that parent happens to be out of earshot. Both of these maneuvers can seriously undercut the authority of the other parent. If you totally disagree with the way your partner is handling a particular parenting issue, call a parenting timeout and discuss the issue out of earshot of the kids. Or, better yet, wait until cooler heads prevail and discuss the issue calmly over a cup of coffee. The only time you should intervene immediately is if your partner is being abusive to your child. Obviously, you wouldn't want to let that kind of behavior go unchecked.

- **Give 'em a break.** Wherever possible, give your partner the benefit of the doubt if he seems to be having a bad day on the parenting front. We all have days when we are less patient, less creative, and less forgiving than we would like to be with our kids. Before you start getting on your partner's case in a major way, cut him a bit of slack. Assuming this is just a temporary misstep, chances are he'll find his parenting groove again before you know it.

- **A compliment can be a parent's best friend.** Be generous with the praise when your partner handles an especially challenging parenting situation with particular finesse.

Parents don't get enough accolades from society in general, so make sure you hand out plenty at home.

- **Keep your eyes on the prize.** Bear in mind that, day-to-day differences aside, you both have the same long-term goal in mind: raising a happy, healthy child. As Maria, a 34-year-old mother of three puts it, "I think it's important to remind yourself that you are on the same team."

Note: You will find additional tips on parenting, particularly related to parenting after separation and divorce, in Chapter 6.

MOTHER WISDOM

"The family is probably the most complex organization that exists. You've got a minister of justice, a minister of recreation, a minister of food, and a minister of education."

—*York University psychologist Harold Minden, quoted in an article in the October 1999 issue of* Today's Parent

---

Childproofing your relationship with your partner

It's easy to lose touch with your partner when you're busy raising a family. There are, after all, a million-and-one other demands on your time. The situation tends to be particularly challenging for dual-income families, who often end up sacrificing time for one another and for themselves, as they scramble to keep all the work- and kid-related balls in the air.

It's important to take drastic steps to prevent couple time from falling off the radar. Rather than thinking of the time you spend with your partner as a luxury the two of you simply can't afford to indulge in at this point in your lives, try to think of it as a necessity the two of you can't afford to live without, suggests Elouise, a 33-year-old mother of two. "If you don't take time for your marriage, no one else will. Your husband will be living with you longer than your children (hopefully!), so it is worth the investment to make it a good relationship. Besides, it provides good modeling for the kids on how to treat someone with love, respect, and intimacy."

Lisa, a 37-year-old mother of two, agrees that parents need to give themselves permission to make their marriage a priority. Like Elouise, she finds it tough to find the time to invest in her relationship with her partner, but she sincerely believes that the entire family functions better when she and her husband are feeling connected: "My husband and I both strongly believe that a good relationship between the two of us lays the necessary groundwork for a good family," she explains. "When we feel disconnected from each other, everything goes less well: We have less patience and tolerance for the chaos; we find ourselves yelling at the kids more; and we just generally feel miserable. When we stay connected to one another and remember what made us decide to have kids, we love each other and wanted to have a family together, everything else goes more smoothly."

Of course, even if you know exactly what you should be doing, it's easy to let the kids and the countless items on your to-do list come between you and your partner: "My husband and I spend so much time just trying to survive the day-to-day work of holding down full-time jobs, keeping up with the household chores, spending quality time with the kids, and so on, that a lot of our personal time has gone out the window," confesses one mother of three. "I have seen the negative effects this has had on our relationship. It is tough. In fact, I have thought about leaving because of it. You start to feel like roommates who only have one thing in common: three kids! It also becomes difficult to see the light at the end of the tunnel. And, all the things I know we should be doing—making dates with one another and setting aside couple time—are good in theory, but hard to do in practice, especially since my husband works shift, and we don't have a lot of time together. I guess what I'm saying is that the *status quo* is not ideal, but it is working for now. It will not be like this forever, but I know we do have to make more time for each other if we're going to make this relationship work."

MOM'S THE WORD

"Our relationship has turned into more of a medical practice than a marriage. Our marriage has suffered greatly because of the many medical needs of our children, but we try to talk things through—to tell one another what we are feeling and why. Nothing is ever completely resolved between us, unfortunately: there is no time. But we try to respect one another and our struggles."

—*A mother of five*

MOTHER WISDOM

Sign up for your phone company's call display feature so that you and your partner can ignore all but the most urgent telephone calls when you're enjoying some couple time together in the evening. You'll also find that the same phone feature can reap big dividends at family mealtimes. You'll no longer have to put up with having your dinner interrupted by a carpet cleaning company or that kid in your neighborhood who insists on calling at least 10 times a day.

Stealing moments away with your partner

Because pre-existing problems in the relationship can lead to conflicts on the parenting front, which, in turn, can lead to further problems in the relationship, it's important for parents to check in with one another on a regular basis. Try to find at least a few minutes a day to touch base over a cup of coffee or via e-mail—whatever it takes to hold you over until you can have a more detailed heart-to-heart. If you're struggling to find time for that heart-to-heart chat, you may want to try one or more of the following:

- **Meet your partner for lunch during the day once a month.** If you're at home with your kids during the day, arrange a childcare swap with another mom so that she can "do lunch" with her partner on a different day.

- **Carry on a conversation via e-mail.** Just make sure that you don't let the conversation stray into overly steamy territory if you or your partner are e-mailing each other at work: You would hate to inadvertently violate your companies' no smut policies!

- **Put on a video for the kids after dinner and then retreat to your bedroom for coffee and conversation.** Depending on the ages of your kids, you may have to do periodic spot checks to make sure that the kids are staying out of mischief, but you should at least be able to speak in full sentences between interruptions!

- **Send the kids to bed early.** Hint: Ignore the phone so that you don't miss out on this special time together if your super-chatty girlfriend happens to call for a late-night yak.

- **Go for a Sunday afternoon drive.** With any luck, the kids will fall asleep, and you'll be able to have an uninterrupted tête-à-tête.

- **Go for a family walk in the woods.** Let the kids run just far enough ahead so that they're out of earshot, and you'll have yet another chance to touch base with one another.

- **Hire a babysitter or swap childcare with another family so that you can enjoy an evening or weekend away.** If you find yourself feeling disconnected from your partner (e.g., you haven't discussed anything more meaningful than the kids' homework assignments in weeks!), this could be just what you need to start feeling like a couple again.

Of course, this list is just the tip of the iceberg in terms of what's possible. If you talk to other parents you know, you're bound to hear some pretty amazing stories about the lengths to which other parents have gone in order to keep their relationships on track—staying up all night to talk even though they both had to go to work the next morning or leaving love notes for one another on the door of the microwave oven because that's the only surface in the entire kitchen that's not buried in a sea of kid-related clutter. It may not be easy to keep the home fires burning when you've got a houseful of children, but it definitely can be done. Don't let anyone tell you otherwise.

Note: If you're interested in picking up a guide to staying connected as a couple, I highly recommend *Getting the Love You Want: A Guide for Couples* by Harville Hendrix and his other book the *Getting the Love You Want Workbook: The New Couples' Study Guide.* It will help you to uncover any "stuff" that's getting in the way of a warm and nurturing relationship between you and your partner (something that is practically guaranteed, by the way, to reap huge dividends on the parenting front).

 **NO KIDDING!**

According to John Gottman, Ph.D., author of *Why Marriages Succeed or Fail*, couples typically experience eight times as much conflict after the birth of their first child as they did before. What's more, two-thirds of couples report a notable drop in marital satisfaction after becoming parents. By the way, don't assume that if you fumbled your way through the post-baby haze following the birth of baby number one that your marriage is in the clear. Sometimes it's the birth of a second or subsequent child that brings hidden marital conflicts to the surface.

Keeping the sizzle in your sex life

No discussion of staying connected as a couple would be complete without at least a quick mention of what parents can do to keep sex from falling off the radar screen for weeks—even months—at a time. Although there will be times when sex has to take a back seat to whatever else happens to be going on in your life, it's important to ensure that your sex life's disappearing act is a temporary, and not a permanent, state of affairs.

Here are some practical tips from real moms and dads on keeping the sizzle in your sex life while you're raising a family:

- **Remind yourself that sex starts outside the bedroom.** "In order to stay connected sexually, you have to stay connected emotionally and mentally," says one mom of three. "That's really at the root of it all. Once you stop talking, you stop doing everything else. Stay interested in each other's day-to-day stuff, hug and kiss often, and remember that small, loving gestures like a simple touch on the hand or shoulder really help a couple to stay connected, even without words. If you stay connected emotionally and mentally, then the physical comes along for the ride!"

- **State the obvious.** If your partner has not yet made the connection between how you're feeling about the way he is dealing with issues involving the kids and the likelihood that he's ever going to have sex again during this lifetime, do him a favor and point out the link. Better yet, hand him a copy of the June 2002 issue of the *Journal of Family Psychology* that talks about just how emotionally disconnected women feel to their partners when the two of them don't see eye-to-eye on parenting issues. Dads don't experience this phenomenon to the same degree as moms, so they're often puzzled to discover that a disagreement over a child-rearing issue can lead to the big chill in the bedroom. So, don't assume that he's being an insensitive swine because he's giving you lustful looks a mere half-hour after the two of you had a major disagreement over a child discipline issue. He may not realize that sex has completely fallen off your radar screen for the time being. ("There's no

sex if mom doesn't feel connected to dad, even if dad believes
it would bridge that gap!" according to one mother of two.)

- **Stockpile sleep whenever the opportunity presents
  itself.** After all, it's pretty hard to feel romantic if you can
  barely stay awake past the kids' bedtimes, and your partner
  isn't going to feel terribly confident in his sexual prowess if
  you inevitably head off to dreamland midway through each
  romantic encounter. Some couples find that early morning
  sex works out best, because both partners should theoreti-
  cally feel well rested and receptive after having just spent
  the night together. (Of course, if you've got a baby who gets
  up repeatedly in the night and a toddler who gets up before
  it's even daybreak, you may have to start coming up with
  Plan C.)

- **Give your body a workout outside the bedroom, too.**
  The endorphins that are released during exercise boost your
  energy level, improve your mood, and can even help to
  jump-start your libido. You're also bound to feel better
  about your body—something that can't help but reap
  tremendous dividends in the bedroom.

MOM'S THE WORD

"By the end of the day, we're both pretty tired, but I think it's very
important to stay connected sexually, whether you're tired or not. If being
tired was our reason for not having sex, then we'd never have it. Ever!"
—*Mother of three*

- **Allow for some decompression time before you hop in
  the sack.** Whether it's taking 20 minutes to soak in the tub
  so that you can make the transition from being someone's
  mommy to someone's lover or simply heading up to bed a
  half-hour ahead of your partner so that you have some time

to read a novel in bed alone, you're much more likely to be receptive to your partner's sexual overtures if you've had a little time to yourself.

- **Off-load some of your responsibilities.** Don't be afraid to ask for help if you're feeling overwhelmed by all the other demands in your life. Martyrs don't make very good lovers. Pent up resentment is, after all, the sexual equivalent of a cold shower!

- **Don't stick one partner with the job of always having to be the one to initiate sex.** According to Anne Semans and Cathy Winks, coauthors of *The Mother's Guide to Sex*, there's no surer way to get stuck in a sexual rut: "The worse-case scenario is that you get stuck in a classic initiation standoff, with one of you assuming the role of 'insensitive horndog,' and the other assuming the role of 'frigid wet blanket.'"

- **Retrace the steps of your wayward libido.** If your sexual passion has gone AWOL, realize that you may have to play an active role in bringing it back home. Don't expect your partner or your fairy godmother to do your sexual homework for you. "If your libido has taken a hike, you don't have to sit and wait for it to come back into view over the horizon," note Semans and Winks. "You can get out your sexual compass and track it down."

- **You may never see another perfectly passionate moment.** Don't hold off on having sex until the perfect moment—a day when you're feeling totally rested and totally in the mood. If you hold out for the perfect moment, you may find yourself settling for abstinence instead. Besides, it's amazing how quickly your energy level and libido will pick up as you get into the swing of things. So, rather than postponing your moment of passion until you've got ideal weather conditions on the passion front, go with the conditions you've got. "Sometimes you have to take a lesson from Nike and 'Just do it,'" insists one mother of two. "I find that once you get started, the mood always comes back."

MOM'S THE WORD

"I found after the birth of my first child that my sex drive dipped below the freezing mark. Right or wrong, I have chosen to keep that fact from my husband. I don't think there is anything to be gained from full disclosure. Until that happens, I'll keep on re-creating the restaurant scene from *When Harry Met Sally* and letting him think I'm having as good a time as he is in bed. Either my sex drive will return in time, or I'll be nominated for an Oscar!"

—*Mother of two*

- **Scheduled or not, it's still sex.** Abandon that crazy notion that says that scheduled sex is less satisfying than spontaneous sex; on the other hand, be prepared to seize the moment if opportunity comes a-knockin' on your door. "One time, the older kids had gone inside to watch a movie, and the babies had fallen asleep in their car seats," recalls one mom of six. "So we opened up the van and were going to pull weeds in the garden as it is right beside where the van is parked. Well, let's just say the weeds didn't get pulled that day." Or, even if you're sure that you don't have time, find ways to fit sex into your busy schedule. "A five-minute quickie in the shower can be great!" says one mom of two.

- **Prevent—not pardon—the interruption.** If your fear of being interrupted is cramping your lovemaking style, put a lock on the door of the room where you have sex, your bedroom or in the case of families who are co-sleeping some other corner of the house that you turn into your after-hours love nest! Your odds of being able to relax enough to enjoy some truly mind-blowing sex are pretty much slim-to-none if you're constantly listening for the pitter-patter of little feet.

- **Play it cool when you are interrupted.** Don't assume you've scarred your children for life if they do happen to catch you in a, *ahem,* compromising position. Your reaction to their impromptu visit is more important than whether or not they actually managed to catch a bit of risqué bedroom action. If you shriek and carry on about how disgusting it is that they caught you prancing around in the nude, you've pretty much guaranteed a therapist a steady stream of work for years to come. On the other hand, if you take a more matter-of-fact approach to the interruption and give your kids the message that sex is a natural, healthy activity between consenting adults and nothing to be ashamed of, you don't have to worry about the psychological effects of their badly timed middle-of-the-night visit.

 MOM'S THE WORD

"Let's put it this way: if we wanted to use the 'withdrawal' method of birth control, we'd be total pros by now! I can't tell you how many times one or both of us have gone, ahem, *unfulfilled* because of an interruption. We've tried having sex when we thought they were playing at the neighbors—only to be interrupted. Now we put on a movie or make them clean up the mess in the basement. Then we know we're safe for a few minutes at least. It's hard for me as I never get to climax. I only get to when we are either out of the country without them or they are at least a 10-minute or more drive away. And even those times, it's hard as I just keep expecting to hear one of them coming up the stairs."

—*Mom of three*

- **Schedule the odd mini-vacation without the kids.** Even just a single night away may be all that it takes to recharge your sexual batteries. If you can't get away, take a vacation at home by having sex in a place other than your bedroom, suggests one mom of six: "We co-sleep with our two youngest children. This has made our sex life more interesting in a way. Before, the bed was so convenient. It's not as convenient with a sleepy baby or two in it. But, boy, is it romantic in front of the woodstove with candles and soft music! There are a couple of comfy chairs in our bedroom that work nicely. And, the shower is a nice rendezvous location." Of course, if you're going to move from room to room, you'll want to make sure that your birth control method is equally mobile. Either that, or you'll want to follow the advice of the authors of *The Mother's Guide to Sex* and stash some condoms in the various rooms of your house—and then just hope like heck that your preschooler doesn't make a mental note of your stash and then decide to go and dig out the "extra balloons" in front of all the party guests at his next birthday party!

MOM'S THE WORD

"It can be hard to find the time, energy, and inclination to remain sexually active. However, if you make the time, you will find the energy, and you will remember how much fun it is to have sex—and then you'll be inclined to do it more often!"

—*Mother of two*

MOM'S THE WORD

"We schedule time for one another. We have to. Every once in a while, one of us will say, 'You know, it's been a while. How about tonight?' Sometimes that gets us through the frustration of the bedtime routine. We know that once the kids are in bed, it will be our time. Then we lock our bedroom door, have a glass of wine, talk, and enjoy one another."

—*Mother of five*

- **Don't be afraid to try new things if you feel like you're getting into a sexual rut.** "We shower together every morning and that sometimes leads to a morning quickie," says one mother of one. "And, on advice from my doctor, we visited a local sex shop and picked up some edible body paints and a sex toy. The idea was just to reconnect and to add a little sizzle to our sex life. It certainly did the trick!" Being willing to experiment a little can definitely help to rekindle the flames, agrees one mother of two: "We've been together for 12 years, and I'm learning and trying new things all the time. That's the best thing about a long-term relationship: I trust him enough, and vice versa, to try things I might otherwise be afraid to try. And sometimes the results really do sizzle!"

- **Reap what you sow.** Realize that the effort you put into maintaining or rebuilding your sex life will reap dividends in other parts of your relationship. "Don't tell anyone, but hub and I are just as hot now as when we first met," confesses one mother of four. "We are fortunate that he works shift work, two of our children are in school, and the other two take afternoon naps at the same time. We make time for each other—sometimes mid-afternoon, sometimes early morning, sometimes late at night. With four children, his full-time job, my work-at-home job, our volunteer activities, and our children's activities, we are certainly busy, but we're never too busy for each other. Our partnership is the reason we are a family, and we do everything we can to protect it."

Safety Valves, Safety Nets, and Other Parenting Tricks of the Trade

Just as it's important to invest in your relationship with your partner during your children's growing-up years, it's also important to invest in yourself. Consider what Perri Klass, M.D., had to say on the subject in a recent issue of *Parenting* magazine: "It's a funny paradox. A child should be at the center of your universe—and yet, all should not revolve around that child. . . . If you keep an eye out for the occasional fun, child-centered weekend activity, that's great; if you haven't looked outside the 'Just for Kids' listings in your local paper in years, that's not so great. If you're living in a child-friendly house, you're doing fine; if your home resembles a playground, you need to get a life."

Not quite sure how to go about getting a life—or even holding on to the life you've got? Not to worry! Here's a quick crash course:

- **Don't allow your parenting responsibilities to take over your entire life.** It's important to maintain some of your outside interests so that you don't lose touch with the person you were before you had kids. And, if that means bowing out on the odd motherhood commitment so that you can do something for yourself, sometimes that's what you have to do. "My daughter started kindergarten this year, and I was encouraged to join the PTA," recalls Lisa, a 41-year-old mother of one. "I thought this was a good idea until I found out that the PTA meetings were on the same night as my monthly book club. I agonized over this decision. I really enjoy my book club meetings because they force me to read at least one book a month, and I am guaranteed at least one evening a month of adult company. But what kind of a parent forgoes the PTA for a book club? Finally, my husband said that my daughter would benefit more from a mother who goes to book club once a month because she enjoys it than from a mother who goes to PTA meetings because she feels she has to. It's true what they say: you can't be good to your children unless you are good to yourself."

- **Be conscious of what else is creeping onto your to-do list.** Setting aside a day of your life to help out on a school field trip or to make a bunch of cookies for the annual bake sale could very well prove to be the proverbial straw that breaks the camel's back, so make sure that you've got it in you to do this before you say yes. If you can't quite muster up the guts to say an outright, "No," at least say, "Not this year." Oh, by the way, if you're feeling guilty because you feel like you should be volunteering with this, that, and the next cause, you may want to consider what my ever-wise family doctor had to say on the subject when, like many mothers with young children, I found myself feeling guilty for ditching a lot of my volunteer work because I was so busy with my kids: "Parenting *is* volunteer work."

- **Remember the activities that work for you.** Make sure that the things that will replenish your stores make it on to your calendar—and that they stay there. "It sounds crazy, but I cherish my coffees out with the girls and my runs," says Natalie, a 32-year-old mother of two. "If you nurture yourself, you have something left to offer your family."

- **Learn how to seize the moment—literally.** Rather than holding out for some far-distant day in the future when you may have the luxury of enjoying an entire day of solitude, train yourself to recharge your batteries on a day-to-day basis in bite-sized five-minute chunks of time. Whether it's sitting down to enjoy a cup of tea while you read the newspaper or climbing into a bubble bath, it's important to teach your kids to respect the fact that you need a few minutes to yourself everyday. Although they're very young, you may need to have someone else run interference to ensure you get that time; for example, you may have to ask your partner to stand guard at the bathroom door to handle any requests for juice or other "emergencies" that arise when you're chin deep in bubbles! As your kids grow older, you can teach them to respect your need for a bit of time and space. It's an important life lesson—learning how to respect and honor other people's boundaries—after all.

- **Don't set the bar too high for yourself.** Although there's nothing wrong with having high standards for yourself when it comes to parenting, expecting too much from yourself will increase your risk of parent burnout.

- **Build your personal support group.** Make sure that you've got at least one person you can talk to about the joys and frustrations of parenting. "If you don't have anyone you can talk to in real life, go online and find a mom's support group," suggests Stephanie, a 30-year-old mother of one. "There are literally thousands of groups out there. I belong to one such group that is a tremendous support to me. I actually find it easier to spill my guts and get feedback from these people because I don't really know them in real life."

- **Find other ways of working off some of the stress associated with being a parent.** Write in your journal, call a friend, or do like Sherri, a 36-year-old mother of three, and hit the gym by yourself. "After having my third tot, I took up karate and earned my black belt," she explains. "Stress release for me often involves heading to the club where kicking, punching, and making primitive sounds is expected! My kids all do karate too, so it has become a family way to blow off steam."

- **Recognize when it's time to call for backup.** After all, we all have our breaking point. It's important to recognize the signs that you're approaching yours and to know who you can ask to step in. If you've got a partner and he's on hand at the time you reach your breaking point, you may choose, like Stephanie—a 30-year-old mother of one—to pass the parenting baton to him: "My husband and I work well off one another," she insists. "We can tell by the tone in one another's voice when one of us has had enough. At that point, the other knows that it's time to step in and take over." If, however, you're a single parent or your partner is unavailable a lot of the time, you may have to find other people in your life who can step in when you need to wave the white flag.

- **Be aware of the warning signs of parent burnout.** If you spot these warning signs in yourself, let others in your life know that you're struggling and that you're in need of a break:

  - persistent feelings of resentment toward your children and/or your partner

  - feeling unappreciated

  - irritability, anger, and frustration

  - feelings of emptiness and sadness

  - emotional exhaustion

  - a loss of enjoyment of life

  - feelings of guilt if you attempt to take time for yourself

  - a lack of motivation

  - difficulty concentrating

  - sleep disturbances

  - a strong desire to run away or otherwise escape from your life

  - physical symptoms such as headaches, backaches, gastrointestinal symptoms, lethargy, cardiovascular problems, and skin conditions

I hope this laundry list of physical and emotional ailments convinces you that you absolutely have to take care of yourself. The price of not investing in a little self-preservation is simply too great to pay. If you absolutely cannot, for whatever reason, convince yourself to take care of yourself for your own sake, at least stop and think of the model you are providing to your children. Do you want to play the role of the infamous Mommy Martyr (an image that's getting rather tired and dated, by the way), or do you want to be a living example of what it means to love yourself enough to take proper care of your own needs?

I don't know about you, but I hope that when my daughter grows up, she'll remember that I took time to nurture myself in all kinds of small but important ways: lighting scented candles, having bubble baths, ensuring that there's always some of my favorite herbal tea in the house, and otherwise acting like my own best friend. Ditto for my sons. These will be valuable life lessons for my kids to learn whether they become parents or not. So, I kind of owe it to them to go and book that pedicure now, don't I?

FRIDGE NOTES

Want to pick up some additional strategies for keeping your life as a parent in balance with the rest of your life? Visit Parentinglibrary.com.

CHAPTER 2

Kid Under Construction

> "Childhood . . . is a deeply furrowed path of developmental
> biology that constantly intersects with culture as
> children grow, physically and mentally."
> —Meredith Small, Kids: How Biology and
> Culture Shape the Way We Raise Our Young

Although the majority of species of animals opt for a method of childrearing that can best be described as express-lane parenting—you do your biological duty; you teach your offspring a few basic survival skills; and then you exit stage left—we human beings choose instead to do our childrearing in the slow lane. In fact, most of us end up devoting the better part of 18 years to equipping our offspring with the skills needed to survive—and, with any luck, even thrive—after they leave the nest.

During the early months of our children's lives, the bulk of our efforts are devoted to attending to their basic physical needs, but as they become a bit more self-sufficient, we're able to switch gears and focus an increasing amount of our parenting energies to teaching them how to become fully contributing members of society. That is the toughest part of parenthood, of course—the unpredictable and sometimes messy part that can frustrate you

end and leave you wondering whether you've actually got
stamina required to see this marathon through to the end.
Not only can you find yourself doing battle with societal norms
that may not exactly mesh with your own personal morals and
values (how's that for an understatement?), but also you may
find yourself engaged in a battle of wills with a child whose temperament gives a whole new meaning to the word stubborn. It's
enough to make even the most committed of parents wave the
white flag.

Don't wave that flag quite yet—at least not until after you
read this chapter. The situation may not be quite as hopeless as
you may think. In the pages ahead, I talk about what you can do
to increase your odds of ending up with a happy, well-adjusted
child at the end of the day, namely:

- accepting your child for who she is—not who you wish
  she was

- ensuring that your parenting style is bringing out the best
  rather than the worst in your child

- deciding upfront what types of morals and values matter
  most to you and how you're going to go about transmitting
  those standards to your child

- doing what you can to tilt the self-esteem roulette wheel in
  your child's favor

Before we get into all that, it's time to wade into the age-old
nature-nurture debate and look at who's to blame for your child's
behavior—good, bad, and ugly.

When Nature Meets Nurture

Previous generations of mothers didn't have to waste a lot of time
wondering who was to blame for their children's imperfections.

If little Johnny was caught bicycling through the next door neighbor's flower garden or, *horrors!,* peering into her bedroom window, it was pretty obvious who was to blame.

Just Blame Mom. It might as well have been emblazoned on bumper stickers, T-shirts, and coffee mugs. The message was that clear. Fortunately, we've come a long way since that time, not the least of which is in our understanding of the role that both nature (the child's temperament) and nurture (the environment in which she is raised) have to play in explaining that child's behavior. We start out by tackling the nature piece of the equation first.

Your child's personality type

The "nature" part of the nature-nurture equation refers to the basic temperament your child is born with—in other words, her personality type. Although every psychologist or medical doctor who has ever written a parenting book seems to have come up with a slightly different laundry list of terms to describe children's temperaments, linguistic nuances aside, they pretty much boil down to the same three basic types that psychologists Alexander Thomas and Stella Chess described way back in the 1950s:

- **The difficult or spirited child:** a child who doesn't adapt well to new situations and who tends to have a negative attitude much of the time

- **The slow-to-warm-up or shy child:** a child who is very cautious and shy when faced with new situations and who is slow to warm up to new people

- **The easy child:** a child who is upbeat, adaptable, and mild to moderate in intensity of response

Child development experts have attempted to fine-tune this list of categories further by coming up with a list of major characteristics that help to define temperament. Here's a quick rundown of the key characteristics and what they mean:

- **Energy Level:** This refers to the amount of energy a child has, whether she's the kind of kid who can sit quietly long enough to read a book or whether she's in perpetual motion. A child's energy level doesn't just affect her behavior during the day, of course; it can also affect the quantity and quality of the sleep she gets at night—something that can, in turn, affect her behavior the following day. And so on, and so on, and so on . . .

- **Regularity of patterns:** This refers to the presence or absence of daily rhythms or patterns when it comes to basic biological functions such as sleeping, eating, and elimination. Some children have highly regular biological rhythms; others are much more erratic.

- **Approach and withdrawal:** This refers to a child's initial response to something new, be it a new person, a new situation, a new food, or a change in routine. Some children find it very easy to go with the flow; others require a lot of coaching to cope with even the most minor deviation from their normal routine.

 MOTHER WISDOM

"The same temperament that can make for a criminal can also make for a hot test pilot or astronaut. That kind of little boy—aggressive, fearless, impulsive—is hard to handle. It's easy for parents to give up and let him run wild, or turn up the heat and the punishment and, thereby, alienate him and lose all control. But properly handled, this can be the kid who grows up to break the sound barrier."

—*David Lykken, Ph.D., behavioral geneticist, University of Minnesota, quoted in "Beyond You,"* Parenting, *May 2002*

- **Adaptability:** This refers to the difficulty a child experiences in adjusting to a new situation and whether that reaction changes over time. For example, if your child is initially uncomfortable when your family is visiting someone new, does she warm up to her surroundings after a few minutes?

- **Intensity:** This refers to the intensity of a child's emotional reactions, either positive or negative. If your child is prone to tremendous exuberance or huge tantrums, she would likely be described as an intense child. (Either that or a drama queen!)

- **Mood:** This refers to the overall mood that a child sends out to the world—positive or negative. Some children are naturally happy and upbeat, and others are much more melancholy.

- **Attention span and distractibility:** This refers to a child's ability to stick with a task without becoming distracted. If your child is unable to do her homework while someone is talking, it could be because she has a short attention span, and/or she is easily distracted.

- **Sensory threshold:** This refers to the amount of stimulation a child requires in order to respond. Some children respond to very small amounts of stimulation; they find even the smallest amount of noise annoying, for example. Others can put up with a steady bombardment of TV, radio, and computer noise all at once. It all has to do with sensory threshold.

It's interesting to consider how these temperamental traits can play out in either positive or negative ways, depending on the circumstances. Table 2.1 describes the eight character traits, how they can play out for better and for worse in various situations, and what you can do to bring out the best in your child.

TABLE 2.1

For Better and For Worse: How Different Types of Character Traits Play Out in Different Situations

Energy Level	When It's a Good Thing	When It's Not Such a Good Thing	Bringing Out the Best in Your Child
High Energy	A high-energy kid tackles life with great gusto and can often keep herself entertained in even the most boring of circumstances. Who has time to get bored when there are couches to dive over, banisters to slide down, chandeliers to swing from . . . well, you get the picture!	A high-energy kid can be impulsive, even reckless, and can get herself into trouble in the blink of an eye. You need to have eyes on the back of your head when you're dealing with a kid like this. It also helps to be psychic!	You have to stay five steps ahead of a kid like this by constantly anticipating her next move. It's also important to provide her with opportunities to burn off some of her endless energy reserves and to provide for a cool-down period when it's time to switch from one activity to another.
Low Energy	A low-energy kid is generally pretty calm and laid back—the kind of kid who is content to sit at the kitchen table drawing a picture or gazing out the window for extended periods of time.	Teachers or other adults may accuse a low-energy kid of being lazy because of the slow pace at which he tackles tasks—something that can do a real number on his self-esteem.	Low-energy kids don't respond well to being rushed, so be sure to allow for enough transition time between tasks. It's also important not to criticize them because they like to take things a little more slowly: They're simply marching to the beat of a different drummer (a much slower drummer).

Regularity of Patterns	When It's a Good Thing	When It's Not Such a Good Thing	Bringing Out the Best in Your Child
Low Regularity	A child with low regularity is not easily upset by changes to her daily routine. It's no big deal if the regular teacher is off sick and a substitute teacher is filling in: She's the kind of kid who will "go with the flow."	A child with low regularity doesn't have a lot of clearly established patterns. Therefore, it can be difficult to predict ahead of time when she's likely to want to eat, sleep, or use the toilet again—something that can make for a bit of a challenge when planning a family road trip!	It's important to respect the fact that your child's eating, sleeping, and elimination patterns may vary from day to day and to cut her a bit of slack accordingly. Although you'll probably want her to sit at the dinner table with the rest of the family whether she's hungry or not, it's a good idea to let her decide whether she's actually hungry enough to eat.
High Regularity	If your child's eating, sleeping, and elimination routines are well established, it's easy to predict his needs from one day to the next—something that can make life easier for both of you.	Your child may not cope well if something necessitates a change to his regular routine—if you get stuck in traffic, for example, and he has to wait an extra hour for lunch or dinner.	If you know that your child will be completely thrown by any sort of deviation to his normal routine, try to anticipate these types of situations ahead of time and to plan for them accordingly (for example, keeping a snack in the car in case you're stuck in traffic and mealtime has to be delayed).

continued

TABLE 2.1

For Better and For Worse: How Different Types of Character Traits Play Out in Different Situations (*continued*)

Initial Withdrawal	When It's a Good Thing	When It's Not Such a Good Thing	Bringing Out the Best in Your Child
Boldness	A bold child tends to be very enthusiastic about encountering new people and new situations. A child like this has a largely carefree and fearless approach to life.	A bold child may put herself at risk because she may not stop long enough to consider whether any dangers may be associated with the new person or environment she has just encountered.	A child who has few inhibitions requires extra monitoring because her carefree, fearless attitude may lead to unnecessary risk-taking.
Slow and Hesitant	A child who is slow and hesitant to adapt to new situations is less likely to become involved in risky situations than a less inhibited, more impulsive child.	A child who is slow and hesitant to adapt to new situations may miss out on a lot of the fun that typically goes along with being a kid. He may also be stigmatized by peers who find it difficult to understand why she would rather sit on the sidelines than join in the fun.	Help your child to prepare for new experiences ahead of time so that they won't be quite so overwhelming for him. Don't force her to do things he's not comfortable with, which will only increase his resistance to trying new things in future.

Adaptability	When It's a Good Thing	When It's Not Such a Good Thing	Bringing Out the Best in Your Child
High Adaptability	A child who is quick to adapt to new situations doesn't have a lot of difficulty coping with life's curve balls. He tends to be highly resilient.	A child who is quick to adapt to new situations is more likely to succumb to peer pressure and other negative influences.	Make sure you know who your child is with and what he's doing. You want his high adaptability to be used for good, not evil!
Low Adaptability	A child who is slow to adapt to new situations is less likely to succumb to peer pressure and other negative influences. Your child's friends will give up in frustration long before they ever manage to convince her to take a puff from a single cigarette!	A child who is slow to adapt to new situations may find it difficult to switch from one task to the next or to accept major changes to her daily routine.	Because your child thrives on routine, try to make family routines as consistent and predictable as possible. When deviations from the regular routine are necessary (we're talking family life, not a scientific experiment, after all!), try to prepare your child in advance so that she won't be so easily thrown.

continued

TABLE 2.1

For Better and For Worse: How Different Types of Character Traits Play Out in Different Situations *(continued)*

Intensity	When It's a Good Thing	When It's Not Such a Good Thing	Bringing Out the Best in Your Child
High Intensity	A high-intensity child demands and receives the attention of adults. You never have to worry about his needs being overlooked because he would never allow that to happen. He's good at looking out for number one.	A high-intensity child's theatrics can get a bit tiresome at times—like if you just want to hit the hay yourself, but he refuses to go to bed because his favorite pillowcase is in the laundry.	Patience in the extreme is required when you're parenting a high-intensity child—not just because you need it in order to avoid blowing your top, but because you want to model this particular virtue for your child. (High-intensity kids tend to be a little bit lacking in the patience department.)
Low Intensity	A low-intensity kid is pretty easy to get along with—someone who cruises through life without making a lot of waves.	If you've got a low-intensity kid and a high-intensity kid, it's easy to overlook the needs of your low-intensity kid. The reason is obvious: Little Miss High Intensity has a knack for demanding and receiving the lion's share of your attention.	Don't penalize your lower intensity kid for being less demanding than her higher intensity siblings or peers. Make sure that her needs get met, too.

Mood	When It's a Good Thing	When It's Not Such a Good Thing	Bringing Out the Best in Your Child
Positive Mood	A generally happy kid is fun to be around. Consider yourself lucky if you ended up with a kid with this type of temperament.	It can be easy to overlook the needs of an "easy kid" who always seems to be in a good mood, simply because a child like this tends to be less demanding.	Don't overlook the needs of your "happy kid," just because he may not be as demanding as some of his siblings or peers. It's not fair to punish him for being easy to get along with!
Negative Mood	A consistently negative kid can be a major challenge for any parent. No matter how much you do to try to make her happy, you may not be able to turn her negative attitude around. You may also find that this particular child demands more than her fair share of the attention in your family—something that can cause conflict within the family.	You're likely to be very tuned into the needs of a child who displays a consistently negative attitude. (Given how much complaining a child like this tends to do, what choice do you have but to hear her grievances?)	Accept the fact that your child's mood may be hard-wired, and you may not be able to alter this aspect of her temperament, no matter how hard you try. That doesn't mean you should abandon all efforts to try to encourage her to see the sunnier side of life; it simply means that you should stop blaming yourself or your melancholy baby for her down-in-the-dumps moods.

continued

TABLE 2.1

For Better and For Worse: How Different Types of Character Traits Play Out in Different Situations *(continued)*

Attention Span and Distractability	When It's a Good Thing	When It's Not Such a Good Thing	Bringing Out the Best in Your Child
High Attention Span (Low Distractibility)	A child with a high attention span is able to zero in and focus on the job that needs to be done, whether it's cleaning his room, finishing his homework, or winning a game of hockey. It's not surprising that having a high attention span is often linked with high levels of achievement.	A child with a high attention span may focus in on a particular task and tune out all other distractions in his life. It's great if he's focusing on his homework and ignoring the TV, but not so great if it's the other way around! It's also easy for kids like this to get out of balance if they get obsessed with a particular activity, such as playing video games.	Make sure that your child is leading a balanced lifestyle. Don't let him indulge his love of video games to such a degree that he never manages to step outside to toss around a basketball with a group of friends.
Low Attention Span (High Distractibility)	A child with a low attention span can be easily distracted— something that can work to your advantage if circumstances necessitate a last-minute change in plans.	A child with a low attention span may have difficulty completing tasks— something that can cause him grief on the home front, at school, and in his relationships with his peers.	Be on the lookout for signs of attention deficit disorder, a medical condition that may require treatment. See Chapter 5 for more information on this condition.

Sensory Threshold	When It's a Good Thing	When It's Not Such a Good Thing	Bringing Out the Best in Your Child
High Sensory Threshold	A child who is very sensitive may be very tuned into the feelings of others—something that can really help to lay the groundwork for a lifetime of rich and satisfying personal relationships.	A child who is very sensitive may overreact to even normal levels of everyday stimuli—lights, noise, smell, bumps and bruises—as well as social slights.	Anticipate situations that may be overwhelming to your child and help your child to prepare for them. Also, try to see your child's increased sensitivity as a gift of sorts: some of the most sensitive people on the planet also happen to be among our most creative artists.
Low Sensory Threshold	A child who is less sensitive to external stimuli may be able to sleep through thunderstorms and may seem oblivious to the pain from a bumped head or a scraped knee. It can take a lot to faze a kid like this!	A child who is less sensitive to external stimuli may have difficulty figuring out how to interpret other people's emotional signals—something that can contribute to social awkwardness.	Emotional literacy (the ability to understand what other people are feeling) doesn't come naturally to every child, so be prepared to step in and coach your child a little if it's obvious that her skills are lagging a little on this front.

Parenting a "difficult" or spirited child

...ing an easy child tends to be relatively easy, but parenting a difficult or spirited child can try the patience of a saint. Here are some tips for holding on to what's left of your sanity if you've been blessed with an extra-challenging kid:

- **Remind yourself that your child's temperament is something with which she was born.** She isn't being intense or moody just to drive you crazy, even though there may be days when you swear that's the case! "One of my children is much more challenging than any of the others," says Kerri, a 37-year-old mother of six. "I have to remind myself that this is just the way she is. It is not intentional, and she deserves as much love and respect as my other children do."

- **Try to see your child's more challenging character traits in a more positive light.** Instead of thinking of your child as stubborn, see your child as persistent. Instead of seeing your child as bossy, recognize your child's budding leadership abilities. Also recognize that a supposedly negative trait can be a good thing under different circumstances, and vice versa. As Sal Severe notes in *How to Behave So Your Preschooler Will, Too!*: "On some days, persistence creates a 'can-do' attitude. On other days, it creates a 'won't do' attitude."

- **Accentuate your child's positives.** Rather than focusing on the things about your child that are driving you crazy, focus on the things that you like and admire most about her. Instead of complaining about how picky my daughter is about everything—the downside to her extreme sensitivity— I try to remind myself how she is going to use her sensitivity to change the world through her art, her music, and her writing.

- **Keep your expectations realistic.** Make a point of praising your child for any improvements you note in her behavior. *Remember:* it's progress, not perfection that you're after.

- **Learn how to pick your battles.** If you've got the kind of child who is willing to battle you on everything from sun-up to sun-down, you're going to have to choose your battles. Otherwise, you're going to feel totally fried before you even get through breakfast. If you're not sure how to tell the difference between the big stuff and the stuff that is merely masquerading as big stuff, flip to Chapter 5. It's one of the issues I talk about at length in that particular chapter.

- **Everyone remain calm.** Try to keep your cool as much as possible, even if your child is somehow managing to push each and every one of your buttons at the same time. (Hey, that kind of fancy fingerwork may mean she's got a future as a pianist!) Although emitting a primal scream may feel good in the heat of the moment, becoming overly emotional or angry with your child tends to be counterproductive in the long run; if you need to let off steam, do yourself and your child a favor and pick up the phone and call a friend instead.

- **Anticipate the knowing sidelong glances of other parents.** Some parents with easy kids are unlikely to understand the challenges with which you're dealing. They may even label you a "bad parent" and your child "a bad kid!" Although the kind of temperament your kid ends up with is pretty much a roll of the dice, parents of easy kids are sometimes guilty of giving themselves too much credit for what simply amounts to biological good luck. As Harriet Lerner notes in *The Mother Dance: How Children Change Your Life:* "Such a mother sincerely believes that you can easily get your frisky, attentionally challenged, rebellious, and colorful offspring 'under control' if you just take charge in the appropriate manner." The moral of the story? You'll be more likely to find support and understanding if you turn to other parents who are dealing with challenging kids than if you attempt to raid the ranks of the parents with the easy kids. (Frankly, the parenting skills of the parents of the easy kids tend to be a wee bit underdeveloped, if you ask me!)

- **Take breaks from your child.** Parenting is exhausting at the best of times, and parenting an extra-challenging child will drain your parenting reservoirs all the sooner, so make sure that you schedule breaks from your child on a regular basis. Despite what some people would have you believe, martyrdom is not part of the motherhood job description, so don't ask yourself to play the part.

 MOM'S THE WORD

"Our third child is what some might call a 'spirited' child. She is so very different from her sisters and sometimes leaves me feeling frustrated and exhausted. Patience is most definitely a key to dealing with her. What I have found works is not yelling but talking to her and being firm when necessary. You must say exactly what you mean and mean exactly what you say. You cannot make idle threats. If you say 'don't touch that again, or you will go to your room,' then you must follow through. If you don't mean it, then don't say it because children like this will call your bluff."

—*Karen, 34, mother of three*

When worlds (and personalities!) collide

Of course, another factor needs to be considered when you're considering your child's temperament: what child psychologists like to refer to as "goodness of fit"—whether there's a good fit between your child's temperament and your own.

There's no denying it: life is easier if you and your child happen to be temperamentally in step—if you're both very outgoing or if you're both very shy, for example. Where you run into difficulty is with a major personality conflict between you and your child.

You've no doubt seen this play out in your own circle of friends and perhaps even in your own family: a sports-loving father ends up with a book-loving son who can't imagine using a hockey puck as anything other than a paperweight. The father has two choices in this situation:

1. Drag his son kicking and screaming to the hockey arena each Saturday morning and hope that his love of sports will somehow rub off on the little tyke. A more likely scenario, of course, is that junior will stuff his novel inside his hockey jersey and read it whenever the coach sends him to the bench, where he'll be more and more often as it becomes increasingly obvious to the coach that the kid would rather read than skate.

2. Deal with the fact that his son is never going to be a sports nut and learn to love and accept his son just the way he is.

There can be a bit of an adjustment if you end up with a kid who is somehow different than the one you ordered. I grew up in a family of four girls, and we spent our entire childhoods reading books, making Barbie houses out of cardboard boxes, and making forts in the ravine behind our parents' house. You can imagine what a shock it was to my system to end up with a teenaged daughter who chose for a time to express her total disdain for the whole Barbie thing by pinning a decapitated Barbie head to her purse (okay, I have to admit I have a bit of grudging admiration for that particular feminist *pièce de résistance!*) and two boys whose idea of a good time involves either playing video games at top volume or playing road hockey at full intensity. My third son is the only one who seems to be following in my footsteps in any way: he loves books; he likes peace and quiet; and he has yet to rip the head off a doll. But then again, he's only five. There's still plenty of time for that yet. . . .

Anyway, what I'm trying to say in my characteristically long-winded way is that you sometimes have to give yourself an attitude adjustment in order to be the kind of parent you want to be to the kids with whom you ended up. It didn't take me long to figure out that applying "quiet little girl" parenting techniques to my two Tasmanian-devil middle boys was simply not going to work. I used to think the methods my parents used on me were different because I grew up in a kinder, gentler time, but recently I've concluded that it was because I was a kinder, gentler kind of kid. All it took to get me to give on a particular issue was my mortal fear that my dad might be mad at me or—even worse—disappointed in me. (I can hear my kids laughing hysterically at this one. Excuse me? Did I just hear someone mutter the word "Wimp?")

As you can see, I've been hit with this temperamental disconnect thing in my very own family. The first time it happened, it rocked my world—just like getting stuck with a party animal for a roommate did in my university days. Now, I see the whole parent-child temperament mismatch as a bit of a challenge—an opportunity to take my creative thinking abilities to a whole new level. (Did I happen to mention that my kids are smart as well as incredibly high energy?)

In fact, over the years, I've actually learned to take the whole thing as a compliment, as proof that the universe somehow has faith in my ability to rise to the occasion and raise this motley assortment of kids to age 18. Of course, that's how I feel on a good day. On a bad day, I figure that there's been some terrible mistake and they've mistaken me for some other Ann Douglas (a much more energetic one, who is pretty much a shoo-in for sainthood).

If you're in the same boat as me, sharing your life with one or more kids who you swear must have been switched at birth, here are a few bits of advice for the sake of your sanity and theirs:

- **Accept the fact that you're dealing with a mismatch of temperaments.** That should allow you to sidestep the thoroughly energy-zapping and time-wasting blame game. It's not your fault that you're the way you are, and it's not your kid's fault that she's the way she is. You simply are the way you are; deal with it and move on.

- **Figure out what you can do to make your interactions as pain-free as possible for the two of you.** If you have a tendency to overreact, and she has a gift for pushing your buttons, you may have to work on summoning up every iota of patience before you allow a single word to pass through your lips. (Hint: This involves knowing yourself inside out, so if you haven't done much navel-gazing since your pregnancy days, it's time to get friendly with your navel again.)

- **Resist the temptation to label your child the difficult one.** It may become a self-fulfilling prophecy. You don't want your child to feel obliged to live up to that vision of herself. Besides, how can you be 100 percent sure that she's the one who is being difficult? What if some of the difficulties that are playing out in the parent-child melodrama stem from your own finely cultivated stubborn streak? (I know, I know: I'm back to blaming Mom again!)

- **Recognize that parents who have children with recognized physical or developmental disabilities often find it particularly challenging to find someone with the skills necessary to step in and take over so that they can get a break from the frontlines of parenting.** If you find yourself in this situation, you may want to talk to other parents who have children with special needs (or to get in touch with agencies serving families who have children with special needs in your community) to find out what sorts of childcare or respite care services may be available to you.

- **Remember to give yourself plenty of time off for good behavior, whether you feel like you've earned it or not.** If you've already forgotten all the important pamper thyself stuff that I covered in the last chapter, pour yourself a cup of coffee and reread it before you do anything else. That's an order, soldier!

Your parenting style

Although genes dictate what traits our children are born with, it's the environment in which the child grows up that determines how those traits play out. According to psychologists, the split between inborn and acquired personality traits is roughly 50/50, so you still have a major role to play in determining the type of person your child ultimately becomes. Because you have so little control over the natural factors, you'll want do to everything you can to influence the factors on the nurture side of the equation, adopting a parenting style that will bring out the best—rather than the worst—in your child.

Although each parent has his or her own *modus operandi,* experts have identified three basic types of parenting styles: authoritarian, permissive, and authoritative (what parenting book author Barbara Coloroso likes to refer to as the brickwall, jellyfish, and backbone schools of parenting, respectively).

Here's what you need to know about each of the three parenting styles:

- **Authoritarian:** As the name implies, authoritarian parents tend to be big on control. Their motto? "I'm the one in charge." They expect immediate obedience from their children and have a strict, unwavering code of conduct that offers little, if any, opportunity to question their edicts. What's more, they're prepared to enforce their rules through spanking or yelling. Children of authoritarian parents learn to obey authoritarian parents not because they believe their parents' rules are fair or reasonable, but rather because they fear the consequences of not obeying. These children have less opportunity to learn how to control their own behavior and are, consequently, less independent and confident than children raised by less controlling parents. Because the focus of this particular discipline style is on stamping out the bad rather than celebrating the good, children raised in this sort of environment may not feel particularly loved by their parents, which can put them at risk of developing an array of self-esteem-related problems. Bottom line? This ain't exactly the formula for raising happy, well-adjusted children!

- **Permissive:** Permissive parents can be found at the opposite end of the discipline spectrum. Their motto? "Anything goes." They allow practically any behavior so long as their child isn't in any immediate danger. Consequently, they don't have a lot of rules for their children, and what rules they do have tend to be enforced on a rather haphazard basis (such as whenever Mom or Dad can be bothered). Kids raised by permissive parents lack structure and don't have a clue about how society expects them to behave. They tend to be impulsive, self-indulgent, aggressive, and highly inconsiderate because their parents have always given in to their needs. Because they have yet to master any self-control or self-discipline, they're held hostage by their own needs and wants, doing anything and everything on a whim simply because they've got the urge. Although they tend to be highly creative, even that can get them into trouble if they choose to exercise that creative streak in the wrong way, such as by coloring on the walls at Grandma's house, picking flowers from the neighbor's garden, or trying to upstage the bride at a family wedding. (You've encountered kids like this, now haven't you?)

- **Authoritative:** Most parenting experts agree that an authoritative parenting style works best for parents and kids. The motto that these types of parents choose to adopt? "We're in this together." They set clear limits and have high expectations of their children's behavior, but, unlike authoritarian parents, they encourage two-way communication and tend to be a bit more flexible in applying the rules. They're known for being fair, consistent, and willing to discuss problems and work through solutions with their kids, a parenting approach that can reap tremendous dividends for the entire family. Authoritative parents tend to be rewarded with well-adjusted, self-confident children who respect themselves and others around them and who demonstrate good self-control. These children tend to be more achievement-oriented than those raised by other types of parents, and as an added perk, they tend to be less rebellious during their teen years (reason enough to buy into this particular parenting style, in my humble opinion).

As you can see, there's really no choice to be made when it comes to picking a parenting style—unless, of course, you are secretly hoping to be a less-than-effective parent. Although you may have to do a bit more work upfront, you dramatically increase your chances of ending up with the parenting holy grail: a happy, well-adjusted kid.

Doing Yourself Out of a Job

Parenting is one of the few professions on the planet where becoming redundant is actually a good thing. After all, you spend roughly 18 years readying your child for that momentous day when she'll finally be ready to face the world on her own. When that day arrives, you want to make sure that she's equipped with three pieces of equipment that will help her to weather life's storms: a fully functioning moral compass, a life raft to help her swim against the growing tide of commercialism, and a virtually foolproof self-esteem toolkit. Here's what you need to know to achieve each of these three goals.

Setting your child's moral compass

It's a lot easier to make your way through life if you have a strong moral compass to guide you. You don't have to second-guess every step you take because you instinctively know whether or not you're heading off in the right direction. What parent wouldn't wish that kind of life for their child?

What's wrong with "family values"?

Although it sounds terribly old-fashioned to talk about morals and values (it kind of reeks of Big Brother, mind-control, the ultra-conservative right, and other scary stuff), I think we need to get past all that "Family Values" paranoia and realize that "family values" can actually be a very good thing.

I don't know about you, but I feel terribly old when I flip through channels on the TV and realize just how much our moral standards have decayed over my children's lifetimes. Although swearing on TV was still a rarity in the late 1980s when I gave birth to my first two children, it's now become commonplace— so commonplace, in fact, that the censors don't even bother to bleep out some of the supposedly less offensive words. (I guess they had to give up because of the sheer volume of bleeping that would have been required. The Parents Television Council found that the number of swear words on TV increased fivefold between 1989 and 1999. Holy bleep, Batman!)

So why haven't we parents wrestled the remote controls away from our kids or permanently set our TVs to the nature channel? I think there are a few things going on:

- First, there's the undeniable fact that TV is the world's most available babysitter, someone who can pinch-hit for you when your kids are fighting, you've got a headache, and you're trying to make dinner.

- Second, TV has become a huge part of our culture that it's practically inescapable. Your kids don't even have to watch TV to find out what happened on a particular show the night before. They are likely to receive detailed plot summaries and dialogue recaps courtesy of neighborhood kids who don't have such tight restrictions on their TV viewing.

- Third, we're made to feel like fuddy-duddies if we object to the declining moral standards of what passes for programming on television. *Temptation Island?* Please!

Of course, the problem with our declining moral standards is much bigger than TV. Much, much bigger. Somehow, we've gotten the message that it's old-fashioned to set the bar too high for your kids when it comes to basic things like good manners and respect. The result has been a willingness to allow the pendulum to swing alarmingly far in the opposite direction. I remember how shocked I felt the first time I showed up at an elementary school during the day and heard little kids swearing at one another. (My own kids were still preschoolers at the time, so this was my first exposure to an elementary school playground since my own growing-up days.) Talk about culture shock! I felt like I had stepped into an episode of *The Twilight Zone.* Were little kids actually talking like this within earshot of their teachers? Why wasn't anyone doing anything about the problem?

I feel like we're at a bit of a moral crossroads when it comes to raising our kids. Things have gotten pretty bad, and they're only going to get worse unless we are prepared to take a stand. I was shocked to discover, for example, that junior high school girls are routinely subjected to comments from their peers that meet the legal definition of sexual harassment and that sex and drugs and rock 'n' roll are no longer the stuff of which high school fantasies are made; they're alive and well and living in your child's elementary school.

It's enough to make you want to grab your preschooler and head for the nearest desert island. I find it terrifying to consider just how toxic our culture has become and how powerless we as individual parents can feel to hold back the tidal wave that is threatening to drag our children under. But, we can make a difference if we lock arms with other parents, join forces with our kids' schools, talk to our neighbors, and resolve to raise the moral bar a little higher for our kids. It's not too late.

Fighting the battle on home turf

The most important front of the battle is the one that has to be waged on home turf, under your very own roof. It may not be easy to fight back against our increasingly toxic culture, but you've got the ultimate weapon at your disposal: the power of the parent-child bond. This bond can serve as an anchor that will give your child the courage to say no to whatever temptations may come her way. Although you may feel that parents exert little, if any, influence over their children's morals as they grow older, research has shown quite the opposite to be the case. When children feel a strong emotional bond with their parents, they are less likely to stray from the moral path.

Despite what you may think, children don't learn the difference between right and wrong purely by chance. Like walking, talking, and riding a bike, moral intelligence is a skill that has to be taught.

Just in case you're not quite clear what I'm talking about when I use the term *moral* intelligence, here's a quick definition. Michele Borba, Ed.D., author of *Building Moral Intelligence: The Seven Essential Virtues That Teach Kids to Do the Right Thing*, defines moral intelligence as "the capacity to understand right from wrong." Basically, it involves having "strong ethical convictions and [the ability] to act on them so that one behaves in the right and honorable way." (Basically, Michele Borba is saying the same thing that Dr. Laura says when she tells her radio show listeners to "Go do the right thing" at the end of each radio show—albeit in a much less in-your-face kind of way.)

The thought of being entrusted with another human being's moral education can be more than a little overwhelming, I know; particularly if you've got a few skeletons in your closet that may cause some people to question your fitness for the job! Fortunately, you've got 18 years to work on the project, so you don't have to produce dramatic results overnight. (It's a darned good thing, too, because your child's moral education is likely to be one of those one-step-forward-two-steps-back kind of scenarios.)

MOTHER WISDOM

You may want to think of your family's core values as belonging to your family's written or unwritten code of ethics. (It's up to you whether you actually put it down on paper, but it's important that every member of the family knows exactly what your family stands for, morally and ethically speaking.) It's not unusual for corporations and professions to operate in accordance with clearly defined codes of ethics, so why shouldn't families have their own code of ethics, too? Besides, a copy of it may look kind of nice hanging beside your family photo and your family coat of arms on the family room wall!

Here are some tips on getting your child's moral education project off the ground:

- **Decide which values matter most to you and zero in on them first.** With dozens and dozens of core values to choose from (see Table 2.2), you'll only succeed in driving yourself and your kids crazy if you decide to try to focus on them all at once. Besides, you risk becoming the moral-intelligence world's equivalent of one of those 1980s superparents who bombarded their kids with flashcards at every possible opportunity in the hope of making them smarter. (Trust me, you don't want to go there!)

- **Start with the basics.** If you're having a hard time deciding which values to start with, you may want to focus on what Michele Borba refers to as the seven essential virtues: empathy, conscience, self-control, respect, kindness, tolerance, and fairness." If you think you can swing an eighth, I would like to suggest that you pick optimism; without an optimistic world view, it's easy for cynicism and a "who cares" attitude to set in—something that will derail your moral intelligence program before it even gets off the ground.

- **Be prepared to model the virtues you are trying to teach your child.** This is definitely one of those situations where you have to be prepared to walk the talk. "Kids learn morals and values from the examples they see from the people around them," says Ellen, a 30-year-old mother of two. "If you don't treat the people in your life well, how can you expect your kids to be any different?"

- **Teach your kids some basic "emotional literacy" skills.** They need to be able to recognize and read other people's emotions. Talk about the feelings that the characters are experiencing in the stories you read together at bedtime. Hit the mute button during a video and have your child either describe the character's feelings or make up the dialogue herself. Play a game of "name that feeling" the next time you watch the pedestrian traffic whiz by from a park bench at the mall. Or, if you've got a preschooler or school-aged child who still enjoys role-playing games, give her the opportunity to practice her emotional literacy skills and nurture her inner ham at the same time. "There is at least one situation every day that you can use to your advantage in teaching your kids right from wrong," says Mary, a 36-year-old mother of three.

- **Take a new look at current events.** Older children are more likely to be hooked by discussions of moral dilemmas that are being played out in the newspaper headlines—celebrities who have been charged with shoplifting, accounting firms that have been charged with dubious financial practices, politicians who have been caught running their personal expenses through the government coffers—you know, the usual fare!

- **Monitor your children's entertainment choices.** What types of shows are your children watching on TV? What types of Internet sites are they visiting? What kind of music are they listening to? What types of video games are they playing? In addition to watching for racist, sexist, and violent content, you'll also want to be on the lookout for material that promotes values that are incompatible with your own—perhaps lyrics that promote casual sex, drug use, and disrespect toward oneself and others. You may not want to pull the plug or hit the power switch in every case, but you'll at least want to talk about why you find the material so objectionable. (If your kids don't want to listen to what you have to say, then hit the power switch!) Note: See Chapter 7 for additional tips on monitoring your child's TV and computer use.

- **Be conscious of what types of entertainment you're tuning into as well.** The high moral ground that you're standing on will quickly be washed away if your kids catch you watching movies, visiting Web sites, or reading books and magazines that undercut the types of values you're trying to model for them.

- **Don't be afraid to set high moral standards for your kids.** If you've been lax in the past about things such as attitude and manners, it may take them a while to catch on to your family's new code of behavior, but in most cases, they will rise to the occasion. In the meantime, you may have to be prepared to follow through with consequences if your child displays a lot of negative attitude each time you insist on some basic civility. See chapters 3 and 4 for some points on choosing a method of discipline that's compatible with the moral standards that you're trying to model for your child.

- **Praise your child when she displays the kind of behavior you're trying to encourage.** Be as specific as possible in your praise so that she'll understand exactly what she did right and how that made the other person feel: for example, "I noticed the way you shared your blocks with your little sister. That was very generous of you. That made your sister very happy."

- **Don't be afraid to let your child experience some negative emotions if she's acted insensitively and hurt someone's feelings.** Although it's tempting to want to prevent our children from experiencing a lot of guilt and shame, we deprive our children of the opportunity to learn from their mistakes if we protect them from these emotions. It's also important to make sure that a child who has acted wrongly understands what she did wrong, why it was wrong, and what she can do to make it right. (Hint: Try to let your child come up with the restitution plan on her own; she'll learn more that way.)

- **Remind yourself that a few missteps are inevitable.** What you're aiming for is evidence that your child is making progress on the moral front. "There will always be situations in which their morals and values will be challenged and they will fail," says Ellen, a 30-year-old mother of two. "All I can hope is that, in most cases, that 'good feeling/bad feeling' will lead them in the right direction."

- **Spend time with your kids.** It's not just necessary so that you will have the opportunity to teach your child these all-important values; it's also important so that you will be able to forge the emotional bonds that will make these values truly matter at the end of the day. Remember, the bond between you and your child is your ultimate weapon against any and all competing value systems.

- **Be prepared to play an active role in creating a healthier, more connected community.** Give your time to causes you believe in and encourage your children to do the same. Better yet, adopt a charity as a family and spend time volunteering together. It's a terrific way to cement those family bonds.

TABLE 2.2

What's on the Menu? Defining Your Family's Core Values

The following is a list of some of the kinds of values that you may choose to stress in your family. The list is by no means exhaustive; you probably can think of some other ones that should make it on to the list, too. The purpose of the list is simply to get you thinking about the values that matter most to you and that you most want to pass along to your kids.

Altruism	Friendliness	Peacefulness
Assertiveness	Frugality	Perseverance
Calmness	Generosity	Politeness
Caring	Gentleness	Purposefulness
Charitableness	Genuineness	Reliability
Civic-mindedness	Graciousness	Resilience
Communicativeness	Gratitude	Resourcefulness
Compassion	Helpfulness	Respectfulness
Compatibility	Honesty	Responsibility

Connectedness	Humility	Self-control
Conscientiousness	Idealism	Self-discipline
Consideration	Industriousness	Self-motivation
Cooperation	Initiative	Sensitivity
Courage	Insightfulness	Serenity
Courtesy	Integrity	Simplicity
Creativity	Inventiveness	Sincerity
Dependability	Joyfulness	Steadfastness
Determination	Justice	Stewardship
Discipline	Kindness	Tactfulness
Discretion	Love	Tenacity
Empathy	Loyalty	Thankfulness
Excellence	Mercy	Tolerance
Fairness	Moderation	Trustworthiness
Faithfulness	Modesty	Truthfulness
Fidelity	Obedience	Understanding
Flexibility	Optimism	Unselfishness
Forgiveness	Patience	Virtue

This is all I'm going to say about morals and values for now, but we'll be returning to this topic again and again throughout this book. I have a lot to say on the subject!

MOM'S THE WORD

"I have been told by family, friends, and even strangers how amazing my kids are. They are very kind, thoughtful, and helpful. My older daughters volunteered to help restore an old schoolhouse around the corner from us—the last one left in our country. They, along with a few other pre-teens and teens—received a community service award this past fall for their efforts in recognition of the many hours of their own time that they devoted to the project."

—*Kerri, 37, mother of six*

MOTHER WISDOM

Unless you're fortunate enough to live in a natural setting, you may have to go out of your way to help your kids to develop an appreciation for the natural world. Here are some steps you can take if you decide to make environmental stewardship one of your family's core values:

- Go for a walk on the wild side—literally. Head deep into the woods so that you can immerse yourselves in the sounds of nature. If you bring along a tape recorder, you'll be able to make a game out of identifying the various nature sounds after you get home.

- Hop on your bikes and observe your part of the world by bicycle. Talk to your kids about the impact of the automobile on living things and ask them to count the number of cars that drive through a busy intersection during a typical five-minute period. Talk about ways in which your family could use the car less and walk more and the health, financial, and environmental advantages of doing so.

- Write an environmental history of your family. Encourage your kids to ask their grandparents about ways in which they practiced recycling (if they did) during their own growing-up years and when our society's "throw-away mentality" first emerged. Your kids may want to find out, for example, when paper cups, microwave popcorn bags, and other garbage-producing goods first hit the grocery store shelves.

- Make some garbage resolutions as a family. Calculate how much garbage your family uses in a week or a year and then come up with some practical strategies for reducing the amount of trash you produce. Have each member of the family commit to one personal "garbage resolution"—for example, carrying a reusable cup to the drive-thru the next time you buy take-out coffee.

- Organize a fundraiser for a local environmental organization. Have a garage sale, a bake sale, or whatever else comes to mind. You'll have a great time and raise money for a worthwhile cause at the same time.

- Encourage your kids to write letters to the local newspaper asking politicians and industry leaders to take action to protect the environment. Letters from kids tend to have a far greater impact than letters from grownups, so it only makes sense to let your kids fight this particular battle for you!

Swimming upstream: parenting in a commercial culture

It's one thing to protect your kids from graphic violence and gratuitous sex during their growing-up years; it's quite another to be able to protect them from the steady bombardment of advertising images that are specifically aimed at children.

According to the Center for a New American Dream (a non-profit association whose motto is "more fun, less stuff"):

- The average American child is exposed to more than 20,000 commercial messages each year.

- Brand loyalty is now beginning by as early as age two.

- By age three, 20 percent of kids are making specific requests for brand-name products.

Here are some tips on swimming against the growing tide of commercialism and encouraging your children to be happy with less:

- **Limit the amount of time your kids spend watching TV.** You'll want to help minimize their exposure to those oh-so-seductive TV commercials. When they are watching TV, hit the mute button during commercials or—better yet—tape the TV shows so that you can skip over the commercials entirely by using the fast-forward button on your VCR.

- **Give your kids a crash-course in media literacy.** Talk to them about the high-pressure techniques and outlandish claims advertisers make in an effort to sell their products. Encourage your kids to challenge product claims by conducting their own product tests at home: Does that frozen pizza really taste as good as homemade—or is it more accurate to say that it tastes about as good as cardboard? You can pick up all kinds of great tips on teaching kids to be media literate by visiting the Center for Media Literacy Web site at www.medialit.org, the Center for a New American Dream's Web site at www.newdream.org, and the National Institute on Media and the Family's Web site at www.mediafamily.org. You can encourage your kids to hone their consumer skills by visiting the following three Web sites aimed at kids:

- Consumer Reports: www.zillions.org

- PBS Kids' Don't Buy It: http://pbskids.org/dontbuyit

- The World Wildlife Federation and the Center for a New American Dream's "I Buy Different" Web site for young people: www.ibuydifferent.org

- **Be realistic about your child's level of discernment.** Don't expect children under the age of five to be able to differentiate between regular TV programs and commercials or children under the age of eight to be able to think critically about advertising messages. They simply don't have the skills to be able to differentiate between the two types of messages.

MOTHER WISDOM

Want to learn more about the impact of advertising on children and what the advertising industry is doing to regulate advertising messages targeted at children? Visit the Children's Advertising Review Unit Web site at www.caru.org.

- **Teach your kids to work for what they want rather than expect you to buy everything for them.** Kids need to know that adults have a finite amount of money and that, like them, we have to make conscious choices about what we are going to spend our money on. Besides, doing chores to earn money is good for kids: Studies have shown that kids who were required to do chores from the age of three or four were less likely to get involved with drugs, more likely to get a job, and more likely to develop healthy adult relationships. So, why not give your kid a break by hiring her to do some odd jobs for you. That leaf pile in the backyard is practically calling her name. . . .

- **Try to connect with other parents who are trying to encourage their kids to be happy with less.** "I think the hardest part about being a parent today is living in an era of instant gratification when everyone wants everything right now," says Mary, a 36-year-old mother of three. "I was not brought up that way and I don't believe in it, but none of my children's friends' parents seem to have any problem with it. This creates tension between my children and me because 'well, so-and-so has one' is a common phrase around our house. I am trying to teach our children that life is not handed to you on a silver platter and that you have to work for what you have. I feel like I'm being undermined by almost every other parent around me. It can be very challenging." Although you may feel like you're the only parent who is trying to promote a less materialistic lifestyle, you're not. If you talk to other parents in your community or connect with other parents via online discussion boards, you'll find that a growing number of parents are trying to wrestle back their children's childhoods from the clutches of the big corporations. And, yes, Virginia, it can be done.

NO KIDDING!

Feel like your kids are constantly nagging you for something? It's not all in your head. A study by the Center for a New American Dream found that a typical kid will nag her parents nine times to get something the parent had already said no to. The worst offenders of all are 12- and 13-year-olds, sometimes nagging their parents up to 50 times after the no verdict has come down. So much for "Just say no."

The self-esteem toolkit: the gift that keeps on giving

Forget about the flashy electronic gizmos and the high-priced sports equipment: One of the greatest gifts that you can give your child is the gift of self-esteem—the ability to feel good about yourself no matter what kind of curve balls life happens to toss your way. Self-esteem is important because it can have a major influence on a person's accomplishments, ability to form friendships, and happiness throughout childhood and adulthood. Here are some tips on promoting your child's self-esteem:

- **Start with yourself first.** It's hard to encourage your child to feel good about herself if you positively radiate "I hate myself" vibes each time you look in the mirror. If a self-esteem tune-up seems like it may be a good idea, there's no time like the present to start working with a counselor to get your own psychological house in order.

- **Accept your child for who she is and encourage her to celebrate her own unique qualities.** Remind her how boring the world would be if we all looked and acted the same. (Note: If body image seems to be a particular struggle for your child, be sure to check out the body image material in Chapter 13. You'll find all kinds of practical tips on promoting a healthy body image.)

- **Keep your expectations for your child realistic.** It's one thing to celebrate your child's achievements, but don't make your child feel pressured to perform to a level that is impossible to achieve—something that can be very detrimental to a child's feelings of self-worth.

- **Encourage your child to set realistic standards for herself, too.** The closer the match between what sociologists refer to as her "perceived self" (the way she sees herself right now) and her "ideal self" (the way she would ideally like to be), the higher her self-esteem will be. Obviously, setting the bar too high for herself may mean setting herself up for disappointment.

- **Make your love unconditional.** Let your kid know that you love her no matter what. When you need to discipline your child, make sure you do so in a way that says, "I may not like the way you are acting, but I sure love you." (You'll find tips on pulling off this particular bit of parenting sleight of hand in chapters 3 and 4.)

- **Encourage your child to try something new.** When she succeeds, she'll experience the self-esteem burst that goes along with achieving something for the very first time. Resist the temptation to jump in too soon if she starts becoming frustrated; otherwise, you'll rob her of much of the sense of accomplishment that goes along with mastering a new skill.

- **Give your child the freedom to make choices.** Increase the number of choices she's able to make as she demonstrates she's able to make good choices.

- **Declare your home a putdown-free zone.** Don't allow family members to engage in name-calling or any other sort of putdown behavior.

- **Help your child rethink any negative ideas she may have developed about herself.** For example, if she's concluded that she's a bad student just because she struggles with math, or that she's no good at sports just because hockey doesn't happen to be her forte, remind her that she is always at the top of her class in English and that she's got a natural talent when it comes to shooting hoops.

- **Be on the lookout for the warning signs that your child could be suffering from a self-esteem problem.** Although most kids will exhibit some of these signs on occasion, you may have cause for concern if your child exhibits a lot of the following behaviors on an ongoing basis:

  - an unwillingness to try new things for fear of leaving herself open to failure

  - difficulty accepting either praise or criticism

  - extreme sensitivity to other people's opinions

  - quitting a game or abandoning a task at the first sign of frustration

  - cheating in sports in order to improve her performance

  - acting controlling and bossy or silly and babylike as a means of hiding her feelings of inadequacy, frustration, or powerlessness

  - making excuses or blaming other people for her failure to achieve, or downplaying the significance of those failures

  - losing interest in activities that have previously been a source of enjoyment

  - a decline in academic performance

  - spending less time socializing with friends

  - moodiness (sadness, crying, anger, or frustration)

  - consistently making negative comments about herself.

- **Encourage self-praise.** Teach your child to acknowledge her own achievements so that she will ultimately be able to assume full responsibility for her own self-esteem maintenance program.

MOTHER WISDOM

Want to tilt the self-esteem roulette wheel in your child's favor? Researchers have discovered that the following factors can play a major role in contributing to a child's healthy self-esteem:

- Feeling safe and secure about the present and the future
- Feeling like she is accepted and loved by others
- Having a sense of purpose and direction
- Feeling like she is competent and capable
- Taking pride in her own achievements
- Being able to trust in herself and those around her
- Feeling like she's a responsible person and that other people can count on her
- Feeling like she's making a contribution to her family and her community
- Being given real choices and decisions to make as opposed to always having other people make those decisions for her
- Feeling like she is in control of her emotions
- Knowing that she has the self-discipline required to carry through on a task, even when the going gets rough
- Feeling that others in her life will support and applaud her efforts, not just her achievements
- Being able to accept and learn from her mistakes and failures rather than being defeated by them
- Belonging to a caring, nurturing family that feels good about itself and that takes pride in the achievements of its individual members

CHAPTER 3

The Dirt on D

"I find discipline to be one of the biggest challenges of parenthood. Sometimes I don't know how far to take it, which battles to fight and which ones to bow out of gracefully."
—Maria, 34, mother of three

"I believe you have to have a consistent structure, but you need to be flexible within that framework. All-or-nothing rarely works in parenting."
—Jill, 34, mother of four

No doubt about it: if there's one part of the parenting job description that parents find particularly challenging, it's the need to discipline our kids. Not only do many of us feel like we're out of our league when it comes to matters of discipline, we also may be more inclined to be our child's buddy rather than to play the role of the heavy.

If you catch yourself indulging in momentary fantasies about hiring your own Mary Poppins or Maria von Trapp look-alike to step in and do all the parenting dirty work for you, you had better give yourself a quick reality check. Not only is there a worldwide shortage of singing nannies, but the discipline portfolio is too critical to be handed off to anyone else (even someone capable of g your kids such important life skills as the words to percalifragilisticexpialidocious" and "Do-Re-Mi"). As tough as this part of parenting may be at times, discipline plays a critical role in shaping the kind of person your child ends up being. It's simply too important a task to be downloaded to someone else. Like it or not, the buck stops with you, Mom and Dad.

Yep, discipline is a major challenge for most parents—and for most parenting book authors, too. There's a lot to say on the subject—so much, in fact, that I wasn't able to shoehorn everything into a single chapter; you're getting three discipline chapters in this book for the price of one. Here's what you'll find in each chapter:

- In this chapter (Chapter 3), I talk about what discipline means and why your child needs it, what you need to know in order to be able to sidestep the most common types of discipline mistakes, the most—and least—effective methods of discipline, how your discipline methods evolve as your child gets older, and how to deal with your feelings of guilt when your best intentions go up in smoke and you blow it on the discipline front. (I hate to break it to you, but it's not really a question of *whether* you will blow it, but *when*.)

- In Chapter 4, I discuss why power struggles occur and what you can do to avoid them, what kids have to gain by getting you locked in a power struggle (and what you have to lose), how to spot situations that tend to trigger power struggles between you and your child, and how to help your child to manage strong emotions while finding ways to manage your own.

- In Chapter 5, I focus on problem behavior—how to deal with routine behavior problems as well as more serious behavioral problems that may signify the need for outside help, and how to decide how high you should be setting the behavioral bar for your child (that is, high enough to challenge your child, but not so high that he trips and falls flat on his face!).

As you can see, we've got a lot of turf to cover on the discipline front. Our first order of business? To pin down the definition of discipline so that we can all be sure we're speaking the same language—literally.

What Discipline Means and Why Your Child Needs It

Although a lot of parents seem to think that discipline is about punishment—they have a powerful mental image of some stern, nineteenth-century schoolmaster tucked away in the deepest, darkest recesses of their brains!—*discipline is actually more about teaching.* In fact, if you flip open a copy of whatever dictionary you happen to have at home (for instance the *Webster's New World College Dictionary*), you're likely to find a definition for discipline that reads something like this: "training that develops self-control, character, or orderliness and efficiency."

That discipline-as-teaching definition certainly rings true for Catherine, a 33-year-old mother of four. She believes that when she disciplines her children, she is teaching them important lessons about what it means to get along with other people and to follow society's rules. "Discipline means teaching my children what is acceptable and what is not," she explains. "They need to know that there are rules we need to follow all through life, regardless of our age. Discipline means setting them on the right path to becoming good and decent human beings."

Aubyn, a 38-year-old mother of one, agrees with Catherine's take on the matter: "Discipline is a means to an end—a way to encourage our children to behave in appropriate ways and to learn right from wrong."

You won't go too far wrong with discipline if you keep Aubyn's simple definition in mind. You'll find that you naturally gravitate toward discipline methods that emphasize teaching rather than punishment—in other words, discipline methods that are designed to encourage your child to learn something from his mistakes so that he won't keep making the same mistakes, rather than discipline methods that are simply designed to punish him for getting it wrong.

Keep your eyes on the prize

Disciplining a child can be a tough and thankless job. You may have to wait a good 10 or 20 years before you get even the most grudging expression of gratitude from your child for all the hard work that has gone into raising him to that point. Before you get to that point, he's likely to challenge your authority, complain about your rules, and test your limits approximately 10,000 times. It's definitely not what you would call an instant payoff scenario!

You really have to keep your eyes on the prize on the days when the going gets especially tough—you know, when your 10-year-old seems determined to get you embroiled in a lengthy debate about the merits of soap, and it's not even 8 A.M.

At times like this, you have to stop and remind yourself that you are giving your child a tremendous advantage in life by teaching him to follow society's rules (the use of soap being one of those rules) and to be a well-disciplined human being. In fact, if you think about it, some of the most successful people on the planet also happen to be the most self-disciplined: they set high standards for themselves; they get along well with other people; and they have the necessary drive and discipline to keep on track. Why would you want to settle for anything less for your child?

The more immediate payoff

Fortunately, there's a more immediate payoff to your discipline strategy (good news if you're finding it hard to live for that distant day when your child finally acknowledges that soap is not the enemy). Having clearly defined limits, and parents who enforce those limits, helps a child to feel safe, secure, and valued—something that can, in turn, encourage a child to value himself. After all, if your parents can't be bothered to make sure that you have a shower and that you use soap, they really can't care all that much about you, now can they?

Don't let the fact that your child insists on challenging each and every limit that you set act as evidence that he doesn't appreciate the fact that you care enough to set those limits. Although he probably talks up a storm about wishing he could live at so-and-so's house because they have no rules and the kids are allowed to do whatever they please, chances are he feels at least a little sorry for those kids. (Of course, he can't actually admit this. Doing so would be as much as admitting that he's grateful to have rules to follow at home—a major infraction of the Kid Code of Ethics, from what I understand.)

That's not to say that it's easy to play the heavy—to ground your child on the night of his best friend's birthday party because he stole some money from your purse or to take away his TV privileges on the night his favorite show is on because he whacked his little brother on the head with the remote control. You may feel your child's disappointment every bit as acutely as he does. ("When our parents said it hurt them more than us to punish us, they were right!" insists Christine, a 38-year-old mother of four.) Chances are what will allow you to stay the course is the knowledge that the bitter medicine that you're forcing your child to swallow will make him a stronger and better person. You're simply doing your job as a parent.

MOTHER WISDOM

"While criticism or fear of punishment may restrain us from doing wrong, it does not make us wish to do right. Disregarding this simple fact is the great error into which parents and educators fall when they rely on these negative means of correction. The only effective discipline is self-discipline, motivated by the inner desire to act meritoriously in order to do well in one's own eyes, according to one's own values, so that one may feel good about oneself—may 'have a good conscience.'"

—*Bruno Bettelheim,* A Good Enough Parent

The Most Common Types of Discipline Mistakes and How to Avoid Them

The road to discipline nirvana is paved with good intentions. It's one thing to know where you want to end up in 18 years' time (with a reasonably well-disciplined young adult in your life); it's quite another to figure out how you're supposed to get there.

Although a few missteps are inevitable, with any luck, this section will help you to steer clear of any major disasters on the discipline front, starting with a list of the biggest discipline mistakes parents make (think of it as the discipline world's not-so-greatest hits):

Not understanding what discipline is all about

If you don't have a handle on what discipline is supposed to accomplish, you can easily fall into one of the following traps.

- **Being apologetic about the fact that you have to discipline your child.** For whatever reason, this is a major stumbling block for parents of our generation; many of us seem to question our right to discipline our children, possibly because we're so busy trying to be our child's buddy that we haven't quite figured out what it means to be some-one's parent. "I think a lot of parents today try too hard to be their child's friend," says Mary, a 36-year-old mother of three. "What they don't seem to realize is that their child already has friends. What they need is a parent—someone who will tell them that they can't do this or that or stay out until 2 A.M."

- **Refusing to discipline your child because you don't like to see him experiencing any discomfort.** Although you may think you're doing your child a favor by going light in the discipline department, you're actually setting him up to experience a whole lot more discomfort down the road. Individuals who are lacking in the self-discipline depart-ment tend to experience difficulties at school and at work, as well as problems in their personal relationships, and—in more extreme cases—they may come into conflict with the law. Rather than increasing the odds that your child will end up taking a rockier road, why not do your best to help him to master the art of self-discipline early on in life? That, of course, means setting age-appropriate limits for him right from day one and backing up those limits with suitable consequences.

- **Sounding indecisive when you make a discipline deci-sion.** If there's even an iota of hesitation in your voice when you are dealing with a discipline matter, your child is likely to seize upon it and do his best to fan the flames of mother (or father) guilt in an effort to have you rethink your deci-sion. You may find yourself backtracking, giving in, and surrendering what's left of your parental credibility—not exactly the recipe for success on the discipline front.

- **Being an absolute control freak.** Of course, some parents have the opposite problem. They're total control freaks when it comes to matters of discipline—a strategy that is pretty much guaranteed to backfire over time. Although you can get away with being controlling toward little kids, you'll have a mutiny on your hands long before your kids enter the teen years. (Note: Chapter 4 addresses the control freak issue more thoroughly, in the context of power struggles.)

 MOM'S THE WORD

"From the day a toddler issues her first declaration of independence with a loud, emphatic 'NO!,' the parent-child relationship becomes a tug-of-war between holding on and letting go. The sooner we allow our child a greater say in her own life, the smoother and more loving our relationship will be. And, more importantly, the more ready we and our children will be for adolescence when the separation process becomes a necessary, inevitable, and often painful source of conflict."

—*Nancy Samalin with Martha Moraghan Jablow*, Loving Your Child Is Not Enough

MOM'S THE WORD

"For the most part, there is uniformity—'You hit, you sit!'—but obviously you have to recognize the child's age and his ability to understand what he's being taught."

—*Chonee, 38, mother of three*

Not knowing what techniques to use

If you use the wrong techniques—or you apply them incorrectly—you risk making the situation worse, not better.

- **Applying a "one-size-fits-all" discipline strategy to all of your kids.** That approach is likely to be about as successful as ignoring your kids' individual likes and dislikes and insisting they each eat the very same meal at a restaurant. You'll find it more effective and far less stressful if you come up with a few basic rules that apply to everyone across the board (no hitting, no swearing, no stealing other people's stuff) and then fine-tune the rest of the rules as well as the consequences for breaking those rules based on the age, temperament, abilities, and individual strengths and weaknesses of each child. "Discipline is a trial-and-error process since every child is different and what worked with one child does not always work with another child," explains Karen, a 34-year-old mother of two.

- **Repeatedly finding fault with a particular child.** If one of your kids tends to be on your wrong side more often than your right, you might want to ask yourself whether this is a case of the reverse halo effect in action. (Just in case you dozed off in Psych 101, the *halo effect* occurs when you can see only the good things about a particular person; the *reverse halo effect* occurs when you can see only that person's faults. Neither gives you a particularly accurate snapshot of the person because you keep gathering evidence to support the label you have developed for that person. For example, you'll look for evidence of how cooperative your "easy" child is and how uncooperative your "difficult" child is.) It's not hard to see why this can cause difficulty for parents and kids. If you're determined to see the worst in a particular child, chances are you'll find it, whether or not the "bad kid" label that you've stamped on his forehead is deserved. After you've found fault with your "bad kid," you'll probably be a little tougher on him in the discipline department, too. After all, he was pretty much convicted before he even did the crime.

MOM'S THE WORD

"What works for one child doesn't work for all three of them. Different consequences lead to different outcomes depending on the child, so I try to pick whatever consequence will work best for each child. Unfortunately, my husband doesn't agree with this strategy. In fact, he accuses me of favoritism in so far as our kids are concerned."

—*Margaret, 27, mother of three*

- **Attacking the child rather than criticizing the behavior.** It may seem like mere semantics, but your child is likely to hear an entirely different message, depending on the words you use when you're disciplining him. If you criticize your child ("You're a bad boy") rather than the behavior ("It was unkind of you to eat your sister's Halloween candy"), you're likely to put him on the defensive, and what's more, you risk doing a number on his self-esteem. (It's much easier to fix problem behavior than to shed the label of being "a bad kid.")

- **Resorting to punishment too soon.** Instead of focusing on ways of punishing your child, look for ways to put the spotlight on all the positive behaviors he's exhibiting. Positive reinforcement feels good to you, it feels good to your child, and—just as important—it puts the emphasis on the behavior you're trying to reinforce, not the one you're trying to eliminate. It also encourages cooperation, promotes healthy relationships between family members, and teaches children to deal positively with other people. It's even easy to use, something that makes it a hit with tired and busy parents who find it hard to muster up the energy to go another round with the less positive methods of discipline. Who knows—positive reinforcement could very well be the answer to your discipline prayers!

- **Allowing good behavior to go unacknowledged.** It's easy to get so caught up in dealing with your child's bad behavior that you fail to recognize his truly shining moments on the behavior front. For example, you may notice only the six out of seven days when he leaves his socks in the middle of the bathroom floor as opposed to the seventh day when the socks mysteriously make it into the laundry hamper without any coaching from you. Like adults, kids respond well to praise, so don't be afraid to use praise to your advantage; your future basketball star will be more likely to toss his socks into the laundry hamper tomorrow morning if he thinks he's going to score big points with you for making the effort.

- **Making too many excuses for your child.** Most of us can come up with an entire laundry list of excuses to explain away our child's problem behaviors: he's tired; he's young; he's sick; he's hungry; he's worried about his exams; he just had a falling out with his best friend. But the fact is, we all have to be accountable for our behavior, even if we happen to be having a less-than-ideal day. (Just try telling your boss that you bit off a customer's head because you didn't get enough sleep the previous night, and you'll see what I mean.) Besides, when you make excuses for your child, you're sending out the message that you don't think he's up to the challenge of dealing with whatever curveballs life is currently sending his way—not exactly a guaranteed way to boost his self-esteem. Of course, there's yet another reason for having a "no excuses" policy when it comes to matters of discipline: if you get in the habit of making a lot of excuses for your child, you're giving him a license to misbehave—something that should pretty much leave you quaking in your boots!

- **Becoming overly emotional.** Not only are you likely to make poor discipline decisions if you allow yourself to become overly emotional, but you're also going to lose a lot of your credibility the next time you give him your trademarked mini-lecture on the importance of anger management. Besides, if your child's whole goal in acting up is to find out whether he could push your buttons effectively enough to get you mad, well, bingo, he just hit pay dirt! (See Chapter 4 for some tips on controlling your emotions when you're embroiled in a frustrating situation with your child.)

- **Rewarding bad behavior.** If your child manages to wear you down after making his ninth consecutive demand for chocolate breakfast cereal at the grocery store, you've just created a monster. (Son of Count Chocula, I presume?) Not only have you taught him that "No" doesn't necessarily mean "No," but also you've allowed him to walk away with top prize. You can expect future trips to the grocery store to be even more tortuous—your penance as handed out by the Great Court of Parenthood, it would seem.

- **Reinforcing bad behavior.** This isn't quite as major a *faux pas* as giving in completely (as in the preceding bullet), but it can still come back to haunt you. Let's assume you manage to get out of the grocery store without the dreaded box of chocolate breakfast cereal, but only after spending the entire trip arguing with your child. If your child was more interested in pushing your buttons than walking away with the box of breakfast cereal, it looks like he won this round hands down. He's also learned that if he wants your attention, he need only whine . . . and whine . . . and whine—not exactly the life lesson you were hoping to impart on this particular grocery shopping expedition, I would imagine.

- **Making idle threats.** Idle threats can spell the kiss of death to your discipline strategy as well as your effectiveness and credibility as a parent. As Barbara Coloroso notes in her book *Kids Are Worth It*, "Children need parents who say what they mean, mean what they say, and do what they say they are going to do." The "no idle threats" rule may not be rocket science, but it can make a huge difference in your day-to-day functioning as a parent, so this is one discipline tip you'll definitely want to keep in mind.

- **Embarrassing your child in front of other people.** Child development experts stress the importance of avoiding any sort of discipline method that will cause your child undue embarrassment or humiliation. Try to be discreet when it comes to discipline. If your child misbehaves when other people are around—when you're at a family reunion or when he's hosting a sleepover with a group of friends, for example—you should take him aside briefly to let him know that the issue will be dealt with later in private. Then make a point of following through; you don't want to get sidetracked and leave things hanging, or your child will think he has a license to misbehave whenever other people are around.

Failing to ensure that the crime fits the punishment

Some parents go overboard when it comes to punishing their kids; others barely hold their kids accountable at all. Here are the key pitfalls to avoid on the punishment front.

- **Allowing too long a delay between the crime and the sentencing.** Even our criminal justice system recognizes the accused's right to a speedy trial. After all, it's hard to see any link between the punishment and the crime if you can no longer remember exactly what it was you did wrong! The only situations that would warrant a delay in sentencing are situations in which you are very angry with your child (you're likely to make a poor discipline decision) and situations that are likely to cause undue embarrassment to your child (you're better to wait until you are able to deal with the situation in a more private setting). Otherwise, you should plan to move on to sentencing as soon as possible.

- **Choosing a punishment that is overly lenient.** If you choose a punishment that's a little soft, it isn't going to act as much of a deterrent in preventing a future recurrence of the behavior in question. Bottom line? If your child weighs the cost of the punishment against the rewards of the crime and decides that the punishment is definitely worth it, you're definitely in the market for a new form of punishment. Sometimes, parents let kids off with too light a punishment because they don't feel entirely confident about their right to discipline their kids. If you suspect that you may be falling into this particular parenting trap, it's time to give yourself a bit of a pep talk. Remember, you're well within your rights to discipline your child; in fact, it's your job as a parent.

MOM'S THE WORD

"I aim for uniformity when it comes to punishing my kids, but not all punishments work equally well for all kids. If you have a kid who doesn't watch TV, taking away that privilege won't change his life. However, asking him to clean toilets might!"

—*Melanie, 39, mother of eight*

- **Choosing a punishment that is overly strict.** It's also important to make sure that the punishment isn't stronger than the crime. If you choose a punishment that's way over the top—such as grounding your child for the next 18 years because he happened to spill a can of pop on the living-room couch—you're falling into another all-too-common discipline trap. This mistake tends to happen if parents attempt to make discipline decisions when they are feeling far too angry, tired, or stressed to think rationally; if they have unrealistic expectations about a child's behavior; or if they make some assumptions (often unfounded) about the child's underlying motive. If you feel your blood pressure shooting through the roof as a river of soda pop cascades down the front of the couch, there's nothing wrong with taking a deep breath and telling your child that you need time to think about a suitable punishment. (Hint: If you have a strong desire to get even with your child, you are too angry to make a rational discipline decision.) After walking around the block a few dozen times (or better yet, sleeping on it), you may decide that a more suitable punishment would be for your child to do enough extra chores to earn back the money to pay for having the upholstery on the couch steam-cleaned. (You may even decide that you've hated that tacky floral-print couch for years and that your child has done you the biggest favor imaginable by drenching it with cream soda—but, of course, you'll have to keep your true feelings to yourself or else you'll totally blow your discipline cover. Some things are better left unsaid, particularly if your partner happens to be particularly fond of the couch in question and may hereafter have a very strong suspicion that you planted the can of soda pop in your child's hand with this dastardly deed in mind!)

- **Choosing a punishment that is designed to humiliate your child.** Most childrearing experts agree that it's important to steer clear of discipline techniques that are designed to embarrass, humiliate, or degrade your child. Your child may toe the line initially, but he's likely to see your tactics as unfair or even cruel, something that can lead to feelings of resentment and weaken the parent-child bond. Your child may even be motivated to get back at you, something that can lead to repeated episodes of misbehavior, humiliation, and retaliation—a truly vicious circle.

- **Choosing a punishment that is overly difficult to enforce—that is, one that turns you into a full-time prison guard!** If you choose a punishment that is too difficult to enforce—that is, you tell your child that he has to sit in a chair facing the corner for an hour without talking or giggling—you're pretty much sentencing yourself to spending the next hour supervising your child to make sure that he does just that. If you don't provide the necessary supervision, your child may not necessarily do what he's told (for example, unbeknownst to you, he may carefully position his chair so that he can tune into whatever other family members are watching on TV in the next room).

 MOM'S THE WORD

"We need to remember that children are human beings. Think about how children are sometimes treated. An adult would never treat another adult friend or co-worker the way they sometimes treat their own child. Yet they feel it is okay to do so."

—*Kerri, 37, mother of six*

 MOTHER WISDOM

If you've overdone it in the discipline department and grounded your child for the next three weeks (something that may feel like a life sentence to him), you may want to consider allowing him to earn some time off for good behavior. Simply agree to knock an extra day of his grounding off for each day that he manages to follow the family rules. The hope of "early parole" is often enough to get even the most uncooperative child to fall into line. Hey, it's worth a try.

- **Choosing a punishment that punishes other family members, too.** (Maybe even you.) If you decide to deal with your child's rude behavior by canceling the family trip to the amusement park, you aren't just punishing him; you're punishing the rest of the family, too. Although the old school of thought was that the other children in the family would apply not-so-subtle peer pressure to the child who had blown the trip to the amusement park (think 1970s-style sibling revenge!), thereby preventing the need for similar trip cancellations in the future. Modern-day parenting experts are less willing to condone this approach because it tends to cause unnecessary friction between siblings. As you'll see in Chapter 6, siblings don't need any outside assistance when it comes to finding things to fight about; they do a pretty good job on their own!

- **Making the punishment last too long.** Although you may be tempted to take away privileges for weeks or even months at a time, it's best to start by taking away privileges in smaller increments, such as days or even hours. Here's why grounding your child until he's 30 or taking away his privileges for the next month may not actually be such a great idea (although it may feel oh-so-good at the time):

  - *You reduce the number of things you have left to take away.* If you take away your child's TV privileges for a month all at once, you've used up one of your major discipline tools. What are you going to do when your child loses his computer, video game, and telephone privileges, too? If you take each privilege away in bite-sized pieces—a day at a time as opposed to a month at a time—you immediately turn that one-month chunk of time into 30 separate things you can take away. (Yes, Mom and Dad, it's slice-and-dice fun night here on the Discipline Channel!)

  - *You plant the seeds of rebellion.* Making the punishment drag on for too long can actually be counterproductive. If your child knows that he's grounded for weeks or months at a time, he may lose all hope of being able to be good long enough to get his privileges back. When he loses all hope, he loses all incentive to behave, and you're bound to find yourself in for a major battle.

A better bet is to either keep the number of days of grounding to a minimum or to allow your child to earn time off for good behavior.

It's all in the details

Learn to sidestep these potential problems and you'll find yourself spending a lot less time dealing with discipline difficulties and a lot more time simply enjoying your kids.

- **Being inconsistent when it comes to dealing with a particular type of problem.** Although it's okay to allow minor deviations from the family rule book from time to time—you'll no doubt allow your child to break the family rule about eating Popsicles in the living room if he's camped out on the couch watching TV while he's trying to recuperate from a tonsillectomy—you don't want to have rules that are every bit as unpredictable as the weather. You can hardly blame your kids for breaking the rules if they don't stay the same from day to day, let alone from week to week. Imagine the mutiny in a typical workplace if the policy and procedures manual was rewritten that often.

MOM'S THE WORD

"Consistency is key. If it was wrong yesterday, it is still wrong today, and it will still be wrong tomorrow. No if, ands, or buts. How else can they learn right from wrong if on some days mommy says it's okay and on other days she flies off the handle?"

—*Catherine, 33, mother of four*

- **Being overly rigid.** Consistency is important, but you do have to be prepared to show some flexibility on the discipline front. "I strive to be consistent in that the same misbehavior would generally result in the same consequences," says Cathy, a 40-year-old mother of two. "I think this helps to reinforce the family rules. But, I do try to be flexible if the child is extremely overtired or upset over something else in order to teach compassion and empathy. It can be a difficult balance because it can also depend on what kind of day I've had!"

MOM'S THE WORD

"We holidayed this year with another couple and their six-year-old son. Every night, they dragged him inside at 7 P.M. and had him in bed by 8 P.M., even though he was on vacation. Meanwhile, Meagan, who is a full year younger, was outside playing, and we were not at all strict about her bedtime.

"I have very fond memories of sitting around the campfire, roasting marshmallows and singing campfire songs when I was a kid. It was so cool to be allowed to stay up after dark when you were on holidays.

"When I gently asked my friend if she'd consider letting her son stay up a bit later while he was on holidays, she responded by saying, 'If I give him an inch, he'll take a mile, and I'll spend the rest of the summer trying to get him back on schedule.'

"I don't know. I always thought that's what summer was for."

—*Judy, 33, mother of one*

- **Giving excessively long-winded explanations if your child asks why he's being disciplined in a particular way.** Although you owe it to your child to give him a reasonable explanation, there's nothing in the parenting rule book that says that your explanation has to be lengthy or repeated more than once. State the facts simply and then end the discussion.

- **Backtracking or losing track of the punishment.** A lot of parents start out well when it comes to deciding upon particular consequences, but then they seem to lose steam along the way. They may decide after the fact that the punishment that they decided upon in the heat of the moment was unnecessarily harsh, in which case they decide to cancel the punishment; or—even worse—the busy pace of family life may lead them to forget that their child was even being punished at all. The net result is the same in both cases: the child gets off with little or no punishment. Rather than committing yourself to something you may not be able to follow through on, you would be better off telling your child that you need a bit of time to come up with a suitable punishment.

MOM'S THE WORD

"I often get into arguments with my daughter, Heather, who refuses to take anything I say or ask her to do at face value. If I ask her to put on her coat, she asks why. It's very easy to get drawn into an argument with her, and I usually end up feeling hopelessly frustrated. Lately, I've been working on saying in certain situations, 'I'm sorry, but this is not up for discussion,' and then just walking away. She'll usually take a moment to protest and then proceed to do what I've asked her to do."

—*Kelly, 32, mother of three*

MOM'S THE WORD

"I grew up under the 'do as I say, not as I do' regime, and that just doesn't cut it these days. Families today seem to be ruled more by democracy. Of course, that isn't a bad thing, but it does make it easy to give away your authority as a parent."

—*Paula, 33, mother of one*

- **Waving the discipline white flag because you're too tired, too busy, or too distracted to deal with the problem.** I don't think there's a parent on the planet who hasn't pleaded guilty to this particular discipline crime on at least one occasion. After all, it's hard to muster up the energy to discipline your preschooler for refusing to pick up his toys if you were up most of the night before caring for his newborn baby sister. Unless you want to be tripping over your son's stuff or—even worse—be picking it up yourself until he's ready to move out on his own, you'll need to find a way to deal with the problem.

- **Choosing a discipline style that emphasizes blind obedience to adult authority figures.** Although it may be tempting to insist on blind obedience when it comes to matters of discipline, it's important to keep the big picture in mind if you insist that your children do whatever you tell them to do without questioning you. You could be leaving them vulnerable to other adults who may not necessarily have their best interests at heart. "I try to teach my children to think independently but to behave themselves respectfully," says Tara, a 32-year-old mother of two. "If they are taught to obey blindly or get punished, they may believe that they must obey all adults. If they are empowered to think independently, then they may be encouraged to listen to their gut feeling in such situations."

There you have it—a whole laundry list of things not to do on the discipline front. The next section zeroes in on your various discipline options and talks about what does—and doesn't—work when it comes to dealing with problem behavior.

The Most—and Least—Effective Methods of Discipline

If you talk to other parents about the methods that they use to discipline their own children, you'll quickly discover that there are a lot of different methods at your disposal—everything from distraction to verbal discipline to time outs. Here's what you need to know about the best and worst methods of discipline that the parenting world has to offer.

The top 10 discipline techniques

Although it's hard to get parenting experts to agree on anything these days, most pretty much see eye to eye when it comes to defining an effective method of discipline. According to the current thinking, a discipline method is considered to be effective if it

- fits into your overall discipline strategy and childrearing philosophy

- is fair and reasonable

- is suited to your child's developmental stage and temperament

- can be implemented relatively quickly and easily

- is designed to teach your child to make better decisions in the future, rather than merely punishing the current incident of misbehavior

- both promotes and models respect

- is not embarrassing, humiliating, or degrading toward your child

- serves to make the undesirable behavior less appealing

- is effective at encouraging the desired behavior

- leaves your child feeling good about himself

- leaves you feeling good about yourself as a parent

- helps to build upon the bond between you and your child

You'll probably find that you use different discipline techniques in different situations and that you have to go back to the discipline drawing board every now and again in order to come up with something new. (Kids go through some remarkable changes between the preschool and preteen years, so it only makes sense that your discipline method would evolve in order to keep pace with those changes.) Fortunately, plenty of terrific discipline techniques are at your disposal. Here's the scoop on 10 discipline techniques that tend to work particularly well with the preschool through preteen crowd:

1. **Prevent problems from occurring in the first place.** An ounce of prevention is worth a pound of cure—actually 10 pounds of cure when we're talking discipline. Because this is the easiest method of all—not actually having to discipline your child—I put it at the top of the list. You'll find you can greatly reduce the need to discipline your kids if you learn to anticipate and avoid problem situations. You already mastered this technique when your child was younger—putting breakables out of reach so that you wouldn't have to wrestle your priceless Royal Doulton figurine away from your intrepid toddler on a daily basis. Now it's time to apply that same technique to slightly older kids. If your 10-year-old keeps getting up in the middle of the night to sneak downstairs to play video games, perhaps the video game controller needs to spend the night in your night table until he's better able to curb his urges. Likewise, if your preteen can't manage to follow the family rules about Internet usage, perhaps he needs to lose his Internet privileges for a while. Although it's unrealistic to expect to be able to sidestep every possible discipline problem—you'd need to have a crystal ball in order to anticipate every potential parenting hot spot!—you'll be amazed at how many conflicts can be eliminated by using this preventative technique on a regular basis. This is definitely my personal favorite discipline method.

2. **Find creative alternatives to saying no.** Kids tend to dig in their heels if they hear the word "no" all the time, so

you'll want to come up with all kinds of creative ways to steer clear of the dreaded "n word." Here are a few tried-and-true parenting tricks of the trade:

• Instead of telling your child what *not* to do ("No jumping on the bed."), tell him what *to* do ("Jump on the floor."). Not only does this technique allow you to avoid saying no, but it also increases the impact of your message by giving your child a specific action to follow.

• Instead of uttering a non-descript "no" when your child is about to do something dangerous, aim for a more powerful word such as "stop." Your words will have greater impact, and as in the preceding example, you'll be telling your child exactly what you want him to do.

• Instead of telling your child that he can't do something, tell him *when* he can do it: "You can go rollerblading with your friends just as soon as you're finished cleaning your room."

• Instead of vetoing a particular activity, give your approval to a modified version of the same request. If your 12-year-old asks whether he can hang out at the neighborhood park until 11 P.M. with a group of friends, you might reply, "You can go if you are home by 9 P.M." If your child chooses to argue, you are free to take your offer off the table. It's kind of like negotiating a real estate deal; you either accept the offer that's come your way, or you write it back on your terms and risk having the other party walk away from the negotiating table. You may choose to negotiate, but you're not obliged to, and it's probably in your best interests not to; unless, of course, you want every parenting decision you make from this point forward to devolve into an episode of *Let's Make a Deal!*

3. **Give your child the opportunity to make choices.** As you've no doubt gathered by now, most kids are closet control freaks; they like to be the ones running the show. So, why not tap into your child's deep-rooted need to be the one in charge by allowing him to make some of the decisions about his own life? If you use this technique effectively, you can head a lot of discipline problems off at the pass. The secrets to making this technique work for you—not against you!—are

- to offer only choices that you are prepared to live with (don't ask your child whether he would like to miss his grandmother's birthday party because of his bad behavior unless you're prepared to live with the fact that he may utter a wholehearted yes!)

- to steer clear of false choices—situations in which only one of the choices is a valid option (for example, "Do you want to clean your room or be grounded for life?")

- to limit the number of choices (a dozen choices is enough to make a typical adult's head start spinning and will be completely overwhelming to your average child; studies have shown, in fact, that children under five do best if you limit the number of choices to two)

- to limit the amount of time your child has to make his choice (if he refuses to make his choice within the time period, you tell him that he's chosen not to choose, so you'll be making the choice for him)

4. **Allow your child to experience the natural consequences of her actions.** You've basically got two types of consequences to draw upon here: natural consequences and logical consequences:

- *Natural consequences:* Natural consequences are consequences that result from the child's own actions; if your child throws his math book across the kitchen in a fraction-induced fit of rage and it takes out the coffee pot as it slides along the counter, he should be on the hook for a new coffee pot. Natural consequences can be a powerful way of helping your child to learn from his mistakes because they are so clearly linked to the child's actions. Even though he's feeling angry about having to spend his birthday money on a new coffee pot, he knows in his heart that he has no one to blame but himself. This method of discipline actually lets you off the hook for a change!

- *Logical consequences:* Logical consequences are consequences that you come up with in the hope of teaching your child an important lesson. You see, as wonderful as natural consequences are, they can't be applied to every situation; getting a concussion is too big a price to be paid, after all, for learning that it's not a good idea to ride your bike without a helmet. (Besides, it's against the law.) So, if your pint-sized biking enthusiast is caught riding his bike without a helmet, you're going to have to come up with a logical consequence as opposed to a natural consequence—perhaps confiscating his bike for a couple of days or signing him up for a bike safety workshop at the local police station. The trick is to make the logical consequence as logical as possible; your child is going to have a hard time figuring out what folding laundry has to do with forgetting his bicycle helmet if you sentence him to a couple of hours of laundry patrol in order to "teach him a lesson." ("What lesson?" he may rightfully ask!)

MOTHER WISDOM

Don't fall into the trap of making most of your child's decisions for him just because it's quicker, easier, or more efficient for you to do so. Children need to have the opportunity to develop their decision-making skills, and the only way they can do that is if their parents back off and let them make some key decisions. Besides, parents who micromanage every aspect of their children's lives don't merely deprive them of the opportunity to hone their decision-making abilities; they can also inadvertently undermine their children's self-confidence by giving them the impression that they aren't capable of making these types of decisions on their own.

5. **Take away a privilege.** Taking away privileges is another popular method of disciplining children—one that parents tend to use a great deal as their children grow older. Privilege removal generally works best if the privilege being removed somehow relates to the crime at hand (a natural or logical consequence). For example, if you were to overhear your preteen swearing up a storm while talking to a friend on the phone, you may want to take away his phone privileges for a couple of days in order to motivate him to clean up his telephone vocabulary. That's not to say that you can't use privilege removal if the privilege being removed doesn't relate directly to the behavioral issue that's being addressed—in other words, it's not that you *can't* take away your child's computer game privileges for being rude to his teacher; it's just that you'll get more bang for your discipline buck if you find a way of making the punishment fit the crime (for example, having your child write his teacher a letter apologizing for his behavior or otherwise taking steps to make amends).

6. **Master the art of selective ignoring.** This technique is the ideal method of handling bothersome but nonlife-threatening behaviors such as rude noises, silly faces, and all-round goofiness—provided that the behavior in question isn't

getting completely out of control. What you're trying to do is pretend not to notice the annoying behavior in the hope that your child will get bored and move on to something else. If he doesn't—that is, if he's still making silly burping sounds a minute or two after you started pretending not to hear him—you'll have to step in and deal with the problem in some other way. Nine times out of ten, however, the problem will resolve itself, and you'll have saved your discipline energy for the battles that really count: hitting, biting, pinching, swearing, lying, cheating, stealing, and so on. You're not ignoring the problem; you're ignoring the attention-seeking behavior.

 MOM'S THE WORD

"We clean every Saturday. I remind the kids on Friday night that we will be dusting and vacuuming the next day and that I don't pick up anything. All it takes are a few barrettes and building blocks getting sucked up the vacuum cleaner hose to convince them to clean up."

—*Kerri, 37, mother of six*

---

7. **Offer a distraction.** Part of the beauty of this particular technique is its sheer simplicity: your three-year-old is about to have a total meltdown about the fact that it's bedtime until you remind him that there's a brand new library book waiting to be read at story time that night. Assuming your parenting fairy godmother is working her magic on your behalf, this distraction may be all it takes to head off the pre-bedtime temper tantrum. There's just one thing you need to know about this particular discipline technique: although it works wonders with preschoolers, it tends to lose some of its effectiveness with older kids, who have a remarkable ability to latch on to a particular issue with bulldogged determination. Besides, after they catch

on to the fact that you're trying the old bait-and-switch technique, this particular tactic is history!

MOTHER WISDOM

Don't be surprised if you get hit with a flurry of bad behavior if you start trying to ignore a particular bad habit, such as whining. This phenomenon is so common, in fact, that behavioral scientists have actually given it its own name—*extinction burst.* (Just for the record, it's the behavior that's on the endangered species list, not your child!)

An extinction burst is your child's last-ditch effort to make a behavior that has always worked for him in the past (such as whining up a storm) come through for him again this time around. (Hey, you can't blame a kid for trying.)

Although an extinction burst can be extremely frustrating to deal with, if you stick to your guns and give your child attention only when he's exhibiting the desired behavior—in this case, not whining—you'll slowly but surely reduce his incentive to whine.

If, on the other hand, you finally crack after listening to an hour or two of whining and reward him for that whining, you've just taught him that those marathon whining sessions do, in fact, pay off, and consequently, you've just undone all your hard work.

If this stuff all sounds eerily familiar, chances are you're having flashbacks to your Psych 101 lecture about B.F. Skinner's work with pigeons. (As you may recall, Skinner's pigeons were rewarded with food only every now and again, but it was just often enough to convince them to keep pecking . . . and pecking . . . and pecking at a metal disk.) This intermittent reinforcement schedule is pretty powerful stuff for animals and people alike—an important point to keep in mind the next time you're about to give in to your child simply to buy yourself a reprieve from the whining. Talk about sacrificing long-term gain for short-term pain!

8. **Apply positive reinforcement.** Positive reinforcement is the twin sister of selective ignoring, but in this case, you're making a point of reinforcing praiseworthy behavior. (To look at it from the flip side, not reinforcing good behavior may cause the good behavior to become extinct. Your child

may figure that it's not worth the effort of trying not to fight with his brother if no one even notices anyway.) Here's the scoop on the two key types of positive reinforcement, praise and rewards:

- **_Praise:_** When you're praising your child, make the praise as specific as possible (tell your child exactly what he did right), keep it sincere (if it sounds fake, your child will feel worse, not better), and try to word it in a way that will help to build your child's self-esteem (say "You should be proud of yourself" as opposed to "I think you did a great job"). Also be sure to praise improvements in your child's behavior rather than holding out for perfection, and try to work in some honest recognition wherever possible. (Honest recognition involves pointing out how your child's behavior is genuinely helpful; for example, "Now that you've picked up all the paints, you won't have to worry about your little brother getting into them and spilling paint on your things. You really know how to take care of your stuff.")

MOTHER WISDOM

Although they become increasingly less willing to admit it as they grow older, most children and preteens are secretly pleased if their parents take them aside to praise them for handling a situation particularly well. This is good news for you as a parent. It means that one of the most powerful tools you have in your discipline arsenal also happens to be one of the easiest and most pleasant to use: the simple act of praising your child.

MOM'S THE WORD

"Not only do kids need discipline when they are doing things incorrectly, they also need recognition when they are doing something right. This is an absolute must if we want to raise children with self-esteem."

—Kerri, a 37-year-old mother of six

- *Rewards:* Although rewards are an accepted part of the adult world—we earn paychecks for going to work, collect frequent flyer points for doing our grocery shopping, and get cash back on our mortgages and credit cards for rewarding our banks with our business—many adults have trouble with the idea of extending those types of rewards to children. I think the problem is that adults tend to confuse rewards and bribes. A reward is something you earn after the fact for a job well done; a bribe is something you demand while the job is still ongoing as payment in advance for holding up your end of the bargain. (It would be like telling your boss that you aren't going to come to work on Monday morning unless he deposits Friday afternoon's paycheck in your account right now!) A reward doesn't have to be a hugely expensive item. In fact, it doesn't have to be an item at all: it could be a little thing like a chance to play *Monopoly* with you after dinner or a bonus drive to the mall. Note: Some parents find it helpful to use charts, checklists, and behavior contracts to encourage their children to work on problem behaviors. Chapter 5 has more about this.

9. **Discipline your child verbally.** Verbal discipline plays an increasingly important role as your child grows older. Although it's sometimes easier to physically redirect a young child who is refusing to cooperate by picking him up and carrying him out, that particular tactic isn't going to get you very far with a six-foot-tall teenager, so you may as well start honing your verbal discipline skills now. Verbal discipline basically involves stating your behavioral expectations clearly, reminding your child of those expectations if he seems to be getting off track, and following through with an appropriate consequence if your child chooses to disregard your instructions. Note: You'll find all kinds of

tips on making verbal discipline work for you in the discussion about avoiding power struggles in Chapter 4.

10. **Give your child a time out.** A time out forces your child to remove himself from a particular situation so that he can reconsider his behavior. If your six-year-old is making rude faces at his sister at the dinner table and he's sent to time out, he may be more inclined to focus his energies on eating rather than provoking his sister by the time he comes back to the dinner table. Note: While time outs were very popular a few years back, some child development experts are giving time outs the thumbs down these days, claiming they are overused or misused in many cases. Here are some important points to keep in mind if you decide to use time outs to discipline your child:

- *Make sure that your child understands why he's getting a time out and how a time out works.* You may have to explain the mechanics of the time out if this is his first experience with this particular method of discipline.

- *Choose a time-out location that's free of distractions so that your child can focus on his behavior.* If he's still quite young, you may want him to serve his time out in the same room so that you can keep an eye on him (both to make sure he's serving his time out and to ensure that he's safe). If he's older, you may find it works better to send him to another part of the house. (Just make sure it's a *boring* part of the house, like the laundry room! Serving your time out in the downstairs TV room hardly qualifies as a punishment, after all.)

- *Make sure that your child can see the timer or clock that you're using to time his time out.* That will eliminate his need to ask you how many more minutes there are left before he's "sprung."

- *Don't go overboard with the length of the time out.* A time out isn't meant to be a life sentence. It's simply designed to give your child enough time to think about his behavior before he re-enters the situation that was causing him difficulty. One minute for each year of age is a good rule of thumb. Anything more than that is probably overkill and may actually start to work against you. (Your child may use some of that time in the time-out chair to start plotting revenge against you!)

- *Make serving the time out your child's problem, not yours.* If your child refuses to serve his time out, let him know that his world is going to grind to a halt until that time out has been served; the TV stays off, phone calls from friends don't get answered, and the usual shuttle run to hockey practice doesn't happen. That should be enough to motivate him to get with the (time out) program. Note: If he still digs in his heels and refuses to cooperate, you may want to check out the behavior modification strategies in Chapter 5. Extra persistent kids require extra creative and resilient parents!

- *Allow time out to be postponed.* If your child can't reasonably serve his time out at the moment when it's earned (perhaps he's on the way out the door to school), let him know when you would like him to serve it (when he arrives home from school at the end of the day).

- *Don't talk to your child while he's serving his time out.* If he insists on talking, yelling, kicking the chair, playing head games with his siblings, or otherwise acting out, calmly reset the timer and let him know that the time out has not yet begun.

- *Observe your child carefully for a couple of minutes after the time out has been completed.* With any luck, you'll have the opportunity to praise him for his newly improved behavior. If, however, you notice a recurrence of the behavior that triggered the initial time out, you'll want to send your child back to time out. (Some experts say that you should simply repeat the length of the original time out. Others suggest that you add on a few additional minutes because you're dealing with a "repeat offender"!) When your child comes out of time out this time around, you'll probably want to provide him with a little bit of coaching to help him avoid getting into trouble yet again, restating your expectations of his behavior and possibly helping him to identify some other ways of handling the situation that has been causing him so much difficulty.

- If you have to call a time out when you're away from home, you may need to be a little creative in coming up with a suitable place for your child to serve his time out. If you're at the mall, you may decide to turn a table in the food court into Time Out Central. You can camp out beside him and read a novel while he does his time. It's a little trickier if you're zooming down a superhighway. You may decide to pull off at the nearest exit and let your child serve his time out at the side of the road, or you may tell your child that he'll be serving his time out as soon as you arrive at your destination.

- Resist the temptation to send your child to time out each time he steps out of line. Most experts agree that time outs are most effective if they're reserved for a few specific situations as opposed to being used for pretty much any behavioral infraction. They tend to lose their effectiveness if they are overused. Rather than wasting them on the small stuff, save them for the stuff that really matters.

Three discipline methods you'll want to avoid

Not all discipline methods are created equal. Here's the scoop on three discipline methods that you'll definitely want to avoid:

1. **Threatened abandonment.** The big problem with this so-called discipline technique is that it's based on a lie; you're not really going to abandon your child in order to teach him a lesson. This technique will have one of two possible effects on your child, depending on his age: either he'll catch on to the fact that you're bluffing (something that will instantly shoot holes in your credibility), or if he's still quite young, he'll secretly worry that you may actually abandon him after all. Neither of these scenarios will play out particularly well, which is why threatened abandonment doesn't tend to be a particularly effective method of discipline.

2. **Bribery.** To bribe or not to bribe? That is the question! Although bribing your child to behave may be awfully tempting and can provide the parenting quick fix you're looking for on a really bad day, you could end up creating a whole new set of problems for yourself. Do you really want to have to wait in the parking lot on Junior's first day at University so that you can reward him a gummy bear for going to class? Note: It's important not to confuse incentives (a reward that has been earned for past good behavior) with bribes (a down payment on a promise of future good behavior). Incentives can be a useful tool in a behavior modification plan, but bribes are just plain bad news.

3. **Spankings.** In recent years, the American Academy of Pediatrics has given spanking and other forms of physical discipline a firm thumbs down. Because spanking relies on negative reinforcement (it emphasizes the bad behavior that

you want to eliminate rather than the good behavior that you're hoping to encourage), young children may find it difficult to see the link between the behavior that landed them in trouble and the spanking that they just received. Of course, there are some even more compelling reasons not to spank your child: not only does spanking teach your child that it's okay to hit other people, but also spanking is typically done in anger, which makes it oh-so-easy for a supposedly harmless spanking to cross the line and escalate into child abuse. Studies have shown that spankings do tend to escalate in intensity if they don't get the desired results right away. Although a lot of parents find that the urge to spank is almost instinctive—a carry-over from their own growing-up years—a growing number are choosing to break with the past and find creative alternatives to spanking. You can, too. (See Appendix A and Appendix B for the contact information and Web site addresses for organizations such as the American Academy of Pediatrics that promote alternatives to spanking.)

FRIDGE NOTES

Unsure how to handle the discipline issue with a child who has special needs? The Internet Resources for Special Children Web site is a terrific launching pad to online resources for parents raising kids with special needs. You can find it at www.irsc.org.

MOTHER WISDOM

"The child supplies the power, but the parents have to do the steering."

—*Benjamin Spock*, **Dr. Spock's Baby and Child Care**

How your discipline methods evolve as your child gets older

Teaching your child to become self-disciplined is not unlike teaching him to ride a bike. At first, he has to rely on training wheels, then a bit of balancing help from you, and then finally he's riding down the street on his own. With any luck, when that moment arrives, instead of wobbling from side to side and veering off into a ditch, he will have the necessary skills to navigate the bike on his own, steering clear of the inevitable potholes on the road of life.

Of course, none of this happens overnight. In fact, it takes years. It's a painstakingly slow process that requires truckloads of time and patience on your part and an equal measure of faith in the universe. You'll increase your odds of ending up with a highly self-disciplined child if you place increased emphasis on discipline methods that promote your child's inner self-discipline as opposed to your own external control over your child as your child matures. Otherwise, you could be headed for trouble the moment your child enjoys that first intoxicating taste of freedom. Remember, it won't be that many years before your child is spending the bulk of his waking hours in the company of other people, away from your watchful eye. (You can pretty much count on the fact that you won't be invited along on his first hot date.)

Here's how to make the most of the time you have left by choosing age-appropriate forms of discipline.

Discipline methods that work well with preschoolers

Unlike toddlers, preschoolers generally are willing to accept the fact that there are rules to be followed and that there are things they can and cannot do. That's not to say that they're necessarily great at following rules, but at least they're willing to at least tac-itly acknowledge your right to make them. (Hey, that's progress!)

Preschoolers respond extremely positively to both approval and praise, so these are your best bets on the discipline front. If some sort of punishment seems to be in order, you'll want to turn to time out, redirection (that is, focusing your preschooler's attention on something other than the problem at hand in the hope of defusing the situation), and small consequences.

In terms of what to steer clear of, lengthy explanations and heavy-duty lectures are wasted on a child this age, so save your breath.

Discipline methods that work well with school-aged kids and preteens

After they start school, children become increasingly independent with each passing year—something that can lead to more battles on the discipline front.

They still respond well to praise and approval, but rewards tend to be particularly motivating for kids in this age group.

Other solid bets for disciplining school-aged kids and preteens include providing natural or logical consequences, withdrawing privileges, and instituting time outs.

You'll also want to avoid heavy-duty lectures with kids of this age group; they'll just tune you out anyway.

Mother (and Father) Guilt

Despite our best intentions, most of us find it's pretty hard to measure up to the standards that we set for ourselves on the dis-cipline front. The result? Truckloads and truckloads of mother (or father) guilt. Here's how to cope with parenthood's most abundant yet useless emotion:

- **Accept the fact that you're a less-than-perfect parent.** Where is it written in the parenting job description that perfection is required? Nowhere, I tell you! Cut yourself a little slack and don't demand anything more of yourself than you ask of your own kids; in other words, progress, not perfection. "I have no guilt," says Catherine, a 33-year-old mother of four. "I am not perfect. I will never be perfect. I am only human. I don't expect perfection from my kids, and I sure as heck don't expect perfection from myself. I am a work in progress, and every mistake I make is a learning experience. I continue to grow as a human being right alongside my children."

MOM'S THE WORD

"I don't feel guilty about being a less-than-perfect parent. I don't think my daughter feels any guilt when she's being a less-than-perfect four-year-old either. We just go along as best we can and accept that."

—*Mary-Tim, 37, mother of one*

MOM'S THE WORD

"You can't let the guilt overwhelm you. On a bad day, I try telling myself that part of my job as a parent is making sure that my kids have something to talk to their therapists about when they get older!"

—*Lisa, 37, mother of two*

- **Don't be afraid to apologize to your child if an apology is warranted.** It won't undercut your authority as a parent if you own up to the fact that you were wrong; in fact, it is likely to enhance your credibility. Your child will have a lot more respect for you if you admit that you blew it than if you try to make excuses for your own bad behavior. You'll also feel a lot better yourself. "The apology is the key for me," says Mary, a 36-year-old mother of three. "If I didn't apologize, I think the guilt would kill me!"

- **Resist the temptation to overcompensate if you come down too hard on your child.** You aren't doing your child any favors if you swing too far in the opposite direction. You'll come across as wishy-washy or, worse, totally incompetent, and nothing is scarier to a child than feeling like Mom and Dad don't have a clue what they're doing. You also risk teaching your child a very dangerous lesson—that he has an excellent chance of getting his own way if he can push your buttons enough to make you lose your cool so that you'll give in out of guilt.

MOM'S THE WORD

"I definitely have moments when I question my abilities as a parent. Am I doing the right thing? Did I say yes or no for the right reasons? There are a hundred questions that go through my mind when I'm dealing with situations that require some thought. I am usually fairly confident in my decisions, but there are times when I question my decisions or kick myself for making a poor decision."

—*Mary, 36, mother of three*

- **Don't feel guilty for doing your job.** The one thing you shouldn't feel guilty about is doing your job as a parent—coming up with a series of clearly defined family rules that are designed to give your child the skills he will need to thrive as an adult. Some parents fall into the trap of believing that it's their job to make their kids happy 24 hours a day, when in fact, it's actually their job to do their best to raise happy, healthy, well-adjusted kids. That means saying no sometimes, whether or not your child wants to hear it. (And chances are he won't.)

There you have it: the lowdown on the art of discipline—and, as you can see, it truly is an art. Whether you decide to use one of the techniques described in this chapter or to come up with something much more creative on your own (perhaps your idea of the perfect discipline technique involves bursting into a chorus of "You Can't Always Get What You Want" in your best Mick Jagger voice the next time your child embarks on a whine-fest), what matters is that you come up with a smorgasbord of discipline methods that work for you and your child. After all, although he's unlikely to thank you anytime soon for playing the role of the heavy, your child is counting on you to do your job as a parent, discipline portfolio and all.

CHAPTER 4

Short-Circuiting Power Struggles before Someone Gets Zapped

"I wish I'd learned sooner that it's important to come at discipline from a position of love rather than control."
—*Natalie, 32, mother of two*

Although most parents understand that handing over too much power and control to their kids can be a recipe for disaster, what some parents fail to realize is that holding on to too much power can also be a bad thing. Rather than maintaining control over your children, you may actually be setting yourself up for an in-house *coup d'état!*

If you think back to all the employers you have had to deal with over your lifetime, you'll have a pretty good idea of what I'm talking about here. There are bosses who choose to rule with an iron fist, bosses who try to be your best friend, and bosses who somehow manage to strike that perfect balance between making you like them and reminding you that they're the ones in charge.

It's pretty easy to get along with the last kind of boss—hey, what's not to like about them?—as well as the buddy-bosses, ept for the fact that the buddy-bosses' careers tend to be rather short-lived. (They have a tendency to get fired by the powers that be when it comes to light that they spend their days shooting the breeze with their employees rather than engaging in such drudgery as filing reports and serving customers!) The ones who tend to make life miserable for their employees and who set themselves up for endless power struggles with their disgruntled underlings are the Mr. and Ms. Iron Fists.

Although these micromanagers like to think that they are running a super-tight ship and that they are genuinely liked and respected by their employees, a mutiny always seems to be in the making. If the boss in question ever managed to catch an uncensored snippet of conversation between two employees or to intercept a misdirected e-mail or two, he or she would know that at least one employee is always plotting revenge against this particular manager and his boot-camp-like *modus operandi*. Who knew that too much power and control could actually leave you pretty much powerless at the end of the day?

The same thing applies to parenting, of course. Although you may be tempted to go into control-freak mode when it comes to raising your kids, it's a strategy that can backfire on you big time. A better bet is to share just enough power with your child to prevent an out-and-out mutiny, but not so much that your child feels that she has a license to walk all over you—you know, the management tricks of the trade that all the really good bosses of the world seem to know instinctively.

As you've no doubt gathered by now, this chapter is all about power struggles: specifically,

- what kids have to gain by getting you locked in a power struggle and what you have to lose

- how you can go about recognizing the triggers that tend to lead to such power struggles

- the important role you have to play, both in helping your child to manage her own emotions and in finding effective ways of managing your own

This chapter builds on the material on discipline covered in the previous chapter and sets the stage for the material on managing problem behavior that is discussed in the next chapter, which is why I chose to put it smack dab in the middle of this discipline discussion. After all, you can't even begin to address your child's behavior problems if she's got you locked into a power struggle from the moment you drag yourself to the breakfast table each morning. It's pretty much game over before your day even begins.

Why Power Struggles Occur and What You Can Do to Avoid Them

Have you ever noticed that your kids are able to push your buttons like no one else on the planet?

Even power struggles in the workplace can't get to you the same way that power struggles with your own kids can. You may not be particularly happy watching some Machiavellian, power-hungry colleague trying to score points with the boss at your expense, but you're unlikely to have the same visceral response to those machinations as you are to your eight-year-old's ongoing challenges to your parental authority. (Just think about how you felt the last time your child crossed her arms, rolled her eyes, looked at you with complete disdain, and uttered those two simple words that are pretty much guaranteed to send any parent's blood pressure skyrocketing: "Make me!")

Unfortunately, power struggles tend to be a losing proposition for parents and kids alike—reason enough to try to avoid them whenever possible. If you can learn to identify some of the root causes of the power struggles between you and your child, you'll be well on your way to brainstorming some possible solutions. Here's the scoop on some of the most common causes:

- **Your child's temperament.** Your child's temperament plays a large role in determining both the number and intensity of the power struggles you can expect to experience. A spirited child is more likely to engage her parents in power struggles than a shy or easygoing child—something that's hardly likely to qualify as news to you if you happen to have been blessed with one of these spirited kids. Although it's pretty much impossible to change your child's temperament, there's plenty you can do to bring out the best in her. See Chapter 2 for a detailed discussion of the types of parenting strategies that tend to work best with children of particular temperaments.

- **Your temperament.** It takes two to tango, so you'll also want to factor in your own temperament, too, and consider how it may be playing into any power struggles you've been experiencing with your child. (Hint: Before you label your child as stubborn, you might want to take a look in the mirror to see whether she has come by that stubborn gene honestly!)

- **Your parenting style.** You'll also want to give some thought to whether your parenting style may be at the root of a lot of your parenting struggles. Studies have shown that authoritative parents are much less likely to run into power struggles with their children than authoritarian or permissive parents. (Note: If you want a quick refresher course on what these parenting styles are all about, flip back to Chapter 2.)

- **Your confidence in your parenting abilities.** Your child is less likely to be able to drag you into repeated power struggles if you feel confident in your parenting abilities. You leave yourself much more vulnerable if you're constantly second-guessing your parenting decisions.

MOM'S THE WORD

"My husband isn't nearly as tolerant with the kids as I am. In fact, I think he is too severe and gets embroiled in a lot of unnecessary power struggles. One night as the children were getting ready for bed, he was brushing their teeth. Our three-year-old daughter Jenna doesn't like the mint-flavored toothpaste, and he had put that on her toothbrush. She started to cry and insisted on the berry-flavored toothpaste instead. I didn't see it as a big deal at all—all he needed to do was rinse off the first tooth-paste and put some new toothpaste on the toothbrush instead—but he wouldn't give in. He shoved the toothbrush in her mouth and brushed her teeth with her screaming her head off. He got very upset with her about this and yelled at her, and then he got mad at me for spoiling the kids for giving them a choice of toothpastes. It was a classic example of a non-issue blow-ing up into something totally ugly and unnecessary."

—*Margaret, 27, mother of three*

- **Your ability to deal with little problems as they arise.** If you have a tendency to allow little problems to snowball into much bigger problems, you could be setting yourself up for power struggles down the road. This tends to be a particular problem if you're inconsistent about enforcing family rules—something that can trigger a huge backlash from your kids when you finally find the time, energy, and inclination to play disciplinarian.

- **Whatever it is that pushes your buttons.** Understanding what types of situations are most likely to push your but-tons will make it easier for you to come up with ways of managing the powerful emotions that are dredged up. If, for example, you become positively enraged if you feel that your child is being totally unappreciative of something you've done for her, you may want to make a point of telling her up front that you are doing her a special favor and that you will be expecting a thank you. That way, she'll know right from the start what you will be expecting from her. If she doesn't come through for you, at least she may understand why you may be less willing to agree to similar requests in future.

- **Your child's triggers.** Parents aren't the only ones with buttons, of course. Kids have triggers, too. If they have brothers or sisters, they can generally count on those siblings to push their buttons on a regular basis. After you become aware of your child's triggers, you can start coming up with strategies for minimizing the number of times that she loses her cool—perhaps monitoring siblings closely to minimize the amount of teasing or bullying that is going on within the family.

- **The time of day.** Don't overlook simple biology when you're coming up with a list of triggers. Most parents find that mornings and late afternoons are the toughest times of day for themselves and their kids. You may find that a bit of extra patience is required at these times of day because everyone tends to be at their hungriest and/or grumpiest and there is generally a lot that needs to be done. Getting a head start on a casserole the night before or allowing an extra 15 minutes in the morning for a preschooler to dawdle over breakfast may be all that's required to short-circuit power struggles during these two particularly challenging times of day.

MOTHER WISDOM

Because our kids know us so well, they know exactly how to push our buttons. You'll probably find that the situations that push your buttons the most are situations in which your children are stomping on one or more of your core values or challenging your beliefs—true motherhood issues in every sense of the word!

- **Other sources of stress in your child's life.** Don't be surprised if the number of power struggles between you and your child increases if there has recently been a major change in your child's life—for example, if you have just welcomed a new baby into the family, moved to a new home, or if your child has just switched schools. It may take everything that she's got to handle the stress associated with these changes, something that may cause her to dig in her heels on supposedly minor issues, such as what kind of juice she's willing to drink at breakfast or what color of pajamas she's willing to wear to bed. This is definitely one of those situations where allowing her to make as many choices as possible will work to your advantage: giving her a semblance of control over some areas of her life may gradually soothe her inner control freak and reduce the number of battles she has with you about things that really matter.

- **Other sources of stress in your own life.** If you're experiencing a lot of stress in your own life (for example, marital problems, conflicts at work, or the worry associated with caring for a sick parent), you may find yourself experiencing more conflicts with your child. It can be difficult, after all, to find the patience to deal with the day-to-day challenges of raising a child if you're already being stressed to the max. If you're experiencing conflicts in your relationship with your partner, it's not at all unusual for some of those conflicts to carry over into your relationship with your child, particularly if your child has certain mannerisms that remind you of your partner—you know, the mannerisms that drive you crazy, now times two. Obviously, you'll want to get a handle on this right away, because it's not fair for your child to have to put up with round-the-clock nagging from you just because you're peeved with your partner.

Wounded animal syndrome

Although we like to put a *Brady Bunch* type spin on family life—to assume that there isn't a problem in the world that a frank discussion in the den can't solve—things don't always play out quite as neatly in real life as they do on TV. Kids push our buttons in sudden and sometimes shocking ways, we react powerfully and emotionally, and the next thing you know, we're saying things that we regret saying even before the words are finished coming out of our mouths. How can things spin out of control so fast?

Whether we're prepared to admit it or not, we're reacting like wounded animals. When we sense a frontal assault to our parenting authority, we either retreat into a corner to lick our wounds or, in an attempt to prevent further injury to ourselves, we go into counterattack mode, launching verbal counterstrikes at the one who wounded us—in this case, our child. It's a totally irrational response, but that's because our child has managed to trigger an emotional response that has momentarily managed to override all the sensible things we know we should be doing and saying. What's called for in this situation is an immediate time out—a chance for both parties to regain their cool before any lasting damage is done. Because the parent should be the one with the stronger self-control skills, it's the parent's job to call the time out.

An ounce of prevention

A better bet, of course, is to try to find ways to prevent these types of power struggles from occurring in the first place. That means

- communicating your message in a manner that increases the odds that you'll be heard

- understanding what your child is looking for when she goes into button-pushing mode and then refusing to take the bait

- helping kids to manage their difficult emotions and mastering the skills to manage your own

- learning more about child development so that you will know which kinds of annoying behaviors are age-appropriate—and, therefore, pretty much par for the course—and which ones are indicative of a possible behavior problem

- coming up with creative strategies for managing problem behaviors

These strategies are discussed at length throughout the remainder of this chapter and in Chapter 5.

MOTHER WISDOM

"Discipline isn't just about winning or losing. Every power struggle offers you the opportunity to connect with your child or to disconnect. The relationship you will have with your child when he's an adolescent lies in the words and actions you use today. Ultimately, your real power is in that emotional bond."

—*Mary Sheedy Kurcinka*, Kids, Parents, and Power Struggles

Making your message heard

You can reduce the number of power struggles that you experience by learning how to communicate effectively with your child. Here are some important tips to keep in mind:

- **Do a sound check first.** Make sure that you have your child's undivided attention before you make a request or start issuing instructions. Barking out orders from the next room doesn't cut it. Not only do you increase the odds that you'll be ignored, but by communicating in a less-than-respectful manner, you undercut your credibility as a parent.

- **Use eye contact to your advantage.** Get in the habit of establishing eye contact with your child before you communicate an important message. It's much more difficult for your child to tune you out (or, alternatively, to claim after the fact that she didn't hear what you were saying!) if you're looking her straight in the eye the entire time you're speaking. You can also pick up some immediate cues about whether or not your message is sinking in and/or likely to meet with some hefty resistance. (Hint: Heavy-duty eye-rolling is seldom a positive sign!)

- **Keep your instructions simple and to the point.** If your child is very young or your message is quite complex and you're concerned that your child may not necessarily have grasped all the important details, ask your child to summarize what you've said. If your child is missing some key points, you'll know you need to go over some of those points again.

- **Don't get in the habit of turning statements into questions.** You undercut your parenting credibility by routinely tagging "Okay?" on to the end of each instruction you give your child. By doing so, you turn each statement into a question. If you say, "It's bedtime, okay?" you're basically asking your child's permission to send her to bed!

- **Watch out for the "why trap."** Although there's nothing wrong with providing your child with a simple explanation for a particular parenting decision, you want to be wary of being lured into a "why trap." Although you may think that you will eventually get buy-in from your child if you take the time to explain your reasoning at length, you're losing sight of your child's motivation in initiating this discussion. She isn't interested in finding out why you vetoed her co-ed sleepover party plans; she's hoping to find a flaw in your logic and/or to wear you down so that you'll have little choice but to overturn that veto. Yes, Mom and Dad, sometimes too much information can be a bad thing!

- **Pay attention to your body language.** Make sure that your body language reinforces rather than undercuts the meaning of your words. If you come across as apologetic rather than confident in your parenting decisions, you're likely to sacrifice a lot of your credibility as a parent and leave the door open to repeated power struggles.

- **Be respectful and polite.** Don't make the mistake of adopting a bullying tone in the hope that doing so will make you come across as a more confident parent and help to discourage power struggles. Not only will you score more points with your child by being respectful and polite but you'll also model the very types of behaviors that you hope to see in your child.

- **Write notes or use pictures to communicate important reminders.** If your child complains that you're always nagging her about something, you may want to use notes, charts, checklists, or (for children who are too young to read) pictures to remind your child about important tasks that need to be done. (Granted, "always" may mean that you asked your child to pick up her wet towel once, but, hey, why not work with her on this one and go to a nonverbal system of "nagging?" Not only will you save her the aggravation of hearing you issue the wet towel reminder every time she steps out of the shower, but you'll also save yourself the aggravation of having to repeat yourself *ad nauseum.*) See Chapter 5 for more on this important technique.

MOTHER WISDOM

"Caring for children is a dance between setting appropriate limits as caretakers and avoiding unnecessary power struggles that result in
unhappiness."

—*Charlotte Davis Kasl*, Finding Joy

- **Come up with a family rule book—literally.** If there's
  on-going disagreement about your family rules, put those
  rules in writing and post them in a place where everyone
  can re-read them on a regular basis, such as on the refrigerator door. This can eliminate the need to constantly rehash
  the rules—an exercise in frustration for all concerned—
  while helping to encourage consistency.

- **Refuse to get into a shouting match with your child.** If
  your child starts shouting at you because she's not getting
  her way, respond in a calm, quiet voice. This may be
  enough to encourage your child to regain control over her
  own emotions. If she continues shouting, let her know that
  you're not interested in continuing the conversation while
  she's acting that way and that you're ending the conversation until she regains control over her emotions. (Note:
  You'll find some tips on helping kids to manage difficult
  emotions toward the end of this chapter.)

What your kids have to gain by getting you locked in a power struggle . . .

Kids rarely do anything without carefully considering the payoff, so
if your child seems determined to push your buttons day after day,
the resulting power struggle must be working to her advantage.

Although it's a rare child indeed who has truly Machiavellian
intents—who deliberately sets out to stage an in-house *coup
d'état* and overthrow the current rulership (a.k.a., Mom and

Dad)—many children will attempt a power grab within the family if given sufficient opportunity.

A child has a lot to gain from getting a parent locked in a power struggle. After all, there's always the hope that you'll give in and concede defeat on a particular issue, in which case the child will get his or her way. If you have a history of losing your cool and then giving in out of guilt, your child may try to lock you into future power struggles in an attempt to get you to repeat this pattern.

Of course, for some kids it's the overwhelming desire to come out the winner—to emerge as the victor in any power struggle against Mom and Dad—that motivates this repeated need for drama. If your child seems to fall into this pattern, you may wish to seek help from a family counselor so that you and your child can learn healthier patterns of relating to one another. Sometimes, it just makes sense to call in the pros.

. . . And what you have to lose

Because kids don't have to worry about mortgages, car payments, job-related worries, and the 1001 other worries that tend to float around inside the head of a typical adult, they have the advantage of being able to approach Operation Power Struggle with a single-minded focus that can leave you at an immediate disadvantage unless you resolve up-front not to play the game.

Although it can take a tremendous amount of self-discipline to avoid taking the bait on days when your child seems determined to trap you in a power struggle, it's important to do just that. Here's what you stand to lose:

- **Your credibility as a parent.** If you become angry and your child was deliberately seeking that kind of reaction from you, you lose some of your credibility as a parent and tip the power balance in your child's favor.

- **Your effectiveness as a parent.** You may find yourself giving in to your child to make up for losing your cool. These sorts of flip-flops are confusing to a child and make you a much less effective parent.

- **Your decision-making abilities.** Getting trapped in a power struggle impairs your judgment and makes it difficult for you to make well-reasoned parenting decisions. You may find that you are so busy reacting to your child's recent behavior that you find it difficult to plan your next parenting move. (Trust me—this reactive strategy doesn't play out any better in the world of parenting than it does in the world of chess!)

- **Your enjoyment of parenting.** You may find yourself feeling increasingly disconnected from your child and increasingly disenchanted with your parenting responsibilities. No one likes to feel as if they are being manipulated, parents included. If you feel like your child has managed to wrestle away some of the power and control that is rightfully yours as a parent, you may be angry at yourself for allowing that to happen and resentful toward your child for gaining the upper hand—something that can put you on the fast-track to parent burnout.

Because power struggles can quickly escalate into something big and ugly, it's important to have an action plan in mind for dealing with power struggles before they get out of hand. Here are the three key points to keep in mind:

- **Go into power-saving mode.** Realize that a less controlling parenting style may actually boost your power as a parent because your child may feel less of a need to challenge you every step of the way.

- **Remind yourself that it takes two to tango.** The best way to short-circuit a power struggle is to call a quick time out. If you feel yourself beginning to act emotionally and impulsively rather than with logic and control, take a break from the situation until you regain your sense of control.

- **Keep in mind that practice makes perfect.** Over time, you will become more adept at steering clear of power struggles and quickly defusing any power struggles that do happen to arise between you and your child.

Teaching Your Child to Manage Her Emotions and Finding Ways to Manage Your Own

According to a recent study conducted by the nonprofit think tank Public Agenda, 83 percent of parents feel that it's important to teach children how to manage difficult emotions, but only 34 percent of parents feel that they have succeeded in doing so.

Anger Management Jr.

If, like many parents, you're not quite sure about how to go about teaching your child how to manage strong emotions such as anger and frustration—the very types of emotions that tend to fuel power struggles—this next section of the chapter is for you. Here's what you need to know in order to help your child to master this important skill:

- **Make sure that your child understands the importance of mastering self-control.** Your child will be more motivated to work at mastering self-control if she has a clear idea of how she can use it to her advantage in her own life. Michele Borba, author of *Building Moral Intelligence*, suggests that parents ask their kids to consider what it means to have good self-control, why some people are better at exercising self-control than others, what makes some people lose control, and what people can do to regain their control once they've lost it.

- **Let your child know that frustrations are part of life.** Everyone has to deal with them. "I make a point of letting my daughter know that adults experience these kinds of frustrations, too," says Kerri, a 37-year-old mother of six. "I remind her of last year when I was drawing a picture of our house for our Christmas cards, and how many times I had to draw and redraw the picture until I was finally satisfied with it."

- **Don't be afraid to play censor.** Make sure that the TV shows your child watches and the video games she plays aren't undercutting all your efforts to teach your child self-control. It's pretty difficult to teach your kid that losing your cool is, well, uncool, if she finds it hilariously funny each time Homer Simpson does it.

- **Give your child a crash course in emotional literacy.** You can help your child to deal with her emotions by helping her to develop the vocabulary she needs to put her feelings into words. Start with the basic emotions—happiness, anger, sadness—and then add more words to your emotional literacy repertoire over time. Who knows? Your seven-year-old may surprise you one day by telling you that she's feeling "agitated" or "apprehensive"! (Table 4.1 has a list of words that may be helpful as you teach your child the language of feelings.)

TABLE 4.1

The Language of Feelings

Children find it easier to express their own feelings and to tune into the feelings of others if they have the appropriate words to describe those feelings. You can build your child's emotional literacy skills one word at a time by regularly introducing new words to her "feelings vocabulary." Here are some words that will quite literally help your child learn how to speak the language of emotion:

I am feeling . . .

abandoned	assertive	cheerful	determined
accepted	astonished	comfortable	devastated
accused	awed	compassionate	disappointed
adventurous	awful	competent	discontented
affectionate	awkward	concerned	discouraged
afraid	bashful	confident	disgusted
aggressive	belligerent	confused	disheartened
agitated	betrayed	content	disillusioned
alarmed	bewildered	creative	distressed
alienated	bitter	critical	disturbed
alone	blissful	cross	double-crossed
amazed	blue	crushed	down
ambivalent	boastful	curious	drained
angry	bored	cynical	dreary
annoyed	bossy	deceived	eager
antagonistic	brave	defeated	ecstatic
anxious	bubbly	defensive	edgy
apathetic	calm	defiant	elated
appreciated	capable	dejected	embarrassed
appreciative	cared for	delighted	empty
apprehensive	caring	depressed	encouraged
ashamed	cheated	desperate	*continued*

The Language of Feelings (continued)

I am feeling . . .

energetic	giddy	insecure	moody
enraged	giggly	inspired	morbid
enthused	glad	intense	needy
envious	gleeful	intimidated	neglected
euphoric	gloomy	irate	nervous
exasperated	goofy	irritated	numb
excited	grateful	isolated	offended
exhausted	greedy	jealous	optimistic
exhilarated	grief-struck	jittery	outraged
exploited	grouchy	joyful	overloaded
explosive	grumpy	lazy	overwhelmed
exuberant	guilty	leery	panicky
fatigued	happy	lively	patient
fearful	hateful	lonely	peaceful
fidgety	helpless	lost	perturbed
foolish	hesitant	loved	pessimistic
forgiving	hopeful	loving	playful
forgotten	hopeless	mad	pleased
frazzled	horrible	manipulated	powerful
free	hostile	mean	powerless
friendless	hurt	melancholy	preoccupied
friendly	hysterical	mellow	pressured
frightened	ignored	merry	protective
frustrated	impatient	miffed	proud
fulfilled	indifferent	mischievous	put down
funny	indignant	miserable	put out
furious	inferior	misinformed	puzzled
generous	infuriated	misunderstood	rambunctious

I am feeling . . .

reassured	selfish	tranquil	useless
regretful	sensitive	traumatized	valued
rejected	shaky	troubled	vengeful
relieved	shocked	trusted	vicious
reluctant	shy	trusting	victorious
resentful	silly	unappreciated	vindicated
responsible	sleepy	uncertain	vindictive
responsive	somber	uncomfortable	vulnerable
restless	sorrowful	understood	wacky
restrained	sorry	unfulfilled	weak
revengeful	spirited	unhappy	weary
ridiculous	stressed	unloved	whiney
sad	surprised	unsafe	wonderful
safe	suspicious	unsettled	worried
scared	sympathetic	unsure	worthy
scornful	terrified	upset	zany
secretive	threatened	used	zealous
secure	tired	useful	

- **Acknowledge your child's feelings.** No matter how upsetting a particular situation may be to your child, she will tend to calm down when her feelings have been heard. On the other hand, if she feels like no one is acknowledging what she is feeling, her frustration level may shoot sky high.

- **Show your child how to put on the brakes when she's starting to become upset.** Teach your child how to recognize the physical sensations of anger so that she can spot the warning signs before she completely loses her cool. Here are some questions that can help even very young children begin to recognize their own feelings of anger:

- Does your heart feel like you've been running a race?

- Do you feel like you want to hit something or someone?

- Do you keep turning your hands into fists?

- Does your body feel all tight and knotted up?

- Does your body feel stiff as a board?

- Are you breathing more rapidly than you normally do?

- Do the muscles in your face feel really tight?

- Are your eyes all squinted together?

Note: You may have to be on the lookout for these warning signs yourself so that you can point them out to your child. Then, after a little coaching from you, your child will start to spot the warning signs that she is beginning to feel angry—something that will then allow her to take steps to soothe or calm herself.

NO KIDDING!

Emotionally intelligent individuals are less likely to have to turn to substance abuse as a means of coping with their emotions. They already have the necessary coping tools within. They also have fewer relationship problems because they are more tuned into the feelings of others—something that can reap huge dividends on the personal and professional fronts.

- **Remind your child that she doesn't have to react right away.** Encourage your child to stop and think of the consequences of her actions before she reacts. If she's really upset, she may want to take a few deep breaths and walk away from the situation before deciding what she should do next.

- **Set clear standards for managing anger.** Let your child know in no uncertain terms that hitting other people is not an option, nor is being verbally abusive, throwing things, or otherwise having a hissy fit. Let her know that it's okay to feel angry, but that she is expected to find ways of managing her anger in more appropriate ways.

- **Help your child to find physical outlets for her anger.** If you know that your child has had a particularly bad day, you may want to challenge her to a game of basketball or invite her to go for a walk so that she'll have a chance to let off some steam. You'll be helping her discover for herself the important role that exercise can play in helping to manage stress.

- **Encourage your child to take a deep breath—literally.** Encourage your child to use deep breathing as a means of calming herself down when she's feeling totally stressed. If you're not quite sure how to demonstrate deep breathing to a young child, reach for the bubble-blowing solution. The deep-breathing action that produces the best bubbles also happens to be the deep-breathing action that is most effective at relieving stress!

MOTHER WISDOM

If your child is having difficulty putting her feelings into words, encourage her to draw you a picture instead. This is definitely one of those situations where a picture can be worth a thousand words.

- **Teach your child the power of positive self-talk.** Show your child how positive self-talk (repeating an encouraging message to yourself) can help you to maintain control when you encounter a frustrating situation. If your child is getting very frustrated with her math homework, encourage her to put down her pencil for a moment and say to herself, "I can handle this." (It's up to her whether she wants to repeat her math mantra out loud or in her head, or make an "I can handle this" sign to stick inside her math book. To each her own!)

- **Encourage a variety of sensory activities as a means of relieving stress.** Soaking in a warm bath, creating a picture with fingerpaints, or playing the piano are examples of the types of sensory activities that tend to be soothing to kids and parents alike. Encourage your child to experiment with various types of activities until she finds the stress-busters that work best for her. Note: While it might be tempting to try to soothe your child's hurt feelings or anxiety about her upcoming math test by handing her a glass of cold milk and a plate of fresh-from-the-oven chocolate-chip cookies, doing so may encourage her to turn to food for comfort whenever she's feeling upset—something that could potentially lead to ongoing problems with emotional eating. So it's best to encourage other strategies for managing stress.

- **Give your child some space.** If your child needs to be alone in order to regain her control, be sure to give her that space. Crowding her when she wants to be alone will only add to the problem. (Of course, if your child is still quite young, you'll still need to supervise her from close by. The trick is to find a way to do so without hovering.)

- **Offer to lend a listening ear.** Make yourself available to your child in case she wants to talk about whatever it is that is making her so angry and/or to brainstorm some possible solutions.

- **Provide the opportunity for role playing.** Give your child the opportunity to practice her anger management skills through role playing. Pinpoint some situations that your child finds particularly difficult—teasing or bullying, for example—and then allow your child to experiment with different ways of handling those situations.

MOTHER WISDOM

Here's yet another reason to teach your child some basic anger management techniques. A study reported in the May 2000 edition of the *Journal of the American Medical Association* revealed that young adults who score highly on tests designed to measure hostility were already well on their way to developing heart disease.

- **Use positive reinforcement.** When you observe your child keeping her cool in a difficult situation, be generous with your praise. Let her know that you noticed how well she controlled her anger in a particular situation and that you were very impressed by her restraint and her self-control. Try to be as specific as possible and make a point of reminding her to give herself a much-deserved pat on the back: "I noticed how patient you were being with your little brother. You didn't get angry with him at all when he kept grabbing your markers. You must be really proud of yourself for keeping your cool like that!"

Anger Management Sr.

Of course, the best way to teach your child to manage her emotions is to serve as a solid role model yourself. This is definitely one of those situations where you have to be prepared to walk the talk. Here are some tips on keeping your anger under control on those days when you swear you've completely reached the end of your rope! (Note: You will also want to re-read the preceding section because many of the anger management tips for kids also apply to parents.)

- **Figure out what's making you so angry.** Try to pinpoint the cause of your anger. Are you angry because your child won't stay in bed after she's tucked in at night or because your partner always seems to leave all the discipline dirty work to you? The more honest you are with yourself about whatever it is that's causing you to see red, the better your odds of being able to get to the root of the problem.

- **Pay attention to the voices in your head.** If you engage in a lot of negative self-talk—in other words, if you have a tendency to undercut your parenting abilities by constantly telling yourself, "I just don't have the patience to be a good parent," or "I always lose my cool when my child starts talking to me that way"—you may want to replace those messages with something a little more positive. For example, you may want to get in the habit of telling yourself, "I am really working at becoming a more patient parent," or "I really handled that frustrating situation with my daughter particularly well." Otherwise, these negative messages in your head could quickly turn into a self-fulfilling prophecy.

- **Don't be afraid to say what's on your mind.** Rather than expecting your partner and your children to figure out what's got you feeling so ticked and to adjust their behavior accordingly, spell out your feelings in black and white so that they are perfectly clear about what you want and need: for example, "I am feeling very angry right now because I am the only one who cleaned up the kitchen after dinner and now the kitchen is messy again. I need everyone to clean up their snack messes before they go to bed."

- **Steer clear of name-calling, insults, or nasty or inflammatory language.** Although it's tempting to resort to colorful language when you're feeling particularly angry, hostile attacks will serve only to add fuel to the fire. Your goal is to get your needs met so that the flames of anger gradually subside, not to fan them into a raging inferno!

- **When in doubt, call a time out.** Exit stage left until you've regained your cool. Note: Don't use this time to stew over the situation; use this time to take a genuine break so that you'll come back feeling renewed and refreshed, and with some fresh thinking about the situation.

- **Work on your stress management skills on a day-to-day basis.** You'll find it easier to chill out in the heat of the moment if you practice stress management techniques on a regular basis. You may want to get in the habit of adding the following five techniques to your stress management repertoire: deep breathing, positive self-talk, exercise, yoga-like stretches, and positive visualization. (For example, you may want to visualize yourself managing a difficult situation with your child particularly well in order to convince yourself that you really do have what it takes to parent this child effectively.)

- **Know when to ask for help.** If your anger is affecting your relationships with other people—particularly your kids—don't be afraid to seek help from outside the family. A counselor can help you to develop strategies for dealing with the frustrations in your life and channeling your anger in healthier, more productive ways. You've got nothing to lose and everything to gain.

CHAPTER 5

Ain't Misbeh
Coping with Behavior
Problems

"*I believe we need to pick our battles. If every single thing becomes a huge deal, then the importance of the bigger lessons gets lost in all the noise.*"
—*Catherine, 33, mother of four*

"*We try not to sweat the small stuff, but sometimes even the small stuff can grow into something big, and then you have to deal with it.*"
—*Donna, 33, mother of three*

D on't sweat the small stuff. It's great advice in theory, but it can be a bit trickier to apply in practice. The problem? Figuring out how to distinguish between the truly small stuff and the stuff that's merely masquerading as small stuff. Given how much work can be involved in convincing your child to get rid of even just one annoying habit, you definitely need to learn to choose your battles. It's either choosing your battles or running

in a permanent state of battle fatigue—the result of too
h time spent battling it out in the parenting trenches.

In a nutshell, that is what this chapter is designed to do—
to help you to learn how to choose your battles. I start out by
discussing strategies for coping with garden-variety behavior
problems—everything from whining to lying to cheating to talking back. Then, after we take a tour of the behavior minor
leagues, we move up to the major leagues and talk about some
serious behavior disorders—attention deficit hyperactivity disorder, oppositional defiant disorder, and conduct disorder. Finally,
I wrap up the chapter by talking about the importance of setting
reasonable standards for kids—standards that are high enough to
motivate and inspire, but not so high as to be completely overwhelming. After all, you don't want your kids to feel like throwing in the towel before the game even begins.

MOTHER WISDOM

"Some parents take the Puritan road and see their child[ren] as
ruffians in need of strict rules. Others may think of childhood as a carefree
time of fun and play and are less likely to set limits lest such rules destroy
this perceived childhood nirvana."

—*Meredith Small*, Kids: How Biology and Culture Shape the Way We
Raise Young Children

The Minor Leagues: Dealing with Routine Behavior Problems

Dealing with behavior problems can be a frustrating and time-
consuming aspect of parenting. According to the American
Academy of Pediatrics, most parents can list five or six things
about their child's behavior that they would like to change at any
given time.

Get with the program: modifying your child's behavior

Of course, it's one thing to identify a problem behavior in your child; it's quite another to come up with a game plan for getting rid of it. Here are some tips for dealing with whatever types of behavioral challenges your kids happen to be throwing your way these days:

- **Figure out which behavior(s) you would like your child to work on.** Identify one (or, at most, two) problem behaviors that you would really like your child to zero in on right now. You can deal with any additional problem behaviors after you get those initial behaviors under control. If you try to tackle all of your child's problem behaviors at one time, he may think you've signed him up for Problem Behavior Boot Camp—not exactly the best way to guarantee his buy-in for the behavior modification program.

- **Try to get inside your child's head.** See whether you can figure out what's motivating your child's misbehavior. You want to try to determine whether it's ineffective coping skills, a desire for attention, or something else entirely that's triggering the behavior problem. Understanding what may be causing your child to behave in this way will make it easier for you to come up with a behavior modification program that will work for him.

- **Come up with a game plan for dealing with the problem behavior.** Set a goal for your child and encourage him to work towards achieving that goal. Make sure that the goal is both *specific* and *measurable* ("I will get to the school bus on time every morning this week") as opposed to vague and wishy-washy ("I will try to be on time"). It's also important to state the behavior goal positively ("I will get to the school bus on time every morning this week") rather than negatively ("I will not miss the school bus any mornings this week") because you want to put the emphasis on the desired behavior, not the behavior you're trying to correct.

- **Make sure that whatever goal you set for your child is realistic.** Not only is it a complete waste of time to pick something that's too difficult for your child to achieve, but setting your child up for failure isn't exactly the most effective method of building up his self-esteem. Let your knowledge of your child's strengths and weaknesses enable you to pinpoint a goal that is just challenging enough to be inspiring, but not so challenging as to be discouraging.

- **Consider your timing before you launch the program.** If your child is dealing with another major stress in his life right now—for example, his dog has just died or his best friend has just moved away—this may not be the best time to get on his case about his swearing. You may want to make like Scarlett O'Hara and face up to his behavior challenges tomorrow. On the other hand, some behavior challenges simply can't wait for tomorrow to come; if your child is showing the signs of developing a serious behavior problem, you'll want to deal with the problem right away.

- **Map out your next move.** Decide in advance what you're going to do and say the next time your child exhibits the problem behavior—whether you're going to engage in selective ignoring, send him for a time out, or remove a particular privilege. Having your strategy figured out ahead of time will leave you feeling much more confident about your ability to manage your child's particular behavioral problem.

- **Make sure that you remember to accentuate the positive, too.** If your behavior modification program focuses mainly on enforcing consequences for behaving badly, you're going to have a hard time keeping your child motivated. That's one reason why it's a good idea to work some rewards or incentives into any behavior management program. Here are some important tips to keep in mind when you're using rewards to reinforce your child's good behavior:

- **Choose rewards that will motivate your child.** You may want to choose a combination of activity rewards (rewards that involve doing a particular activity that the child enjoys) and material rewards (items that the child would like to have). For obvious reasons, you'll want to put a cap on the dollar value of the material rewards: you don't want your child's behavior modification program to force you into bankruptcy! Besides, there's no need to go overboard with material rewards—not when activity rewards can be so effective. (See Table 5.1 for a list of the types of activity rewards you may wish to use to motivate your child.)

TABLE 5.1

Examples of Effective Activity Rewards

The following activity rewards tend to be highly effective at motivating good behavior and, as an added bonus, most involve little or no expense:

➜ Extra time on the computer
➜ Extra time on the telephone
➜ Extra TV viewing time
➜ An extra bedtime story
➜ Having a friend over to play
➜ Having a friend over for dinner
➜ Having a friend over for a sleepover
➜ Going to a friend's house
➜ Going rollerblading, bicycling, skateboarding, and so on
➜ Playing basketball or road hockey with Mom or Dad (or both)
➜ Having a picnic at a nearby park
➜ Borrowing Dad's binoculars after dark to check out the night sky

continued

Examples of Effective Activity Rewards (*continued*)

➔ Playing a board game with Mom or Dad (or both)
➔ Making a long-distance phone call to Grandma and Grandpa
➔ Choosing the radio station in the car
➔ Choosing the family TV show
➔ Making popcorn or some other favorite snack
➔ Renting a movie at the video rental store
➔ Getting to sign books out of the library
➔ Going to the park or the playground
➔ Getting to choose the restaurant the next time the family eats out
➔ Being allowed to stay up an extra 15 minutes at bedtime
➔ Earning the right to a chore-free day

- **Understand that activity rewards are a very individual thing.** What serves as a great activity reward for one child may be totally useless at motivating his brother or sister. There's no point offering to take your child to a football game if he hates that particular sport; he may misbehave in order to avoid the reward! The key is to zero in on something that your child absolutely loves doing and to make that activity the reward. If he's crazy about board games, having the chance to play Chutes and Ladders with you after dinner may be just what he needs to motivate himself to make it through dinnertime without tormenting his little sister.

- **Reward good behavior promptly.** Studies have shown that the more immediate the reward, the stronger the link the child makes between the reward and the desired behavior. Taking your child rollerblading on the weekend because he did a great job with his geography project on Tuesday night isn't nearly as effective at rewarding good behavior as strapping on your rollerblades and heading out for a weeknight rollerblade while the ink is still drying on his project.

- **Reward your child consistently.** When you're first starting out with your behavior modification program, you'll want to make a point of rewarding the good behavior each and every time it occurs. Offering rewards only intermittently will decrease the effectiveness of your behavior motivation program. (Note: You needn't worry that you'll have to drive to your child's workplace when he's 30 to give him a sticker for working quietly at his desk all morning. Over time, you can ease off on the rewards as the good behavior gradually becomes more automatic.)

- **Recognize that inconsistency is the enemy.** Being inconsistent with your child's behavior management program is like forgetting to give him the rest of his antibiotics. You're helping your child to develop resistance to future attempts at behavior modification by teaching your child that you're not going to bother following through if you're too busy, too tired, or too distracted to deal with his behavior problems. You actually risk making the problem worse; it's better not to tackle a behavior problem at all unless you've got the time and energy to devote to it in a consistent fashion, than it is to attempt to deal with your child's behavior problem in a half-hearted way.

- **Re-evaluate your strategy after a week or two.** If you haven't noticed any changes in your child's behavior after a week or two, you may want to tweak your consequences or incentives or consider whether the goal you've set for your child may be too challenging for him right now. Just don't make the mistake of rushing into tweak mode too soon, cautions Mary, a 36-year-old mother of three: "I wait 10 days to two weeks before making any adjustments to any behavior modification program. In the past, I assumed that the habit I wanted to eliminate in my child would be gone within a couple of days of implementing some new tactic.

Wrong assumption! It took time to get the habit, and it takes time to break it, too."

- **Write it down.** Don't rely on your memory when you're trying to decide whether or not your behavior modification program is starting to work. A written record is much more reliable than simple memory. If you get in the habit of recording the number of times each day your child hits his sister, for example, the two of you will be able to spot progress immediately if the number of incidents drops from ten a day to seven. That's a 30 percent improvement over the course of one week—results that would put most corporate turnaround specialists to shame and that definitely warrant some positive recognition. Unfortunately, it's likely you would overlook this improvement entirely if you were just going by the fact that your child was still hitting his sister, and you would miss out on an important opportunity to praise your child for a job well done. (The not hitting part, not the hitting!)

- **Consider using charts and checklists to motivate your child.** Seeing his successes recorded in black and white may encourage your child to try harder, particularly if there are incentives tied to his successes (for example, he gets a half-hour of computer time after dinner if he manages to achieve his behavioral targets for the day). Some parents even come up with tiered systems of rewards, a guaranteed way to capture the attention of members of the video-game generation who are used to games that reward you for getting to the next level! ("Hey, Dad! I only need to get three more behavior points and then I'll get to watch an extra TV show tonight. Cool, eh?" Cool indeed!) (See Appendix B for leads on Web sites that will help you come up with yet more strategies for motivating your child.)

- **Think about introducing a behavior contract.** If your child's behavior is spinning out of control, you may want to negotiate a behavior contract that spells out the rewards your child can earn for so many hours or days of good behavior. Because a behavior contract spells out exactly what your child is agreeing to do and what you are agreeing to do in return, it helps to foster a cooperative atmosphere within the family, encourages children to remember rules and to be accountable for their actions, and provides them with immediate feedback on whether they're on track. If you decide to go the behavior contract route, it's important to target behaviors that are easy to observe and verify. (Hint: It's pretty hard to verify that your child didn't lie about anything all week. What if he's lying about not lying!) If you find that the behavior contract isn't doing its job, you may have run into difficulty for one of the following three reasons:

  - Your child didn't play a big enough role in creating it, and therefore, he doesn't feel obligated to live up to its terms.

  - The rewards that are provided for in the contract aren't sufficiently motivating your child.

  - Your child has to be good for too long a period of time in order to earn a single reward.

- **Help your child to learn from his mistakes.** When your child takes a giant step backwards, as he inevitably will from time to time, ask him *what* he did, not *why* he did it. Asking him why he did it merely invites excuses. Asking him what he did forces him to state the facts about what happened—something that can then set the stage for some creative brainstorming about ways to avoid the problem in the future.

MOM'S THE WORD

"When my son gets up, he has zero privileges. As the day progresses and he demonstrates good and respectful behavior, he is able to earn privileges. He has the choice of what he wants that privilege to be: a TV show or a half-hour of Nintendo, or he may decide to save some of his privilege toward a bigger reward such as a trip to the movies. This has worked best for me because it encourages good behavior right from the get-go."

—*Sandi, 32, mother of two*

- **Be prepared to reap some unexpected dividends.** According to Sal Severe, author of *How to Behave So Your Children Will, Too,* if you help your child to improve his behavior in one area of his life, you can expect to see improvements in other areas of his life, too: "It is like having a two-for-one sale on good behavior: be consistent with priority behaviors and get improvement in other behaviors free. How could you refuse such a deal?"

MOTHER WISDOM

Feel like you're spinning your wheels on the discipline front? Ask your child's pediatrician if she can recommend a family therapist who specializes in child discipline or if she can help you to find a parent support group in your community so that you can swap parenting strategies with other parents.

The most common types of garden-variety behavior problems

Now that we've talked about what's involved in encouraging kids to modify their behavior, this section looks at ways to handle some of the most common behavior problems that tend to arise during the preschool through preteen years.

Attitude

Problem: Your child is full of attitude. His body language and mannerisms convey utter contempt for all the authority figures in his life, and the tone of his voice pushes every single one of your buttons.

How to handle it:

- Let your child know that his attitude is unacceptable. If he tries to argue that he hasn't actually said anything disrespectful, remind him that sometimes our actions speak louder than words.

- Realize that showing attitude is a power-seeking and attention-getting behavior—your child's attempt to wrestle power away from you and to come across as the one in charge.

- Try not to overreact—something that's obviously much easier said than done. If your child's goal was to push your buttons, and you react by completely flipping your lid, he's won this round of the parent-child tug-of-war.

- Refuse to have anything to do with your child while he's being rude and disrespectful. Let him know that the conversation is finished until he gets his attitude under control.

- Keep an eye on what your child is watching on TV and what video games he's playing. Some forms of entertainment glorify the act of showing disrespect for authority figures, making it come across as hip and funny rather than obnoxious and rude. If your child is already struggling with an attitude problem, he doesn't need any additional coaching in the not-so-fine art of being rude.

Talking back

Problem: Your child gets mouthy or challenges your parental authority every time you ask him to do something.

How to handle it:

- Understand that talking back is a power-seeking and attention-getting behavior—your child's attempt to wrestle power away from you and to prove to you and anyone else within earshot that he's the one in charge.

- Try not to overreact to the backtalk. Remember that if you lose your cool, your child wins this round.

- Refuse to talk to your child while he's talking back. Let him know that the conversation is finished until the backtalk ceases.

- Choose an appropriate consequence. At a minimum, your child should lose the right to do whatever it is he's trying to backtalk you into letting him do.

- Make sure that your child understands that he doesn't necessarily have to express every thought that runs through his head out loud. Self-censorship is an important survival skill when it comes to getting along with other people. In other words, it's okay if he *thinks* you're acting like a big jerk, but it's not okay for him to *say it*.

- Keep an eye on what your child is watching on TV and what video games he's playing. Some forms of entertainment glorify backtalk, making it come across as hip and funny rather than obnoxious and rude. Bart Simpson of TV's *The Simpsons* is, after all, pretty much the poster child for talking back!

Defiance

Problem: Your child refuses to do what she is told, either by out-and-out defying you or by choosing to ignore your instructions.

How to handle it:

- Try to figure out what's triggering the defiance. Is your child rebelling against this particular parenting decision or against your overall authority as a parent? Sometimes these types of power struggles can be indicative of a more serious problem in the family (e.g., serious conflicts between the two parents), in which case you'll want to get at the root of the problem.

MOM'S THE WORD

"I don't want my children to be mindless followers. I want my children to think for themselves and, yes, this does mean that there will be times they don't 'behave' as I would want them to."

—*Kerri, 37, mother of six*

- Try to steer clear of situations that are likely to be problematic for your child. If your child seems to tune you out completely when he's in the company of a particular friend, you may want to limit visits from that friend for a while. If he has a hard time remembering that he needs to be home by 8 P.M. on school nights, you may have to institute a "no going outside after dinner" rule until he feels confident that he'll be able to remember the rule.

- Don't make a huge deal out of every single behavior misdemeanor, or you'll end up encouraging defiance in your child. Attempting to exercise too much control over your child is like waving a red flag in front of a bull. It's pretty much guaranteed to bring out your child's inner rebel!

- Be generous with your praise on occasions when your child does a good job of complying with your requests. Positive reinforcement doesn't merely encourage your child to repeat the desired behavior; it also helps to build upon the bond between you and your child.

- Try not to let on that your child's difficult behavior is starting to get under your skin in a major way. Otherwise, he may continue being difficult simply because he knows it will get a great reaction from you. (Who knew you would be relying on your labor breathing exercises so many years after the fact!)

- Don't be afraid to seek outside help if your child's behavior seems to be going from bad to worse: for example, if your child is aggressive or destructive, has been expressing feelings of extreme unhappiness, or appears to be suicidal. It's important to deal with any underlying behavioral problems before your child enters adolescence because the teen years have a tendency to be rocky at the best of times.

Ignoring

Problem: Your child doesn't argue with you when you ask him to clean his room. He just never gets around to cleaning it.

How to handle it:

- Try to figure out whether your child is deliberately ignoring you (passive resistance) or whether he's simply so caught up in playing video games with his friends that he's forgotten he even has a bedroom. A good way to go about doing this is to check in with your child to find out what's *really* going on with him—what the experts refer to as "taking social/ emotional inventory."

- Make sure that any instructions you give your child are totally clear. If you say, "Your room is a mess," your child may take that as a passing comment rather than as a heavy hint that you would actually like him to do something about the problem. You'll also want to avoid

- *chain directions* (a set of directions that involves multiple steps),

- *question directions* (directions posed as questions—"Would you mind cleaning your room?"—that can give your child an out), and

- *directions followed by lengthy explanations* (your child can be so distracted by the explanation that he loses sight of the original direction).

- Don't let your child get away with ignoring you, or the problem will become self-perpetuating. This will require a lot of policing on your part initially—a major drag, for sure!—but it's better to nip the problem in the bud than to allow it to blossom into a full-blown habit.

- Give your child a five-minute warning if he's totally engrossed in an activity and is likely to find it difficult to switch gears. There's no rule that says your child has to drop everything right this second (something that amounts to a boot-camp-style of parenting); what you're looking for is compliance within a reasonable period of time.

Interrupting

Problem: Your child interrupts you constantly whenever you're trying to carry on a conversation in person or over the phone.

How to handle it:

- Let your child know that it's rude to interrupt other people. Children need to learn that conversations are all about give and take: one person talks and another person listens.

- Refuse to listen to your child if he's captured your attention by interrupting. Simply explain to him that it was rude to interrupt and that it will be his turn to talk in a couple of minutes. If he's very young, you may want to set a timer for him so that he'll know that it will be his turn to talk just as soon as the timer goes off.

- Be sure to model the behavior you would like to see in your child. Make a point of apologizing if you have to interrupt your child when he's speaking with someone else. Over time, he'll get the message that interrupting is not acceptable behavior.

Silly behavior

Problem: Your child acts completely goofy and won't stop acting silly when you tell him to get his act together.

How to handle it:

- Let your child know when his behavior is inappropriate. He may think he's being cute when, in fact, he's being obnoxious.

- Practice selective ignoring and see whether the behavior will go away on its own. If your child's goal in acting silly is to get your attention, you reduce the incentive for the silly behavior by refusing to grant him that attention.

- Give your child permission to be silly when he's by himself (for example, if he's playing alone in his room). That way, he still gets to engage in the ultra-annoying behavior, but you don't have the aggravation of having to deal with it.

- Realize that silly behavior tends to come and go throughout childhood and adolescence. There may be times when you swear that your preteen or teen has morphed back into a preschooler again.

Whining

Problem: Your child whines in an attempt to get your attention and/or to blackmail you into giving in to his demands.

How to handle it:

- Avoid situations that tend to trigger major episodes of whining (for example, visits to the video-game store) until your child has proven that he can handle the situation.

- Refuse to respond to your child's demands until he stops whining. Let him know that you're waiting for his "real voice" to return. If he's not sure what you're talking about, pull out a tape recorder and catch him in mid-whine. He'll be amazed to discover just how awful he sounds when he's in whine mode.

- Don't give in. If you give in after 10 minutes, you'll simply be teaching your child to whine longer the next time around.

- Pay attention to your child when he stops whining so that he'll see the benefits of expressing himself in a non-whiney way.

- Try to respond to your child as quickly as possible at times when he's using his non-whiney voice. If you wait until he starts whining to respond to him, you're inadvertently teaching him that whining pays off.

- Praise your child for being patient if he manages to wait for something without whining. Child development experts say that you can expect your child to be patient for approximately as many minutes as he is old. (Obviously, your mileage may vary, but this is a helpful rule of thumb to keep in mind.)

Screaming

Problem: Your child screams in order to get your attention or to blackmail you into giving in to his demands.

How to handle it:

- Avoid situations that tend to lead to screaming. If your child has a screaming fit each and every time you spend a day at the amusement park, he's telling you in no uncertain terms that he can't cope with the demands of that kind of an outing just yet.

- Refuse to respond to your child's demands until he stops screaming. Let him know that it's impossible to understand what someone is trying to say when they're screaming at the top of their lungs.

- Don't give in. If you give in to your child on the ninth scream, you'll simply be teaching him that it pays to be persistent.

- Pay attention to your child when he stops screaming so that he'll see the benefits of expressing his feelings in other ways.

- Praise your child whenever he manages to find ways to express his frustration without resorting to screaming.

Temper tantrums

Problem: When your child is completely frustrated with his math homework, he launches into a temper tantrum and throws his math textbook across the room.

How to handle it:

- Try to identify your child's temper tantrum triggers. Although temper tantrums are fairly common behavior for toddlers and preschoolers, they tend to occur much less frequently in school-aged children. If your child is past the peak age for tantrums but is still losing his cool on a regular basis, you may want to try to figure out what's causing him to lose control—not because you want to make excuses for his behavior (which would be a mistake, by the way), but because you want to come up with strategies for helping him to deal with the problem. If you analyze his behavior, you may be able to pick up on some underlying patterns. Perhaps he's tired, bored, hungry, sick, or dealing with a major source of stress in his life—or maybe he's showing one of the signs of a more serious behavioral disorder (see the material on behavioral disorders later in this chapter). When you're clued into his triggers, you'll be able to come up with strategies for helping him to manage his emotions and creative ways of avoiding those situations that tend to lead to tantrums, perhaps postponing a less-than-urgent trip to the shoe store until a day when your child is in a more cooperative frame of mind and is more likely to be able to put his best foot forward—literally!

- Be prepared to step in if you can sense that your child is about to launch into a tantrum. Rather than waiting for him lose his cool completely (something that's frustrating for you and that can be brutal on his self-esteem), you may want to encourage him to take a break from the situation and to find ways of calming himself down. (See Chapter 4 for some tips on helping kids to control difficult emotions.)

- Try to avoid showing your anger, even if you are feeling totally frustrated with your child. It's important to model good anger management skills for kids—particularly those kids who are finding it exceptionally difficult to control their own emotions. (See Chapter 4 for some tips on managing your own emotions.)

- Don't give in to the tantrum or react strongly to your child's behavior, or your child will quickly learn that he has the ultimate weapon at his disposal. Instead, ignore the tantrum and try to keep your cool no matter how frazzled and frustrated you may be feeling. Who knows? Maybe you'll end up with an Academy Award nomination in addition to your nomination for Parent of the Year!

- Try to ignore the temper tantrum so that you don't inadvertently reward the bad behavior by giving your child your attention. Either look the other way or walk away until he has had a chance to regain his control. Note: If he's about to hurt his baby brother or throw a plate across the room, you will have to step in and deal with the situation. Some types of behaviors simply can't be ignored.

- Seek professional help if your child throws a tantrum every time he feels frustrated, if the tantrums are occurring a couple of times each day, if the tantrums are occurring outside the home as well as at home, if the tantrums are resulting in the destruction of property or resulting in aggression towards other people, and/or if you are finding it extremely difficult to cope with your child's behavior.

Acting bossy

Problem: Your child is determined to boss anyone and everyone around.

How to handle it:

- Realize that a certain amount of bossiness is normal, even healthy. It's an indication that your child is becoming more confident and independent.

- Don't tolerate rude behavior, but don't expect young children to outgrow their bossiness overnight. It simply doesn't occur to a preschooler that he is not the center of the universe.

- Look for books that feature ultra-bossy characters (for example, *Franklin Is Bossy,* by Paulette Bourgeois and Brenda Clark) and talk to your child about how the main character's bossiness tends to make life more difficult rather than easier for him or her.

- Don't be a control freak yourself. The more you allow your child to make some decisions on his own, the less need he'll feel to assert his authority.

Regression

Problem: Your toddler or preschooler suddenly starts behaving like a much younger child.

How to handle it:

- Try to figure out what's triggered the behavior. Regressive behavior is most likely to occur after the birth of a new baby, but it can happen in any stressful situation. It's your child's way of letting you know that he's craving the same type of attention he received during his baby days.

- Resist the temptation to scold your child or insist that he "act his age." It's not unusual for a child to take these minor detours on the path to growing up. The less of a big deal you make of his behavior, the sooner he'll pass through this stage and start acting like a "big kid" again.

- Gently sell your child on the benefits of being a big kid, while making it sound like being a baby is *boring*. Point out that babies can't ride bikes, play in the backyard, or eat ice cream cones. You'll know you've done a great sales job if you manage to make it sound like babies miss out on all the fun.

Lying

Problem: You confront your child about a problem, and he lies about the situation.

How to handle it:

- Try to find out why your child was lying. When you're aware of the underlying causes for the lie (most likely a desire to avoid getting in trouble or a reluctance to take responsibility for a particular action), you can help your child to start brainstorming some creative alternatives to lying.

- Realize that children under the age of three or four don't fully grasp the concept of telling the truth. Lying may be caused by forgetfulness, an active imagination, or just plain wishful thinking. (He wishes he hadn't picked Grandma's tulips, so he tries to convince you—and himself—it didn't happen by making up a story about how he "found" the tulips lying in Grandma's garden, already picked.) Preschoolers believe that parents are capable of reading their minds, so they really don't have any incentive to lie. By the time they turn six, most children are able to understand the difference between lying and telling the truth, so if a child this age fabricates a lie, chances are he knows he is being deceitful.

- Don't set traps for your child by asking questions to which you already have the answer. Asking your child, "Did you eat that cookie?" when cookie crumbs are all over his face is just inviting him to tell a lie.

- Avoid calling your child a liar even if you've caught him in a lie. Otherwise, he may feel a need to live up to the "liar" label in future. Simply focus on his actions—the fact that he didn't tell the truth in this particular situation—and move on.

- Ask yourself if you have a double standard about lying in your family. Do you insist on a higher standard of honesty for your child than you do of yourself? Has your child overheard you calling in sick on days when you were perfectly well enough to go to work or fabricating elaborate excuses for getting out of family gatherings? These kinds of lies and half-truths can come back to haunt you when it comes time to start teaching your child the difference between right and wrong.

MOM'S THE WORD

"I remember one time when Marissa was not doing her homework, but she was saying that she had been doing it. I sat down with her and told her that if she told me right then and there that she had been lying to me, then her punishment would be no TV for the weekend. If she insisted that she was doing her homework, and I found out later that she hadn't been doing it, she would not have any TV nor would she be able to go outside and play for two weeks. She decided to come clean and take the lesser of the two punishments."

—*Ed, 36, father of two*

NO KIDDING!

Researchers at Queen's University in Kingston, Ontario, Canada, have discovered that children as young as three years of age will tell little white lies in order to avoid hurting people's feelings.

The researchers involved in this particular study asked each child to play a board game. When the child won the game, the child was given a dirty piece of soap as a prize. The children then were asked if they were happy with their prizes. Fully 60 percent of the children who had shown clear signs of displeasure upon receiving the pieces of soap pretended that they liked the prize.

The researchers were hit with one unexpected curveball while conducting their research: Some of the children appeared to be genuinely thrilled with the dirty piece of soap—proof positive that any self-respecting three-year-old can foil even the best-designed research study.

- Don't set overly high standards for your child. Otherwise, he may be encouraged to lie in order to cover up any perceived shortcomings or mistakes. He may lie about getting an "A" on his math test because he knows that's what you want to hear, and then quickly chuck the math test with the "D" scrawled on the front into the recycling bin.

- Make sure that your child knows that he'll get in a lot less trouble if he tells the truth about a particular situation than if he gets caught lying, says Olivia, a 31-year-old mother of three: "I try to explain that the truth will come out and that it is usually obvious that she is lying: chocolate breath means that she has eaten chocolate, no matter how loudly she may be proclaiming her innocence!"

- Praise your child each time he tells the truth in a difficult situation. Let him know that you recognize that it was tough for him to come clean about a particular situation and that you appreciate his honesty.

Cheating

Problem: Your child can't seem to stick to the rules when he's playing games, and you've caught him peeking at the answers when he's working on his math homework.

How to handle it:

- Realize that cheating can be the result of an overemphasis on competition. If winning is prized above all else, the desire to do well can be overwhelming. You may want to ask yourself whether you're overemphasizing achievement in your family—something that tends to send the wrong message to kids.

- Make sure that your kids understand why it's wrong to cheat and what the long-term repercussions of cheating could be as they get older—for example, getting expelled from university for cheating on an exam or getting fired from a job for cheating on an expense report.

- Ask yourself whether you're setting a good example when it comes to honesty and integrity. It's pretty hard to sell your kids on these particular virtues if they've heard you gloating about cheating on your income tax return or talking about how you like to sneak out of work early when the boss is out of town. This is definitely one of those situations where you have to be prepared to walk the walk.

Stealing

Problem: Your child has been caught stealing a toy from a friend's house or has been caught shoplifting in a store.

How to handle it:

- Consider your child's age. Children under the age of six may not necessarily understand that you can't just take things that you want without asking someone's permission or paying for the item in question. After their sixth birthday, children are much more likely to be aware that they are doing something wrong by taking something that belongs to someone else.

- Make sure that your child understands that stealing is wrong. Have him return the stolen goods and apologize for his behavior. This is generally all it takes to "cure" a child of the urge to steal. If a child continues stealing after this initial episode, you may want to consider whether an underlying psychological problem is at work. Some children with chronically low self-esteem steal repeatedly in order to boost their own feelings of self-worth and/or to attempt to "buy" themselves friends by giving other children some of the stolen goods.

NO KIDDING!

Stealing tends to peak at age seven, when possessions tend to be particularly important to a child and the desire for something that another kid has can be completely overwhelming.

The incidence of stealing also peaks again at around age 13, when peer pressure and dares tend to be the key triggers. Some teenagers start stealing as an act of rebellion against the authority figures in their life, to acquire brand merchandise that they may not otherwise be able to afford, to support a drug or alcohol habit, because their friends are doing it, or just for the thrill of it. In these situations, the desire to steal may indicate an underlying problem that should be dealt with by a mental health professional.

Swearing

Problem: Your child has learned a swear word and is determined to work it into the conversation at every opportunity.
　How to handle it:

- Understand what's behind the swearing. School-aged kids will often swear in order to impress their friends or to try to come across as being older than their age. (They think that swearing is a grown-up thing to do.) Younger children who swear may not even know the meaning of the words they're saying; they just know that these words are somehow bad, which gives the taboo swear words a very powerful mystique!

- Try to ignore the swear word the first time your child says it, in the hope that your child won't be encouraged to repeat it. If you don't provide him with a reaction, he'll have less of an incentive to continue using the word. (For more on selective ignoring, see Chapter 3.) If he continues using the word, however, you'll have little choice but to let him know that the word in question is off limits.

- Offer your child an alternative expression that's equally appealing—perhaps a highly enthusiastic "Oh man!" combined with a roll of the eyes and some other over-the-top body language. (Remember, you've got to make this new word even more appealing than the word you want it to replace—something that's much easier said than done!) Note: This technique tends to be much more effective with younger kids than with older kids, who are less likely to settle for a swear word that Mom or Dad made up. I mean, who wants a homemade swear word when you can pick up a brand-name swear word from your friends?

- Give some thought to the language your child hears at home. If you're in the habit of swearing like a trooper (for example, the first thing that popped out of your mouth when you heard your child swear was a string of equally colorful swear words!), your child may have difficulty even picking up the fact that a particular word is a swear word. Even if you do make a point of spelling out which words are swear words and which ones aren't, your child may have a hard time heeding your rules about not swearing, if your own language is less than pristine. Perhaps you need to give serious thought to cleaning up your own act first.

- If you tend to swear when you hurt yourself, you may want to institute a rule that says that this is the one and only situation when colorful words are allowed to fly at home. Just be careful that your kids don't start deliberately hammering their thumbs just so they can have a license to swear. Hey, it could happen! You may decide it's safer to come up with a string of colorful non-swearing words that you reserve for such occasions—words that feel almost as good as swearing. (If you make it fun enough to engage in some colorful non-cursing when you're really mad, the kids may learn to follow your lead, which sure beats getting that call from the school to report that your kid has been caught swearing, and that he swears he learned "that word" from Dad.)

- Make sure that your child's friends are clear about your family's no swearing policy. It's not fair to let your child's friends get away with swearing or using other poor language in your home if you're holding him to higher standards of behavior.

- Decide whether or not you're prepared to send the language police out to deal with more than just *bona fide* swearing— perhaps expressions like "that sucks," "that blows," and all the other crude but not necessarily profane expressions that seem to pepper the vocabulary of your typical ten-year-old.

- Try not to be too embarrassed if you have a younger child who is experimenting with swearing. Because much of what toddlers say is intelligible only to you, other people within earshot may fail to pick up on what your child is saying. Even if the swear word ends up coming out crystal clear (odds are, your child will manage to utter it during that millisecond when the busy restaurant where you're dining becomes dead silent), most people will assume that he was trying to say something else. (Surely that sweet-faced little two-year-old wouldn't say a bad word like that!)

- If your child continues to swear or engage in a lot of "potty talk" (another delightful phase that tends to set in at around age three), you'll have to find ways of letting him know that such language is unacceptable—perhaps sending him for a time out to let him know that you don't want to hear any talk like that. (One mom I know sends children who want to engage in "potty talk" to the bathroom.)

Aggressive behavior

Problem: Your child deals with his frustration by threatening, bullying, or hurting other people or by destroying property.

How to handle it:

- Try to figure out what might be triggering this behavior. Aggressive behavior is often a child's response to other stresses in his life.

- Let your child know in no uncertain terms that his aggressive behavior will not be tolerated. Children need to learn how to manage their feelings of aggression and to channel those feelings in socially acceptable ways.

- Don't punish your child's aggression by resorting to physical punishment. Doing so will only add to the problem because physical punishment teaches children to link feelings of anger with aggression.

- If your child has been caught bullying another child, make sure that the problem is being dealt with in a manner that is healing to both the victim and the bully. (See Chapter 9 for more on dealing with bullying.)

 NO KIDDING!

Studies have shown that boys are seven times as likely to exhibit aggressive behavior as girls.

- If your child has damaged someone's property, have him apologize to the person whose property he damaged and pay for restitution. (You may have to pay for the damage up front, but he can pay you back by doing extra chores.)

- Praise your child each time he manages to control his anger in a challenging situation. It's important to recognize the progress he's making toward mastering this all-important skill. (See Chapter 4 for tips on helping kids to control powerful emotions.)

Now that we've talked about techniques for managing routine behavior problems, it's time to talk about spotting the warning signs of more serious behavioral problems.

The Major Leagues: More Serious Behavioral Problems

Finding it hard to tell whether your child has a garden-variety behavior problem or a more serious behavioral disorder? Sometimes it can be difficult to figure out where to draw the line. Not only do children the same age vary tremendously when it comes to maturity levels but parents also often have very different ideas about what constitutes acceptable behavior. Studies have shown that easygoing parents are more inclined to tolerate more misbehavior than parents who are stricter by nature, and that a parent's own mood, temperament, and stress level may also determine to what degree they are likely to see their child's behavior as a problem.

If your child has been exhibiting extreme behavior for a number of months, you may want to at least consider the possibility that he could be dealing with some sort of behavioral disorder— perhaps attention deficit hyperactivity disorder, oppositional defiant disorder, conduct disorder, or some sort of learning disability, mental health disorder, or developmental disorder that is contributing to his difficulties. Or he could be being physically or sexually abused. (Note: Learning disabilities, mental health disorders, and developmental disorders are not behavioral disorders *per se*, but they can all contribute to behavioral problems. In fact, these problems are frequently misdiagnosed as behavior problems. See Chapter 7 for more on learning disabilities and Chapter 10 for more on mental health and developmental disorders.)

If your child is diagnosed with a behavioral disorder, you will want to

- Research the treatment options that are recommended for your child so that you can make informed choices about your child's medical care (for example, medication, individual counseling, family counseling, and/or residential treatment).

- Learn about your child's medical, legal, and educational rights so that you can ensure that his needs are being met within both the educational and healthcare systems.

- Learn which types of parenting strategies work best with children with various types of behavioral disorders so that you can work to bring out the best—rather than the worst—in your child.

Dealing with a child with a behavioral problem can be exhausting and frustrating, so you may want to join an in-person or online parenting support group, call your local crisis line for immediate support, or make a point of comparing notes with a friend or family member who is also dealing with the frustration of parenting an extra-challenging child. Although it can be scary to attend that first parent support group meeting or to open up about the challenges that you're dealing with in your own family, it can also be incredibly liberating. Remember that saying, "It takes a village to raise a child"? Don't be afraid to reach out to your village.

Now that we've discussed behavior disorders in general, the balance of this section considers three specific types of behavior disorders:

- attention deficit hyperactivity disorder (ADHD)

- oppositional defiant disorder (ODD)

- conduct disorder (CD)

Attention deficit hyperactivity disorder (ADHD)

Attention deficit hyperactivity disorder is a behavioral disorder that makes it difficult for children to focus their attention on the task at hand. Rather than not being able to focus enough attention on things, the current thinking is that individuals with attention deficit hyperactivity disorder pay too much attention to too many different things, something that can result in a lack of focus.

Children with ADHD tend to be highly impulsive and easily distracted. They may have particular difficulty with flexibility (specifically, shifting from one strategy to another), organization, planning and goal setting, storing and retrieving information from their short-term memory, separating emotion and reason, and controlling their impulses. (See Table 5.2 for list of the symptoms of ADHD.)

FRIDGE NOTES

Interested in finding out where the American Academy of Pediatrics stands on the use of both medical and non-medical treatments for ADHD? Visit the Academy's Web site at www.aap.org.

TABLE 5.2

Does Your Child Have ADHD?

In order for a child to be diagnosed with ADHD, the child must:

➜ Meet the criteria for the attentional disorder, the hyperactive disorder, or both forms of the disorder

➜ Have experienced the onset of symptoms by age seven

➜ Exhibit symptoms in at least two different settings (for example, at home and at school)

➜ Show signs of reduced social, academic, or occupational functioning as a result of the disorder

➜ Not have any other condition that could better account for the behaviors in question (for example, schizophrenia or another psychotic disorder)

Criteria for diagnosing the attentional form of the disorder.

Your child must exhibit at least six of the following nine symptoms of inattention for at least six months, and these symptoms must be noteworthy in their severity:

➜ Failure to pay adequate attention to details and/or a tendency to make careless mistakes when it comes to schoolwork or other detail-oriented activities

➜ Difficulty maintaining focus on tasks or in play situations

➜ Failure to listen when spoken to directly

➜ Failure to follow through on instructions and to complete tasks such as chores and schoolwork

➜ Difficulty organizing tasks and activities

➜ Tendency to avoid homework that requires sustained mental effort

Criteria for diagnosing the attentional form of the disorder.

→ Tendency to lose items (such as school supplies) that are required for tasks or activities

→ Frequently distracted by nonessential stimuli

→ Often forgetful in daily activities

Criteria for diagnosing the hyperactive form of the disorder.

Your child must exhibit at least six of the following nine symptoms of hyperactivity and impulsivity for a period of at least six months, and these symptoms must be noteworthy in terms of their severity:

→ Often fidgets with his hands or feet or squirms in his seat

→ Often gets out of his seat when he is in the classroom or in other situations where remaining seated is expected

→ Often runs around or engages in a lot of climbing in situations where it is inappropriate to do so

→ Often has difficulty playing quietly

→ Often behaves as if he is being powered by a motor

→ Often talks excessively

→ Often blurts out answers to questions before the questions have even been asked

→ Often has difficulty waiting his turn

→ Often interrupts others in conversation or otherwise intrudes in conversations

ADHD occurs in approximately 3 to 7 percent of children and is three to four times as likely to occur in boys as in girls. Approximately 50 to 60 percent of individuals with ADHD also experience other types of difficulties, including learning disabilities, depression, anxiety disorder, eating disorders, substance abuse disorder, conduct disorder, and obsessive-compulsive disorder.

There is also a strong likelihood that a child with ADHD will have at least one family member with either ADHD or one of the disorders that is commonly associated with ADHD.

Oppositional defiant disorder (ODD)

Oppositional defiant disorder is defined as a recurrent pattern of negativistic, defiant, disobedient, and hostile behavior toward authority figures that lasts for at least six months.

Children with ODD tend to lose their temper, argue with adults, ignore requests, refuse to follow rules, deliberately annoy other people, blame other people for their own mistakes or misbehavior, become easily angered or annoyed, and behave spitefully or vindictively if they feel they have been wronged.

ODD occurs in approximately 6 to 10 percent of children, and it often occurs in children with ADHD. Children who tend to be irritable, impulsive, and intense in temperament are more likely to develop ODD, as are children who are growing up in unstable family environments (that is, families in which there is a lot of economic stress, parental mental illness, harshly punitive behaviors, inconsistent parenting practices, multiple moves, and divorce).

If it is not managed appropriately, ODD can progress into a much more serious disorder known as conduct disorder.

Conduct disorder (CD)

Conduct disorder (which is sometimes known as *disruptive behavior disorder*) is a behavioral disorder that causes children to act out their feelings or impulses in destructive ways and to repeatedly violate the basic rights of others and the rules of society.

The offences committed by children with CD tend to become more serious over time and may include harming or threatening people or animals; lying; theft; skipping school; early drug, alcohol, and tobacco use; early sexual activity; arson; and vandalism.

Children with CD tend to experience higher rates of depression, suicidal thoughts, suicide attempts, and suicide than other kids their ages. They tend to have poor relationships with peers and adults and frequently end up moving from one adoptive, foster, or group-home situation to another. Children with CD are at increased risk of injury, sexually-transmitted diseases, school expulsions, and conflicts with the law.

CD occurs in approximately 1 to 4 percent of kids ages 9 to 17. It is more likely to occur in children who are highly irritable, highly active, or who are poorly attached to their caregivers; or who are growing up in unstable family situations.

Setting Standards for Your Child: How High Is Too High?

Before wrapping up this discussion of discipline, I want to touch upon one final topic: the importance of setting the bar high—but not too high—for your child. What you want to do is motivate your child to try his best, but not set your standards so high that it is impossible for your child to measure up to your expectations.

Here are the important points to keep in mind:

- **Make sure your expectations are age-appropriate.** Make sure that your behavioral expectations are in line with what's appropriate for a child of a particular age. Otherwise, you may end up setting the bar too high for your child—something that can result in unnecessary frustration for both of you.

- **Help your child to understand what is expected of him.** Don't expect your child to understand intuitively what good behavior is all about. Be prepared to both model appropriate behavior and coach your child about the ins and outs of what it means to behave.

- **Choose your battles.** Rather than getting on your child's case about all of his behavioral shortcomings at once, decide which behavioral issues warrant the greatest amount of time and energy at any given time. Obviously, you'll want to give priority to behaviors that put your child at risk (whether physically, emotionally, or morally) and that are potentially harmful or damaging to people or property, as opposed to behaviors that are merely annoying.

- **Ask yourself whether you're the one in need of an attitude adjustment.** If you're no longer enjoying the job of being a parent or you feel like you're getting stuck in a parenting rut, you may want to seek out the services of a professional who can help you to find more effective ways of managing your child's behavior. The stakes in this type of situation are incredibly high, so don't be afraid to make that call. It could make a world of difference for you and your child.

Talking the Talk

"At our house, the optimal time for chat is during the after-school snack. It's relaxed enough for my kids to talk, and things are usually fresh in their minds. Also, they know I'm going to ask about their day, so it's our special time. In fact, if I get sidetracked and don't ask right away, they'll remind me: 'Mom, you didn't ask about my day.'"
—Lisa, 33, mother of four

Communicating with kids is both the easiest and the toughest part of being a parent—easy in that we come biologically hard-wired to want to communicate with our kids right from the moment we first lay eyes on that wrinkled, red-faced bundle of joy; tough in that the methods we use to communicate with our kids have to undergo an extraordinary metamorphosis as our children pass from one developmental stage to the next. After all, the highly exaggerated, gesture-rich speech that is such a hit with newborns isn't likely to score nearly as many points with your teenager—particularly if you use it at the mall when she's surrounded by a group of her friends!

This chapter is all about promoting healthy communication—and healthy relationships—within the family. In addition to discussing what you can do to keep your relationship with your child on solid ground, I also talk about what you can do to help child to develop the healthiest possible relationships with her siblings and grandparents.

Of course, that stuff is an absolute cakewalk compared to helping your child deal with some of the truly heavy stuff that many children encounter during their growing-up years: the death of a family member, their parents' separation or divorce, or other types of stressful or traumatic events. Although we would all like to be able to guarantee our kids a picture-perfect childhood, it's a rare child indeed who manages to make it through to age 18 without having to weather a few of life's storms, so it's important to know what you can do to help your child to cope when the storm clouds move in and temporarily block out the sun. It's definitely one of the tougher parts of the parenting job description, which is why I've chosen to cover this topic.

Promoting Healthy Communication between Parent and Child

Encouraging healthy communication between you and your child may not be rocket science, but it requires a solid investment of time and effort on your part. When you set the stage for that sort of communication to take place, it tends to happen as if by magic. The secret is to find the time and place that works best for you and your child, whether it's during bath time, story time, or while the two of you are putting away laundry together.

Anne, a 45-year-old mother of one, finds that the words tend to start flowing from her four-year-old son, Tom, once she's tucked him into bed. "I cuddle up with him after the bedtime storytelling is over. We have a quiet time together while he gets sleepy and ready to drift off. If something is on his mind, he always brings it up at this time. I simply provide the venue and the sounding board."

MOM'S THE WORD

"I lie down one-on-one at night with each of my kids and ask each one about their day. I find they have an easier time talking to me when the lights are low, their backs are to me, and they don't have to look me in the face. This is especially true when something is bothering them and they don't know how to talk to me or their dad about it."

—*Mary, 36, mother of three*

Mandy, a 27-year-old mother of two, finds that her 10-year-old son, Brandon, is more likely to open up when the two of them are alone in the family minivan: "Perhaps it's because he doesn't have that confrontational, face-to-face contact, but yet we are still in close proximity. For whatever reason, that seems to be where he opens up most. So now that I've figured this out, I try to make sure that we get time alone to go somewhere in the family minivan a few times a week."

Mealtime conversation works best for Lisa, 41, her husband, and their four-and-a-half-year-old daughter, Kathryn. "We try to eat dinner together at the dining room table every day," the mother of one explains. "We have a rule that you can talk about anything at the dinner table with just the three of us there, bad words that you heard—anything. We sometimes ask each other, 'What was the best thing that happened to you today?' and 'What was the worst thing that happened to you?'"

Of course, while providing the right setting is important, it isn't the only thing you need to think about. You'll want to make sure that you steer clear of these common parent-child communication pitfalls:

- **Pretending to listen to your child when you're actually busy doing something else:** Life is full of distractions and competing demands, but your child deserves your undivided attention when she's pouring out her heart and soul. (Think about it: How would you feel if you were telling your best friend about a momentous decision you had just made in your life, but she wouldn't stop peeling potatoes long enough to make eye contact? Of course, some kids immediately stop talking the moment you put down the potato peeler, because they prefer to talk when you're not able to make direct eye contact. You'll have to figure out for yourself whether your child is a potato-peeler or no-potato-peeler kind of kid!) If you can't give your 10-year-old daughter the time and attention that she deserves at the moment that she wants it (such as when the entire family has to be out the door for a soccer game in an hour, and dinner is still far from being made), be honest with her and let her know that you need a rain check until after the soccer game. She may be annoyed momentarily, but she'll be a whole lot less annoyed than if you pretend to be listening while you dash around the kitchen doing a dozen different things. Of course, there's just one small caveat if you decide to go this route. If you ask for a rain check, make sure that you initiate the conversation at the agreed-upon time. If you drop the ball, you'll give her the message that talking with her is low on your list of priorities—not exactly the best way of forging the bonds between parent and child!

- **Interrupting your child before she's finished telling her story:** I'm sure you have at least one friend or business acquaintance who is guilty of doing this to you—cutting you off when you're in the middle of talking and finishing your story for you. People like this don't really care whether they get the ending of the story right, of course; all they're interested in doing is getting you to stop talking so that they can take over the conversation. If you've had this maneuver pulled on you, you know how frustrating it is, so don't do it to your child. It's a guaranteed conversation stopper.

- **Jumping to conclusions before you have all the facts:** I
  don't think there's a parent alive who hasn't been guilty of
  falling into this trap at least once. Your child is in the middle of breaking some bad news to you about the brand new
  scratch on your car when you immediately jump to
  conclusions—the wrong conclusions—and pin all the blame
  on her. It's not until after you've flipped your lid, grounded
  her unfairly, and caused her to burst into tears that you
  finally learn that it was the kid next door, not her, who
  came up with the bright idea of practicing archery shots in
  between the parked cars and who scored a bull's eye on the
  driver's side front door. The only good thing about making
  this particular mistake is that you quickly get to eat your
  serving of humble pie and apologize to your child. (Of
  course, by then she may be sitting in her room, swearing up
  and down on the phone to her best friend that she will
  never, ever tell you anything again, in which case you'll just
  have to hope that you've got an extra generous forgiveness
  gene kicking around your family gene pool!)

- **Failing to read between the lines:** Sometimes what kids
  aren't saying is every bit as important as what they *are* saying. If your child leaves out some key details and doesn't
  respond to your comments or questions, or her body language alerts your mommy radar to the fact that she's trying
  to hide something from you, this is a sign that you need to
  put down that potato peeler right now so that you can
  devote your full attention to decoding her verbal and nonverbal signals. (If you keep peeling, you're bound to do a
  real number on your thumb—particularly if she blurts out
  something particularly shocking or unexpected. Don't say
  you weren't warned!)

- **Coming down on your child because you don't like
  what she has to say:** One of the surest ways to slam the
  door on parent-child communication is to get angry with

your child because you don't like what she has to say. Maybe she's just launched into a 10-minute-long whinefest about how mean her teacher is, how unfair her math test was and how much she hates school. Rather than giving her the 1950s style "Well, it sounds like you need to buck up and stop whining, young lady" lecture, you'll be further ahead if you acknowledge her feelings ("It sounds like that math test was a lot tougher than you thought it was going to be") and wait for her to calm down enough to be able to start coming up with some possible solutions on her own. Getting angry at her for expressing her feelings of anger—or, worse, labeling her "a whiner"—will only teach her that you don't want to hear about the bad stuff that is going on in her life, not exactly the message you want her to carry into the sometimes rocky preteen and teen years.

- **Failing to appreciate the fact that something may be a huge deal to your child, even if it seems completely insignificant to you:** "We forget, in our adult world of mortgage payments and car payments and credit card debts, that our children's problems and dilemmas are as significant to them as ours are to us," notes Catherine, a 33-year-old mother of four.

MOM'S THE WORD

"My husband tends to start labeling our four-year-old whenever Jake is being whiney about something. He says things like 'you're a whiner' or 'you're being a brat.' These kinds of statements only exacerbate the problem. They really upset my son. If he was merely whining before, now he's hurt, mad, and crying."

—*Abby, 40, mother of one*

- **Asking too many—or not enough—questions:** If you launch into a line of questioning that gives your child flashbacks to her recent history class on the Spanish Inquisition, chances are you've overdone it in the interrogation department. On the other hand, you can count on having the conversation with a less-than-communicative child grind to a complete and utter standstill if you never interject as much as a single "So what happened next?" The challenge is knowing when to open your mouth and when to keep it shut—no easy feat given that the rules of the game tend to change as kids get older. ("With teenagers, sometimes a simple question can stop the communication entirely, but with younger kids you have to ask lots of questions to get the information flowing," explains Lillian, a 39-year-old mother of three.)

- **Offering unsolicited advice:** Although it's tempting to offer advice when your child is describing a problem that she's struggling with at home or at school, it's best to keep that advice under wraps unless your child specifically asks for it. Even then, you'll want to encourage her to try to come up with her own solutions before you offer to play the role of in-house Dear Abby. Kids need a chance to give their problem-solving muscles a workout on a regular basis—something you'll prevent your child from doing if you offer advice rather than a listening ear. However, there's nothing wrong with coaching your child through the problem-solving process. Some kids need a bit of extra help defining the problem and brainstorming some possible solutions. What you want to avoid doing is taking over the problem and delivering a ready-made, gift-wrapped solution to your child. She won't learn anything from the experience if you do all the work.

- **Lecturing your child:** Remember how you used to tune out after your parents switched into lecture mode? You would daydream, look out the window, play with your cutlery—basically do whatever you could to ignore what they were saying until their lips stopped moving. If you were really good at this, you actually stopped hearing the words—or only allowed yourself to hear a Charlie Brown–version of grown-up speak: "Blah blah blah—blah blah." So, rather than forcing your child to master this tuning-out technique for herself, why not simply skip the lecture and state your point calmly, concisely, and without that oh-so-annoying schoolmarmish tone. (Hint: If you catch yourself putting your hands on your hips and saying things that only a 1920s school teacher would say, you can pretty much figure that you've slipped into lecture mode. Time to step back inside the time machine and rejoin the twenty-first century!)

As you can tell, keeping the lines of communication open between you and your child is every bit as much of an art as it is a science. Because what works well with a preschooler is very different from what works with a preteen, you can expect to be spending a fair bit of time fine-tuning your intrafamily communication skills over the course of your parenting career.

Fortunately, you won't have to reinvent the rules from scratch every time. Although the language and gestures you use to communicate with your child will evolve quite markedly as your child matures, some of the same "tricks" that help to encourage a preschooler to talk can work equally well with a preteen or teen, too. As long as you can keep coming up with plenty of excuses to schedule long drives with your child and continue to listen to your gut when it tells you that your child wants you to listen rather than to talk, your odds of being able to communicate effectively with your child over the long term are pretty darned good.

MOTHER WISDOM

Family meetings can be an effective tool for problem solving as a family, or they can quickly turn into everyone's worst nightmare (parents included). Here are some important tips to keep in mind:

- Family meetings work best when they are combined with a pleasant activity that helps to keep the mood light and upbeat (such as eating pizza). A family meeting that is held at the kitchen table while the entire family folds laundry is pretty much doomed to failure from the get-go!
- Be sure to lay down any ground rules at the start of the meeting so that everyone knows what to expect: "Each person gets a chance to speak without fear of being shot down or interrupted."
- Have a clearly defined goal in mind for each meeting. Without such a goal in mind, the meeting can devolve quickly into a whinefest—something that will serve to demoralize rather than inspire the members of your family.
- Make sure that your meeting goal is positive rather than negative. You'll get much greater buy-in from your kids if the purpose of the meeting is to plan an upcoming family vacation or to talk about ways of fitting all of the chores in on Saturdays so that you can go off and do something fun as a family on Sundays. A family meeting should not be used as an excuse to rehash old grievances, blow off steam, or (worst of all) put one person on the hot seat. Otherwise, everyone will simply tune out, and you'll have a hard time rallying up any support at all for future family meetings.
- Keep your meetings short—ideally 20 to 30 minutes. If you try to turn them into all-day proceedings like a corporate board of directors, you're likely to spark a hostile takeover bid from a new management team (a.k.a., your kids) that is determined to do away with family meetings altogether!
- Last but not least, make it clear to your kids that while the purpose of the family meeting is to gather their input on important issues affecting the entire family, you will not be operating like a democracy. Parents have the final say in any decision, which means that the family meeting political model is, at most, a benevolent dictatorship!

Oh Brother! (Oh Sister!) Dealing with Sibling Relationships

When you made the decision to have more than one child, you were no doubt thinking about all the great things that can go along with having a brother or sister; by giving your first-born a younger sibling, you would ensure that both kids would have a built-in playmate and in-house confidante.

In a perfect world, that's exactly how things play out. Kids share their toys without as much as a squabble; they willingly step aside so that their sibling can take his or her turn first on the slide; and they never, ever argue about who has the blue cup versus the red cup.

Of course, most of us happen to be raising our kids in a decidedly imperfect world—a world in which siblings are as likely to grab one another in a headlock as they are to embrace one another with a hug, and in which turf wars over everything from TV privileges to computer privileges tend to erupt at regular intervals.

If you were raising your kids a generation ago and you expressed concern to a child-rearing expert (a.k.a., your child's doctor) about the fact that your kids were thumping one another on a daily basis, he no doubt would have shrugged his shoulders, muttered something about kids being kids, and turned the other way. The conventional wisdom has always been that a certain amount of sibling warfare is to be expected. ("Nobody's bleeding, and there are no broken bones. So what seems to be the problem, Mrs. Cleaver?")

Expert thinking on the sibling issue has done a major turn-around in recent years. The current thinking is that although a certain amount of bickering is to be expected—these are real children we're dealing with, after all, not wind-up dolls!—it's not appropriate for parents to look the other way when siblings are being downright nasty—or even abusive—to one another.

MOM'S THE WORD

"It's as hard for kids to share their parents as it is for parents to be divided."

—Kristina, 34, mother of two

Why sibling relationships can be a minefield for parents

Of course, knowing how and when to step in is yet another one of those situations in which a little parenting finesse is required. You may understand *in theory* when it's important for parents to intervene in referee-type fashion and call a quick time out between squabbling siblings, but making the right call in real life is nothing less than an art.

What makes things even trickier is that you're emotionally hooked into both parties—something that your typical referee doesn't have to deal with when he's making a tough call at the hockey arena. Can you imagine how much more complicated a ref's job would be if he were related to every player on both hockey teams? He would have a hard time calling even the most painfully obvious penalties. That's why sibling relationships can be such an emotional minefield for parents; you have a powerful bond with both of your children, which means that it's easy for them to drag you into even the most minor of squabbles—situations that they really should be learning how to resolve on their own.

Besides, if you've spent much time playing parent referee, you already know it's a thoroughly thankless job. You're always vulnerable to getting conned into siding with the kid who happens to be in the wrong, just because she got to you first or made a more persuasive argument—something that can cause you to lose a lot of parental credibility with your other child. Unfortunately, this trap is extremely difficult to sidestep if you're still determined to play the role of on-call referee. Unless you witnessed every single verbal exchange—to say nothing of those oh-so-fast sibling pokes and shoves—from the very moment that the fight first erupted, you're in serious danger of sizing up the situation inaccurately.

If you're crazy enough to try to tackle the whole question of intent while you conduct your post-game analysis with the two less-than-happy combatants, you're really setting yourself up for trouble. After all, if proving intent in a courtroom can tax the brains of an entire team of legal eagles, what makes you think you're going to be able to make a convincing enough argument to the jury (a.k.a., your two kids) to prove without a doubt that your 12-year-old did *not* intend to toss his smelly socks on his eight-year-old sister's half of the couch when the two of them were watching TV together in the family room? It was an accident, pure and simple.

MOTHER WISDOM

Refuse to play the blame game. If your children are fighting, don't waste your energy trying to figure out who started the fight. It takes two to tango.

MOTHER WISDOM

"The parent who intervenes in every conflict will inevitably discover that the conflicts multiply in proportion to the number of interventions."

—*Nancy Samalin,* Loving Each One Best

How to handle sibling conflicts

If playing the role of on-call referee and in-house lawyer doesn't work particularly well when it comes to minimizing the amount of sibling bickering, then what's an exhausted and frazzled parent to do?

The current generation of parenting experts are recommending a back-to-basics approach: allow your kids to work out their conflicts on their own *as much as possible.*

Now be sure to take note of that "as much as possible" fine print. What they aren't recommending is that you let the law of the jungle prevail at your house—that you let the stronger kids in your family bully your weakest kid into submission à la *Lord of the Flies.* Nor are they suggesting that you watch Darwin's theories of natural selection play out around the dinner table. What they *are* suggesting is that you slowly but surely teach your kids the skills they need to resolve garden variety sibling disputes on their own.

That's not to say that your mediation services will never be required. You're bound to get called in whenever your kids are really and truly over their heads. If, for example, your five-year-old opens up his ten-year-old sister's hamster cage because he wants to give the hamster a pat, and the hamster accidentally gets loose, you'll no doubt want to help him break the news to his sister. (In this case, more than the hamster's life may be in danger!)

You may also need to monitor (ideally from a distance, but in a more hands-on way, if necessary) the way that siblings sort out conflicts between themselves if one of the siblings is considerably older than the others. There's always the chance that the older sibling will try to take advantage of the younger sibling by cutting a deal that's less than fair.

Assuming that both siblings are reasonably close in age, however, there's no reason why they shouldn't be able to resolve a lot of conflicts on their own. You may have to coach them through the problem-solving process initially (hey, Rome wasn't built in a day!), but they'll probably amaze you by how quickly they're able to pick up the basic concepts and lingo of mediation.

The next time you hear that telltale "Mommy" shriek from the other side of the house, simply take a deep breath and prepare yourself to start teaching your would-be combatants the fine art of mediation. Start out by listening to both parties state their side of the situation ("She ate my chocolate bar." "It was my chocolate bar. Hers is in the fridge."), and then summarize the situation as you understand it ("Jenna ate the chocolate bar that was in the bedroom. She thinks it was her chocolate bar, but Lisa thinks it was her chocolate bar.")

MOM'S THE WORD

"Parenting multiples can be extremely rewarding and yet at the same time very stressful. You can never appeal to the older of the two to be reasonable during a conflict because you're dealing with two children who are developmentally at the same stage. You are constantly wondering if you are being 'fair.' You second-guess yourself about whether they should take part in the same activities if one or the other doesn't seem interested in something, but the interested one refuses to attend without her sister. It's a balancing act for sure, but at the same time, there's something powerful about their relationship when you see them sticking up for one another, sharing with one another, and holding hands and dancing and singing together. They share a bond that I see growing by the day but cannot possibly hope to fully understand. It makes me wish I had a twin sister of my own."

—*Kelly, 32, mother of four-and-a-half-year-old twins and a six-month-old baby*

When both parties agree that you've got an accurate handle on the actual problem (which, by the way, is a major achievement on your part if you had to gather the facts about the great chocolate bar fiasco from two sobbing kids!), you have three basic options open to you:

- You can calmly state that you are absolutely sure that the two kids will find a way to solve this problem on their own and then quickly exit stage left (a good bet after your kids have made it through mediation 101, but these two members of the Junior League of Chocolate Appreciators may not be able to handle that quite yet).

- You can point out that they are both too upset and angry to be able to resolve this problem right now and that you are, therefore, going to call a brief time out until cooler heads prevail (just be sure to make a point of getting both parties back to the negotiating table as soon as possible so that the problem isn't left hanging for too long),

- You can help the kids with brainstorming some possible solutions to the problem (the secret is to let them come up with as many of the ideas as possible on their own so that they can both create a final game plan that they will both be able to live with (for example, "Jenna and Lisa will check in the refrigerator to see whether there's still a chocolate bar in there. If there is, it is Jenna's chocolate bar, which will mean that Jenna ate Lisa's chocolate bar by mistake. If Jenna ate Lisa's chocolate bar by mistake, Jenna will give Lisa her chocolate bar.").

MOTHER WISDOM

Don't try to give your kids a primer in conflict resolution when they're on the verge of coming to blows. You'll be wasting your breath. Instead, wait until they've both had a chance to cool down before you start the discussion. At that point, you can help them conduct a post-mortem on the conflict that got out of hand and talk about ways that they might handle future conflicts more constructively. You'll also want to get them involved in brainstorming some family ground rules about fighting (no hitting, no name-calling, no yelling, no tattling) and setting some consequences for breaking those rules (for example, they both lose their computer turn for the day if they can't figure out a way to share the computer without screaming at one another).

When your kids have worked out a solution, either by themselves or with a little bit of coaching from you, resist the temptation to second-guess that solution. If it feels fair to both of them and it resolves the conflict, it's a good solution. The solution doesn't always have to be objectively "fair" in order to work: Lisa may be willing to accept Jenna's chocolate bar as a replacement, even though there's a piece missing. She may not care about the missing piece unless you make an issue out of it, in fact. So, do your kids and yourself a favor and bite your lip before you accidentally torpedo the Cadbury Treaty. Simply focus on all the great career skills you're acquiring by dealing with your kids; by the time you're finished doing your time in the parenting trenches, you'll pretty much be a shoe-in for any job that happens to come up at the United Nations.

 MOTHER WISDOM

Sibling squabbles particularly severe? You may want to consider family therapy if one or more of the following situations applies to you:

- Your kids' fighting is so severe that it's causing conflict between you and your partner.
- You are worried that one of your children may harm the other one physically.
- You are concerned that the sibling abuse may be taking its toll on the psychological well-being of one or more children.
- You suspect that a more serious problem (for example, depression or drug abuse) may be contributing to the conflicts between your children.

 **MOM'S THE WORD**

"I remove a privilege from both of them if they can't work out a particular issue. I do this because I don't always know who started the argument; it takes two to continue it, and I want them to learn problem-solving skills that they'll be able to use later in life."

—*Cathy, 40, mother of two*

Other things you can do to promote healthy sibling relationships

Of course, there's more to promoting healthy sibling relationships than circumventing the odd fistfight or wrestling match. Here are some other things you can do to help the relationship between your kids get off on the best possible foot:

- **Resist the temptation to play one sibling off against the other.** It's tempting to try to motivate one of your kids to do a better job cleaning her room by pointing out what a great job her brother did cleaning his, but all you're likely to do is to plant the seeds of sibling dissent (assuming, of course, that you haven't already got an entire garden of dissent growing already!). If you ever had a boss who made a point of praising one of your coworkers and pointing out how much superior her monthly sales reports were to your own, you'll have at least an inkling of how thoroughly demotivating this particular strategy is—and how likely it is to encourage all kinds of wild and crazy revenge fantasies. (Come on, 'fess up: you were always secretly hoping that your coworker's computer would crash the moment she finished slaving over one of those super-impressive sales reports, now weren't you?)

- **Don't favor one child over another.** Showing favoritism can be poisonous to sibling relationships. After all, it's expecting a lot of your daughter to ask her to feel anything but animosity toward her brother if you've made it painfully obvious that he is your sun, moon, and stars, and she's merely some sort of unidentified flying object that somehow found her way into your family. Although you may think it would be the least favored child who would suffer the most in such a situation, studies have shown that it's actually the more favored child who tends to experience the greatest psychological fallout. These kids often suffer from what is known as "golden child" syndrome—an overwhelming pressure to live up to their parents' sky-high expectations. If they feel that such star billing is unearned, they may become anxious and withdrawn—their way of refusing to play the game any longer.

- **Make sure that you let each child know how much you value his or her own unique strengths.** Your less-than-athletically inclined older daughter may come to resent her more athletically inclined younger brother if she thinks that the only place to score points with you is on the soccer field. Let her know that you value all the things about her that make her unique and special—her artistic flair, her organizational wizardry, and her razor-sharp wit.

- **Don't fall into the trap of assuming that things have to be equal in order to be fair.** Kids have different wants and needs, and if you try to treat them all the same, you'll end up shortchanging each child. Besides, a study published in the September 2002 issue of the *Journal of Family Psychology* concluded that kids don't mind if their parents don't treat them exactly the same as they treat their brothers and sisters, as long as things generally seem fair overall. So, rather than handing out the same number of crackers to each child, whether they're hungry or not, simply focus on meeting the needs of each child. Maybe one child wants six crackers while another child doesn't want any at all. Who's to say that's "unfair?" As author Phyllis Theroux once noted, "Rearing three children is like growing a cactus, a gardenia plant, and a tub full of impatiens. Each needs varying amounts of water, sunlight, and pruning."

MOM'S THE WORD

"In my experience, the root of most of my children's conflicts is their perception of 'fairness.' It seems to also stem from a fierce competitiveness and a fear that they are being shortchanged of anything from time to affection to food to praise. I try to remember something my sister-in-law, Joan, a mother of five, once said to me: 'Fair doesn't always mean equal.' It's a hard concept for a child to grasp, but it helps me out during the times when I'm not even sure myself what the fair thing to do is."

—*Kelly, 32, mother of three*

- **Refuse to tolerate putdowns and insults between siblings.** Not only is such name-calling disrespectful, it can be highly damaging to a child's self-esteem. Besides, calling someone an idiot will serve only to fan the flames of an already heated argument. Although it's important to give kids the opportunity to express feelings of anger toward their siblings, they need to be taught right from day one to fight fair and to treat their siblings with the same degree of respect you expect them to show others outside the family. Why should her brother be worthy of any less respect, after all, than what your daughter offers the kid next door?

- **Don't allow violence between siblings to go unchecked.** Studies have found that physical abuse between siblings is far more common than parent-child or spousal abuse, and yet parents have a tendency to look the other way. There should be clear rules and firm consequences for violating your family's no-violence policy. I kind of like Barbara Coloroso's "You hit, you sit" rule. It's simple and it's memorable! If you lose your cool and smack your brother, you've just sentenced yourself to a time out in the closest chair.

- **Teach your kids to respect one another's space and belongings.** Siblings shouldn't be able to barge into one another's rooms or rifle through one another's backpacks without asking the sibling's permission first. (My five-year-old has major issues when it comes to anyone sitting in his chair at the dinner table, or even putting an elbow on his part of the table. "You're invading my personal space!" he declares in a way that would do any 1960s flower child proud, but that totally freaks out his preteen and teen siblings to no end!)

- **Make sure that chores are divided fairly, even though it's unlikely that you'll be able to divide them equally if you have children of different ages.** If everyone hates cleaning the kitchen after dinner because they're eager to get back outside to play with their friends, rotate dish duty so that it moves from kid to kid. (We used to have "dish nights" in our family, but this got to be a nightmare to police as the kids got older and started having more dinners out at their friends' houses. Funnily enough, those dinner invitations almost always seemed to land on the night that a particular child was supposed to do his or her dish night. So, we've recently switched to "dish weeks"—seven consecutive days of dish nights. We're getting a lot less kvetching at the dinner table as a result.)

- **Try to discourage tattling.** If you allow tattling, you may be inadvertently encouraging your child to tell on her brother or sister in order to score points with you. Of course, it's important to distinguish between "tattling" (telling tales in the hope of getting someone in trouble) and "telling" (letting a grown-up know about a potentially dangerous situation). You don't want your six-year-old daughter to hesitate to tell you that her three-year-old brother is playing with the stove.

 MOM'S THE WORD

"Find a family with children about five years older than your own whose children reflect the kinds of qualities you want your own children to have, and whose marriage reflects the kind of relationship that you want to have with your partner, and approach them to see whether they would be willing to 'mentor' your family in some way."

—*Tracy, 31, mother of two*

- **If you feel like you're in need of some fresh ideas on the sibling front, assemble your own "parenting board of directors."** It's important to have a few trusted friends that you can turn to—whether face to face over a cup of coffee or via phone or e-mail—on those days when you need a second opinion on a tough parenting issue.

- **Remind yourself that your goal is progress, not perfection.** Although a certain amount of sibling dissention is to be expected, you want to try to minimize the amount and reduce the intensity of that conflict, for your sake as well as your kids. After all, living in a war zone isn't much fun for anyone, parents and kids included.

Parenting Your One and Only

Although society's take on *only children*—that is, children with no siblings—has progressed a great deal since nineteenth-century sociologist G. Stanley Hall declared that an only child was "a disease in itself," stereotypes about only children being selfish, spoiled, and egocentric social misfits still abound more than a century later.

Fortunately, we're also getting the other side of the story—that being raised as an only child can be a blessing as well as a curse! Studies have shown that only children generally have excellent verbal skills and tend to score highly on intelligence tests—the result of spending so much time in the company of adults. As an added bonus, they also tend to have exceptionally close relationships with their parents that continue well into adulthood.

There are, of course, a few drawbacks to having only one child. Only children often feel more pressure to succeed, knowing that their parents have all their eggs in one basket. It's easy for them to fast-forward through childhood at an unusually rapid pace because they spend so much of their time with their parents and other adults. They miss out on the unique interplay between siblings. "There's a whole arena that can be played out with siblings that only children miss out on," noted psychologist Rebecca Eder in a recent article in *Parenting* magazine. "They don't get to work out basic conflicts with other kids in the safe way that siblings can. That's the trade-off for not having to deal with sibling rivalry."

Fortunately, there's plenty you can do to offset some of these drawbacks if you're parenting an only child:

- **Accept the fact that your child isn't a "mini you."** Although all parents tend to fall into this trap to a certain degree, parents of only children are particularly vulnerable to trying to encourage their kids to emulate them. The reason is simple: they have only one kick at the parenting can. If you're a hockey nut, it's only natural to want your only child to share that interest, but you have to accept that it's completely the luck of the draw. If your kid acquired the Zamboni gene and is as wild about hockey as you are, great, you lucked out; but, if her vision of hell involves spending time in a freezing-cold building watching grown men bump into one another on ice skates, you had better start shopping around for a new parent-child bonding ritual to enjoy with your child!

- **Help your child to learn the socialization ropes.** Provide your child with plenty of opportunities to socialize with other children as soon as she gets that urge to switch into social butterfly mode, usually around age three. Because she doesn't have any built-in playmates at home, you'll need to make a concerted effort to ensure that she has the opportunity to play with other kids on a regular basis—perhaps by enrolling her in a group daycare, family daycare, or nursery school program; signing her up for kid-related activities in your community; or making regular visits to the local family resource center.

- **Don't go overboard with material possessions.** Before you fill an entire shopping cart with kid-related paraphernalia during your next visit to the nearest kid superstore, ask yourself whether you would be buying this amount of stuff for each child if you had four kids to shop for. If the answer is no, you may want to think about whether your child actually needs all this stuff. While we're talking stuff, here's another important point to keep in mind: you may have to ask grandparents and others to limit the amount of money they spend on gifts for your child. They may be willing to spend more on gifts for your child because she's the only one they have to shop for—something that can quickly result in a full-blown case of Pampered Princess Syndrome.

- **Resist the temptation to be overprotective.** Being under constant surveillance by overprotective parents isn't fun for any kid, but it's a lot less fun if you're the sole focus of attention. (If you've got a brother who's sharing the spotlight, you can always hope that he'll do something really bad and distract Mom and Dad momentarily.) Ease up a little and give your one and only the time and space she needs to blossom into her own person. Besides, the more tightly you try to restrict her every move, the greater the incentive she'll have to make a jail break once she reaches the teen years. (For more on the parent-teen tightrope act, see Chapter 14.)

Dealing with Grandparents

Grandparents vary greatly in the approach they choose to take to the grand-parenting role. Some dive in with great gusto, eager to make the most of the opportunity to get to know their grandchildren. Others are decidedly hands-off, feeling that they've done their time in the parenting trenches, and they're quite happy with their child-free existence, thank you very much!

The amount of grandparent involvement also tends to evolve over time, depending on which age of children the grandparents enjoy most and with whom they are most comfortable. If the grandparents are totally baby crazy, they may want to embark on the grand-parenting adventure right away—perhaps even before the baby is born. (A growing number of grandparents are choosing to take special grand-parenting classes before their grandchildren arrive so that they'll be fully up to speed on the do's and don'ts of modern grand parenting.) If they're not quite so keen on the baby stage, they may be a bit more low-key about the whole experience until the child is a little older. A grandfather who seemed quite cool and standoffish may suddenly get right into the swing of things when his grandson is old enough to carry on a conversation and ask questions about Grandpa's tool collection.

MOM'S THE WORD

"My seven-year-old daughter Meg and her great-grandmother have a standing date every Friday night for a sleepover. I love the fact that they get to spend this time together. Such memories Meg will have!"

—*Jodi, 29, mother of one*

Troubleshooting problems before they arise

Of course, not every grandparent-child (or grandparent-parent) relationship is necessarily made in heaven. Some grandparents try to play too much of hands-on role in raising their grandchildren, second-guessing the parents' decisions on everything from breast-feeding to toilet-training to discipline. "It's frustrating to be using gentle discipline with my children, only to have my mother-in-law yell at me that my kids must need a good spanking to smarten them up when she knows that we have chosen not to spank our kids," notes Kendra, a 35-year-old mother of six.

If you find yourself in such a situation, you'll want to have a private conversation with your parents or in-laws, out of earshot of your kids, so that you can kindly but firmly let them know that although you respect and value their input and you understand that they only have their grandchildren's best interests at heart, ultimately you're the one who is responsible for making the parenting decisions.

You'll also want to let the interfering grandparent know in no uncertain terms that you do not appreciate having your parenting decisions questioned in front of the children: "If a grandparent disagrees with the parent about a particular childrearing issue, it should be discussed at a later time—not in front of the children," stresses Jacqueline, a 35-year-old mother of four.

If one of the grandparents has a mental health condition, substance abuse problem, or other condition that may potentially impact on their relationship with their grandchildren, you'll no doubt find yourself walking a very fine line as you attempt to balance off your need to see that your kids are protected from any potentially dangerous or damaging situation and your desire to see that your kids have as "normal" a relationship with this particular grandparent as possible.

"I think it's important for parents to teach their children to treat their grandparents with respect," notes one mother of three. "My mother was an alcoholic, and, when my girls were old enough, we had to explain the problem to them. We treated the problem sensitively, however, not harshly and critically; I explained that no matter what my mother did, she was still my mother, and I would always love her. My children have respect for all of their grandparents and I am grateful for that."

Maintaining the bond with a long-distance grandparent

If your child's grandparents happen to live at a distance, you can foster a healthy relationship between your child and her grandparents by encouraging the two of them to talk on the phone; swap audio or videotapes (perhaps an audiotape of a Grandma reading a treasured bedtime story or Grandpa telling a funny story about Mom or Dad's growing-up years; or a videotape of your child making her world theatrical debut in the school's Thanksgiving pageant); exchange cards, letters, and artwork (your child's, presumably, though your daughter may be thrilled to place Grandpa's garden shed design on your refrigerator door); and, if your family is set up to send and receive e-mail, blast off messages containing everything from short one-line recaps of that day's soccer game score (complete with digital photo of your daughter's game-winning goal) to scanned-in versions of their latest report card. So, momentarily put aside all the bad things you may be hearing about the Internet; it can also serve as a terrific intergenerational lifeline in keeping kids and grandparents connected.

 MOM'S THE WORD

"Even if your kids don't have the opportunity to see their grandparents very often, they can have a good relationship if you make a bit of effort—especially in this Internet-connected world. We scan pictures—both photos and artwork—and send them to the grandparents. We make videotapes and audiotapes of the kids. And we talk on the phone fairly regularly. My husband's parents have never met our three-year-old son—they are older, and we have not been able to travel to see them. But Keeghan is very aware of Nana and Papa. He talks with them on the phone and he looks forward to the packages they send with little trinkets they've found: shells, rocks, coins, used books, etc. He has no relationship like this with anyone else, and I will work to help him remember these special people in his life."

—Lisa, 37, mother of two

Getting Through the Tough Stuff Together

Up until now, we've dealt with the day-to-day challenges that are part and parcel of raising children: finding the time and energy to squeeze in a heart-to-heart chat with your child at the end of a busy day; deciding when you should ignore sibling squabbles, and when you should intervene; and figuring out what you can do to promote healthy relationships between your kids and their grandparents.

This next part of the chapter deals with some of the really heavy-duty stuff that you may have to support your child through: the death of a family member or the break-up of your marriage.

A death in the family

Dealing with a death in the family is a painful experience for parents and kids alike. Because many of us didn't receive a lot of coaching from our own parents on how to deal with death, dying, and grief, we may be unsure about what to tell our own kids about these difficult subjects.

How much a child is able to understand and how she reacts to the death of a loved one varies according to the age of the child. Here's a rough guide to what kids understand when:

- **Three- to five-year-olds:** Three- to five-year-olds often have a difficult time understanding the fact that death is permanent, even if this fact has been explained to them repeatedly. They may also have a lot of questions about the physicality of death: where the person is, what's happening to the person's body, and whether it hurts to be cremated or buried. After they accept the reality of the person's death, they may react by becoming extra clingy or anxious when they are separated from their parents; they may also experience night terrors or bedwetting; they may become very whiney; and they may develop stomach aches and other physical symptoms associated with stress. (Note: I talk more about the symptoms of stress later on in this chapter.)

- **Six- to eight-year-olds:** Six- to eight-year-olds are able to understand that death is an irreversible event, but they are likely to have a lot of questions about the death that they may or may not be willing to put into words. For example, "Where did Grandma go when she died?" or "Will I ever get to see her again?" and the Really Big Question, "Are you going to die, too?" Children this age sometimes mistakenly conclude that something they did caused the loved one's death, or they draw similarly illogical conclusions about what went wrong around the time that the loved one died. One young girl involved in a research study about death refused, for example, to talk to the researchers about the possibility of her mother's death for fear that the mere act of talking about it would make it happen. Rituals such as funerals or memorial services can be very helpful in allow-ing children this age to work through their feelings of grief, so it's important to make an effort to include them in such rituals, wherever possible.

- **Nine- to fourteen-year-olds:** The emotions of grief tend to be even more intense for nine- to fourteen-year-olds. Some kids this age choose to handle the powerful flood of emo-tions by simply refusing to deal with their grief at all. What may come across as extreme insensitivity on your child's part—her refusal to acknowledge any feelings of sadness at all about her grandmother's death—may actually be her way of protecting herself against the tidal wave of grief that threatens to sweep over her, should she let down her guard.

Dealing with grief and death is challenging at any age, and will be doubly difficult for you if you had a significant relation-ship with the person who has died. As much as you may be tempted to try to protect your kids from the painful process of grieving the death of a loved one, however, that simply isn't pos-sible, nor is it desirable. It is much healthier—and much less painful in the long run—to deal with grief head-on. Here are some tips that may be helpful to you and your child as you begin to make the grief journey together:

- **Be a healthy role model for your child when it comes to dealing with grief.** Children have a more difficult time dealing with the death of a loved one if their parents refuse to acknowledge or deal with the death appropriately. Show your child through your own words and actions that it's possible to grieve someone's death deeply and yet go on living yourself—a very powerful lesson for a child to learn at any age.

- **Let your kids know that it's okay to feel the way they are feeling.** Get the message across that grief is a very individual thing. Some people cry a lot. Others cry very little, or maybe even not at all. They need to know that there's no right or wrong way to grieve.

- **Realize that children tend to grieve differently than adults.** Although adults tend to become fully immersed in their grief for a period of time following the death of a loved one, children tend to move in and out of grief. They can be terribly upset one moment and laughing and playing the next. If you're not aware that this is how kids work, you might assume that they are being disrespectful or showing a lack of caring toward the person who died. This isn't the case at all. Kids simply choose to process their grief in tiny chunks rather than immersing themselves in it on an ongoing basis.

- **Understand that the latest loss can trigger memories of other losses.** If your child has already faced some other significant losses in his life—her grandfather died last year and her best friend moved away last month, for example—she may completely fall apart if she finds her pet canary lying in the bottom of the cage one day. Don't assume that this means that your daughter loved her canary more than her grandfather just because she happens to shed a lot more tears over her canary then she did at her grandfather's funeral. She may be actually grieving all three losses simultaneously: the loss of her grandfather, her canary, and her best friend. The poor little kid's world has been rocked in a major way. The death of the canary may simply have been the final straw.

 MOM'S THE WORD

"My first three kids lost their birth mother when they were very young. I married their father when the oldest was eight, and I adopted them. We talk about Mommy Corri a lot. Our two youngest children know a lot about her, too. Because of what has happened in our family, we have always been very honest about death—the right to grieve and the fact that your feelings are valid no matter how trivial a particular loss may be to someone else. We always acknowledge the feelings, comfort them, and try to help them to move on. I believe that honesty is very important when you're talking to kids about death. If the dog dies, explain it. Cry with them. Hug them. If Grandma dies, let them see you grieve also. It is important that kids know that it is okay to be sad and that it is also okay to be happy again. Life goes on."

—Susan, 37, mother of five

MOM'S THE WORD

"My daughter lost her beloved cat, and I let her choose what she wanted to do in terms of burial or cremation, and—after she chose cremation—I let her decide what to do with the cat's remains. (They are in the living room in a box wrapped in kitty wrapping paper, much to my dismay!) I let her know that she was a good owner and that it wasn't her fault that her cat died. And I gave her lots of hugs and gave her total permission to feel the way she was feeling."

—Kristina, 34, mother of two

- **When you're explaining death to a child, use the most straightforward language possible.** Using euphemisms (for example, "Grandpa is sleeping," or "Uncle Jim is now at rest") isn't merely confusing to a child, it may be down-right frightening. Your child may fear that, like Grandpa or Uncle Jim, she, too, may go to sleep and never wake up.

- **Be prepared for some tough—even morbid—questions.**
  Sometimes parents are shocked by the graphic questions that kids can ask when they find out that someone has died. Kids aren't trying to be morbid when they ask what is going to happen to the dead person's body. They're simply look-ing for simple factual information. Although these ques-tions can be a bit distressing to have to confront when you're deeply immersed in your own grief, you might find them a little easier to cope with if you remind yourself that questions about death are simply the flip side of questions about birth—another perennial favorite topic of discussion for young children.

- **Check for misinformation, even if you're sure that your child has a solid grasp of what has happened.** Sometimes children appear to understand more than they actually do—something Lillian, a 39-year-old mother of three, dis-covered during the weeks following her husband's death. "When my first husband was killed in a car accident, Jaclyn was just three days away from her fourth birthday and Sarah was just 14 months old. Jacyln was a very mature, independent four-year-old, and I tried to explain things to her as they were happening, in a simple sort of way. I thought she was handling things pretty well until one day, about two months later, her junior kindergarten teacher called me to say that when they were talking about family in school, Jaclyn had told them that Daddy had gone to live at Grandma's house. Jacyln and I talked about this, and I asked her where she thought her Daddy was and she told me that she didn't know."

- **Realize that the questions may resurface months—even years—after the death.** "Taylor was only a year-and-a-half old when my mother died, and, at the time, I didn't think she was stressed at all," recalls Janice, a 34-year-old mother of one. "Now that she is three-and-a-half, however, the questions and comments are finally coming."

- **Give your child a chance to participate in funerals and other rituals.** Although parents sometimes worry that children may be frightened by funerals, memorial services, and cemetery visits, children tend to be more frightened if they are excluded from these important rites of passage. They may conclude that funerals must be really terrible or scary if you wouldn't allow them to go—an attitude that they could carry with them into adulthood. If you deprive your child of the chance to participate in a family funeral or memorial service, you deprive her of the opportunity to give and receive support.

MOM'S THE WORD

"Our first daughter, Jeneca Marie, was born at only 31 weeks and lived for just 9 days. Our girls both say a prayer for their big sister Jeneca every night when they say their prayers. And on Jeneca's birthday each year, Meghan—our four-year-old—draws a picture and writes a letter to Jeneca, and we put it into a balloon and release the balloon into the wind."

—*Stacey, 28, mother of two living children, and baby Jeneca*

- **Try to keep the rest of your child's life as normal as possible.** Although it may take a superhuman effort on your part to take her to her soccer game when you're still grieving deeply yourself, the more you can stick with your child's normal routine during this challenging time, the easier it will be for her to cope with her grief and the other fallout resulting from the death of this significant person in her life.

- **Don't be afraid to seek outside support for yourself or your child if you find that you are having trouble coping with your grief.** Individual or group support can make a world of difference if you are overwhelmed by feelings of loss.

Separation or divorce

The death of a significant person or a much-loved family pet isn't the only type of loss that children may face at some point during their growing-up years. Many children also have to work through the grief associated with a parent's separation or divorce.

Despite the massive amount of research that has been conducted in this area, the experts are still battling it out over the long-term effects of separation and divorce on children. Some experts, such as University of Virginia psychologist E. Mavis Hetherington, have found that the majority of kids come through their parents' divorces relatively unscathed: her research has shown that, within six years of the divorce, 75 to 80 percent of kids from divorced families are as happy and well-adjusted as children from so-called "intact families."

The research of other experts, including California psychologist Judith Wallerstein, has painted a decidedly less rosy picture. Wallerstein has repeatedly made the case that the negative fallout from divorce is something that children may carry with them well into adulthood.

One thing the experts *do* agree about is that the way the breakup is handled has a major effect on the way the children cope, both in the short-term and over the long-term. Here are the key points to keep in mind if you and your partner are thinking of parting ways:

- **Don't tip your hand until you're sure you're going to follow through with your plans.** There's no point in upsetting

your child unnecessarily by talking about your plans to separate from your partner if you subsequently end up chang-
ing your mind.

 **NO KIDDING!**

A study conducted at Iowa State University revealed that boys in
divorced families face a higher risk of depression during their teen years than
girls do. The researchers concluded that "perhaps even optimal post-divorce
circumstances are not sufficient to compensate for the sadness experienced
by boys because of the departure of their father from the home."

NO KIDDING!

A recent study conducted at the Harvard School of Public Health
found that parental divorce by age seven was associated with a higher lifetime risk of depression. The risk was most pronounced when there was a
great deal of conflict between the parents. Such depression is by no means
inevitable, however. A separate study conducted at Arizona State University
found that children of divorced parents were less likely to develop mental
health problems in adolescence and adulthood if they participated in family
counseling following the breakup. The researchers involved in this particular
study found that 11 percent of teens of divorced parents who participated in
family therapy, as opposed to 23 percent of teens of divorced parents who did
not participate in family therapy, subsequently experienced health problems.

- **Give careful thought to your timing.** It's best to avoid
  making your announcement right before your child has to
  go to bed or the night before a big track meet or test at
  school. Your child will need some time to absorb the news.

- **Break the news at a time when both partners can be
  there so that one parent doesn't get stuck playing the
  heavy.** You want your child to get the message that this was
  a mutual decision, not merely one parent's doing. If it isn't
  possible or practical for both parents to break the news

together, then the parent who has played the most hands-on role in parenting should be the one to break the news. The child will likely find the news a little easier to take if it is delivered by this parent.

- **Make sure you provide your child with some sort of concrete explanation about what went wrong.** If you leave her to fill in the blanks on her own, she may find ways to blame herself for the breakup. Obviously, you don't want to hang out all your marital dirty laundry in front of your child, so you'll want to keep your explanation simple and to the point, perhaps something along these lines: "Your father and I have decided we would be happier living apart instead of living together and fighting all the time. What happened was a problem between us. It had nothing to do with anything you said or did. Even though we will no longer be living together as a family, I will always be your mother and your father will always be your father, and we will both always love you and take care of you."

- **Make sure that your child understands that she didn't do anything to cause the breakup.** Your child is more likely to feel this way if she has overheard you and your partner arguing about parenting issues. She may conclude that fights about her were what caused the two of you to part ways.

- **Be sure to reassure your child that both parents love her and that nothing will ever change that.** It's important to stress that the love between a parent and a child is unconditional: you're not about to divorce *her*, no matter what.

- **Realize that it can be difficult to predict in advance how your child may react to the news.** Your child may be depressed, withdrawn, angry, spiteful, or uncooperative—or she may react in some other way entirely.

- **Let your child know that she has a right to feel angry or sad or whatever else she is feeling, but be prepared to set limits on her behavior.** She needs to know that rude and hurtful behavior directed at either you or your ex will not be tolerated. There are other, healthier ways of dealing with painful emotions.

- **Get ready for a lot of tough questions.** After the basic facts have had a chance to settle in and the initial shock has worn off, your child is likely to approach you with an entire laundry list of questions about how the divorce is likely to impact his or her life—everything from where she will be living to who gets "custody" of the family dog. Although some of her questions may seem downright bizarre—you may wonder why she's so hung up on finding out where her bathing suit is going to be stored in the off-season—her fact-finding mission will slowly but surely help her to make sense of her new world.

Life after divorce

Breaking the news to your kids about your plans to separate from your partner is one of the first challenges you will face as a single (or almost single) parent. Here are some important points to keep in mind that will help to minimize the divorce-related fallout on your kids after you've overcome that initial hurdle:

- **Resist the temptation to trash your ex when you're within earshot of the kids, even if you're totally furious about the circumstances that led to the breakup.** That late-night venting session with your girlfriend may feel oh-so-good to you, but it could be extremely damaging to your child to hear you slamming her dad. Besides, mutual respect is the name of the game for separating partners, says Ed, a 36-year-old father of two: "My ex-wife and I have been able to put our feelings toward each other aside and focus on doing what's right for the girls. I am very proud of that and I think we have a very good relationship as a result."

- **Insist that family members abide by the same policy.** Let them know that you want them to avoid criticizing your ex anytime your child is within earshot. You don't want your child to be hurt as a result of inadvertently overhearing relatives, who are bitter about the breakup, tearing her other parent to shreds.

- **Be creative when it comes to carving out a workable co-parenting relationship with your ex.** "Let go of any preconceived notions you may have about what your kids' dad should or shouldn't do for you," suggests Natalie, a 32-year-old mother of two. "Carve your own path."

- **Accept the fact that even though you may feel tremendous relief about the breakup, your child is likely to be missing her other parent.** Don't dismiss her feelings or feel threatened by her love for her Dad; instead, encourage her to phone and e-mail her Dad on a regular basis so that the two of them can stay in constant contact in between face-to-face visits.

- **When you talk to your child about your ex, focus on his positive qualities as a parent rather than anything else about him.** Remember, it's possible for someone to be a terrible partner but an awesome Dad.

- **Resist the temptation to make up for any guilt feelings you may have about the breakup by showering your child with material goods.** You'll also want to be careful to avoid allowing your child to manipulate you into buying her all kinds of stuff. What your child really needs is a little extra love and attention from both of her parents. No electronic game system can take the place of that.

- **Kindly but gently nip any reunion fantasies in the bud.** You're not doing your child any favors by allowing her to harbor any illusions about you and your ex getting back together. You're simply allowing her to postpone the painful but necessary process of grieving the breakup of your marriage.

- **Watch for any behavioral changes that may indicate that your child is not adjusting well to the divorce.** If your child is having trouble eating or sleeping, having difficulties at school, or exhibiting behavior that is out of character for her, you may want to schedule an appointment with a child therapist or mental health professional who specializes in working with children whose parents have separated recently. (*Note:* I talk more about stress at the end of this chapter.)

 MOM'S THE WORD

"Parents who have never had to raise a child on their own do not realize what it is like. There is no one around to share in the joys and no one to stand beside you during the hard times."

—*Jodi, 29, mother of one*

- **Don't forget to take care of yourself.** It's easy to be so focused on your child's needs during this challenging time that you may lose sight of your own needs. "I was a single parent for nine years after the death of my first husband," recalls Lillian, a 39-year-old mother of three. "The best advice I could give to someone else who finds themselves in this situation is this: don't forget to live for yourself. The first couple of years are kind of a blur to me as I turned into a parent who would do everything for my kids. When I got home from work, it was kids, kids, kids. There were gymnastics lessons, jazz lessons, swimming lessons, T-ball, baseball, piano, karate, and so on—and I was volunteering to help coach and taking them on day trips to the zoo, the museum, the science center, and so on. There was nothing left for me. I'm not saying that you shouldn't spend time with your kids. Of course, that is important. But, for a while, I went a little overboard, trying to compensate for the loss of their daddy."

- **Connect with other single parents.** "It's hard for your married friends to understand what you're dealing with," says Natalie, a 32-year-old mother of two. "It helps to know you're not alone."

Beyond Cinderella: Step-parenting success

Just as kids need a period of time to adjust to the changes that happen at the time of their parents' separation or divorce, they also need time to warm up to any new stepparent who subsequently arrives on the scene.

It's a challenge that's being faced by a growing number of American families. In fact, according to the Census Bureau, 1300 new stepfamilies are formed daily and 500,000 adults become stepparents for the first time each year.

Here are some tips on promoting healthy stepparent–stepchild relationships:

- Have a frank discussion with your new partner about child-rearing issues before he or she assumes step-parenting duties. You need to make sure that you're in synch when it comes to the really key childrearing fundamentals.

- Make it a given that your child has the right to spend some one-on-one time with you, her biological parent. Not every activity has to include the stepparent.

- Encourage your new partner to spend some one-on-one time with your child, too. Doing so will allow the two of them to start building up their own storehouse of shared memories and experiences.

- Stepparents should be clear right from the start about the behaviors that they are willing to tolerate from their stepchildren. Although some anger, sadness, and acting out may be understandable initially, the stepparent should not be expected to put up with the doormat treatment.

- Be patient when it comes to stepsibling relationships. It can take time for these relationships to gel. If you're expecting life between your kids and your partner's kids to instantly play out like an episode of *The Brady Bunch*, you're dreaming in 1960s sitcom Technicolor!

Other Traumatic or Painful Events

Although death and divorce are the biggies when it comes to traumatic life events for children, your child may also be significantly affected by a parent's or sibling's illness, a parent's job loss, or a move to a new neighborhood. Any event that significantly rocks a child's world can trigger feelings of grief or stress.

It can be easy to overlook the needs of your child when you're in the midst of dealing with a crisis yourself. If, for example, you've had to focus a huge amount of energy on helping a child with a physical, mental, or emotional disability or disorder, or a life-threatening health problem, you may temporarily lose sight of how her brother is reacting to the crisis. (Don't beat yourself up about this; you're simply playing triage nurse, obtaining help first for the child who needs it the most urgently.)

It's not unusual in situations like this for the behavior of the child who is not ill to become extreme: he may either behave extremely well—too well—because he doesn't want to worry you, or he may act out in an effort to steal back "his share" of your attention from his sick sibling. Obviously, neither strategy is particularly healthy, so you'll want to give your son a chance to talk about his feelings about his sister's illness and the ways her illness has affected the rest of the family. He needs to be allowed to have his say about how his life has been changed by this crisis in the life of your family.

How Stress Plays Out for Kids

Stress is a fact of life for kids today. Even if kids are lucky enough to sidestep any major traumas such as death, divorce, a parent's job loss, a natural disaster, or other life-altering events, they're still likely to encounter such garden-variety sources of stress as math tests, gymnastics recitals, and the stress that goes along with learning how to ride a bike.

Although we may not be able to completely stress-proof our kids' lives, there's plenty we can do to inoculate them against the most harmful effects of stress. Studies have shown that children are less likely to experience the negative effects of stress if parents make a point of

- fostering a climate of love, trust, and respect within the family

- encouraging kids to contribute to the family in meaningful ways

- helping kids to develop strong problem-solving skills

- keeping their expectations of their kids flexible and realistic

- using humor to help kids to see the lighter side of challenging situations

- teaching kids relaxation techniques and conflict-resolution strategies

Of course, it's possible to do all the right things and still end up with a thoroughly stressed child on your hands. Whether it's a matter of nature, nurture, or a little of both, some children end up being more affected by stress than others. You should at least consider the possibility that your child may be having difficulty coping with stress if she exhibits some of the following symptoms:

- She has developed some of the physical symptoms of stress: headaches, neck pain, tense muscles, an upset stomach, skin rashes, fatigue, and more colds and flus than usual.

- She has acquired some nervous habits such as nail biting, hair-twisting, thumb-sucking, or sighing deeply.

- Her eating habits have changed. She either has little appetite or is overeating.

- She is having difficulty sleeping and may be experiencing nightmares, too.

- Her behavior patterns have changed rather markedly. She is either extremely volatile and prone to tantrums or is much more quiet and withdrawn than usual.

- She is anxious or afraid a lot of the time.

- She is consistently getting into trouble at home or at school.

- She is having difficulty concentrating at school.

- She has lost interest in activities that she previously enjoyed.

- She seems sad or depressed a lot of the time and seems hopeless about life in general or the future.

If your child appears to be having a difficult time coping with stress, you should discuss your concerns with your child's doctor. Children who suffer from anxiety during childhood are at increased risk of developing depression during the teen years, so you'll want to do whatever you can to help her to weather this particular storm and find her way back into the sunshine again.

Note: I talk more about childhood anxiety disorders and other childhood mental health conditions in Chapter 10.

CHAPTER 7

Playing It Smart

"The joys of being a parent lie in those quiet moments when your child asks you a question or makes an observation that is so profound that you wonder if your child is 5 or 45."
—*Natalie, 32, mother of two*

Children come hard-wired to want to learn everything they can about their world. You can witness that desire in the quiet wakefulness of a newborn who drinks in every detail of his mother's face or the unrestrained glee of a toddler who figures out how to open a doorknob for the very first time. The joy that accompanies learning is pure and unbridled, intoxicating and contagious. It's pretty heady stuff.

But as natural—even instinctual—as that drive to learn may be for kids, parents have an important role to play in getting kids hooked on learning (a subject I discuss at length in this chapter and the next). A parent is a child's first teacher, after all, and, as the years go by, his coach, cheerleader, and mentor, too.

Because there's so much to say about kids and learning, I devote two chapters of this book to the topic. In this chapter, I talk about the types of learning that occur in the classroom and what parents can do to ensure that their kids get off to the best possible start in school. (Assuming, of course, that they actually choose to send their kids to school: a growing number of American parents are choosing to home-school their kids.)

Then, in Chapter 8, I zero-in on what parents can do to encourage the types of learning that take place during nonschool hours, when your child is crawling around in the backyard, looking for bugs; surfing the Internet in search of cool science experiments to try; floating on his back in the middle of a lake and watching the clouds float by; or otherwise going about the business of being a kid.

Countdown to Kindergarten

The letter from the school or local newspaper article announcing the deadline for kindergarten registration often comes as a bit of a shock.

You've always known—at the intellectual level at least!—that your child's first day of school would eventually roll around. But, you may still find it difficult to believe that the tiny, helpless infant that you were cradling in your arms not so long ago has already morphed into a free-spirited four- or five-year-old who is eager to hop on board the school bus and head for whatever exciting adventures may await him at school.

Is your child ready to start school?

Of course, not every four- or five-year-old is necessarily ready to start school just because the number of candles on his birthday cake indicates that he should be. Just as it takes some children a little longer than others to learn how to walk, some children may lag behind other children the same age when it comes to school readiness. Here are the key points to keep in mind when you're trying to determine whether your child is ready to start school:

- **Does your child cope reasonably well when he is separated from you?** If your child finds it extremely stressful to be away from you, even for a short period of time, the first few weeks of kindergarten could prove to be a major adjustment for him. That's not to say that sending him to kindergarten would necessarily be the *wrong* decision, however. In fact, enrolling him in kindergarten may actually help, over time, to ease his separation anxiety. You simply need to know right from the start that your child is likely to face a rockier-than-average transition to kindergarten.

- **Is your child able to get his coat and his shoes on and off by himself?** Although no one is going to ban your child from kindergarten because he has not yet mastered the art of tying his own shoes and zipping up his own jacket, he'll feel much more comfortable in the kindergarten classroom if he's able to do some of these things for himself. Of course, being able to get his clothes up and down (and the necessary fastening devices open and closed) in the bathroom without assistance will make a huge difference in terms of how well he settles into the whole kindergarten routine: he won't have to worry about whether anyone will be around to help him with his clothes when nature calls.

- **Is your child able to control his temper reasonably well when he's frustrated?** The kindergarten teacher isn't going to expect your child to show up sporting the negotiating skills of a career diplomat, but she will appreciate it if your child has at least a few coping skills under his belt. If he doesn't, he'll need to work on developing them both at home and during his time in the kindergarten classroom, but be prepared to participate early on in a few parent-teacher conferences.

- **Does your child enjoy playing with other children?** If your child has reasonably good social skills and tends to gets along well with other children most of the time, he's likely to thrive in the kindergarten setting. You'll probably find that he looks forward to going to school each day because he's so eager to play with his friends. It also helps if he's able to resolve conflicts with other children on his own without requiring constant intervention from an adult. He'll feel a lot more secure and in control if he can resolve a lot of the more run-of-the-mill disputes on his own.

- **Is your child able to follow basic instructions?** Military-style obedience may not be required of kindergarten students (good thing, too, because the chances of any four- or five-year-old falling in line to that degree are pretty much zilch!), but it's helpful if your child is capable of following basic instructions: for example, "Please hang up your coat on your coat hook and then join the rest of the boys and girls for circle time."

- **Is your child capable of working independently for short periods of time?** Even a kindergarten teacher who lucks out and ends up with a small class of around a dozen students is still outnumbered 12 to 1, which is why she will be hugely grateful if your child is capable of working on his own for short stretches. If each child in her class requires her undivided attention during each moment of the school day, the poor teacher will be completely fried by Thanksgiving! Besides, your child will also be a lot less stressed if he's able to keep himself busy while he waits for his turn to talk to the teacher. It's a win-win situation all around.

- **Is your child capable of sitting still and listening to a story without disrupting his classmates?** Think orchestra leaders are highly skilled professionals? Imagine the skill that is required in convincing a dozen or more four-year-olds to all sit down and listen to a story at the same time. Now *that* takes some fairly high-level conducting! The kindergarten teacher will appreciate it tremendously if your child is able to sit still for at least a few minutes at a time.

Life will be a lot more pleasant for your child if he has the necessary attention span to be able to sit still for a few minutes: he won't have to deal with constantly being sent back to the story corner by the conductor.

- **Is your child able to communicate his needs effectively?** Imagine how frustrating—and scary—it would be to find yourself in a strange classroom with a strange teacher and to be unable to get your message across. That's why most educators recommend that children starting kindergarten be capable of expressing themselves, either verbally or otherwise. (Note: Speech and language delays aren't unusual among kindergarten students, so some students may start school relying on a combination of words and gestures for communication.)

What you can do to prepare your child for the first day of school

After you've made the decision to sign up your child for kindergarten, you'll want to start preparing him for his first day of school. How much preparation he needs depends on whether he's been at home full-time up until now or whether he's been involved in some sort of group daycare experience.

If he's been attending a preschool or group daycare program, he'll already have a rough idea of what to expect from a kindergarten program, but you'll still want to give him a detailed briefing on how kindergarten is going to be different.

If, on the other hand, he's been at home full-time and has had little exposure to other children his own age, you'll probably want to enroll him in swimming lessons or some other group activity during the summer months so that he can master a few of those all-important social skills before he has to face his first day in the kindergarten trenches.

Here are some additional tips to keep in mind:

- **Get an all-clear on the health front.** Schedule a prekindergarten checkup for your child so that your child's doctor can screen him for any hearing, vision, or other problems that may make it difficult for your child to benefit fully from the kindergarten program. While you're at the doctor's office, you'll want to find out whether your child is due for any immunizations. (See Chapter 10 for more on vaccines.)

 MOM'S THE WORD

"Take your children for a visit to the school, so they can see the facilities and meet the teachers. Talk to them about how the day will go and what types of activities they will be enjoying. Make sure they know that you will be coming back to get them after snack or naptime or playtime. Then let them ask all the questions they want."

—*Jill, 34, mother of four*

- **Prepare your child for his first visit to his new school**. You will probably find that there is a time set aside for your child to visit his classroom and meet his teacher before his official first day and that there are staggering start times so that only a few students start on any given day. (This way, the "veterans" who started two days ago can help teach the "newbies" the ropes!)

- **Try to hook up your child with a buddy ahead of time.** It's a whole lot less scary walking into the kindergarten classroom that first day if you know at least one other kid in the class. "I put an ad in the local paper asking who was going to be in this particular kindergarten class and ended up getting lots of responses from other parents," recalls Kristina, a 34-year-old mother of two. "A bunch of us got our kids together before school started so that they would all have friends that first day."

- **Give your child the chance to socialize with other children on a regular basis.** Practice makes perfect when it comes to mastering the social graces, and most four- and five-year-olds can use all the practice they can get! If your child spends his days in a group daycare setting, you won't have to go out of your way to make these types of play opportunities happen. If he's home alone with the nanny or his baby sister, however, you may want to arrange for him to attend a neighborhood day camp or playgroup a couple of times a week so that his social skills get a bit of a workout before that all-important first day of kindergarten.

- **Make sure that your child knows what to expect in terms of the whole kindergarten routine.** If you are able to arrange a classroom visit, the teacher will handle this for you. If you aren't able to arrange such a visit, you'll want to give your child the lowdown on the key ground rules of kindergarten: the teacher is in charge; the toys are for everyone to share; and one person talks at a time. (Hey, those rules can come as quite a shock if you're not expecting them!)

- **Give your child a chance to practice important self-care skills.** If your child has been prancing around in sandals all summer long, he may have forgotten how to do up the Velcro or tie his shoes (assuming, of course, he knew how to do them up in the first place). There's no time like the present to sign him up for Velcro or Shoe Tieing 101. While you're at it, you may want to sign him up for a few other important refresher courses, such as Bathroom Basics and Fundamentals of Zippering.

- **If your child seems to be exceptionally anxious about kindergarten, try to figure out what's got him so stressed.** After you have a handle on what's at the top of his worry list, you can take steps to try to ease his mind. Is he worried that he won't be able to make it to the bathroom on time (a very common worry, by the way)? You may want to reassure him that there's likely to be a bathroom right in his kindergarten classroom, but, even if there's not, the teacher will definitely make a point of showing the entire class where the bathroom is as soon as everyone arrives at school that first day. If your school district sends school buses to pick up kindergarteners, is your child afraid that he won't know what bus to get on when it's time to come home? Once again, you can reassure him that the teacher will be looking out for him when it comes time to get back on the bus at the end of the day. (Despite his fears to the contrary, no one's going to expect him to be able to read the signs in the various buses or to decipher the bus schedules on his own that first day.)

- **Help your child to pack his backpack the night before.** (Or a week before if he's super keen!) In addition to making sure that he's got all the items the school requested, which may include a towel to lie on at quiet time, an extra pair of shoes, a backpack, a lunch bag with his name on it, and so on, you may want to send along a family photo or some other little memento (such as a picture of his dog) that will remind him of home if he happens to get lonely. Just make sure that it's something that can be replaced easily if he loses it. You don't want his school career to get off to an overly traumatic start! It goes without saying that you'll want to label all your child's belongings clearly so that they don't get mixed up with all the other kids' belongings. (Pity the poor teacher who has to figure out which of the six pairs of seemingly identical blue shoes belongs to which kid!)

When the moment of truth finally arrives, whether kindergarten or first grade, and it's time for your child to hop on that bus to go to school, make sure that your body language is conveying the message that going to school is a good thing! (I know, I know, it's hard to pull this off when it's your baby who is stepping on board that huge hunk of steel being driven by some strange bus driver you've never laid eyes on in your life. But, you've got to act the part of the calm, cool, and collected parent, if only for the 45 seconds that it takes for the bus to pull out of view. So, take a deep breath, give your child a hug and a kiss, and calmly let your child know that you'll be looking forward to seeing him at the end of the day.)

Of course, if you walk or drive your child to school, this routine will play out a bit differently. You'll either escort your child to the edge of the playground or right to his classroom, depending on how the kindergarten teacher likes to handle the drop-off. Once again, an Academy Award–worthy performance is required from you as you smile calmly and confidently and exit stage left.

Although most kindergarteners do just fine with waving goodbye to Mom and Dad, if your child happens to get teary-eyed and beg you not to go, your best bet is to keep the goodbyes relatively brief. Dragging them out just tends to make things worse. Besides, as most experienced teachers will tell you, the majority of kids who burst into tears when saying their goodbyes to Mom and Dad settle into the kindergarten routine quickly and relatively painlessly. Those who are still having a great deal of difficulty adjusting after a few days or weeks clearly aren't ready for kindergarten or may be dealing with some underlying issue that's causing them a lot of stress and anxiety. In this case, you may wish to keep him at home or in his current daycare arrangement for an extra year. There's no point forcing the kindergarten issue if your child isn't ready.

Don't be surprised if your child is extremely tired and maybe even a bit grumpy at the end of his first day of school. Kindergarten requires a lot of stamina, even with that middle-of-the-day quiet time built in. You may find that your child comes home and crashes on the couch for the first week or two.

MOTHER WISDOM

If you pick up your child at school at the end of the day, be sure to show up on time. If the end-of-day school bell rings and your child is the only child without a parent there to pick him up, he may be seriously worried that you've forgotten all about him.

Even if he does somehow manage to make like the Energizer Bunny and keep going at the end of the day, you'll want to make sure that you schedule in some downtime after school. The school environment tends to be fairly structured, so he may be less-than-thrilled if you try to hustle him off right after school to another highly structured activity, such as music lessons.

Besides, you've got other reasons for wanting to keep your schedule relatively light. You want to have plenty of time to hear all about your child's all-important first day. This is the stuff of which memories are made, after all.

What you can do to prepare yourself for your child's first day of school

Up until now, this chapter has focused on what you can do to prepare your child for school. Now it's time to tackle an equally important topic—and a topic that far too many parenting books choose to ignore: how to go about preparing *yourself* for this monumental milestone in your child's life.

MOM'S THE WORD

"I was scared the first few days about how she would handle being away from me. But, if the truth is to be told, I was also worried about how I would handle not having her with me all day. But, we both survived and now she is truly thriving at school."

—Janice, 40, mother of one

"I put them on the bus, waving gaily, and smiling bravely. But I was scared for them. Still am. My babies, out in the world? Defenseless? Without my protection? Terrifying. I put them on the bus and ran—ran!—all the way home, jumped in the van and raced to the school. They were already off the bus and inside the school when I arrived, so I ran to their classroom and found them standing in the coatroom, hanging up their backpacks and putting on their shoes. They looked quite comfortable, not at all nervous, and were surprised to see me. I snapped a few photos, left, and cried all the way home. Sure, I was excited that they were embarking on a new adventure and that they would be exposed to all kinds of new ideas and experiences. And I was happy for them because they were so happy and excited. But mostly I was scared and sad."

—Anita, 40, mother of four

"I once read that a mother's life is a life-long weaning process, and this is so true," says Karen, a 36-year-old mother of four. "First the umbilical cord is cut, then your kids start solids, then you stop nursing, then you get them out of diapers, then they're on to kindergarten, high school, college, and marriage. It is so true. I find that on the first day of school, I always feel this strong sense of separation. You're happy for them, but at the same time, you're feeling them letting go."

Maria, a 34-year-old mother of three, agrees that the start of school can be a bittersweet time for parents: "My five-year-old daughter got on a school bus for the very first time in her little life just today. She was so excited and willing to go that she left me standing there without so much as a goodbye. I am excited that she is able to go to school, to learn, to meet new friends, and to grow, but I'm very apprehensive that my baby is not a baby anymore and that the years just flew by too quickly."

Many parents also experience a lot of worry and anxiety when their children start school. Putting your precious babies in the hands of total strangers can seem like an almost impossible leap of faith. These feelings hit Jacqueline, a 35-year-old mother of four, quite suddenly and unexpectedly: "I never imagined I would cry. But cry I did. All the way home and all day long. It just happened. It was like he was growing up, and I was scared for him and me, too. What if a stranger took him? Could the one teacher look after all those kids by herself? What if they had to go to the bathroom? How about lunchtime? In the end, the teacher helped to put all my fears to rest, and so did the other parents. And, I found out I wasn't the only one to have those feelings. That was very comforting to know."

What You Can Do to Help Your Child Succeed in School

Now that you've got the first day of kindergarten under your belt, it's time to stop and consider the major role you have to play in your child's school success. Yes, Mom and Dad, your story reading, math help, and old-fashioned cheerleading are a far greater predictor of your child's long-term academic fortunes than any computer software package or educational game you purchase in an effort to give your child the scholastic edge.

Here's what you need to do to get your child's school career off to the strongest possible start and to help keep him on solid ground academically in the years to come:

- **Model a love of learning.** There's no better way to get your child hooked on learning than to show your child on a daily basis what great delight you take in learning new things. So, if you stumble across a fascinating fact while you're reading your favorite science magazine, share what you've learned with your child. Your enthusiasm is bound to shine through.

- **Plant the seeds of discovery for your child.** Make a point of having a variety of interesting books and magazines on hand so that your child can thumb through them whenever the urge strikes. You don't have to purchase all these materials, of course. In fact, it's better if you don't. If you make a point of borrowing books from the library and swapping magazines with friends and neighbors, you'll always have something new sitting on the coffee table.

MOM'S THE WORD

"Show enthusiasm for what your children are learning and take pride in their discoveries."

—*Brenda, 31, mother of one*

- **Make a point of asking questions about your child's hobbies and interests.** Your child will get a huge kick out of being able to teach you things you didn't already know—a guaranteed way to get him hooked on learning. (Can there be any greater motivator, after all, than the thrill of being able to stay one step ahead of Mom or Dad?)

- **Plan field trips to interesting attractions.** If your child is studying trees as part of his science unit at school, you can help to bring the curriculum to life for him by organizing a family walk in the woods. The secret is to be low-key about what you're doing and to make the excursion fun in its own right. No kid is going to be thrilled to death at the prospect of a "bonus" science class on a Saturday afternoon. (Note: Chapter 8 has more tips on organizing fabulous family excursions and finding other ways of extending your child's curriculum at home.)

- **Let your child know that you value education.** Talk about the payoffs—both material and nonmaterial—of doing well in school, and make a point of celebrating your child's various successes during his school career: everything from his first day of kindergarten to his graduation from high school or college.

- **Speak positively about your own school experiences.** If you had a tough time at school during your growing-up years, you may want to keep this information to yourself for now. Who knows? Your child may take to school like a fish to water. If it turns out that he ends up struggling in school at some point down the road, you can always share your own experiences then. Just make sure that the prevailing message is one of hope and inspiration—that you struggled, but in the end you managed to get through school, and he can, too.

- **Set the bar high (but not too high) for your child.** Although it's important to have expectations that are sufficiently high to be motivating, you don't want to set the bar so high that your child is doomed to trip and fall flat on his face. No matter how high (or low) you choose to set the bar, you'll want to make a point of rewarding effort rather than performance. (Rewarding performance alone penalizes those children who have to work harder than others to achieve the same results—a sure-fire way to discourage less academically gifted kids.)

- **Make sure your child understands that effort—not luck—plays a key role in academic success.** Don't let your child get away with thinking that the schoolmate who got an A on his science project was just lucky; chances are that A was the result of a lot of behind-the-scenes hard work (although, of course, the kid in question may be reluctant to boast about the hours that went into his science project for fear of appearing uncool).

- **Be the poster child for perseverance.** Show your child how much you value perseverance by setting some long-term goals for yourself and then talking to your child about the slow but steady progress you're making toward achieving that goal.

- **Teach your child how to problem solve and negotiate.** If you make a point of thinking out loud when you're struggling with a real-life problem, your child will begin to figure out how people go about solving problems, and he'll start to get the message that even grownups have to master the fine art of give and take. (After all, contrary to what every 12-year-old believes, grownups don't always get to do whatever they want. *As if!*)

- **Encourage creative thinking, too.** Children who are creative thinkers also tend to be good problem solvers—reason enough to encourage your child to think outside the box.

- **Set the stage for learning.** Children respond well to structure and routine, even though they claim to hate it. (What? You want your eight-year-old to thank you for sending him to bed at a decent hour? Unless your parenting Fairy Godmother happens to grant you this particular wish, it would appear that you're out of luck!) They find it easier to learn when there are regular times for sleep, meals, play, homework, and (dare I say it?) when there are clear limits about how much time they are allowed to spend camped out in front of the TV or staring zombie-like into the nearest video-game console or computer screen. (See Chapter 8 for more on setting limits on screen time of all types.)

- **Encourage your child to set goals for himself and to strive to achieve them.** Although you may be tempted to set goals for your child, these goals won't mean much to him unless he buys into the goal-setting process. (Just think of the number of employers who have had to learn this particular lesson the hard way! No doubt you've worked for a few such bosses.)

- **Keep tabs on your child's performance in school by going over his tests and school assignments with him on a regular basis.** Being tuned in to how he's doing on a day-to-day and week-to-week basis will allow you to get a handle on your child's academic performance long before report card time rolls around.

- **Help your child to master important study skills.** It's easy to forget that note taking, studying for tests, and other academic tricks of the trade don't necessarily come easily—or intuitively—to every student. Something as simple as teaching your child how to "budget" the marks on his test so that he divvies up his time according to the worth of the various questions (for example, don't spend half your time working on a question that is only worth 10 percent of the marks) could have a huge effect on his academic fortunes.

- **Encourage your child to talk about his day at school.** It doesn't matter whether you're waiting for your child with the proverbial cookies and milk at the end of the school day or whether you have this conversation at bedtime. What matters is that you let your child know that you're interested in hearing all about what he learned in school, how his day went, and anything else he would care to tell you. (See Chapter 6 for more tips on communicating with kids.)

- **Get involved with your child's school.** "I try to become involved in every aspect of Austin's schooling," says Ellen, a 30-year-old mother of two. "I am secretary of the PTA, and I volunteer with his class one morning a week. I think if children see their parents valuing the school system, it helps to create a respect for education within the child." Ellen isn't the only one who sees the value of parent involvement in schools, whether that involvement means volunteering in the classroom or merely showing up for open houses and other school events. Studies have shown a clear link between the degree of parental involvement with the child's school and the level of student achievement. A recent study made a particularly powerful case for having fathers involved in schools: researchers from Northwestern University and the University of Michigan found that children whose fathers were involved in parent-teacher associations tended to complete more years of schooling and to have higher wages and family incomes as adults than children whose fathers were less involved.

MOM'S THE WORD

"I have found that parents spend a lot of time being very interested and very involved in their children's learning when their children are preschoolers, but that the involvement slowly dies down once their children start school. When I volunteer in my daughter's grade four classroom, I am astonished by how little the parents are involved in their children's schoolwork. The children's homework is not finished; they don't get their paperwork signed by their parents; and they come to school without pencils and erasers."

—Karen, 36, mother of four

Reading really is fundamental

There's no denying the benefits of reading. Study after study has proven that children who are avid readers tend to do better in school than their less book-minded counterparts. Although there's no proven formula for raising a reader, there's plenty you can do to increase the odds that your child will develop a lifelong love of books (and not just because they happen to make great ramps when you're playing with your favorite race-car set). This section discusses what you can do to tilt the reading roulette wheel in your child's favor.

Before your child starts reading:

- Point out the words on the page so that your child will begin to recognize print. Over time, he'll start to recognize letters and words when they crop up on food packages, on TV, and on highway road signs.

- Teach your child the letters of the alphabet and encourage him to play word games that allow him to blend sounds to form words (for example, "h" + "at" = "hat"). Over time, he'll begin to understand that each letter of the alphabet has its own name and makes its own unique sound or sounds, and that you use these sounds to form words.

- Expose your child to a variety of different types of books: alphabet books (which emphasize letter and sound recognition), poetry and rhyming books (which demonstrate word patterns), counting books (which promote number recognition), concept books (which teach colors, shapes, sizes, opposites, and so on), nonfiction books (which increase your child's knowledge of the world around him), and storybooks (which help to promote a general enjoyment of reading and—if a lot of repetition is used—can also help to encourage word and phrase recognition).

MOTHER WISDOM

Give your child the opportunity to practice his reading and writing skills by writing messages, notes, grocery lists, and anything else that he is interested in writing. The tasks of reading and writing are intrinsically linked, so the more writing practice your child gets, the more easily—and naturally—reading will come to him.

- Teach your child about the mechanics of reading: for example, we read words from the left to the right, we read books from the front to the back, and the words on the page tell us something about the picture.

- Help your child to develop the listening and speaking skills that are the building blocks for reading:

    - Ask questions that require more than a *yes* or *no* answer.

    - Constantly expose your child to new words so that his vocabulary will continue to grow day by day.

    - Encourage your child to use his imagination to make up stories.

    - Ask your child to tell you the story behind recent family photos.

    - Talk about books you've enjoyed together.

- Find fun ways to bring books to life and to turn reading into an adventure: for example, reading books in a tent or a fort, acting out scenes from a favorite story by using puppets and costumes, and drawing pictures and trying other activities that are based on something you've read in a book—like whipping up a batch of Dr. Seuss's delicious *Green Eggs and Ham!*

After your child starts reading:

- Keep reading to your child even after he is capable of reading on his own. You'll be able to expose him to more challenging books than what he may be willing to tackle by himself, and you'll both get to enjoy the pleasure that comes from sharing a great story. (Hint: It can be particularly fun to read a book together and then go see the movie based on that book. You and your child can have fun talking about how the book compared to the movie. Did the main character look like what your child imagined he would look like? Did the movie stick to the plot in the book? Who knows? Maybe this is how Roger Ebert got his start!)

- Resist the temptation to be a literary snob when it comes to your child's reading choices. Any type of reading should be encouraged, whether your child's current literary fare happens to be a kids' comic book, the sports section of your local newspaper, or the back of a breakfast cereal box!

- Stock up on children's magazines (or better yet, get your child a subscription: your kid will get a huge kick out of getting mail addressed to him); keep word puzzle books on hand (crosswords, word searches, and word scrambles); play word games like Scrabble, Boggle, and Hangman; and visit kid-friendly Web sites (for example, the Web site of your child's favorite author or sports team).

- If your child is a reluctant reader who has difficulty sticking with books, look for ones with short chapters that feature cliff-hanger endings. If the cliff-hanger is sufficiently spellbinding, he'll want to plunge into the next chapter to find out what happens next. Or, at least that's the theory.

- Write notes to your child to give him some extra practice reading. Thanks to the invention of sticky notes, you can leave notes for your child pretty much anywhere, anytime.

- Host a book party or form your own parent-child book club by inviting other parents and kids in your neighborhood to drop by to share the pleasure of a good book. (And, to enjoy some good eats, too, of course.)

- Listen to books on tape when you're taking a long car trip as a family. Just make sure that you choose a book that will be sufficiently enthralling to hold everyone's attention despite the inevitable interruptions (think food stops and bathroom breaks!).

- Get other adults involved in your child's reading program. Ask friends, neighbors, relatives, and others who care about your child to pass along the names of books that they enjoyed during their growing-up years or that their children have enjoyed.

- Encourage your child to keep a reading journal. Your child can record the title and author of each book he reads, along with a mini-review. He can either keep his reading journal in a notebook or post it to the family Web site (a great way to pass along your child's reading picks to cousins and other far-flung relatives, by the way).

- Find other ways to encourage your child to practice his writing (and, therefore, his reading) skills by writing stories, updating the family Web site, publishing a family newspaper or e-zine, writing a family cookbook, keeping a travel diary the next time you head out on a holiday, writing a letter to the editor about an issue he feels strongly about, cataloguing his hockey card collection, writing to an e-mail or snail mail pen pal, and so on. The possibilities are endless.

A parent's guide to homework

If you've got friends with older kids, you've no doubt heard a lot of grumbling about homework—about how much homework is being dumped upon this generation of kids and how much hands-on help is being demanded of parents. You probably know of at least one parent who had to leave work early in order to get his science project (I mean, *his son's* science project) finished on time.

There's no doubt about it. Homework can be a major stumbling block for parents and kids, particularly if there's a lack of communication from the school about how much homework is required of kids in various grades and what the homework assignments are supposed to accomplish. (Does your child's teacher primarily assign homework in order to give the kids in her class a chance to review material that was covered that day at school, or does she use homework as a way of getting parents involved in introducing new material to their kids in a relaxed one-on-one setting? You and your child need to know this right from the start.)

Here are some other important points to keep in mind on the homework front:

- **Give some thought to the time of day when you expect your child to tackle his homework.** Some parents find it works best to encourage their kids to plunge into their homework assignments right after school so that everyone's homework is out of the way before dinner. (Obviously, this only works if a parent or other adult is available to help answer any homework-related questions after school.) Other families find that kids put a greater effort into doing their homework if they're allowed to unwind and play after school and to leave their homework until after dinner. You may have to experiment a little to find out what works best for you and your child.

- **Don't banish your child to his bedroom when it's time for him to hit the books.** If you allow him to do his homework in a shared part of the home, such as the kitchen or the family room, he won't feel as isolated, and you'll be right there if he needs some extra help. Just make sure that the area where your child is doing his homework is comfortable, well-lit, and free of distractions. Your child will have a hard time focusing on his essay if the TV set is blaring in the next room.

- **Keep an eye on your surfer boy or girl.** If your child is using the Internet to research school assignments, make a point of monitoring his Internet use closely. Not only do you want to make sure that he's steering clear of the unsavory characters who like to prey on kids on the Internet but also you want to make sure that he's actually doing his homework (as opposed to sending endless instant messages to his friends). You'll also want to make sure that he understands the need to avoid plagiarizing material and to consider the source and the quality of the information he finds online. Note: See Chapter 8 for more on kids and Internet use.

NO KIDDING!

According to researchers at the University of Michigan, kids today are doing more homework than ever before—and at a younger age. A recent study found that while 6- to 9-year-olds were spending just 44 minutes a week on homework in 1981, by 1997 their workload had jumped to 2 hours a week on average.

MOTHER WISDOM

Limit the amount of time your child spends watching TV, playing video games, and surfing the Internet. All of these activities cut into the amount of time that is available for homework. What you don't want to do, however, is to drastically curtail the amount of time your child spends playing outdoors. Studies have shown that the current generation of kids isn't getting nearly enough exercise as it is, so you'll want to do whatever you can to encourage your child to hop on his bike and ride around the block a few times after school. (Of course, you'll eventually have to break it to him that he still has to do his math homework. Even Olympic cyclists need to know how to balance their checkbooks, after all.)

- **Give your child the tools he needs to get down to business.** Make sure that your child's homework station is well-stocked with all of the school supplies he needs to do his homework: pencils, pens, erasers, paper, glue, scissors, a stapler, and so on. You don't want your child to have to constantly get up from his desk in order to track down some of these supplies. Otherwise, he may "accidentally" get way-laid in front of the TV set while he's off in search of the missing stapler.

- **Do your "homework" at the same time your child is doing his.** Your child will find it a lot easier to settle down and do his homework if everyone else around him is working on some sort of paperwork, too: paying bills, answering e-mails, writing work-related reports, and so on. He won't have such a strong sense that he's missing out on all the fun (unless, of course, he happens to consider bill paying fun).

- **Keep tabs on the amount of homework your child is doing each night.** As a rule of thumb, homework should last no longer than 10 minutes per grade level. In other words, a child in grade three should be doing about 30 minutes of homework per night. Let your child's teacher know if your child seems to be spending an excessive amount of time on homework. This could be a clue that he's either not using his time well in class or that he's really struggling with the curriculum.

- **Avoid assuming too much responsibility for your child's homework.** Although it's your job to ensure that your child has the time and the tools required to tackle the homework that has been assigned, you shouldn't have to nag him into getting down to business. Whether or not his homework gets done is a matter between him and his teacher. (Of course, the teacher may ask you to help motivate your child by applying subtle or not-so-subtle pressure to ensure that he stays on track. You may find that he's more willing to hit the books if all incoming phone calls from friends are intercepted until he's proven to you that his homework is finished.)

- **Remember who owns the (math) problem.** Although it's okay to coach your child from the sidelines, resist the temptation to do his homework for him in an effort to make everyone's math homework pain go away. You've already proven that you can do long division (haven't you?). Now it's your child's chance to strut his mathematical stuff. Besides, studies have shown that children are more eager to learn when parents take a more laid-back approach to homework.

- **Go easy with the red pen.** Offer to read your child's homework over for him, but don't do a line-by-line edit unless your child's teacher specifically asks parents to do this. Otherwise, the mark that your child ultimately receives will be more a reflection of your editing abilities than your child's actual ability to do the work.

- **Teach your child how to organize his time and to keep track of upcoming assignments.** That way, he'll be less likely to hit the panic button at 10 P.M. on a Sunday night when he suddenly remembers that he has to have a speech written by the next day. Your child should get in the habit of recording all upcoming school assignments on his calendar and of breaking large, seemingly Herculean tasks ("Write a speech") into a series of smaller, more manageable tasks ("Choose a topic," "Do the research," "Write the speech"). He can then assign a series of due dates to each of the smaller subtasks, something that will ensure that work on the speech gets started sooner rather than later and that will help to make the speechwriting process a little less daunting.

 NO KIDDING!

Do siblings make you smarter? Maybe, according to a group of researchers at the University of Essex in Britain. The researchers found that children who have a brother or sister tend to do better in school than children who don't have any siblings. They also found, however, that having a large number of siblings had a negative effect on school performance—proof that you can have too much of a good thing, even when it comes to siblings.

- **Watch for changes in your child's homework habits.** If your child suddenly seems reluctant to do his homework or appears to be avoiding a particular subject, it could be because he's struggling with his schoolwork. You'll want to try to get a sense from your child of what the problem might be. Is the work a lot harder this year than it was last year? Is there a lot more homework to do? What type of work is he finding the most difficult? The more information you can gather from your child, the easier it will be for you, him, and his teacher to brainstorm some possible solutions.

What Report Cards Can—and Can't—Tell You

The mere sight of a white report card envelope sticking out of a backpack can be a major source of stress for parents and kids, particularly if your kid happens to be struggling in school, and you're at a loss about what to do about the problem.

It's important to remind yourself that your child's report card is only one source of feedback about his abilities. It provides a snapshot of your child's performance in a particular classroom environment during a particular period of time. If your child has a major personality conflict with the teacher or there's something else going on in his life (for example, his beloved grandfather is dying of cancer), the report card may not necessarily accurately reflect his strengths and abilities.

It's also important to keep in mind that a report card does not measure intelligence, nor is it a predictor of future performance. So, don't make the mistake of assuming that a single bad report card means that your second grader is automatically on the fast track to a career as a label gluer in the Acme Widget Factory.

How to interpret your child's report card

It's easy to fixate on the letter or number grades on your child's report card. After all, they have a tendency to leap off the page, particularly if they convey exceptionally good or bad news. It's important to remind yourself, however, that you can glean a lot of other valuable information from your child's report card. Here's what else you should be zeroing in on:

- **The teacher's comments:** Sometimes the teacher's comments are much more revealing than your child's marks. Assuming that the teacher has taken the time to comment on your child's strengths, weaknesses, and areas for improvement, you can learn a lot about your child's performance in the classroom by reading his report card. (Of course, if your child's teacher simply relies on a bank of meaningless but impressive-sounding phrases, you may find it difficult to glean any useful information at all from the comment section of your child's report card. Welcome to the scary world of eduspeak!)

- **The learning skills section:** Most modern report cards include a learning skills section that provides parents with feedback on how well their kids are doing when it comes to mastering such basic skills as conflict resolution, class participation, problem solving, and goal setting to improve work. These skills are often a greater predictor of a child's long-term academic success than anything else on the report card, so if you're going to fixate on one set of marks, these are the ones to fixate on!

- **Your child's performance versus the class average:** Many report cards today include the class average for a particular subject along with your child's individual mark—great information to have when you're trying to put that C in math in context!

Make sure that your child knows that his report card isn't a reflection of his value as a person or an indicator of how much—or how little—you love him. Let him know that he'll always have straight A's in that department, as far as you're concerned.

- **Any overall patterns:** After you've read your child's report card from start to finish, go back and read it again, this time looking for patterns. You may notice, for example, that your child does extremely well in subjects that require strong mathematical reasoning skills, but that he really struggles in those subjects that require a lot of writing. After you've identified these types of patterns, you'll have a clear idea of where your child's academic strengths and weaknesses lie and what skills he needs to work on during the months ahead.

Dealing with report card shock

Although parents often have an inkling ahead of time that their child's report card may not necessarily be dripping with good news, sometimes a bad report card comes as a complete shock. Here are some tips on handling a bad report card that seemed to come completely out of left field:

- **Look for the silver lining, even if you have to use a pair of high-powered binoculars to find it.** Find at least one positive thing you can comment about on your child's report card. Perhaps your child did well in one or more of the learning skills areas, such as "cooperation with others" or "class participation."

- **Try not to overreact to the bad news.** Grounding your child for three months or yanking him from the hockey team will only make him feel worse about himself at a time when his self-esteem is likely to be hitting rock-bottom. Although you may want to scale back on some of his extracurricular activities if they are preventing him from getting his homework completed, it's important to remember that students who are struggling in school are in even greater need of the self-esteem boost that comes from doing well on the hockey ice than kids who are bringing home straight A's on a regular basis.

• **Try to find out why your child is having so much trouble in school.** Is the work too difficult? Is there too much of it? Does the teacher breeze through the lessons too quickly, or does she plod through the material at such a tedious pace that your child tunes her out? Are the kids in the class given the chance to ask questions of the teacher, and, if so, is your child taking full advantage of the opportunity to receive extra help with any material he doesn't understand? The more you can figure out about your child's academic difficulties, the easier it will be for you to help him and his teacher come up with a game plan for getting him back on track.

MOM'S THE WORD

"I was shocked to see three areas on my son's report card where he received only a satisfactory grade. I arranged a meeting with the teacher to let her know I was concerned that I hadn't been informed about these problem areas sooner. We came up with a method of communicating daily about how he was doing. If he had a good day, she would send home a piece of green paper; if he had a bad day, she would send home a piece of red paper, with notes about what the problems were. This system has really helped to encourage positive behavior from my son, and he has made a dramatic improvement at school."

—*Sandi, 32, mother of two*

- **Help your child to set some improvement goals for himself for the next semester.** Then help your child to develop a game plan for achieving those goals. Perhaps your child needs to put in some extra hours of study time each weekend. Or, maybe he would benefit from obtaining some hands-on help from a tutor. (Note: See the next section of this chapter for more about tutors.) Just make sure that whatever goals your child sets for himself are realistic and attainable. You don't want to inadvertently set your child up to fail again.

- **Take advantage of the opportunity to meet with your child's teacher to discuss his performance.** The more information you have about what's going on in the classroom, the easier it will be for you to help your child to get back on track academically. To prepare for your parent-teacher interview, ask your child whether there are any specific concerns he would like you to raise with the teacher, and then make a list of your own questions. It's important to go into the meeting with a view to problem solving rather than pinning blame on the teacher or the school (even if you feel that blame is much-deserved). What you want to walk away with at the end of the meeting is a clear action plan outlining next steps, for both yourself and your child's teacher, for supporting your child's learning at home and at school.

- **Minimize report card shock the next time around by getting a better sense of what's going on throughout the entire semester.** Make a point of reviewing your child's homework and assignments with him on a daily basis so that you'll get a clearer idea of whether he's understanding things well. Or find out if your child's grades are accessible to you in between report cards by accessing the school's Web site. Note: If tests and marked assignments don't make it home very often, call the teacher to find out why. Is your child failing to bring his schoolwork home because he's upset or embarrassed by his marks? Or, does the teacher allow students to bring marked work home only at the end of the semester?

Does your child need a tutor?

If your child is struggling with his schoolwork and your efforts to help him have proven to be unproductive, it may make sense to hire a tutor for assistance. Although tutoring doesn't come cheap—and most kids require two or three hours worth of tutoring per week in order to see any significant improvement at school—if the tutoring helps to turn your child's academic fortunes around, you will likely consider this money well spent.

The best way to find a tutor is to ask for referrals from other families you know with school-aged children. If that doesn't result in any leads, you can always ask your child's school for a list of tutors and tutoring services operating in your area, check the bulletin board of the children's department of your local library for leads, do a Web search, or flip through the Yellow Pages.

 NO KIDDING!

Should you pay for those A's on your child's report card? Maybe, maybe not.

Some child development experts say that there's nothing wrong with rewarding kids for a job well done. The adult world is full of similar incentives, the argument goes, so why not extend some of these rewards to kids? Others are less convinced of the merits of reaching for your checkbook just because your child happened to bring home a stellar report card. They argue that teaching kids to rely on external rewards reduces the likelihood that they will develop the ability to rely on internal rewards such as pride in a job well done—not exactly a sure-fire way to program your child for long-term success!

Try to find a tutor with plenty of experience and training, ideally in the subject area with which your child is struggling. If your child has been diagnosed with attention deficit hyperactivity disorder (ADHD) or any other type of exceptionality, you'll want to find a tutor who has the patience and energy to keep him on track. Don't forget to ask for a list of references and to check those references thoroughly. You want to make sure that this tutor is skilled at working with children and that he's capable of helping kids to pull up their socks academically. Otherwise, what's the point of shelling out all that hard-earned cash?

When you've settled on a tutor, make sure that you establish clear goals for your child and that you obtain regular reports from the tutor on your child's progress. Note: It's a good idea to obtain your child's teacher's input, too. You may want her to help you to identify a few key areas for your child's tutor to work on (ideally those areas that will reap the greatest rewards for your child in the classroom), and you may want her to provide you and your child with ongoing feedback about how well the tutoring efforts are paying off.

 **NO KIDDING!**

While kids of a generation ago lived in constant fear of failing a grade, holding kids back a grade (or, to use the correct educational buzz word, "grade retention") is much less common today. When grade retention occurs today, it is typically done in situations in which the child is both socially immature and experiencing academic difficulties.

If the child is socially up to speed but struggling academically, schools generally will allow the child to move up a grade with his peers and provide some remedial instruction the following year in the hope that the child will eventually catch up.

"Retention in a grade has to qualify as one of the most malignant setbacks for a student," says Mel Levine, M.D., author of *A Mind at a Time*. According to Levine, holding a child back leaves that child feeling like the failure is his fault: "How ironic, since in most cases it's the fault of the school for not understanding and meeting the educational needs of that child, for never having uncovered the obstructing neurodevelopmental dysfunctions."

Make sure that you schedule your child's tutoring sessions at a time of day when he's likely to be at his best. Although right after school may work best scheduling-wise, he may be tired and hungry at that time of day and may lack the energy and focus to give the tutoring process his all.

Be sure to let your child know ahead of time what the tutoring is for and how it will help him: with some hard work on his part, it will help him to catch up with his classmates so that he feels happier and more confident when he's at school.

Troubleshooting Common School-Related Problems and Concerns

Not every child takes to school like a duck to water. The following sections help you to understand and cope with some of the most common school-related problems and concerns.

School-related fears and anxieties

Your child develops a headache or a stomach ache every morning at 7:30 A.M. sharp. Every school day, that is. For some reason, his mysterious affliction doesn't seem to strike on Saturday or Sunday mornings. In fact, he bounces out of bed on those two mornings with such energy and enthusiasm that you have to wonder whether you're dealing with your own in-house Dr. Jekyll and Mr. Hyde.

School-related fears and anxieties affect between 5 and 10 percent of children; 1 percent of children are so severely affected that they actually refuse to go to school. So what's a parent to do if a child develops a case of school avoidance or full-blown school refusal?

First of all, schedule an appointment with your child's doctor to rule out any health causes for the headaches, stomach aches, nausea, dizziness, and/or hyperventilating that your child may be experiencing. Then, if no underlying physical cause is identified, you then can start trying to figure out what's at the root of your child's problems.

Here are the key points to consider:

- **Is your child experiencing difficulties with his friends?** The social demands of elementary school are enough to make any kid want to wave the white flag. You either play by the rules of the jungle—the elementary school jungle, that is!—or you risk being ostracized or ignored. Anyone who has lived through the experience can tell you that it makes lying at home in bed all day, bored out of your tree and nursing a real or imagined stomach ache, seem like an absolute walk in the park.

- **Is your child overly anxious about his academic performance?** If your child is completely panic stricken at the thought of doing badly on an upcoming math test or spelling quiz, it may be performance anxiety—academic performance anxiety—that's causing your child to hide under the bedcovers each weekday morning.

- **Is your child experiencing ongoing conflicts with his teacher?** Not every teacher-student pairing is necessarily a match made in heaven. If your child and his teacher just plain rub one another the wrong way, he may lack the strategies to deal with this frustrating situation. He may need a little coaching from you on how to get along with someone he doesn't particularly like—one of the tougher lessons of life!

- **Has something about your child's school situation changed?** It's not unusual for a student who has been perfectly happy going to school in the past to develop some school-related anxieties when he's starting a new grade or going to a new school. Perhaps the rumor mill has been working overtime, and he's heard that his new teacher is really strict—or that the crowd of kids at his new school are really tough. Either scenario is likely to have him quaking in his boots until you remind him that rumors are often just that—rumors—and that it would be best for him to size up the situation for himself.

- **Is there something upsetting happening on the home front?** School avoidance and school refusal can also be triggered by events unrelated to school. Your child may be reluctant to go to school if he's worried that something may happen to you while he's gone (a not-so-unusual fear if you or his other parent have recently been diagnosed with a serious illness or there's been another source of trauma in the family). In this type of situation, you may need to line up counseling for your child to help him to deal with his fears. Sometimes, the world can seem like a scary and unpredictable place, particularly when you're a kid. (See Chapter 6 for more about helping kids to manage stress.)

Regardless of what's at the root of your child's fears, it's important to let him know that you think it's important that he attend school on a regular basis. On those rare occasions when you do allow him to stay home because he seems to be genuinely ill, you'll want to make a point of making staying home as unappealing as possible (that is, by banning TV, computer, and video-game use during the school day).

You'll also want to communicate with your child's teacher about the difficulties your child is experiencing at school. This way, you can ensure that the teacher is fully up to speed on the situation so that she can provide some additional support for your child during his school day.

Working cooperatively with your child's school

You'll find it easier to troubleshoot any problems that your child encounters at school if you make a point of working cooperatively with your child's teacher and the school community as a whole right from day one. Here are a few tips:

- **Get to know your child's teacher.** Establish the lines of communication between yourself and your child's teacher before there's any sort of problem to deal with. It's much more pleasant to get to know one another under friendly circumstances than in the midst of a crisis.

- **Be generous with your praise.** Something as simple as writing a quick note in your child's daily planner to let the teacher know how much your child enjoyed a particular classroom activity can help to generate a lot of goodwill.

- **Meet other school officials.** Make a point of participating in parent-teacher interviews and of attending school barbecues and family information nights so that you can get to know the rest of the school staff.

- **Show your willingness to support the school.** Volunteer to serve on a school committee, to lend a hand in the classroom as a volunteer assistant, or to help with a school fundraiser. (Hint: If you don't have time to make an ongoing volunteer commitment to the school, think of a way you can donate your skills on a one-time basis—such as offering to speak about your job on career day.)

- **Get in touch with your child's teacher right away if a problem arises.** It's easier to deal with a problem before it has a chance to snowball into something huge. A minor misunderstanding can develop into a major problem if it's not dealt with promptly and decisively.

- **Don't trash the teacher or school in front of your child.** Cutting up the teacher will make it hard for your child to respect the teacher's authority at school. If you have a beef with something the teacher has said or done, approach the teacher or principal directly. Don't drag your child into the conflict.

- **Accept the fact that you may be bringing some emotional baggage along for the ride.** If you had some negative experiences with school during your growing-up years, you may have a tendency to pin the blame for any difficulties your child is experiencing on the school. If you were a top student who loved every minute of school from kindergarten right through grade 12, you may feel frustrated, angry, and embarrassed if you get dragged into the principal's office to talk about your child's misbehavior at school. You may have to make a conscious effort to remind yourself that you're the parent this time around and that it's your kid—not you!—who's in the hot seat!

Home-Schooling: Is It a Good Fit for Your Family?

If the neighborhood school doesn't seem to be the best place for your child, you have another option: home-schooling.

The number of home-schooled (or home-educated) children increased dramatically during the late 1990s—by an estimated 15 to 20 percent each year, in fact. By the fall of 2000, more than 500,000 American children were being home-schooled. Although the home-schoolers of the 1970s tended to withdraw their kids from neighborhood schools for reasons of ideology or religion, today's generation of home-schoolers are more apt to opt to educate their kids at home because they feel that doing so will allow them to more ably meet their kids' academic needs than what is possible in a standard school setting.

Home-schooling requires a major commitment from parents. It's definitely not for everyone. If you decide to home-school your kids, you will need to design a curriculum that meets your state's requirements for home-schooling families. Note: If you don't think you're up to the challenge of designing your own curriculum from scratch, you can purchase a ready-made curriculum from one of the growing number of educational publishing companies serving the home-schooling market. Or, you can swap curriculum modules (homegrown or commercially purchased) with other home-schooling families.

Most parents who choose to home-school their kids make a point of networking with other home-schooling parents. Not only does getting together with other home-schoolers help to reduce the isolation that can go along with home-schooling, but it also allows you to swap your skills and expertise. Perhaps you're a whiz when it comes to math but hopeless at art. You could swap teaching duties with a more artistically minded friend and reduce the teaching workload for both of you.

Of course, there's nothing to say that all your resource people have to be drawn from the ranks of other home-schoolers. Some families hire tutors, sign their kids up for classes in the community, or partially enroll them in school if there's a subject area that Mom and Dad simply don't feel equipped to handle on their own. Home-schoolers may be some of the most resourceful people on the planet, but even they have their limits!

Exceptional Kids, Exceptional Challenges

If your child happens to be exceptional in any way—if he has some sort of special need or learning disability, or has been identified as gifted, for example—you are likely to find yourself playing the role of your child's advocate as he makes his way through the school system. It's not that educators and administrators are out to make life difficult for you and your child; it's simply that the system is designed to meet the needs of average students with average needs.

In most cases, if you know what to ask for and what you need to do to get it, you can ensure that your child's needs are met to at least a reasonable degree within the school system. The trick is to learn how to jump through the appropriate hoops as early on as possible in your child's educational career—something that is often easier said than done. Fortunately, people in your community can help you to figure out how to go about advocating on behalf of your child. The special education coordinator for your local school district, as well as local parent support groups for children with learning disabilities and other exceptionalities, can be excellent sources of information on everything from having your child formally identified within the school system (without a formal identification, your child won't be eligible for special equipment and services within the school system) to ensuring that your child's individual education plan (see Table 7.1) is updated appropriately from year to year. There are also federally funded services in each state to support families with children with special needs. If your school district isn't providing you with much information about what's available in your district, contact your state Department of Education or the Governor's Council on Special Education in your state.

Note: If your child has been identified with a special need or diagnosis, be sure to mention this at the time of kindergarten registration (or any other school enrollments) and to provide all medical (and related) reports so that the school can line up appropriate support for your child as soon as possible.

TABLE 7.1

Your Child's Individual Education Plan: What It Includes

An individual education plan (IEP) is a detailed document that spells out the school's commitment to your child for the current or upcoming academic year. An IEP typically includes the following types of information:

→ the reasons for developing an IEP

→ a statement about who was involved in drafting the IEP (for example, classroom teacher, resource teacher, principal, and parents)

→ details about any outside agencies that are currently working with your child, or health support services that your child is currently accessing

→ information about medical conditions that are relevant to your child's identified learning challenges

→ details about the subject and skill areas to which the IEP applies (such as math or writing)

→ a description of the assessment and evaluation methods that will be used with your child and the accommodations that will be made on his behalf

→ a summary of the key teaching strategies that will be used when the teacher is working with your student

Note: While the powers that be don't always do a very good job of making you feel like you're a key player in the IEP process, you are. And, what's more, you have every right to bring other people into the process to provide additional information or to help advocate on behalf of your child (e.g., your child's pediatrician, special education advocate, after-school teacher, counselor, lawyer, etc.). All you need to do is to alert the person who is in charge of scheduling the next IEP meeting that you're bringing one or more additional parties to the meeting with you to help represent your child's various interests so that the other players will know to expect them.

MOM'S THE WORD

"As the parent of a child with special needs, you always need to be advocating for your child. When it comes to funding and such, it is very hard to learn that you have to talk about the 'not so good' things about your child when, as a parent, you like to focus on the best things about your child."

—*Dorothy, 36, mother of three, including a five-year-old who is autistic*

Does your child have a learning disability?

If your child seems to have a lot of difficulty with his school work and exhibits a lot of anger, frustration, and sadness at school, it's possible that he could be struggling with a learning disability.

Learning disabilities affect approximately 11 percent of American children between the ages of 6 and 13. They can be mild or severe in nature and typically occur in children of average or above-average intelligence. Some common types of learning disabilities include the following:

- **Academic skills disorders** (difficulty mastering reading, writing, and arithmetic)

  For example:

  - *Developmental reading disorder* (formerly known as dyslexia): difficulties with word identification or word comprehension.

  - *Developmental writing disorder:* difficulties with vocabulary, grammar, hand movement, and other tasks associated with writing.

  - *Developmental arithmetic disorder:* difficulty recognizing numbers and symbols, memorizing facts (for example, multiplication tables), manipulating numbers, and/or understanding abstract concepts.

- **Speech and language disorders** (difficulties with listening, speaking, and comprehension)

- **Motor-sensory integration skills disorders** (difficulties with coordination, balance, and the physical mechanics involved in the writing process)

- **Developmental disorders** (various types of developmental delays that may interfere with the learning process)

- **Attention disorders** (attention deficit hyperactivity disorder, for example)

- **Memory disorders** (difficulty processing and retrieving information)

Other types of educational challenges include mental disability (a condition that affects 2 to 3 percent of children and that is characterized by lower than average intelligence) and autism (a condition that occurs in approximately 1 to 2 per 1,000 births and that is characterized by difficulties communicating with others, and, in some cases, mental disability). Early and ongoing intervention can significantly improve outcomes for children with autism, so it's important to have your child identified as early as possible if you suspect autism.

Note: It's unusual to diagnose a learning disability before the age of six or seven. Although a parent or teacher may suspect that a younger child is struggling with a learning disability, the formal identification process may not be started until he's a little older because there is such wide variation in what young children are able to do at any given age. If there still appears to be cause for concern by the time your child is in grade one or two, you may wish to begin the process of having your child formally identified.

Is your child gifted?

Kids with learning disabilities and special needs aren't the only ones who may find it a struggle to get their needs met within the school system. Gifted kids can also find school to be a frustrating experience and may develop behavioral problems that make it difficult for their teachers and parents to tell whether they are gifted, struggling with attention deficit hyperactivity disorder, or both (see Table 7.2).

TABLE 7.2

ADHD or Gifted: How to Tell the Difference

Children with attention deficit hyperactivity disorder (ADHD) and children who are gifted often exhibit very similar types of behaviors—something that can make it difficult for the adults in their lives to figure out what's at the root of their behavioral problems. Here's what you need to know in order to distinguish between ADHD and giftedness:

Behavior Characteristic	How This Behavior Might Present Itself in a Child with ADHD	How This Behavior Might Present Itself in a Child who is Gifted
Attention span	A child with ADHD may have difficulty focusing his attention for sustained periods of time in almost all situations. In other words, he has trouble sticking with tasks both at home and at school.	A child who is gifted may have difficulty focusing his attention in specific situations (such as, if the child is bored or feels that the school assignment is irrelevant).
Persistence	A child with ADHD may have difficulty persisting with a particular task in situations where there is no immediate feedback on his performance.	A child who is gifted may have difficulty persisting with a particular task in situations where the task seems irrelevant to him. If he can't see the point of doing something, he doesn't want to do it.

continued

ADHD or Gifted: How to Tell the Difference *(continued)*

Behavior Characteristic	How This Behavior Might Present Itself in a Child with ADHD	How This Behavior Might Present Itself in a Child who is Gifted
Impulsivity	A child with ADHD may have difficulty controlling his impulses. If he wants something, he wants it right now.	A child who is gifted may be less emotionally mature than intellectually mature—something that can cause difficulties in the area of impulse control.
Cooperation	A child with ADHD may find it difficult to comply with adult requests that he behave.	A child who is gifted may find himself locked in power struggles with authority figures.
Activity level	A child with ADHD may be more restless and active than other children.	A child who is gifted may have a higher-than-average activity level and may be able to get by with less sleep than other children (to say nothing of his parents!).
Willingness to conform	A child with ADHD may find it more difficult to follow rules and regulations than other children.	A child who is gifted may have an overwhelming need to understand the reasons behind rules, customs, and traditions—something that may result in a refusal to follow any rule that he doesn't accept or agree with.

Contrary to the popular stereotype about the super-brainy kid who sits there with his nose stuck in a book, gifted children often appear quite restless because they are bored. Studies have shown that gifted kids typically spend one-quarter to one-half of their time in the classroom waiting for their classmates to catch up—hardly surprising given that their level of academic achievement is often two to four grades above the grade in which they are actually placed.

Here are some other clues that a particular child may be gifted:

- **He has an exceptional ability to engage in abstract thought.** A gifted child may have a solid grasp of highly advanced mathematical and linguistic concepts and may come across as someone much older than his years when he is engaged in discussions about complex and abstract subjects such as religion, philosophy, and ethics. Not surprisingly, gifted kids often prefer to be in the company of adults. They typically describe kids their own age as boring.

- **He is capable of puzzling out complex concepts before they are formally taught in school.** This is the kind of kid who figures out how multiplication, fractions, and decimals work long before anyone ever gets around to explaining them to him!

- **His concentration skills and ability to focus are exceptional for a child his age.** Of course, he's only willing to concentrate on things that he finds genuinely fascinating. Present him with rote math that he considers to be simplistic or stupid, and you'll end up with a riot on your hands!

- **He has an exceptional ability to memorize facts.** If you've ever seen that episode of *Malcolm in the Middle* where Malcolm starts reciting a dizzying number of decimal points of pi, you know exactly what I'm talking about!

- **He has a well-developed vocabulary.** The good kind of vocabulary—and perhaps the more colorful kind, too. (If a gifted kid is given the chance, he'll absorb any kind of language, good, bad, or downright obscene.)

- **He has strong leadership abilities, which he can use for either good or evil, depending on his mood.** Ever wonder where the term "evil genius" came from? Now you know!

- **He is confident in his abilities and accomplishments.** Sometimes he can be a little too confident, in fact, which may tend to get under the skin of his peers at times. After all, who wants to have a "perfect" friend?

Here's something else you need to know about gifted kids—something that many people find quite surprising: it's possible for a gifted child to have a learning disability. Such a learning disability is typically diagnosed if there's a large discrepancy between the child's scores on intelligence and achievement tests.

As you can tell, your child isn't the only one who will be grappling with new ideas once he starts school. You'll be learning right along with him. Of course, only a fraction of the learning that will occur during the next few years of his life will actually take place in the classroom. The world is his to explore, and you're lucky enough to be invited along for the ride.

CHAPTER 8

The Joy of Play

"I think everyone wants their kids to have all of the opportunities that they themselves didn't have growing up; but all of these children today are seriously lacking the opportunity to cultivate their own relationships and to be creative. It is a hard cycle to break. There are a few kids out on the street playing, like there were in our day, but many days when my kids want to have a friend over, there's no one around. They go through the list: 'Becky has volleyball, Molly has piano, Bryanna is at her skating lesson. . . .' It goes on and on. It is a racket! It is as if your child has to be enrolled in something just to be able to socialize."
—Christine, 38, mother of four

A t some point over the past 30 years or so, simply being a kid went out of vogue. Simple childhood pleasures, such as kicking a pebble up and down a driveway or tossing a rubber ball against a wall, which could be counted on to kill a bit of time on a lazy summer day back in our growing-up years, became painfully passé, horribly unhip for today's generation of entertainment-hungry kids.

Even if you do happen to stumble across the odd kid who would be perfectly content to while away an entire summer watching leaves floating down a stream or making necklaces out of dandelions, odds are good that the child's well-meaning parents have signed her up for some sort of sports camp or computer camp designed to help her make productive use of the summer

.months and give her an athletic or academic edge come fall. The art of doing nothing—a skill I myself perfected on an air mattress at my parents' cottage when I was a kid—is slowly but surely going the way of the dodo bird.

This chapter is all about kids and play—specifically, what you as a parent can do to create an atmosphere in which learning through play is celebrated. I start out by talking about how easy it is to fall into the trap of over-programming your child's life with too many extracurricular activities—something that forces some kids to stick to a grueling schedule that would have most boot camp recruits begging for mercy! Then I talk about another major challenge that many families face in trying to free up time for good old-fashioned play of the dandelion-necklace-making variety: the need to limit the amount of "screen time" kids get. (That's no easy feat, I know, when you're dealing with a generation of kids who seem to consider the TV remote, game console, and computer mouse extensions of their own bodies. How else can you explain the extreme possessiveness that is shown whenever a child is asked to share the remote, game console, or mouse with a sibling? You would think you had just asked her to hack off her arm.) Then, I wrap up the chapter by talking about some of the fun and (dare I say it?) educational activities you may enjoy doing with your child now that you've freed up a little space in her schedule. (Hint: If you keep the emphasis on having fun, more often than not the learning will take care of itself.)

 MOTHER WISDOM

"Playing should be fun. In our great eagerness to teach our children, we studiously look for 'educational' toys, games with built-in lessons, books with a 'message.' Often these 'tools' are less interesting and stimulating than the child's natural curiosity and playfulness. Play is by its very nature educational. And, it should be pleasurable. When the fun goes out of play, most often so does the learning."

—Joanne E. Oppenheim, Kids and Play

MOTHER WISDOM

"We're taking away childhood. We don't value play in our society. It has become a four-letter word."

—*Dorothy Sluss, a professor of early childhood education at East Tennessee State University, quoted in* Time *magazine (April 30, 2001)*

Stop the Extracurricular Insanity

A 1998 study at the University of Michigan revealed what parents have long suspected: the current generation of children has a lot less free time than kids in generations past. Back in 1981, kids could count on having approximately 40 percent of their time free after doing all the things that needed to be done—eating, sleeping, and going to school, for example. By 1998, the amount of free time had nose-dived to just 25 percent. If what I've witnessed in my own neighborhood is any indication, we've no reason to hold out any hope that the trend has started to reverse itself.

Of course, you don't have to be a social scientist to pick up on this particular trend. All you have to do is stand outside on a suburban cul-de-sac that, a generation earlier, would have been a beehive of kid-related activity and notice the decided absence of children. Rather than gathering together for an after-dinner game of street hockey or tag, the kids on the street have been shuttled off to soccer practice, guitar lessons, and all kinds of other highly worthy but sometimes exhausting extracurricular activities.

What's motivating this shift to formalize play is fear: fear that your child will be left behind her peers if she doesn't have the necessary athletic skills; fear that she will have nobody left to play with if you don't hop on board the extracurricular bandwagon; fear that your child will miss out on some key childhood experience if you don't ensure that she is exposed to the full gamut of possible experiences—everything from art to music to sports—and, of course, the fear that most of us don't even want to think about, yet alone articulate: the fear that our neighborhoods may no longer be safe places for our children to play.

Whether it's a matter of wanting to keep up with (or exceed!) the Joneses or a desire to keep Johnny safe, the net result is the same: kids are being enrolled in a mind-boggling number of extracurricular activities. "I have a friend who proudly tells me all about her six-year-old son's busy schedule," says Alex, a 40-year-old mother of four. "He's enrolled in soccer, piano lessons, karate, and gymnastics all at the same time. She also has a 14-month-old daughter. She says that her children are her priority, and, with a schedule like that, I'd guess they'd have to be! I'll be watching with interest to see how she handles things when her daughter is old enough to start taking lessons, too!"

Although there's nothing wrong with signing your child up for an extracurricular activity or two—assuming, of course, that she's interested in taking swimming lessons or going to science camp with her best friend—what you don't want to do is to schedule every minute of every day with some sort of activity. Not only will it leave her—and you—feeling like you're living in a pressure cooker, but you'll also prevent her from learning how to entertain herself or play with friends when no structured activity is planned. (Think about it: it's one thing to be able to get along with the kids in your class at swimming lessons. It's quite another to invite another kid over to your house to play when there's no grown-up calling the shots!)

Because your kids' friends are likely to be signed up for a-million-and-one activities, you may find that your kids will pressure you to sign them up for a-million-and-one activities, too. Before you start getting hit with all these requests, you may want to decide how many activities you are reasonably willing to commit to per child at any given time. Some of the factors to consider include the following:

- **How many children you have.** If you have four kids and they each sign up for two activities, that's eight activities you need to shuttle kids off to each week!

- **What you figure your budget can swing.** Extracurricular activities can take a hefty bite out of your family's budget, with certain sports like hockey being particularly expensive.

- **How much time you and/or your partner are willing to commit to driving.** If you're a single parent with four other kids, and you don't have anyone else who can help with driving, you may be willing to sign your child up only for activities in which car pooling is a possibility.

- **Whether the activity in question conflicts with other activities.** Unless you figure out a way to clone yourself, it can be pretty tough to arrange to show up at four different extracurricular activities at the same time, something I've learned during my own time in the mom-of-four trenches!

- **Your child's age.** Younger children—particularly children who have just started attending school full-time—need time for unscheduled play, so signing a six-year-old up for too many extracurricular activities can lead to a bit of passive resistance on her part: if she's too tired to play or not really interested in the game, you'll find her standing on the sidelines or chatting with the goalie rather than helping her team chase that soccer ball down the field!

- **How well this particular child is doing in school.** If your child is struggling in school, you may want to limit her to one extracurricular activity so that she'll have more time to devote to her school work until her grades improve.

Even if you do limit the number of extracurricular activities, you may still find it necessary to call the occasional extracurricular time out—putting all of the kids on notice, for example, that the family is taking a break from extracurricular activities during the summer months. "I only allow one activity at a time, but after a few months of running the children everywhere, I need to take a break, or else I start to feel like I am burning out," explains Sheri, a 29-year-old mother of four. "As a single mother, I think it makes it harder to run the children places, and I burn out faster. I do whatever I can, and I hope the children understand and appreciate that."

MOTHER WISDOM

Although you may be tempted to pull the plug on your child's extracurricular activities the moment her grades begin to dip, as noted in Chapter 7, the experts advise against going this route because kids who are struggling in school really benefit from the self-esteem boost that comes from excelling at a particular extracurricular activity—an important point to keep in mind before you yank her from the swim team.

MOM'S THE WORD

"Our unwritten rule is one activity per child. I don't think it's good if you're constantly running from place to place for activities."

—*Dorothy, 36, mother of three*

MOM'S THE WORD

"We only allow one extracurricular activity at a time. Our daughter has taken dancing, gymnastics, and swimming. We give her the choice of which activity she would like to try next. The only stipulation is that she has to finish it once she starts the session."

—*Lisa, 41, mother of one*

NO KIDDING!

Don't forget that extra-curricular activities are for the kids, not the parents (although one could be forgiven for assuming otherwise, judging by the conduct of some of the overzealous parents who show up at certain sporting events). After all, some grownups don't merely settle for overseeing their children's play. In many cases, they take over that play entirely—a point Stacy M. DeBroff makes in her book *Sign Me Up! The Parents Complete Guide to Sports, Activities, Music Lessons, Dance Classes, and Other Extracurriculars*: "Just imagine what would happen if adults took over the game of hide-and-seek," she writes. "We would most likely have volunteer parent coaches, intense training sessions, and weekend tournaments culminating in a national championship. Tryouts for elite teams would start at age 7, aimed at recruiting strategic hiders and aggressive seekers. . . . All of a sudden, it's hard to imagine where the fun has gone."

"Screen Time": How Much Is Too Much?

Remember what they taught you back in science class about nature abhorring a vacuum? The same thing applies to kids and free time. If you follow my advice and build a bit of free time into your child's schedule, there's a very real danger that your child's newly found free time will be swallowed up by "screen time."

"Screen time" is, of course, the term that educators and others use to describe any kind of time a kid spends plunked down in front of a screen, be it a computer monitor, a video-game system screen, or a TV screen. Parents sometimes forget that these three activities are really just variations on the same theme, a point that Holly Bennett and Teresa Pitman make in their book, *Steps and Stages: From 6 to 8: The Early School Years*. "A computer, whether used for games, homework, or personal learning, is still an electronic screen," they write. "Children who rotate from video game to computer to TV can give the impression of doing varied activities, when what's really happening is hours sitting in front of a screen. Those are hours your child is not playing outside, drawing, reading, inventing and acting out detective stories, learning to knit, etc."

The next three sections of this chapter discuss how to do battle with the three specific subspecies of screen time: TV, video games, and computers.

The In-House Brain Drain: Kids and TV

Although TV has lost some of its appeal for the current generation of kids, many of whom have been wooed away by video games and the Internet, American kids still spend a fair bit of time planted in front of the tube—an average of 25 hours per week, in fact. This far exceeds the two-hour daily maximum recommended by the American Academy of Pediatrics.

A pretty solid case can be made for limiting the amount of time kids spend watching television. Studies have shown that excessive television viewing can contribute to a number of different types of problems, including the following:

- **Behavioral problems:** Research has shown that kids who watch a lot of television are more likely to use aggression as a means of dealing with problems and are more likely to engage in irresponsible sexual behavior than kids who watch less TV.

- **Social problems:** Kids who watch a lot of TV don't get along as well with their friends as other kids who spend less time in front of the tube. They also tend to be less imaginative, to be more easily bored, and to have fewer hobbies and interests.

- **Academic problems:** Kids who watch more than four hours of television per day tend to put less effort into their school work and have poorer reading skills than other kids. They are also more likely to exhibit behavioral problems at school.

- **Health problems:** Kids who watch a lot of television are more likely to be obese than other kids—the result of the triple whammy of TV viewing: kids aren't physically active when they're watching TV; they're likely to be snacking in front of the tube; and they're subjected to a steady stream of advertising messages designed to encourage them to eat unhealthy foods—messages that are likely to stick with them long after the TV gets turned off.

Not quite sure how to go about taming the TV monster at your house? Here are some tips.

- **Come up with some sort of TV-viewing limit for your child.** Whether or not you actually tip your child off to this limit is up to you (some parenting experts argue that if you give your child a two-hour limit, they'll feel compelled to watch the full two hours per day!), but it's important that you're clear in your own head about how much TV watching you're prepared to allow. The disadvantage to not providing your child with a clear guideline about how much TV watching is too much is that she'll never be sure exactly how much she's allowed—something that will create a lot more work for you. You'll have to let her know each day whether her planned viewing schedule is okay or not. You'll have to decide what works best for you.

- **Spread the word.** Make sure that your child's childcare providers, grandparents, and the other key adults in her life know about your family's TV-viewing rules. That way, you can ensure that the rules are followed consistently if they happen to be caring for your child. While you're spreading the word about your family's TV-viewing policies, be sure to let friends and neighbors know what you're up to, too. Not only will they be able to help support your efforts by limiting the amount of time your child spends watching

TV while visiting their houses, but you also may inspire them to tame the TV monster at their place, too!

- **Limit your own TV-viewing time, too.** It's pretty hard to sell your child on the merits of leaving the TV turned off if you're sneaking off to the family room at every opportunity to get your own TV fix. This is yet another one of those parenting situations where you have to be prepared to walk the talk. If you get really desperate to find out what's going on with your favorite soap, then you may want to do what I do and catch up via the show's Web site from time to time. Of course, I'm no saint in the screen-time department. I'm not about to confess how many hours a day I spend pounding away at my computer!

- **Insist that your child know what show she wants to watch before she turns on the TV.** This will help to eliminate a lot of mindless TV watching, and it will encourage your child to use her TV-viewing quota wisely—something that will save her (and hence you!) a lot of angst if your child discovers at the end of her daily viewing allotment that her very favorite show is coming up next. It will also force her to practice her reading and time management skills. After all, the only way she's going to find out exactly what her TV-viewing options are for a particular evening is to flip open the TV listings and plan her viewing time.

- **Encourage your kids to tape their favorite shows and watch them later on.** Not only are they likely to make more appropriate viewing choices if their TV-viewing is pre-planned, but they'll also be able to fast-forward through the commercials—something that is likely to dramatically reduce the amount of whining you hear for everything from breakfast cereals to toys.

- **Kick the cable habit.** I know, I know: it can be painful to kiss some of those round-the-clock home renovation channels goodbye if, like me, you like nothing more than to watch other people fix up their homes, but you'll probably find that your kids are much less tempted to watch TV if you don't get any of "the good channels" anymore. (Who knows? You may even be tempted to tackle a home renovation project in real life. I'm actually flirting with the idea of picking up a power tool.)

- **Refuse to allow the TV to become the backdrop to daily living.** The TV should be turned off as soon as the show your child planned to watch is over. If she tries to argue that she's not watching TV anymore—her sister is—you will want to remind her that the clock keeps ticking on her own viewing time so long as she remains in the room. If she wants to save her remaining half-hour so that she can tune into another show later on, she had better plan to exit stage left!

- **Refuse to succumb to the pressure to give your child her own TV.** Kids who have TVs in their bedrooms tend to watch a lot more TV than other kids, and much of this TV viewing tends to take place late in the evening, when their parents think they are sleeping! Not only is late-night viewing undesirable because of the types of shows that tend to air after prime time, but your child also is unlikely to be particularly on the ball in her early-morning science class if she stayed up half the night watching some mindless celebrity dating show. (Then again, if it happens to be on cross-species pollination, she may be better prepared than you think.)

- **Relocate the TV if it has always occupied prime real estate in your home.** If the TV has always been the focal point of your entire family room (that is, you've only just barely fallen short of placing it on a tiny altar, complete with burnt offerings!), you may want to find it a less appealing place to live—perhaps in the downstairs recreation room across from the old, lumpy couch that your kids complain is too stinky. (You'll know they're really eager to tune into a particular show if they head for the basement sporting a pair of nose plugs.)

- **Refuse to dine with Bart Simpson.** If you decide to leave the TV in the kitchen or family room as opposed to relocating it to the basement, have a rule that it gets turned off during mealtimes. It's pretty hard to carry on a conversation with your kids if you're being forced to compete with the inane antics of Marge and Homer's infamous offspring.

- **Have a rule that the TV needs to stay off while friends are over.** Your child will miss out on the fun and the socialization opportunities that go along with having a friend over to play if the two of them spend their entire visit parked in front of the tube. You'll be doing them both a favor by forcing them to find other ways of entertaining themselves while they are playing at your house, even though they may complain bitterly at first. (Note: You may want to alert the other child's parent to your strategy so that she can hold firm at her end, too. Otherwise, the two little TV junkies may simply make a beeline for the TV set at the other child's house the moment you tell them that the TV set at your house is off limits.)

- **Have clear rules about the times of day when TV viewing is and isn't allowed.** You may want to have a no-TV rule in the morning when everyone is busy getting ready to go out the door to work, school, and daycare (I mean, do you really want to have to wait for a particular TV show to end before you can hustle the kids out the door?), and you may also want to ban TV watching after school until everyone's homework is finished (something that may provide just enough of an incentive to encourage the math books to find their way out of the backpacks!).

MOM'S THE WORD

"We have a no-electronics day (for Mom and Dad, too!) on Sunday every week and try to do family activities instead."

—*Sue, 45, mother of three*

Pay attention to quality as well as quantity. It's just as important to monitor the types of TV shows your kids are tuning in to as it is to be aware of exactly how much TV they're watching. Some experts have suggested that the evidence linking media violence to aggressive behavior is even more compelling than the evidence linking smoking to lung cancer! Of course, it's not just violence and aggression you need to watch out for: you also need to be on the lookout for sex, offensive language, and just plain unsuitable subject matter (that is, pretty much anything that shows up on *The Jerry Springer Show!*). If you're not quite sure whether a particular show is suitable for your child, sit down and watch it with her the first few times. That way, if you do decide to veto the show, you'll be able to provide her with a clear explanation of why it didn't exactly earn your own in-house Parent Seal of Approval.

Here are some other ways that you can dialog with your child about what she sees on TV:

- **Talk to your child about TV violence.** It's important for kids to understand that what happens on TV shows isn't real (unless, of course, it's a news story or a documentary) and that violence in real life hurts. Studies have shown that TV violence can have three potentially detrimental effects on kids: making them less sensitive to the pain and suffering of others; making them more fearful of the world around them; and making them more likely to behave aggressively toward others. And, of course, you'll want to be conscious of all the stereotyping that gets served up as entertainment via the tube: sexism, ageism, racism, and so on.

- **Encourage your child to play TV critic.** When you're
  watching a new TV show together, get your child involved
  in sizing up the merits of the show. Is it well-written, well-
  acted, and well-produced, or is it some poorly thrown
  together show that's primarily designed to sell spin-off merchandise? Is the show consistent with your family's values?
  Does your child think the show is suitable for her younger
  cousins? These types of questions can help to jump start a
  thought-provoking discussion between you and your child.

MOTHER WISDOM

Give some thought as to how you use TV in your family. Some
parenting experts say that it's a good idea to use TV as a reward for good
behavior. Others disagree, arguing that doing so only serves to overempha-
size the importance of TV. If your kids are already totally hooked on TV, you
may wish to find other ways of rewarding them for good behavior—such as
offering to take your child on a family outing instead.

And now that you've laid all the groundwork for leading a less
TV-centric life, you can get ready to start reaping the rewards.
Cutting back on your TV viewing time is likely to pay off big-
time for you and your kids. Researchers at Eastern Washington
University found that 99 percent of families who watch less than
six hours of TV per week report that they are generally happy
and satisfied with their home life. Because TV doesn't eat up as
much of their day, they have more time to spend talking to their
kids—something they spend an average of an hour a day doing,
as compared to the mere half an hour per week that families with
heavier TV viewing habits typically spend talking with their
kids.

Note: The above tips assume that you're merely seeking to
reduce the amount of time your kids spend watching TV. If
you're interested in eliminating TV viewing altogether (and
more power to you, by the way, if you decide to go that route!),

you may want to visit one of the growing number of Web sites devoted to leading a TV-free life for some tips on how to pull the plug entirely, like www.tvturnoff.org.

MOTHER WISDOM

If your child complains that she's bored because she's not allowed to watch TV, help her to come up with a list of totally fun 100 percent TV-free activities. (Note: You'll find a list of fun activities at the end of this chapter that may provide her with a few ideas for her list.) If your child hangs her list on the refrigerator door, she can keep adding to her list over time.

Video Games: Do They Get a Bad Rap?

Video games are big business in North America. Video game manufacturers rack up an estimated $10 billion in sales each year. A key market for their products is, of course, children.

Although today's generation of kids are guinea pigs when it comes to the long-term effects of video gaming—video games haven't been around long enough for developmental psychologists and others interested in the study of children to conduct any truly long-term studies—we are starting to get at least a partial picture of what video games mean for kids. Despite what you may think, the news isn't entirely bad on the video-game front. There are actually some benefits to video game playing. Studies have shown that kids who play video games a lot tend to score above average in such areas as eye-hand coordination, information processing skills, spatial abilities, visual strategy skills, and nonverbal problem-solving skills.

That's the good news. Unfortunately, the bulk of the research about kids and video games paints a decidedly less rosy picture. Here's a quick summary of the key concerns that researchers have raised to date:

- **Violent content:** Gone are the days when the scariest thing a kid could expect to see on-screen was poor old Pacman getting gobbled up by a ghost. Today's generation of video games is much more violent and gory than most parents realize. Some video game critics have pointed out, in fact, that the military uses video simulation software similar to the current generation of violent video games to desensitize soldiers to killing. Unfortunately, parents tend to be less tuned in to the violent nature of video games than they are to violence in other forms of media. For whatever reason, parents don't seem to be as alarmed by the thought of their kids playing video games as they are by the thought of their kids playing with toy guns. Not everyone is in denial about the potential effects of video games on kids, however. The kids themselves are prepared to admit that the violent content in today's generation of video games isn't good for other kids; a 1998 study conducted at Simon Fraser University in British Columbia, Canada, found that most kids believe that video games could have a negative effect on their friends.

 NO KIDDING!

A recent Stanford University study indicates that violent behavior learned from violent video games, videos, and TV can be unlearned. The researchers found that when parents limited kids' TV-watching time to seven hours a week and insisted that they stick with less violent videos and video games, the amount of aggression that the previously aggressive children exhibited toward other kids dropped significantly. In fact, by the end of the study, the previously aggressive children were only half as likely to engage in bullying and aggression.

- **Sexist stereotyping of women and/or inclusion of sexual subject matter:** Many video games feature sexist stereotyping of women. Other games that are aimed at an adult audience—but that some kids end up playing nonetheless—feature content of a highly sexual nature. So, don't make the mistake of assuming that if it's a video game, it must be meant for kids: a growing number of "adults only" games are hitting the market these days that are anything but suitable for children.

- **Potential for psychological addiction:** Although there's still some controversy about whether it's actually possible to get addicted to playing video games, it's fair to say that some kids become obsessed. Studies have shown that 7 percent of preteens play video games for at least 30 hours each week. If your child gets hooked on playing video games, he may lose interest in other, more worthwhile activities, such as playing outside with his friends, doing his homework, talking to family members, and so on. (See Table 8.1 for a list of the warning signs that your child may be developing a video-game addiction.)

TABLE 8.1

Is Your Child Becoming Addicted to Video Games?

Although the jury's still out on the question of whether it's actually possible to become addicted to playing video games, if your child exhibits a number of the following classic warning signs of addiction, you may want to consider cutting back on his video-game time or getting rid of the video-game system entirely.

➡ Does your child enjoy playing video games for long stretches of time (for example, three or four hours at a time)?

➡ Does your child find it difficult to control the amount of time he spends playing video-games?

➡ Does your child become restless or fidgety after he's used up that day's allotment of video-game time?

continued

Is Your Child Becoming Addicted to Video Games? *(continued)*

→   Have you noted any unusual moodiness or other changes to your child's behavior that could indicate a possible addiction?

→   Has your child lost interest in most activities (such as social and sporting activities) other than video games?

→   Are your child's grades starting to decline because he's spending so much time playing video games that he's not getting his homework done?

→   Has your child been caught skipping school in order to go home or to the mall to play video games?

→   Is your child starting to withdraw from family members, preferring to spend his time playing video games?

→   Has your child exchanged his old group of friends for a new group of friends who share his video-game obsession?

→   Has your child broken family rules in order to squeeze in more video-game time (for example, sneaking downstairs in the middle of the night to play video games or lying about doing his chores because he's in such a hurry to get out the door to play video games at a friend's)?

→   Is your child skipping meals, eating in front of the video-game screen, neglecting his personal hygiene, and/or failing to get the sleep he needs because he's eager to spend every possible minute playing video games?

→   Does your child become angry or hostile when you confront him about his video-game habit or suggest that he cut back on the amount of time he spends playing video games?

Note: Although video-game addiction can be a problem for both boys and girls, it is much more common in boys than in girls, which is why I use the male pronoun when discussing this subject in this chapter.

- **Illusion versus reality:** Kids who play video games excessively may have a hard time switching to "reality mode" (a.k.a. real life!). Video games provide kids with an illusion of control that doesn't exist in real life. It can be quite a letdown to go from ruling the universe—literally!—to having to function as a member of society. "Video games are about letting kids manipulate reality, bend it to their will, which means that when they get up at last from the console, the loss of power is hard to handle," noted Nancy Gibbs in an article in the November 1, 2001, issue of *Time* magazine. "You can't click your little brother out of existence."

- **Potential for physical injury:** Excessive video gaming can contribute to repetitive stress injuries. Kids as young as seven years of age are starting to show the signs of repetitive stress injuries such as carpal tunnel syndrome—a condition that occurs when repetitive hand motions made over a long period of time put pressure on the nerve that runs through the carpal tunnel in the wrist. The condition may result in numbness or pain in the thumb and first three fingers, especially at night, and, if severe enough, may require surgery. The problem is more likely to occur in kids who play video games on their parents' computers because the monitor and keyboard at these computer workstations are typically positioned at adult height, something that means that the child is generally using the computer in an awkward position. You can reduce the likelihood that your child will develop repetitive stress injuries by:

  - limiting the amount of computer and video-game time (It's not just keyboards that are to blame; joysticks can be a problem, too.)

  - ensuring that the computer system is positioned appropriately for your child

  - encouraging your child to use proper posture while using the computer

  - insisting that your child take a break at least once every 30 minutes (Tip: Set the timer on your computer to ring every 30 minutes so that your child won't forget that it's time to get moving. Or, better yet, set an alarm clock in the next room so that he'll have to walk away from the computer to turn it off!)

You can prevent video games from becoming a problem for your child by limiting their use in your household and being conscious of what types of games your child is playing. Here are a few tips:

- **Try to hold off on buying a video-game system for as long as you can.** You may be able to get away with not owning one if you agree to rent a game system and a few video games on the odd occasion as a special treat. You may also consider doing what we did at our house; we told our kids that we weren't prepared to buy them a video-game system ever. They would have to save up the money themselves. This strategy bought us a few extra video-game-free years than we might otherwise have enjoyed. (My oldest son didn't manage to scrape together the funds needed to buy his own game system until he was 12.)

- **Have clear rules about video-game playing.** You may want to have rules about how much time your kids are allowed to spend playing video games each day, what times of day video-game playing is allowed, what responsibilities need to be attended to first (such as chores and homework), and what types of games your kids are allowed to play.

- **Monitor your child's video-game use carefully.** Pay careful attention to the games he borrows from the video-game store as well as the games that he borrows from other kids. You want to be sure that the games he plays are suitable for kids his age. In addition to reading the box and sitting down to watch your child play the game, you may also want to read software reviews (in magazines and online), talk to other parents about their knowledge of particular games, and ask the staff of the video-game store that you do business with whether a particular game is suitable for children.

- **Be on the lookout for games that allow the player to adjust the amount of violence, sexual content, or profanity.** Your child may play the game at its most parent-friendly setting when you're looking over his shoulder, but then switch to another setting the moment you leave the room.

- **Be wary of any game that can be played over the Internet.** You may want to veto online gaming unless you know for a fact that your child will be playing only with classmates or other "real world" friends. Cyberpredators are known for hanging out on computer gaming sites, in the hopes of striking up a friendship with kids. Even if your child doesn't happen to bump into anyone other than *bona fide* gamers, you may be less than impressed by some of the language that gets used on these Web sites. (To think that parents in the musical *The Music Man* were concerned about their kids hanging out in pool halls!)

Kids and Computers

The computer manufacturers have certainly done a pretty impressive job of marketing to parents in recent years. They've managed to convince us that we're putting our kids at a huge disadvantage if we don't invest heavily in the latest—but not necessarily greatest—educational software at home and at school.

Although it's important for kids today to acquire some basic computer skills, there's no need for parents to go overboard by overemphasizing computers in the home. In fact, there can be a downside to all that time spent in front of a computer screen.

Studies have shown that kids who spend a lot of time working at the computer may miss out on the chance to master the skills needed for handwriting and simple activities that require coordination, sequencing, and spontaneous movement. They're also likely to pay a hefty price on the health front as a result of too much screen time: obesity, poor posture, eye problems, carpal tunnel syndrome, and an overall lack of strength and coordination. So it's important to ask yourself what else your child could be doing if she weren't plunked in front of a computer doing math drills on that fancy new educational software package you just bought her—and whether these other activities may, in fact, have more to offer from a developmental or health standpoint.

You may also want to take a step back and consider what your child is actually learning from a particular educational software product. If it's a well-designed product that she enjoys using and that appears to be teaching her something, she may be actually deriving some benefit from the product; but if it's not, the software could potentially be doing her more harm than good. Some educational software packages have been demonstrated to limit creativity, promote a poor attention span, over-reward kids for minimal effort, and—even worse—reduce motivation by rewarding or praising the child for repeatedly wrong answers.

 NO KIDDING!

A study conducted by the University of California-Berkeley School of Optometry found that kids who spend longer than three hours in front of a computer screen at any one time are at risk of developing eye problems. Researchers found that 12 percent of these kids have focusing problems and 25 to 30 percent have initial signs of far-sightedness. To screen for such problems, you should ensure that your child's next eye check-up includes tests of focusing and eye-coordination skills—the aspects of vision most often affected by computer-related eye fatigue.

MOTHER WISDOM

Don't get your preschooler hooked on computers too early. Although a small amount of computer time is suitable for kids this age, you don't want to fall into the trap of using the computer as a babysitter. According to the National Association for the Education of Young Children, "Computers supplement and do not replace highly valued early childhood activities and materials such as art, blocks, sand, water, books, exploration with reading materials, and dramatic play." In other words, playing with computerized building blocks is no substitute for dumping a bucket of blocks on the living room floor and building the real thing. Or to put it another way, real-world experiences beat virtual experiences hands down.

Surfer boys and girls: Kids and the Internet

Something that distinguishes the current generation of kids from any previous generation of children is the fact that they have grown up online—something that has earned them the nickname "the Internet generation." While their parents are still struggling to figure out the Internet and to understand its impact on their lives, their kids have long since embraced this new technology and left their parents in the online dust.

Keeping kids safe online

Even though parents and kids may feel like their kids are in relatively little danger because the computer is situated in the family home, the dangers of the online world are very real. A study published in *The Journal of the American Medical Association* revealed that one in five children who are regular Internet users have been on the receiving end of at least one unwelcome sexual solicitation.

Although kids may think they know it all when it comes to the Internet, they sometimes lack the critical thinking abilities required to make good decisions while online. To prevent your kids from running into trouble online, you need to be vigilant.

That means keeping tabs on how much time your kids are spending online and what they are doing while they're connected. Here are some important tips to keep in mind:

- **Write up a family Internet agreement before your kids go online.** That way, your kids will be totally clear about your expectations right from the start. At the very least, your agreement should spell out:

  - what types of Web sites your kids are allowed to visit

  - what types of activities they're allowed to engage in online

  - which search engines they are allowed to use (for example, kids-only search engines versus regular search engines)

  - how much Internet time they are allowed each day

  - what information they are and are not allowed to divulge about themselves

  - what they can do to avoid running into trouble online, and what they should do if they run into a situation that leaves them feeling like they're in over their heads

  - what consequences your kids will face for breaking any family Internet rules

- **Ensure that the computer that your kids use to surf the Internet is situated in a high-traffic area of the household.** That way, you'll able to keep close tabs on what your child is doing while she's online. If you have a laptop computer with a wireless connection to the Internet, be aware that your child may be tempted to sneak the laptop off to her bedroom to try to surf in privacy or to squeeze in some middle-of-the-night surfing time when she's supposed to be asleep. If you have such a computer system in your house, you'll want to make it a firm rule that the computer doesn't leave the kitchen or the family room—wherever it normally resides.

- **Don't make the mistake of assuming that your kids use the Internet in exactly the same way you do.** Although parents are inclined to turn to the Internet as a source of news or information, kids are more inclined to be drawn by its entertainment value—to see it as a place to relax, hang out, meet friends, and have fun. While you may not be inclined to hang out in chat rooms or to spend a lot of time sending instant messages to your friends, these activities are very popular with preteens and teens. Yep, the generation gap is alive and well and living on the Internet!

- **Don't judge an e-book by its cover.** Although you might assume that your child is busy researching her geography assignment because the browser is open at a geography Web site or she has a geography e-book open on her desktop each time you walk by, it's possible that she has chat software running in the background or that she's busy sending instant messages to a friend.

- **Don't assume that you can keep tabs on your kids' Internet use simply by checking the browser history every once in a while.** Most computer-savvy kids know how to hide their online activities by deleting any portions of the browser history that they don't want their parents to see. Even if they haven't figured out these tricks by themselves, there are entire Web sites devoted to teaching kids how to ensure that their parents remain in the dark about their online activities. The only way to find out exactly what your kids have been up to is to supervise their activities closely and/or to rely on Internet monitoring software that captures screen shots of the Web sites your child visits (something that will allow you to determine whether your child is following family Internet rules or getting into trouble by visiting unsuitable Web sites, such as pro-anorexia Web sites), records keystrokes of everything she types (something that can be valuable in determining whether she's set up any secret e-mail accounts), and/or keeps a detailed history of all Web pages she's accessed (one that she can't override unless, of course, she's onto the fact that you're monitoring her activities and knows how to disable the software).

Finally, don't expect a piece of software to do your job as a parent. Although you can purchase Internet software packages that block Web sites containing certain keywords and Internet tracking software that will allow you to monitor what your kids have been doing online, no piece of software is infallible. Nothing can replace the eye of a watchful parent.

 NO KIDDING!

Eighteen percent of parents surveyed by the University of California in 2001 said that they felt that their kids were spending too much time online.

Kids and Internet addiction

Just as academics continue to debate whether it's possible for kids to get hooked on video games, there's still considerable debate about whether Internet addiction actually exists.

What researchers do know, however, is that the Internet can be a highly seductive technology for kids—particularly kids who may be having difficulty relating to friends in the real world. After all, it doesn't matter if you're quiet and introverted in real life; you can morph into a popular, extroverted older teen—a football player or cheerleader even—the moment you grab hold of that computer mouse.

Kids may also be attracted by the ease with which Internet friendships can be made. Internet relationships may feel safer than face-to-face relationships because you don't fear rejection to the same degree when you can't see or be seen by the other person. What's more, the instant intimacy of online relationships can encourage a lonely preteen to pour out her heart and soul to someone who appears to be a soulmate.

Internet use can cross the line into addictive behavior if the real world begins to pale in comparison to the fantasy world that the preteen has created online. Because most preteens tend to lead rich fantasy lives, they can easily get hooked on the larger-than-life dimensions of the Internet, creating a parallel universe—a world in which they're the ones calling the shots. Table 8.2 outlines some of the warning signs of Internet addiction in kids.

TABLE 8.2

Does Your Child Have an Internet Addiction Problem?

You may wish to consider cutting back on your child's Internet use or taking away her Internet privileges entirely if you notice that she appears to be becoming addicted to the online world. Your answers to the following questions should help you to determine whether or not your child has a problem.

→ Does your child go online for long stretches of time (for example, three or four hours at a time)?

→ Does your child find it difficult to control the amount of time she spends online?

→ Does your child become restless or fidgety after she's used up that day's allotment of Internet time?

→ Have you noted any unusual moodiness or other changes to your child's behavior that could indicate a possible Internet addiction?

→ Has your child lost interest in most activities (such as social and sporting activities) other than going online?

→ Are your child's grades starting to decline because she's spending so much time online that she's not getting her homework done?

→ Has your child been caught skipping school in order to go home, to the library, or to a cybercafe to access the Internet?

continued

Does Your Child Have an Internet Addiction Problem? *(continued)*

→   Is your child starting to withdraw from family members, preferring to spend her time in the company of her online friends?

→   Has your child started to receive letters or phone calls from people she has met online, but doesn't know in real life?

→   Has your child broken family rules in order to spend more time on the Internet (for example, sneaking downstairs in the middle of the night to go online or lying about having finished her homework because she's eager to get back online)?

→   Is your child skipping meals, eating in front of the computer, neglecting her personal hygiene, or failing to get the sleep she needs because she's eager to spend every possible minute online?

→   Does your child become angry or hostile when you confront her about her Internet usage habits or suggest that she cut back on the amount of time she spends online?

More often than not, Internet addiction is a symptom of a bigger problem, like dissatisfaction with life in the real world, so you may want to line up support for your child if you suspect that she's becoming overly dependent on the Internet. Your family doctor should be able to refer you to counseling resources in your community.

That's Entertainment? Music and Music Videos

Music videos can become a source of conflict between parents and kids as kids head into the preteen and teen years. It's not just music lyrics laced with profanity, as well as references to sex, violence, suicide, and drug and alcohol use, that have many parents up in arms. The music videos that the music companies release to promote these songs often contain images that some parents may consider inappropriate for their kids. If you are bothered by the content of the music videos your child is tuned in to, you may want to sit down and watch some of these videos with your child and talk about why you find certain elements of certain videos offensive. You may discover that your child shares some of your concerns; but even if she doesn't, it's worthwhile taking the time to make your own views clear.

While you're having a dialog about music anyway, you may also want to raise the issue of copyright infringement with regard to downloaded music. The major record labels are starting to prosecute ordinary citizens—teens included—for illegally swapping copies of copyright-protected music. Unless you're willing to risk being dragged into court by a major record label, you may want to institute a "no illegal downloads" policy in your family.

Setting the Stage for Play

Although you don't want to fall into the trap of taking on the role of full-time entertainment director for your child, you can help to set the stage for play by making sure that your child has plenty of unscheduled downtime so that she can play by herself or with others and ensuring that she's got an interesting mix of materials on hand to play with.

Obviously, the types of materials that appeal to your child at any given time will vary according to her age and interests, so you'll want to ensure that you're providing her with access to new materials on an ongoing basis. (Don't worry. This isn't nearly as expensive a proposition as you may think, as you'll see when you check out Table 8.3 and Table 8.4. Many of these materials are low-cost—even free—and you certainly don't need to purchase everything on the list. Just try to pick and choose items from different categories as birthdays and other gift-giving occasions roll around so that your child will be able to enjoy a variety of different play experiences.)

TABLE 8.3

The Play's the Thing: Great Play Materials for Kids

The following items offer exceptional play value to children ages 3 through 12. Obviously, some of these items will have greater appeal to older kids than younger kids, and vice versa, so you'll want to keep your child's developmental stage in mind when selecting individual items.

Games and Puzzles

Decks of cards

Dominoes

Traditional board games such as Yahtzee, Othello, Memory, and Checkers

Cooperative board games that require players to work together to achieve a common goal

Jigsaw puzzles

Puzzle books (crossword puzzles, word search puzzles, dot-to-dot puzzles, and so on)

Science Fun

Magnets

Magnifying glasses

Flashlights

Binoculars

Microscopes

Periscopes

Telescopes

Kaleidoscopes

Bug collecting kits (for example, ant farms)

Birdfeeder kits

Gardening kits

Science lab sets

Science activity books, field guides, astronomy books, and other science books

Dramatic Play and Music

Finger puppets

Hand puppets

Costumes and related props (for example, a magic wand)

Musical instruments

Tape recorder and a mix of both blank and prerecorded tapes

Building Blocks and Construction Sets

Wooden building blocks

Plastic building block sets (for example, LEGO)

Marbleworks (a construction set that allows you to build ramps for marbles to roll in)

Tool sets

Model-making kits

Arts and Crafts

Basic arts and crafts supplies (see Table 8.4)

Ink pad and stamps

Sketch books

Origami kits

Modeling clay

Candle-making kits

Jewelery-making kits

Disposable camera or a digital camera (assuming your budget can swing it)

Craft activity books

Active Play

Balls of all sizes (bouncey balls, beach balls, and volleyballs)

Other sports equipment (such as skateboards and rollerblades, and appropriate safety gear)

Bicycles (again, be sure to include helmets and other safety gear as needed)

Kites

continued

The Play's the Thing: Great Play Materials for Kids *(continued)*

Active Play (continued)

Frisbees
Boomerangs
Skipping rope
Sidewalk chalk (for drawing hopscotch and four-square courts)

Note: See Chapter 12 for tips on encouraging active play and Chapter 11 for tips on reducing the risk of recreational injuries—a major cause of injuries in children.

TABLE 8.4

Basic Arts and Crafts Supplies for Kids

Although it's not necessary to purchase every item on this list, it's a good idea to try to provide your child with a variety of different types of art materials, if you can afford to do so, because these materials will help to spark your child's creativity.

Tools and Supplies
Chalk (regular and sidewalk)
Colored pencils
Crayons
Fabric crayons
Fabric paints
Glitter glue
Glue gun
Glue sticks
Markers
Masking tape
Paints (tempera, watercolors, and fingerpaints)
Paintbrushes
Paint sponges
Paper (white paper, construction paper, tissue paper, and so on, in all shapes, sizes, and colors)

Tools and Supplies

Pastels

Pencils (regular and colored)

Playdough or modeling clay

Ruler

School glue

Scissors

Sketch books

Sponges

Stamps and a washable pad

Stapler

Stencils

Tape (transparent tape, masking tape, and two-sided tape)

Additional Materials to Collect or Purchase

Aluminum foil

Baskets

Beads

Berry boxes

Boxes (all shapes and sizes)

Buttons

Calendars

Cardboard

Carpet remnants

Catalogues

Cereal boxes

Chalk

Cloth scraps

Clothes pins

Coffee creamers (restaurant-style cream containers)

continued

Basic Arts and Crafts Supplies for Kids *(continued)*

Additional Materials to Collect or Purchase *(continued)*

Coffee filters

Confetti

Cotton balls

Crayon pieces

Deodorant bottles (roll-on style for rolling on paint)

Doilies

Egg cartons

Fabric scraps

Feathers

Felt

File folders

Flower pots

Flowers, artificial or dried

Foam and wood shapes

Foam chips

Frozen juice cans (cardboard style)

Gift-wrap scraps

Gift-wrap rolls

Glitter

Gloves

Greeting cards

Hair rollers

Jars

Jewelry, old or broken

Junk mail (especially the type with stamps)

Lace

Lace doilies

Lacing cord

Additional Materials to Collect or Purchase

Leaves, artificial or dried

Magazines and newspapers

Makeup brushes and sponges

Maps

Milk cartons

Mittens

Modeling clay

Muffin papers

Napkins

Paper bags

Paper plates

Paper towel rolls

Paper towels

Pasta

Pie plates, aluminum

Pinecones

Pipe cleaners

Plastic containers

Plastic cups and bottles

Pom poms

Pop bottles, plastic

Popsicle sticks

Postcards

Raffia

Ribbon

Rice (uncooked)

Rocks

Shells

continued

Basic Arts and Crafts Supplies for Kids *(continued)*

Additional Materials to Collect or Purchase *(continued)*

Shoeboxes

Shoe polish applicators (they make great paint applicators)

Silk flowers

Socks (for puppets)

Spools

Squeeze bottles (for paint)

Stamps

Stickers

Straws

String

Styrofoam trays

Tissue paper

Toilet paper rolls

Toothbrushes

Wallpaper scraps

Wiggley eyes

Wire

Wood scraps

Wool or string

Wrapping paper

Wreaths

Boredom Busters: 22 Fabulous Ways to Banish Boredom at Home

"I'm bored, and there's nothing to do." If that lament sounds all too familiar to you, then this section is for you. I've pulled together a smorgasbord of boredom-busting ideas that are (practically) guaranteed to entertain your kids and (shhh!) get them excited about learning at the same time. (Of course, you'll get more enthusiastic buy-in from your kids if you remember to emphasize fun rather than learning. Remember "educational" sounds like a synonym for "boring" when you're 10 years old!)

This list is by no means complete—you could come up with thousands of ideas along these lines, I'm sure—but what I've tried to do is provide a sampling of different ideas to give you a taste of the possibilities. Anyway, here goes. . . .

1. **Launch a sidewalk graffiti campaign.** Don't worry: I'm not recommending that you encourage your child to embark on a life of crime by spray-painting the sidewalk at the tender age of ten. What I'm suggesting is that you paint words on your sidewalk (or driveway) in front of your house with water and a paintbrush or, if you prefer, engage in some heavy-duty doodling with sidewalk chalk. Your child will get practice writing out words, and you'll have a lot of fun, too, I promise. (When was the last time you got to draw a yard-high happy face or daisy in sidewalk chalk, after all?)

2. **Check out the cookbook shelf in the children's department of your local public library.** Cooking gives kids a great chance to practice their reading and math abilities, to say nothing of their time management and organization skills. After all, if you leave the cookies in the oven for too long, you end up with chocolate chip briquettes rather than chocolate chip cookies!

3. **Organize an "eye spy" scavenger hunt for your kids.** Instead of having your kids run around the neighborhood trying to gather up objects, with an "eye spy" scavenger hunt, they simply have to spot the objects while you're walking around the neighborhood together. Here are some fun themes to work into your eye spy scavenger hunt:

   • *Geometry walk* (look for circles, triangles, squares, and other geometrical shapes while walking around the block)

- *Pattern walk* (keep your eyes open for repeating patterns—for example, "car, car, truck, minivan, car, car, truck, minivan")

- *Alphabet walk* (look for objects that start with a particular letter of the alphabet—for example, sidewalk, sprinkler, sunflower—or each letter of the alphabet in sequence—for example, acorn, bicycle, church, dog)

- *Binocular walk* (bring along a set of binoculars so that you can check out the neighborhood from a different perspective)

- *Texture walk* (take crayon rubbings of textured objects, such as tree bark, that you encounter during your walk)

4. **Climb your family tree.** Research your family history and construct a genealogy chart. If you're feeling really ambitious, you could write up stories from your family's history or write a play based on your family history. Note: If you're looking for some tips on how to get kids hooked on genealogy, look for a copy of my children's book, *The Family Tree Detective: Cracking the Case of Your Family's Story.*

5. **Organize a backyard bug hunt.** Lift up rocks and logs to see what kinds of creepy crawlies you happen to have for neighbors. If you manage to unearth some unusual specimens, make a quick trip to the library to load up on insect identification books. Your kids will have fun trying to figure out just what it was that scurried under the deck. (You may sleep better knowing, too.)

6. **Take a walk on the wild side.** (Literally.) Bring along a picnic lunch, a compass, a pair of binoculars, and a field guide or two and turn your walk in the woods into a bit of an adventure. If you're really ambitious, bring along a field

notebook and take notes about the wildlife and plant species you observe. This could serve as the first entry in a family nature journal that you and your kids keep during all subsequent nature treks. Who knows? You may end up planting the seeds of inspiration for a future botanist!

7. **Help your child to start a collection of some sort.** If she's interested in science, you might encourage her to collect objects from the natural world: leaves, rocks, shells, seeds—basically anything that can be added to over time as you stumble across new specimens. If she's more interested in pop culture, she may be more inclined to collect postage stamps, postcards, or restaurant placemats from any one-of-a-kind truck stops you happen to venture into during your family's travels. (Of course, you may want to discourage your child from collecting sugar packets and other food items from the restaurant stops—unless, of course, you don't mind her acquiring a "bonus" collection of ants!)

8. **Plant a flower or vegetable garden in your backyard.** If you don't have a suitable growing space on your property, find out whether there's a community garden in your neighborhood where you can plant your garden. Then, after you've planted your garden, encourage your child to keep a garden journal so that the two of you can keep track of what was planted, how long it took the seeds to sprout, and (in the case of vegetables and herbs), when the plants were harvested. You might also want to jot down a few notes about the crop's yield, noting the number of vegetables this year's growing season produced and the size of your largest vegetables. It's a great way to help your child learn about the mechanics of gardening while practicing her math skills at the same time.

MOTHER WISDOM

Looking for some ideas for some truly fabulous family field trips? Consider working one or more of the following excursions into your family's day trip itinerary:

- *An auction:* Auctions can be highly entertaining for kids. Just make sure you go over the ground rules before you arrive. You don't want your child to accidentally purchase an expensive gold watch for you, just because she reached up to scratch her head!
- *Flea markets and yard sales:* Although you'll want to steer clear of stores with high-priced collectibles (particularly collectibles of the breakable variety!) when you've got a young family, it's fun to check out flea markets and yard sales with more middle-of-the-road fare, such as toys, books, and games from the 1960s and 1970s. Who knows? Maybe you'll be able to show your kids a replica of the lunch box you carried off to first grade!
- *A hobby or special interest show:* If you live in a large or medium-sized city, you're likely to have your pick of hobby and special interest shows throughout the year—everything from dog and cat shows to model airplane exhibits. These shows can provide a relatively cheap form of entertainment for the entire family since kids typically get in for half-price or even free, depending on their age.
- *Your local airport, train station, or pier:* Kids are fascinated by all modes of transportation, and a trip to your airport, train station, or pier can provide them with the opportunity to check out airplanes, trains, and ships in action. (Note: If you're reluctant to pay hefty parking fees for actually parking at the airport terminal or to deal with the added security in our post 9-11 world, you may decide to simply park in a nearby field and watch the planes zoom by overhead.)
- *A pioneer village:* A trip to a pioneer village can give your kids a sneak peek at what it was like to be a kid before television, video games, and home computers—reason enough to make the trip!
- *A cemetery:* Cemeteries with graves dating back a century or more can also provide kids with a fascinating history lesson. Just make sure you give your kids a crash course in cemetery etiquette before you go so that they won't embarrass themselves or you or upset any mourners who are visiting their loved ones' graves.
- *A factory tour:* Your local tourism bureau should be able to tell you which factories in your area offer tours to members of the public and which of those tours are open to children. Obviously, some types of factory tours will be of greater interest to children than others, so you'll want to bear this in mind when deciding whether or not to go.

- *Other area attractions:* While you're talking to the folks at the tourism bureau, be sure to pick up brochures for other area attractions. Odds are there is at least one museum, park, or recreation area you've yet to take your kids to, so there's yet another possible destination to add to your family excursion list. It's your chance to play tourist in your hometown!

MOTHER WISDOM

You don't have to wait until the summer months to "get growing" with a gardening project. You can give your child a chance to practice her indoor gardening skills during the off-season by growing a bean plant. She may also enjoy flipping through seed catalogues to plan next year's garden— a great way to encourage a reluctant reader to do a little extra reading.

---

9. **Switch into mad scientist mode.** Load up on science activity books at the library and tackle some fun science projects together. Don't assume that you have to have a Ph.D. in chemistry to pull this off, by the way: a simple vinegar-and-baking-soda volcano is generally all it takes to dazzle your typical seven-year-old with your scientific prowess. Of course, if your kids are a little older (and, dare I say, a little more jaded?), you may have to go for slightly more complicated experiments—ideally ones that result in plenty of noise, mess, and smell, the three key criteria for success with the preteen boy crowd, it would seem!

10. **Join a museum, art gallery, science center, planetarium, or other family-friendly facility that offers family memberships.** If you live nearby, you'll easily get your money's worth if you make the museum your destination for those rainy days when you find yourself and your kids at loose ends. That membership could also end up being the answer to your birthday party prayers: a growing number of museums, art galleries, and similar facilities are now hosting sleepovers for kids.

11. **Play mapmaker.** Show your child how to make a map of her neighborhood, her backyard, her bedroom, or anything else in her world. Hint: Your child may find it easier to plot out her map on graph paper rather than drawing it freehand because graph paper makes it easier to keep track of the distance between objects—one of the trickier parts of making a map.

MOTHER WISDOM

Don't pass up the opportunity to take your children to see a first-rate theatrical performance, just because you think you can't afford it. Most professional theaters offer deep discounts to families, in an effort to make the theater experience more accessible to families with young children, so you may be able to scoop up tickets for less than you might think.

---

12. **Help your child to acquire a taste for the arts.** Take in a children's concert or play, or look for a kid-friendly venue for an adult concert or play. (Outdoor concerts and plays work particularly well because your child can always get up and stretch her legs if she gets restless during the performance.)

13. **Weave a great yarn.** Tell your child some stories from your own childhood or, if you prefer, one of those stories that tend to get handed down from generation to generation. The story you tell your child doesn't have to qualify as great literature: a simple ghost story from your days as a kid at summer camp will do! Of course, if you're not the world's greatest storyteller (that is, you have a habit of forgetting the ending midway through the story!), you may decide to read a book to your child instead. If your child is already of reading age, the two of you may enjoy taking turns reading passages of the chapter to one another. (See Chapter 7 for more tips on sharing books with your child.)

14. **Add an educational twist to a classic game like checkers.**
You might add a rule that says that your child has to read a
particular number, letter, or word before she can move her
checker piece. You can also try this same maneuver with
card games such as Go Fish. You can't take your turn until
after you've done a math question or written out one of the
words in your spelling book. The trick is to ensure that the
game is sufficiently motivating to make the child want to
do the associated work. (You would be unlikely to convince
me to balance my checkbook by prompting to let me move
my checker piece one square, for example. But, if you
promised me that you would watch 15 minutes of *The
Sound of Music* with me each time I entered a check in the
electronic register—well, you would have yourself a deal!)

15. **Play with paper.** Make paper dolls, paper boats, paper airplanes—basically paper anything. If you're really feeling
creative, sign a book out of the library on origami—the
Japanese art of paper folding. Or, if you truly want to
secure your nomination for Parent of the Year, teach your
kids how to make their own paper. There are books and
Web sites galore that will show you how.

16. **Build something together.** It doesn't matter whether you
set out to build a birdhouse, assemble a model airplane, or
whip up a set of curtains for your child's bedroom. What
matters is that you zero in on an activity that you and your
child will enjoy doing together.

17. **Pass along a skill that someone taught you.** If you know
how to knit, sew, weave, or needlepoint, chances are it's
because your mother or grandmother showed you how. So,
do your kids a favor and pass these skills along. Who
knows? Maybe you'll end up helping your child to discover
an exciting new hobby, or maybe you'll manage to rekindle
your interest in a hobby you haven't tried in years.

MOTHER WISDOM

Look for ways to reinforce important math concepts as a part of daily living. If someone gives your child a huge jar of jelly beans for her birthday, encourage her to count them and sort them by color before she starts eating them.

Depending on the age of your child, you might also encourage her to take this lesson in Candy Math a little farther by calculating the percentage of red versus yellow jelly beans in the jar and graphing the results. Just don't expect her to do these more advanced math calculations without eating a single jelly bean, or you'll end up with a mutiny on your hands!

---

18. **Start your own garage band.** So what if the neighbors look at you a little funny when you take your roasting pan and metal spoon out to the garage and start making a terrible racket? You can have a heck of a lot of fun organizing your own pots and pans band. Of course, if you prefer to play it straight by playing the guitar, electric keyboard, or harmonica, that's perfectly fine, too. I just happen to be a little partial to the roasting pan myself.

19. **Let your dramatic side hang out.** Encourage your child to organize a play or a puppet show for the neighborhood children. You can offer to help out behind the scenes by printing tickets or programs for the big event, or you can indulge your inner ham by offering to take on a starring role in the play. (That's assuming, of course, that the director will have you!)

20. **Introduce your kids to some classic picnic games.** Preschoolers and young school-aged kids generally get a huge kick out of games like the sack race (use an old pillow case), the bean-bag toss, and the three-legged race. You can even make the games appealing to the hard-to-please pre-teen crowd by challenging them to try the games in the pool or at the beach. (It's anything but easy to balance an egg on a spoon if you have to do so while you're paddling

your way from one end of a pool to another on an air mattress!) Note: You'll find some additional tips on encouraging kids to be physically active in Chapter 12.

21. **Play in the sand.** Either hit your child's backyard sandbox or head for a nearby beach. You can make sandcastles or simply bring along some funnels and have fun exploring the physics of sand. Sand is a lot of fun to play with, whether you're a grown-up or a kid, so go ahead and indulge your inner child in some serious sand therapy!

22. **Simply hang out and do nothing.** This last item is probably the most important item on the entire list. Spend a day hanging out with your child, letting her take the lead when it comes to play. If she wants to ride bikes, grab your helmet and get ready to go for a ride. If she would rather press wildflowers and use them to make greeting cards to send to her relatives, let her know you're up for that, too. If she simply wants to lie on the grass, arms stretched out, watching the clouds go by, let her know that you think that's a perfectly wonderful way to pass the time, for parents and kids alike. Because, of course, it is. We just sometimes lose sight of that.

CHAPTER 9

Social Studies
and Friendship

"A few weeks ago, my six-year-old son Sam and his friends were playing ball hockey on our driveway. Ben came home with a new child on our block, and some of the other kids started teasing this boy about his last name. Sam didn't join in the teasing. In fact, he went up to one of the eight-year-olds who was doing the teasing and said, 'There is nothing funny about his last name.' The older kids continued to snicker. Sam went up to this same kid again and said quite loudly, 'It's not funny. His name isn't funny.' At that point, the older child skated away. The eight-year-old had been put in his place by a six-year-old, and I couldn't have been more proud."
—*Mary, 36, mother of three*

We spend plenty of time helping our kids to master the nuts-and-bolts skills required to thrive in the land of childhood—how to tie their shoelaces, do up their buttons, and ride their bikes—but sometimes we forget that kids can benefit from a little coaching on the friendship front, too. Although some kids seem to have a knack for making friends right from day one, others require a much lengthier apprenticeship as social caterpillars before they are ready to join the ranks of the ever-confident social butterflies.

Make sure that you have a solid understanding of what is—and n't—age-appropriate behavior when it comes to kids and friendship. You don't want to be too tough on your child when he's still a relative beginner in the friendship department, nor do you want to turn a blind eye to overly aggressive behavior.

You can get an indication of what type of behavior is typical for kids your child's age by observing other children on the playground, talking to other parents with kids the same age, or loading up on child development books at the library. Just remember: there's considerable variation in what constitutes "normal," so don't assume that there's necessarily cause for concern if your child happens to be a bit more or less outgoing than other kids the same age.

In this chapter, I talk about the important role that parents have to play in teaching kids the friendship ropes. I start out by talking about how you can go about determining how well your child is doing socially and what to do if your child seems to be having a tougher-than-average time on the social front. Next, I tackle the age-old problem of bullying—specifically, why parents, teachers, and kids have to be prepared to tackle this particular problem head-on. Finally, I wrap up the chapter by talking about the major social occasions in your child's life—think play dates, birthday parties, sleepovers, and summer camp—and how to deal with the fact that another family's rules may not necessarily be quite in synch with your own. (How's *that* for an understatement?)

Friendship 101

Figure your eight-year-old should simply know what it takes to get along with other kids?

Then how come some corporate executives feel compelled to fork over the big bucks to hire high-priced consultants to teach their staff members the kind of skills we expect kids to know intuitively: conflict resolution, assertiveness training, and (my personal favorite!) how to get along with difficult people? After all, if your average 40-year-old can still benefit from a little added coaching in these areas, isn't it asking a lot to expect a typical kid to have all these social skills down pat?

What parents (myself included) sometimes seem to forget is that kids generally need to be taught the ins and outs of being a good friend. This stuff doesn't generally come naturally. After all, we humans don't come programmed with a microchip to tell us when to share our toys, what to do when our best friend makes up an outrageous lie about us, and how *not* to lose our cool when we find out we've just been left off the birthday party invitation list of the kid we *thought* was our best friend. These are all lessons that have to be learned through the Friendship School of Hard Knocks. (Don't you just wish some days that you could enroll your child in a different school?)

 NO KIDDING!

According to a recent study at the University of Michigan, kids' friendships are frequently modeled on their parents' friendships. The researchers found that kids whose parents exhibited strong conflict-resolution abilities and who were consistently willing to go out of their way to help their friends were likely to exhibit these same traits in their relationships with their own friends.

With so many things to teach your child about friendship, the job may feel completely overwhelming. Fortunately, I've got good news for you. You don't have to teach your child everything there is to learn in a day, a week, a month, or even a year. You've got 18 years to conduct this anything-but-crash course. Here are some tips to keep in mind as you go about teaching your child what friendship is all about:

- **Make sure that you're setting a good example for your child in the friendship department.** Everyone knows that kids don't pay nearly as much attention to what you say as to what you do. The best way to teach your children how to be a friend is to set a good example yourself. Let your children see you modeling the very behaviors that you're trying to teach them about: listening, sharing, respect, and so on, advises Mary, a 36-year-old mother of three: "I know so many people who will talk to a friend on the phone and then hang up and start bad-mouthing the person. You need to think about what you're teaching your children."

- **Give some thought to the friendship lessons that are being taught within the family, too.** Children who see mutual respect and caring modeled between family members are likely to find it easier to form friendships with their peers. If, on the other hand, they have been exposed to a lot of unhealthy interactions between family members (that is, your dinnertime conversations are beginning to sound like something that could show up on *The Jerry Springer Show*), the fallout on the friendship front can be highly negative; studies have shown that kids who come from troubled backgrounds are likely to gravitate toward equally troubled peers.

- **Make sure that your child has plenty of chances to play with other children.** Practice makes perfect when it comes to friendship, as with everything else. A child who rushes from school to piano lessons to soccer won't have the opportunity to learn the social ropes to the same degree as a child who has a bit more downtime built in his schedule. Don't assume that your child doesn't need a chance to socialize with his classmates because he's with them all day at school. Incidentally, the school environment tends to be highly structured, so your child is unlikely to get the same opportunity to stretch his social muscles in class as he would by going bike riding with a bunch of his buddies after school.

- **Encourage your child to talk to you about his friends.**
  By showing interest in his circle of friends, you'll show your
  child how important you think it is to have friends, and
  you'll encourage him to work on developing his social side.
  You'll also have the opportunity to get to know his friends
  a little better—something that can provide you with valuable insights into your child's personality and social skills at
  the same time.

- **Turn your child's world into a friendship laboratory.**
  Look for opportunities to discuss other people's behavior—
  the real-life behavior that you witness in the grocery store,
  the TV scriptwriters' version of human behavior, and, of
  course, you'll want to be sure to talk about the behavior of
  the characters in your child's favorite storybooks or novels,
  too. Discussing examples of people acting kindly toward
  one another or treating friends badly can teach your child a
  lot about what it means to be a good friend. It can also lead
  to some fascinating discussions about human psychology,
  ethics, and other heavy-duty topics that will only serve to
  deepen your child's understanding of life.

- **Help your child to learn how to read body language.**
  Sarcasm is often lost on young children because they have
  a hard time interpreting the eye-rolling and other over-the-
  top body language that indicates that what's being said is
  being said in jest. This makes it easy for them to misinter-
  pret what is actually being said—something that can lead
  to trouble on the playground.

- **Teach your child empathy.** Encourage your child to try to
  figure out what other people are feeling—either by reading
  their body language or by considering how they themselves
  would feel if they found themselves in that particular situation. This strategy can work particularly well in helping to
  defuse conflicts between younger and older siblings.

Sometimes, when older kids stop to consider the underlying motivation behind a toddler's out-of-control behavior—he missed his nap and now his favorite teddy bear is missing in action!—they may find it easier to be a little more sympathetic to their younger brother's plight. (Well, at least in theory.)

MOM'S THE WORD

"My kids have been playing tag a lot lately. One child is slower than the others and ends up being 'it' all the time. One day, I went out to see why he was crying and he said, 'I've been 'it' 10 times and I want someone else to take a turn.' I asked the other kids how many times they'd had being 'it,' and they admitted that some of them hadn't been 'it' at all. Then I asked them to put themselves in Bill's shoes and imagine what it was like to be stuck being 'it' all the time. They thought about it, shrugged their shoulders, chose someone else to be 'it,' and came up with a new rule: you only have to be 'it' three times. After that, you can pick someone else to take your place. Do my efforts to teach my kids about kindness pay off? I hope so! I would hate to think I've been talking to them about all this stuff for nothing!"

—*Cathy, 37, mother of two*

- **Help your child to come up with a game plan for potentially difficult situations.** Teach your child how to anticipate problems that he may encounter on the friendship front and then help him to brainstorm some possible ways of dealing with the problems. You may, for example, help your smaller-than-average son to develop a series of comeback lines that he can draw upon if some larger kid decides to tease him about his size. He'll be less likely to feel intimidated in such a situation if he already has a rough game plan in mind for dealing with the teasing.

- **Make sure that your child has mastered the basic social graces.** Although not knowing which fork to use in a fancy restaurant is unlikely to have too big an impact on your seven-year-old's social life, he'll score more points with potential playmates if he knows how to say "please" and "thank you" and how to wait his turn. Kids who don't know how to treat other kids with respect quickly become the outcasts of the playground.

- **Give your child the opportunity to participate in "random acts of kindness."** Doing kind things for others—such as helping you to make a casserole for a relative who just had a baby or raking leaves for an elderly neighbor—can help to encourage such traits as kindness and empathy, the essential building blocks to becoming a good friend.

- **When your child has a friend over, take note of how the relationship dynamics between the two children play out.** Is there a healthy amount of give and take in the relationship, or is one child clearly dominating the other? If you notice that your child always seems to be bossing his friends around or that he always lets other children make the decisions about what the two of them are going to do, chances are he would benefit from a little coaching from you on how to negotiate more effectively with his friends.

- **Be prepared to step in if you think your child is being bossy or mean.** If your child is still quite young and his behavior is obviously causing one of his friends a great deal of distress, you may want to intervene in the dispute. Otherwise, it's generally best to speak to your child about the problem in private, either by calling him into the kitchen for a quick huddle while his friend waits in the family room or by doing a post-visit analysis of his friendship strategy after his friend has gone home.

- **Nip any aggressive behavior in the bud.** Even though a certain amount of aggression is to be expected from very young children (expected, but not excused, mind you), there's no reason to tolerate it in school-aged kids. Aggressive behavior tends to reach its peak between the ages of two and four, but then it declines as kids start to master better self-control and get a better handle on what is expected of them socially. If your child continues to behave aggressively after this age, you will want to help him to work on developing his anger management skills. (See Chapter 4.)

- **Praise your child when you see him behaving kindly toward his friends.** Of course, you don't want to focus exclusively on those behaviors that you don't like; you also want to make a point of letting him know when you think he's done a really nice thing for a friend or when you think he's handled a difficult situation with particular finesse. It's just as important to praise your child for acts of kindness and generosity as it is to gently correct him if he starts showing signs of being overly controlling or mean to his friends. Besides, a healthy dose of praise from you will help to reinforce those friendship behaviors you would like to see a little more often.

MOM'S THE WORD

"My five-year-old recently had a friend over to play. She thought that she should be the one to make the rules and decide what to play. I ended up having to intervene. When my daughter made an even bigger fuss about not getting her own way, I ended up sending her to her room and letting her eight-year-old sister play with the friend instead."

—Christine, 38, mother of four

- **Try to get a sense of how well your child gets along with other children when you're not around.** Your child's childcare provider or teacher should be able to tell you if the social patterns you've observed on the home front jibe with what she's noticed about your child when the two of them are together. She may be able to provide you with some valuable insights into the types of situations that your child finds the most challenging: perhaps he gets along just fine when he only has to work with one or two of his peers, but he can't seem to cope with the added chaos of large group activities, for example.

MOTHER WISDOM

Kids with speech and language delays may experience greater difficulty making friends because they may have a hard time picking up on all the language nuances and verbal and nonverbal cues required to truly understand what's being communicated. Consequently, they may miss out on some of the inside jokes and secret-sharing that help to cement friendships during middle childhood.

- **Be on the lookout for signs of trouble on the friendship front.** If your child seems to have difficulty making or keeping friends, encourage him to talk openly about what he thinks the problem may be. Then make a point of observing him when he's with his friends so that you can try to pick up some clues about what may be causing him so many difficulties. Learning how to make and keep friends is an important skill, so you may want to arrange for your child to see a counselor if he seems to be struggling socially. Note: Your child may be at a disadvantage in the friendship department if he has a behavioral problem or an emotional or learning disorder. If your child comes across as "different" or his behavior is extreme, other kids may simply not want to be bothered with him. A counselor can help your child to come up with strategies to deal with the problem.

MOTHER WISDOM

If your child is painfully shy, try to provide some nonthreatening opportunities to work on his social skills. Encourage him to invite a friend to tag along the next time your family is planning an outing to the movies. Your child won't find his role as host quite so arduous if he only has to worry about engaging in small talk while waiting for the movie to start.

- **Be prepared to rewrite the friendship "curriculum" on an ongoing basis as your child matures.** Realize that the lessons that you teach your child about friendship will become increasingly more complex as your child's friendships become more intricate and more mature. When your children are very young, the toughest lesson they'll have to master is the art of sharing—no easy task, by the way, for a three-year-old who is determined not to let anyone else at daycare come within a yard of his favorite bucket of blocks. Then, by the time your kids start grade school, it's on to the Golden Rule ("Do unto others as you would have others do unto you")—something that is guaranteed to spark endless discussions around the dinner table. (My kids always want to know if this means you can be rotten to someone who was rotten to you first. Hey, it's a legitimate question!) As your children continue to grow older, their friendships will become increasingly complex, and you'll no doubt find yourself being asked to weigh in with an opinion on issues that could give Ph.D. ethicists a rip-roaring headache: when it's appropriate for friends to have secrets and when it's not; why it's not a good idea to gossip about one friend with another friend; and if it's ever okay to lie to spare a friend's feelings.

It's a girl thing . . .

At around grade six, friendships between girls start to become much more intense and more exclusive. The whole idea of having a "best friend" becomes almost irresistible—and not having a best friend a fate almost too painful to contemplate.

You can see the whole "best friend" phenomenon playing out on the schoolyard at recess—two girls huddled together having intense discussions, acting and sounding like an old married couple. Because girls spend so much time talking, there's a much greater opportunity for feelings to get hurt, bickering to start, and best friends to go their separate ways.

"Girls are very fickle," says Karen, a 35-year-old mother of three. "Today, they like you, tomorrow they don't. And when they don't, look out! They talk about you behind your back to everyone else, spreading rumors and lies. True friendships between girls can be very strong—almost unbreakable—but the more ordinary friendships come and go and, unfortunately, can cause a lot of pain, heartache, and frustration along the way."

 **NO KIDDING!**

Although parents often worry that there's something wrong with their child having a single best friend, there's nothing wrong with children having exclusive friendships, other than the inherent risk that goes along with having all your eggs in one friendship basket. As long as the two kids are having a positive effect on one another—that is, they aren't operating like some sort of Dennis the Menace tag team!—child development experts say there's generally no need for parents to worry about the two kids stifling one another's social growth. Odds are they'll start making friends with other children eventually, too.

While Anita, a 40-year-old mother of four, has always known that friendships between girls can be nasty, she hadn't expected the head games to be a part of her twin daughters' grade one experience: "I have been shocked and surprised by how early a pecking order is established—who's the prettiest, who has the nicest hair or clothes, who's a prima donna, who's a bully, etc.—and by some of the cattiness I've witnessed among very young girls. My daughters are only in grade one and right now it seems that friendships change weekly based on who was nice to them recently and who was not."

. . . and a boy thing

Although girls tend to be big on highly intense one-on-one friendships, boys generally prefer to do things in groups, and, more often than not, their friendship is based on shared enjoyment of a particular activity. Rather than limiting themselves to a single best friend, boys are more likely to have a pool of different friends to draw upon at any given time.

 NO KIDDING!

At around age six, kids who happily played with either boys or girls suddenly become more interested in playing with kids of the same sex. Then, after a few years of hanging out with kids of their own sex, mixed-gender peer groups become the norm.

Preteens enjoy spending time hanging around at recess, talking and teasing one another. Although it may look to adults like they're standing around doing nothing, they're actually practicing valuable predating behaviors that will serve them well during the teen years and beyond. (Yes, Moms and Dads, the mating dance starts early!)

With Friends Like These . . .

Most kids can expect to go through at least the odd rough patch while they're trying to figure out what it means to have and be a friend. Here's how to help your child deal with two common but difficult scenarios: making a poor choice in a friend and coping with teasing.

You can't choose your child's friends—or can you?

We've all managed to do it at least once in our lives: striking up a friendship with someone who is just plain bad news. Over time, we manage to figure out that this person is less than all-star material in the friendship area, but the process of making that discovery can be extremely painful for all concerned.

What leads a child to strike up a friendship with this particular child as opposed to that particular child is one of those questions that has fascinated social scientists (and parents!) for years. There's some research to indicate that friendship choices may be influenced by genetics: that, like adults, kids deliberately seek out others who share their interests and who have similar personality traits. Some studies have even shown that kids tend to gravitate toward other kids who hold the same core values as their own parents. Of course, in some cases, opposites attract: your child may be drawn to a friend who has a particular personality trait or ability your child admires. There may also be some truth to your long-standing observation that your kids' friends tend to bring out either the best or the worst in them: a child's traits can be magnified by his peers—something that goes a long way toward explaining why a group of rowdy kids hanging out together suddenly becomes exponentially rowdier! Of course, as your child's hobbies, interests, and needs and wants in a friend change, his group of peers can change dramatically, too. Don't expect to see the same group of kids hanging out in your family room from kindergarten through high school. Odds are there will be at least a bit of turnover from year to year.

Sometimes your child will bring home a friend who is so unlike him that you have to stop yourself from staring at the two of them in an effort to try to figure out what the basis for this friendship may be—what on earth your hockey-worshipping son could possibly have in common with his violin-toting friend. In most cases, these friendships are more cause for fascination than for concern. Sometimes, however, your child strikes up a friend-ship with a child who seems to be just plain bad news—a modern-day Eddie Haskell type who is setting off all the alarm circuits in your parental radar.

In most cases, it's best to allow your child to make his friend-ship decisions for himself. If you've noticed a disturbing deterio-ration in his own behavior since he's started hanging out with a particular friend, you'll find it generally works best to focus on dealing with the behavior problem (that is, having firm conse-quences for any family rules that your child broke while his friend was visiting) rather than attempting to ban the friend. The reason is obvious: if you try to ban a particular friend, you run the risk of making that friend all the more desirable and sim-ply driving the friendship underground. (As Karen, a 35-year-old mother of three puts it, "If you try to tell your child who not to be friends with, you can bet you have just picked your child's new best friend, even if that friendship happens entirely behind your back.") Hopefully, if you're consistent about disciplining your child for any rules he and his friends break while his friend is visiting, he'll get sick of being in trouble every time his friend comes over to play and eventually ditch the friend.

Although there may be times when you may feel a need to take a hard line and ban a particular friend from your home—if, for example, a particular child has been caught stealing money from your purse or bullying one of your other children—you'll be more likely to get buy-in from your child if you ask him to help you to brainstorm a solution to the problem—something that Karen learned when her daughter struck up a friendship with a girl who turned out to be just plain bad news. "Alicia had a friend who was going through some difficulties at home, so we tried to include her in our family outings, and we made a point of welcoming her into our home. Unfortunately, she took advan-tage of the situation. She was rude to us and stole from us. Alicia and I discussed the situation and agreed that, even though we felt badly for her, we did not deserve to be treated in that manner. Alicia did not want to confront her friend about the problem, so asked if it would be okay if she simply stopped being available when her friend called. I wanted to call her parents, but I agreed to follow Alicia's lead on this because it was her friend. Now, several years later, the girl still calls from time to time, and Alicia continues to tell her she's busy."

At the same time that you are gently discouraging a particular friendship, you may also want to make it easier for your child to develop a friendship with another friend who may appear to you to be a more suitable choice. If your child is in the process of ending a friendship with a neighborhood friend who has been in trouble with the police, you may want to offer to take your child and a different friend on an outing to the amusement park or some other area attraction in order to give this new friendship a chance to gel.

MOM'S THE WORD

"You may not be able to 'choose' your child's friends, but you can determine where and when they hang out."

—*Tracie, 27, mother of two*

The truth about teasing

Kids sometimes have a hard time knowing what to make of teasing. After all, name-calling, sarcasm, put-downs, and rudeness are often depicted on TV and in other forms of pop culture as normal—even "fun"—ways for family members to relate to one another. More often than not, however, teasing is a blatant power grab—an attempt to assert control over another person or gain approval from a group of peers by knocking others down.

If your child is the one being teased, let him know that you empathize with him and that you don't consider teasing to be a laughing matter. Help him to brainstorm some possible ways of dealing with the problem—for example, refusing to continue to play basketball with a group of friends who continually criticize his athletic abilities—and make sure that he understands that the less he reacts to the teasing, the less of a payoff the person doing the teasing receives. Depending on the circumstances, your child may want to challenge the teasing by making a joke that makes him look smarter or funnier than the person doing the teasing. If one of the kids on the basketball court likes to take potshots at him because of his height, he may simply respond by smiling and quipping, "Hey, I may be short, but I'm fast!"

If, on the other hand, your child is the one doing the teasing, you may need to remind him that words can hurt and to encourage him to think about how he would feel if he were on the receiving end of all that teasing. You may also want to consider whether there could be some underlying problem in your child's life that's responsible for all the teasing—perhaps feelings of insecurity on his own part or good old-fashioned boredom. (Getting a rise out of another child can substitute for other forms of entertainment on a day when there's nothing else to do, which explains why teasing and bickering between siblings always seems to be at its worst when everyone's restless and at loose ends.) Finally, you may want to remind him that there's a very fine line between teasing and bullying and that you don't want him to take a chance of stepping over that line.

What Every Parent Needs to Know About Bullying

While you may have been hoping that bullying had disappeared since your own growing-up years, like it or not, it's alive and well and thriving in your local schoolyard. According to the National Youth Violence Prevention Resource Center (www.safeyouth. org), approximately 30 percent of students in grades six through ten are involved in moderate or frequent bullying—as bullies, as victims, or both—at any given time.

Bullying can take a variety of different forms:

- Physical bullying (pushing, shoving, hitting, tripping, and other acts designed to physically harm another person)

- Verbal bullying (insults, harassment, taunts, and other verbally aggressive behavior, whether verbally or in writing)

- Emotional intimidation or "relational aggression" (withdrawing friendship or rejecting someone as a means of asserting control over that person)

- Racial bullying (mocking racial traditions, spray painting racist graffiti, uttering racial slurs, and engaging in other racist behavior)

- Sexual bullying (making sexual comments about the victim or engaging in unwanted sexual touching)

 NO KIDDING!
E-mail and instant messaging bullying is becoming an increasingly common bullying problem among the preteen crowd.

 NO KIDDING!
Wondering how often bullying occurs? When a group of Canadian researchers used remote microphones and video cameras to observe students in an elementary school playground, they discovered that acts of bullying occurred once every seven minutes on average.

Although boys tend to resort to more physical forms of bullying—punching, hitting, tripping, and kicking—girls resort to what bullying experts refer to as *relational aggression*—gossiping, excluding, and the withdrawal of friendship to manipulate other people's behavior.

"Boys are physically tough, but girls are just as cruel to other girls," notes Janie, a 34-year-old mother of one. "Some of my most horrible days were in grades seven and eight. I will never forget what it was like to be picked on by a group of girls. I will do anything I can to protect my own daughter from that fate."

The fallout of bullying

There's no denying the fallout of bullying. Children who are bullied frequently experience depression, anxiety, and other psychological difficulties. They are more likely to be absent from school, and they tend to be more susceptible to peer pressure than other children, having learned the hard way what can happen if you don't go along with the group.

The fallout from bullying doesn't stop there. An act of bullying can hurt children other than the victim, too. Research has shown that children who witness bullying can be afraid to go to school, too, worrying that one minor misstep on their part may cause them to become the bully's next victim. Or, they may start throwing punches or firing off insults themselves, figuring that they would be further ahead siding with the aggressor than the victim.

Even the bullies end up with some collateral damage. If they are allowed to get away with their behavior, they learn unhealthy means of relating to other people—something that can set them up for a lifetime of relationship problems.

 NO KIDDING!

That old myth about bullies suffering from low self-esteem is just that—a myth. Bullies tend to be more confident than other children and to make friends with ease. Victims, on the other hand, tend to have greater difficulties forming friendships and are more likely to lack confidence on the friendship front.

What parents and teachers can do
to stamp out bullying

Bullying typically occurs when few adults are on hand to deal with the problem, and, to make matters worse, when victims are often reluctant to report what has occurred, both out of fear of possible repercussions and because they're simply not convinced that adults will actually be able to do anything meaningful to make the bullying stop. Even when adults are aware that bullying is occurring, they may fail to take all but the most life-threatening incidents of bullying seriously, feeling that kids should be left to resolve their problems on their own—the old "kids will be kids" school of thought. The net result is that adults end up intervening in only 4 percent of bullying incidents.

Wondering what you can do to help stamp out bullying? Here's what the experts suggest:

- **Make it difficult for bullying behaviors to take root by fostering a climate of empathy in your home.** Don't tolerate cruelty in any form, whether in real life or in the form of nasty jokes on sitcoms or in other forms of entertainment. Let your child know that he has a right to insist that others treat him with respect and dignity.

- **Make sure that the no-bullying policy in your family applies to grown-ups as well as kids.** You can't very well criticize your child for bullying her friends or her little brother—and then turn around and use the same bullying tactics on her.

- **Keep an eye on your child's choice of entertainment.** Limit your child's exposure to violent video games, lyrics, and TV programs, as well as violent toys such as guns— basically anything that glorifies violence or suggests that violence is an acceptable means of solving problems.

- **Keep an ongoing dialogue with your child about bullying.** Discuss any bullying stories that happen to be in the news. That way, if your child encounters any bullying problems in his own life, he'll be more likely to open up and talk to you about those problems. If he does open up and tell you that he's being picked on by another kid at school, help him to come up with some constructive strategies for dealing with the problem.

- **Encourage your child to make friends.** Bullies are more likely to target children who are loners, so having friends can provide a measure of protection against bullying.

- **Teach your child the importance of body language.** A child who exudes confidence and who appears to be in control is less likely to get picked on than a child who sends off less confident body signals.

- **Be alert to the warning signs that your child could be being bullied.** Children are often reluctant to tell teachers and parents that they are being bullied, either due to embarrassment or a fear of reprisal, so it's important to be on the lookout for the warning signs of bullying. You should at least consider the possibility that your child may be being bullied if:

  - you notice sudden changes to your child's behavior

  - your child is spending more time fighting with his siblings

  - your child has a lot of unexplained cuts and bruises

  - your child's clothing is frequently ripped or dirty

  - your child is suddenly unwilling to go to school (see Chapter 7 for more about school avoidance)

- your child is unusually hungry after school (an i̇ tion that his lunch may have been stolen or his lu money extorted)

- your child's grades begin to slip (an indication that your child's bullying experiences may be making it difficult for him to concentrate on his school work)

- **Explain the difference between tattling and telling to your child.** Make sure that your child understands that there's a world of difference between *tattling*—telling on someone simply because you want to get that person in trouble—and *telling*—reporting a serious problem to an adult. Kids need to know that it's okay to report instances of bullying to parents and teachers.

MOM'S THE WORD

"My son witnessed an incident of bullying, and I contacted the school. I was so proud of him because he had told me what had happened. I told him how much he had helped the children who were being bullied. They hadn't told anyone what was going on."

—*Denise, 35, mother of three*

- **Encourage bystanders to blow the whistle on bullies.** Bystanders have an important role to play in discouraging bullying. According to research by Canadian psychologist Debra Peppler of Toronto's York University, bullying behavior typically stops within 10 seconds if another child intervenes. Given that there are bystanders on hand in fully 85 percent of bullying instances, peer intervention is perhaps the most powerful weapon available to help combat bullying.

- **Find ways to hold bullies accountable.** When parents get involved and insist on restitution—that the bully find a way to make things right for the victim—bullying becomes a much less attractive proposition for the bully. Bullies need to know that the adults in their life will not tolerate such behavior and that they will be held accountable for their actions. Unfortunately, when adults *don't* follow through in bullying situations, they risk letting the victim down in a major way. "My son was the victim of a bully who lives down the street," recalls Jill, a 34-year-old mother of four. "He was picked on and pushed around. When he reported the incident to the duty teacher at school, he was told he was acting like a baby and to deal with it. I was outraged and called the school. The school was no help whatsoever. I then called the child's mother and was told off by her in no uncertain terms. My son was labeled as a crybaby—a label which still persists. We had told him that if he was bullied, he was to tell the person in charge, and, in this case, they failed him miserably."

 NO KIDDING!

Bullying is most likely to occur around age 7 and between the ages of 10 and 12.

The New Kid on the Block: Helping Your Child to Settle in after a Move

Moving can be a highly stressful event in the life of a child. Not only is your child forced to say goodbye to all of his old friends but he also finds himself thrust into the rather unenviable

- your child is unusually hungry after sch′ tion that his lunch may have been stolen oɩ money extorted)

- your child's grades begin to slip (an indication that your child's bullying experiences may be making it difficult for him to concentrate on his school work)

- **Explain the difference between tattling and telling to your child.** Make sure that your child understands that there's a world of difference between *tattling*—telling on someone simply because you want to get that person in trouble—and *telling*—reporting a serious problem to an adult. Kids need to know that it's okay to report instances of bullying to parents and teachers.

MOM'S THE WORD

"My son witnessed an incident of bullying, and I contacted the school. I was so proud of him because he had told me what had happened. I told him how much he had helped the children who were being bullied. They hadn't told anyone what was going on."

—*Denise, 35, mother of three*

- **Encourage bystanders to blow the whistle on bullies.** Bystanders have an important role to play in discouraging bullying. According to research by Canadian psychologist Debra Peppler of Toronto's York University, bullying behavior typically stops within 10 seconds if another child intervenes. Given that there are bystanders on hand in fully 85 percent of bullying instances, peer intervention is perhaps the most powerful weapon available to help combat bullying.

Play Date Do's and Don'ts

A play date can either provide your preschooler or school-aged child with a valuable opportunity to practice his socialization skills or cause him to swear off sharing his toys with any other kid for the rest of his life! Here's what you need to ensure that your child's play date career gets off on the best possible footing:

- **Impose time limits.** Keep the play date short until you're sure that your child is up to playing host for an extended period of time. Sometimes, very young children decide midway through the play date that they want their own toys back and they're tired of sharing their turf (and their stuff!) with other kids.

- **Try to steer clear of threesomes.** It's too easy for one child to get left out if the other two kids buddy up. If you can't convince your child to stick to one guest (not a bad idea, by the way, if he's still learning the play date ropes), make sure that you invite three guests rather than two so that the kids can pair off in two groups of two.

- **Involve your child in the planning.** Encourage your child to decide ahead of time what he would like to do while his friends are visiting. You want him to assume responsibility for coming up with a list of things to do. This is a great time to establish rules regarding TV and video-game use (see Chapter 8). If you don't want your child turning on the television or firing up his video-game system when his friends are over, your child needs to know this ahead of time so that he can avoid making promises to his friends that he won't be able to keep—something that could prove embarrassing if he happened to promise his friend a chance to play his brand new video game before he found out about your "no video games when friends are over" rule.

- **Establish ground rules early.** Make sure that your child is equally clear about which parts of the house are off limits while friends are over. You don't want your child thinking it's okay to entertain his friend by jumping on your bed or digging through your dresser drawers! Make sure that he knows right from the get-go that he's ultimately responsible for any messes that his friend makes while his friend is a guest in your home: that way, he'll have an added incentive to encourage his friend to help him pick up as the two of them go from activity to activity.

- **Entertain your other kids.** Make a point of keeping your child's other siblings at bay while he has friends over. It's not fair to saddle your child with the responsibility of caring for a younger sibling while he's trying to entertain a friend. Doing so will only lead to friction between siblings—a lose-lose proposition all around.

Birthday Parties

Just when you think you've seen it all on the birthday party front, some parent in your neighborhood is likely to up the ante a little, proving that there's no limit to what some parents are willing to do or spend in order to celebrate their child's birthday in style.

If you've long since given up on the whole idea of trying to keep up with the Joneses when it comes to kids' birthday parties, this section is for you. Here are some ideas for cheap and cheerful birthday parties that prove without a doubt that you don't have to take out a second mortgage in order to host a supremely cool birthday party bash for your child. (Obviously, you could come up with hundreds of other terrific ideas of your own. I simply wanted to give you a quick overview of what's possible. So let the birthday games begin.)

- **Gardening Gala:** Give preschoolers the chance to plant bulbs or seeds at this one-of-a-kind birthday bash. (Obviously, you'll want to tip the party guests' parents off to the theme ahead of time so that none of the kids show up in ultra-frilly party dresses!)

- **Potato Printmaking Party:** Ask your three-year-old to pick a theme for his potato print paint party before the guests arrive so that you can carve the potatoes into the appropriate shapes (for example, sun, moon, and stars if you're going for a celestial theme). Then cover the kitchen table with butcher paper and trays of washable poster paints and set the party guests loose with the potatoes and the paints.

MOTHER WISDOM

No matter what theme you decide to go with, it's important to have a few backup activities up your sleeve—unless, of course, you don't mind the kids entertaining themselves by running around the house at breakneck speed and/or trying wrestling moves on one another. Your backup plan could be something as simple as signing a science activity book out of the library so that you can do some kitchen science projects in a pinch or digging up the copy of Twister that you liberated from your parents' home when you headed off to college. (Come on, 'fess up! You're the one who walked off with the game, now weren't you?)

- **Garage Graffiti:** Cover your garage door in heavy-duty craft paper and hand out washable markers, roll-on deodorant bottles filled with washable paint, and art supplies.

- **Crafty Solution:** Got a kid who positively lives and breathes crafts? A craft party is a natural. As an added bonus, the flower pots or picture frames that the party guests spend their time decorating during the party make ideal grab bag fare.

- **Homegrown Magic:** If you're entertaining a group of young school-aged kids, see whether you can arm-twist one of your kid's older cousins into doing magic tricks for the party guests. (Note: If you're hoping to entertain older kids, you'll probably have to spring for a professional magician. It won't be fun for the kids or the magician if they're able to figure out the "magic" behind each of the tricks.)

- **Mad Science:** A lab coat, a wig, a pair of nerdy glasses, a book of science experiments, and—of course—a larger-than-life persona are generally all that's required to play the part of the mad scientist. You can either play the role of Einstein yourself or hire a neighborhood teen to help out.

- **Road Hockey:** If road hockey is the passion *du jour* of your birthday boy or girl, ask each birthday guest to bring a hockey stick to the party. Let it be known that you'll be supplying the three Ps: pop, pizza, and the puck!

- **Backyard Olympics:** Introduce your kids to such classic picnic games as the three-legged race, the bean-bag toss, the sack race, and so on. If you're dealing with an extra-tough crowd (that is, a group of preteens), you may want to throw in an added twist by suggesting that the party-goers try some of the picnic games after dark, in the swimming pool, and/or while blindfolded!

- **Do-It-Yourself Disco:** Make your own music tapes by recording selected tracks from an assortment of albums— either current favorites from your preteen's music collection or picks from some vintage disco albums scooped up at a second-hand store. Borrow a lava lamp or disco ball from a friend or neighbor (that is, if you don't have one stashed in the closet) and prepare yourself for an outbreak of *Saturday Night Fever!*

- **Home Spa Day:** Treat your preteen daughter and her friends to a day at Spa Chez Vous. The party guests can have fun making all kinds of homemade spa delights—everything from cucumber facial masks to lip balm to bath fizzies. (Note: You can find all kinds of terrific home spa recipes in *The Herbal Home Spa*, by Greta Breedlove.)

- **Book Party:** If you've got a child who loves to read and who happens to hang out with an equally bookish crowd, a book party could be the ticket to birthday party nirvana. Everything from the party invitations to the party games can be tied into the book theme, with wonderfully creative results.

MOTHER WISDOM

If you're hosting your child's birthday off-site at a busy children's attraction, make sure to stick to a suitable parent-child ratio and give serious thought to dressing all of the kids in the same color of T-shirt—ideally a particularly vibrant shade of neon green or yellow! Obviously, this particular tactic will only work with very young kids—your odds of convincing a preteen to wear an uncool T-shirt are pretty much slim-to-none!—but it's worth considering if you're planning to take a group of six-year-olds out on the town.

By the way, if you're stuck on ideas of where to take the gang, here's a list of some of the destinations suggested by the parents interviewed for this book: an art gallery, bowling alley, children's museum, aquarium, planetarium, indoor play space or gym, recreation center or swimming pool, miniature golf course, skating rink (ice skating or rollerskating), movie theater, beach, children's theater, or zoo.

MOTHER WISDOM

Rather than loading up on junk and candy for grab bags, send the party guests home with one genuinely useful item that ties into the party theme—a watering can and seeds if they've just attended a birthday party with a gardening theme, or a pair of inexpensive binoculars if they've just spent the evening gazing at the stars.

- **Seeing Stars:** Borrow a friend's telescope and help your child to host a backyard astronomy party. (Of course, you'll want to hedge your bets by renting a few kid-friendly astronomy videos, too, just in case Mother Nature decides to rain on your child's birthday party parade.)

- **Gallery Gala:** Not too keen on the thought of having your house invaded by a tribe of highly rambunctious kids? You can always take your party act on the road and head for the nearest children's museum, recreation center, or other kid-friendly venue.

- **Reel Fun:** Host a midnight movie madness birthday party—a late-night bash where the movie doesn't even get popped into the VCR or DVD player until midnight. While the kids are waiting for the movie to start, they can entertain themselves by making pizza, testing their knowledge of movie trivia, and making a reel-shaped party cake.

Sleepover Survival Tips

If your child's planning to celebrate her birthday party by hosting a sleepover, you've got a few additional issues to sort out. Here's what you need to know to help your child to make her sleepover party a success: (By the way, you'll notice that I'm assuming it's your daughter rather than your son who's hosting the sleepover. Although a growing number of boys are hosting sleepovers these days—and there are even a few co-ed sleepovers happening!—they're still very much "a girl thing," so I thought it made sense to use the female pronoun in this part of the chapter.)

- **Don't start sleepovers too early.** Children under the age of eight may not be ready to spend the night away from Mom or Dad, unless, of course, the sleepover happens to take place at the home of someone they know extremely well—perhaps the next-door neighbor or their favorite cousin.

- **Limit the number of invitees, particularly if your child is still quite young.** The more kids you have under one roof, the lower the likelihood of anyone (parents included!) getting any sleep.

- **Make sure that you've got plenty of snacks on hand.** As any veteran of the sleepover scene will tell you, sleepovers are much more about eating than sleeping. Of course, if you're going to be serving food, you need to find out about food allergies ahead of time. You don't want to find out *after* the pizza arrives that your child's best friend is allergic to tomatoes.

- **Help your child to come up with a list of games and activities for her party.** Sleepover guests are more likely to get lonely and homesick if there's nothing to do than if they're kept busy watching videos and playing games.

- **Make sure that any entertainment you have planned is age appropriate.** You wouldn't want your child tuning in to an R-rated flick at someone else's house, so make sure that you pay careful attention to what the kids are watching while they're in your home. As for horror flicks—the results can be just plain scary when you're dealing with younger kids. Unless you want to spend the rest of the night playing amateur shrink to a room full of terrorized eight-year-olds, you may want to veto anything scarier than *Casper the Friendly Ghost.*

- **Establish a clear "lights out" time—but make sure that it's not unreasonably early.** If you try to hustle the kids off to bed while everyone's still wired for sound, you'll end up fighting a losing battle against whispers and giggles in the dark. A better bet is to wait until the party guests are starting to show signs of genuine sleepiness and then gently encourage everyone to find their way to their sleeping bags.

- **Suggest a solution to the problem of sleeping arrangements.** To avoid hurt feelings about who is sleeping next to whom (a perennial hot potato at sleepovers!), suggest that the party guests sleep in star formation, with everyone's head pointed toward the center.

MOTHER WISDOM

If your child has been invited to a sleepover, make sure that the other child's parents have all the info they need to keep your child safe and happy—the "operating instructions," so to speak. You'll want to pass along information about any allergies, strange fears, bedwetting problems, medications, and so on.

You'll also want to make sure that your child packed the essentials: a novel to doze off with, her favorite stuffed animal—whatever it takes to get her through the night!

- **Make sure that the party guests know that they're welcome to wake you up if they're sick, scared, or lonely.** Be sure to leave a nightlight or two on so that the path to the bathroom is easy to navigate.

- **Firm up middle-of-the-night rescue arrangements with the parents of each of the sleepover attendees.** That way, if someone has a bad dream or becomes seriously homesick and insists that she needs to go home right away, you'll know for sure that it's perfectly okay to call her parents to schedule a 3 A.M. pickup!

Note: If your child is reluctant to accept sleepover invitations out of fear that she may end up wetting her sleeping bag while she's at the sleepover, you may want to talk to your child's pediatrician about medications that can help with the problem. See Chapter 10 for more about bedwetting.

Summer Camp SOS

Summer camp can be the best of times or the worst of times, depending on whether your child is ready for the experience. Here's how to tell whether your child is a good candidate for summer camp and what you can do to help him to prepare for what may very well be his first extended stay away from home:

- Decide whether your child has what it takes to thrive at overnight camp—or whether he may do better in a day camp environment for now. Very shy kids and kids who have never been away from home before sometimes find overnight camp a bit too overwhelming.

- Treat your child's camp-related concerns seriously. Even kids who are looking forward to camp can get hit with some last-minute heebie-jeebies. If there are some specific camp-related worries causing him to toss and turn at night—possibly a concern about being able to find his way from the cabin to the washrooms in the middle of the night—then see whether you can track down some concrete information to help lay that particular worry to rest. (Maybe the camp's Web site has some maps or other information that may help to reassure him.)

- Give your child a clear idea about what to expect. Make sure that your child has a clear idea about what the camp routine will be like—how many roommates he'll have, what the daily routine will be like, what kind of food will be served, and so on. That way, there won't be any last-minute surprises to deal with when he's on unfamiliar ground.

- Help your child to anticipate some of the kinds of problems he may encounter during his time at camp and to brainstorm some possible solutions. Just be careful not to go overboard when you're helping your child to anticipate possible problems. You don't want your child to head off to camp anticipating one nightmare after another. (Fun, wow!)

- Send a letter or "care package" to camp ahead of your child so that there will be something waiting for him when he arrives. Or simply tuck a little surprise away in his suitcase so that he'll stumble across it when he goes digging for his toothbrush that first night. (Of course, if your child tends to be a little, ahem, *hygiene challenged*, you may want to alert him to the fact that there's good reason for him to remember to brush his teeth. Otherwise, he could be on the bus on the way home—with very dirty teeth!—long before he ever finds his special surprise.)

MOTHER WISDOM

If there's any chance that your daughter could start her period while she's at summer camp, make sure you pack some sanitary pads in her suitcase and that you have a talk with her about how to use them. Otherwise, this particular rite of passage could prove to be a very awkward and embarrassing experience for your daughter. If you're unsure how to get the dialog started, plan to visit Tampax.com's "Mother to Daughter" area by yourself or www.beinggirl.com with your daughter.

"The Meanest Mom in the World": Dealing with Other Families' Rules

One of the more challenging issues you'll have to contend with as your child gets older is the fact that other families' rules are likely to be quite different from your own. Although you're unlikely to sweat the relatively small stuff—the fact that vegetables appear to be optional at their house and the kids are allowed to eat doughnuts for breakfast—you won't want to turn a blind eye if there are major discrepancies between the other family's values and your own—if, for example, they don't have a problem with co-ed sleepovers, while the mere idea of your preteen daughter bunking down beside a bunch of her 12-year-old male friends is enough to make your hair stand on end!

Of course, taking a tougher stand than your child's friend's parents pretty much guarantees you're a shoe-in for the title of "meanest mom in the world"—a title that some parents aren't embarrassed to hold in the least. "I cope with being the meanest mommy because I know the rules are set because I care about and love my children, and I make sure they know that," explains Kerri, a 37-year-old mother of six. "We compromise when we can. But I would rather be the meanie and keep my kids safe than to never be able to forgive myself if something happened because I didn't take my parenting responsibilities seriously enough to make the tough decisions."

📢 MOM'S THE WORD

"A big challenge I've just started to face is the fact that other families have far different latitudes when it comes to behavior. For example, one of my five-year-old daughter's little friends is allowed to run through the school and play in the parking lot while her mom speaks to the teachers. Meagan's tried that a couple of times and I've had to come down really hard on her for it—something that's led her to declare that she wishes she was the other mom's daughter! So not only do I have to discipline my child and remind her of some important safety rules, but I also have to keep explaining that other people have different rules than we do. At the moment this issue seems to be ongoing at our house."

—Judy, 33, mother of one

Ellen, a 30-year-old mother of two, agrees: "We cannot be our children's best friends. To do so is ineffective parenting. You can't give them everything; you can't always make them happy; and you can't protect them from everything. Part of being a good parent is doing the things that are difficult and not always taking the easy way out. The meanest mommy on the block may well be raising the most balanced kids!"

Although it would be violating the kid code of ethics to admit it, some kids are secretly happy to have a "mean" mom or dad waiting for them at home, insists Mary, a 36-year-old mother of three. "Our kids respect us for having firm rules. Too many kids are floating around without any boundaries, and this is what gets them into trouble. Having firm rules allows your child to say, 'No, I'm not allowed,' to their friends when they don't want to do something. It makes the parent look like the bad guy, and it also gives the kids an 'out' if they need one."

So try not to sweat it if your kids are giving you a lot of grief about how much nicer Jessica's Mom is—or how they *never* have to help clear off the dinner table when they're sleeping over at Andrew's house. Who's to say that the other parent's rules are right and yours are wrong? "Sometimes you just have to stick with what you are comfortable with," says Christine, a 38-year-old mother of four. "The kids may not like it, but they will appreciate your rules some day."

Shelly, a 32-year-old mother of two, agrees: "I try to take a long-term view. When the nicest mom in the world is visiting her child in prison, I'll be at my child's graduation from medical school. Mind you, I may be paying for years of therapy for him, but, hey, it's a tradeoff!"

CHAPTER 10

The Health Department

Those days of rushing off to the doctor's office every time your baby developed a fever or broke out in an unusual rash may be behind you, but that doesn't mean that health-related worries have fallen off your radar screen entirely. You're still likely to find yourself with lots of health-related questions at this stage of the game.

I've got a lot to say about kids and health—so much, in fact, that I devote the remaining four chapters of this book to health-related issues. Here's what you'll find on a chapter-by-chapter basis:

- In Chapter 10 (this chapter), I talk about doctor's visits; vaccinations; garden-variety childhood illnesses, such as head colds and ear infections; general pediatric health concerns, such as dental care and sleep disturbances; and what it's like to care for a child with a chronic physical or mental health problem.

- In Chapter 11, I talk about what's involved in keeping kids safe—specifically, what you need to know to help your child to steer clear of the most common types of childhood injuries.

- In Chapter 12, I talk about nutrition, fitness, childhood obesity, and what you can do to promote a healthy body image and reduce the odds that your child will develop an eating disorder.

- In Chapter 13, I talk about the challenging health and emotional issues that you can expect to face after your child steps on board that exciting roller coaster ride called puberty.

What's up, Doc?

You're no doubt a veteran of the doctor visit scene by now. After all, you've been taking your child for regular checkups since she was an infant, and you've probably made your fair share of "bonus" doctor visits over the years, whether to get some advice on dealing with ear infections or to pick up some tips on doing battle with the mystery virus du jour.

After your child enters the preschool and school years, you'll probably find that your trips to the doctor become a lot less frequent. In fact, there may be times in your child's life when you don't actually step foot in your doctor's waiting room between one annual checkup and the next. But, that doesn't mean that doctor's visits have suddenly become any less important. They still have a vital role to play in ensuring your child's continued good health. "Well-child" doctor's visits (also known as checkups) allow the doctor to keep tabs on your child's physical and emotional development and to spot the early warning signs of any possible problems.

During such a checkup, the doctor typically will:

- check your child's height and weight and conduct a thorough physical examination to see whether her development is on track

- check your child's blood pressure and vital signs

- screen for vision and hearing problems

- ask you questions about your child's overall health and development (something that allows the doctor to gather information about your child that may not otherwise be picked up during a routine physical examination)

- ensure that your child's immunizations are up to date (see the section on immunizations that follows)

- order follow-up tests if there are any areas of concern (for example, hearing tests if your child has had a history of ear infections and/or is experiencing some speech delays)

- answer any questions you may have about your child's health or development

- give you a heads-up regarding the types of health and developmental issues you're likely to face with your child between now and her next checkup, as well as general guidance on things you need to know about in order to keep your child safe and healthy (e.g., the latest advice on car seats, fluoride supplementation, fire safety prevention in the home, and a whole lot more).

Note: Don't be surprised if you get left in the waiting room for part or all of your child's doctor's visits after she hits the preteen years. Your doctor will want to make it possible for your child to feel free to discuss any health-related issue that may be of concern to her—particularly those issues that she may not necessarily feel comfortable discussing while you're within earshot.

MOTHER WISDOM

Doctors of preteens can find themselves engaged in a bit of a tightrope act as they attempt to balance issues of patient confidentiality with their responsibility to provide parents with essential information about their child's health—information that the child may or may not necessarily be able to convey accurately on her own.

Although the doctor may choose to limit what he tells you about his private discussions with your preteen or teen, you are free to provide the doctor with whatever information you feel he needs to have about your child in order to accurately assess her health and well-being. If, for example, you suspect that your daughter is battling anorexia or bulimia, you would want to let the doctor know about your concerns so that he could be particularly tuned into any possible signs and symptoms of an eating disorder. You could do this by calling your doctor's office in advance of your daughter's appointment or writing your doctor a letter. Remember, patient confidentiality concerns don't limit what you can tell your child's doctor. They only apply to what the doctor can tell you.

The Facts on Immunization

Although they've been the subject of much controversy over the years, immunizations continue to play a vital role in helping to protect children against disease—so vital, in fact, that the Advisory Committee on Immunization Practices (ACIP), the

American Academy of Pediatrics (AAP), and the American Academy of Family Physicians (AAFP) have all spoken out strongly in favor of the current practice of routinely immunizing American children against a number of potentially life-threatening diseases.

Although some side effects are associated with immunization, the vast majority tend to be relatively minor and short-lived. Given the overall benefits to public health, the case for having your child immunized is pretty compelling. Here are some noteworthy statistics from the Centers for Disease Control and Prevention:

- 13,000 to 20,000 cases of polio were reported each year in the United States prior to the development of the polio vaccination. None were reported in 2000.

- Measles vaccinations help to prevent 2.7 million deaths worldwide each year.

- Before the Haemophilus influenza type b (Hib) meningitis vaccination was developed, 600 children died each year as the result of this disease, and thousands of others suffered hearing loss or brain damage.

- Approximately 260,000 cases of whooping cough (Pertussis) were reported in the United States each year prior to the introduction of the Pertussis vaccine. The disease resulted in 9,000 deaths each year.

- Before the United States introduced its Rubella vaccination program, 10,000 infants were born each year with Congenital Rubella Syndrome (CRS), a condition that is characterized by heart defects, cataracts, mental retardation, and deafness. What's more, prenatal Rubella resulted in an additional 1,000 neonatal deaths and an additional 11,000 miscarriages each year.

- Up to 20 percent of children died from Diphtheria each year prior to the introduction of the Diphtheria vaccine.

- 212,000 cases of Mumps occurred each year in the United States prior to the introduction of the Mumps vaccine. Approximately 1 in every 20,000 children developing the disease became deaf as a result of contracting the Mumps. Others experienced other serious side effects, including swelling of the brain, nerves, and spinal cord resulting in paralysis, seizures, and fluid on the brain.

- Tetanus continues to kill 300,000 newborns worldwide each year. A significant number of deaths could be expected each year in the United States if the Tetanus immunization program were discontinued.

How immunizations work

Immunizations help the body produce antibodies against a particular disease. The majority of immunizations are injected (given as a shot). Still, as much as they've revolutionized pediatric health, immunizations aren't 100-percent effective. Studies have shown that up to 15 percent of children will fail to build up antibodies to a particular disease after receiving the appropriate immunization.

Here's what you need to know about the immunizations given to American children. (See Table 10.1 for a schedule outlining when these immunizations typically occur.)

TABLE 10.1

Recommended Childhood and Adolescent Immunization Schedule, United States, 2003

Legend: range of recommended ages | catch-up vaccination | preadolescent assessment

Vaccine ▼ \ Age ▶	Birth	1 mo	2 mos	4 mos	6 mos	12 mos	15 mos	18 mos	24 mos	4-6 yrs	11-12 yrs	13-18 yrs
Hepatitis B[1]	HepB #1 only if Mother HBsAg (-)	HepB #2									HepB series	
Diphtheria, Tetanus, Pertussis[2]			DTaP	DTaP	DTaP		DTaP			DTaP	Td	
Haemophilus influenzae Type b[3]			Hib	Hib	Hib	Hib						
Inactivated Polio			IPV	IPV		IPV				IPV		
Measles, Mumps, Rubella[4]						MMR #1				MMR #2		
Varicella[5]						Varicella				Varicella		
Pneumococcal[6]			PCV	PCV	PCV	PCV			PCV	PPV		
Hepatitis A[7]									Hepatitis A series			
Influenza[8]						Influenza (yearly)*						

Vaccines below this line are for selected populations.

This schedule indicates the recommended ages for routine administration of currently licensed childhood vaccines, as of December 1, 2002, for children through age 18 years. Any dose not given at the recommended age should be given at any subsequent visit when indicated and feasible. Shading with diagonal lines indicates age groups that warrant special effort to administer those vaccines not previously given. Additional vaccines may be licensed and recommended during the year. Licensed combination vaccines may be used whenever any components of the combination are indicated and the vaccine's other components are not contraindicated. Providers should consult the manufacturers' package inserts for detailed recommendations.

1. **Hepatitis B vaccine (HepB).** All infants should receive the first dose of Hepatitis B vaccine soon after birth and before hospital discharge; the first dose may also be given by age 2 months if the infant's mother is HBsAg-negative. Only monovalent HepB can be used for the birth dose. Four doses of vaccine may be administered when a birth dose is given. The second dose should be given at least 4 weeks after the first dose, except for combination vaccines which cannot be administered before age 6 weeks. The third dose should be given at least 16 weeks after the first dose and at least 8 weeks after the second dose. The last dose in the vaccination series (third or fourth dose) should not be administered before age 6 months. Infants born to HBsAg-positive mothers should receive HepB and 0.5 mL Hepatitis B Immune Globulin (HBIG) within 12 hours of birth at separate sites. The second dose is recommended at age 1-2 months. The last dose in the vaccination series should not be administered before age 6 months. These infants should be tested for HBsAg and anti-HBs at 9-15 months of age. Infants born to mothers whose HBsAg status is unknown should receive the first dose of the HepB series within 12 hours of birth. Maternal blood should be drawn as soon as possible to determine the mother's HBsAg status; if the HBsAg test is positive, the infant should receive HBIG as soon as possible (no later than age 1 week). The second dose is recommended at age 1-2 months. The last dose in the vaccination series should not be administered before age 6 months.

2. **Diphtheria and tetanus toxoids and acellular pertussis vaccine (DTaP).** The fourth dose of DTaP may be administered as early as age 12 months, provided 6 months have elapsed since the third dose and the child is unlikely to return at age 15-18 months. Tetanus and Diphtheria toxoids (Td) is recommended at age 11-12 years if at least 5 years have elapsed since the last dose of Tetanus and Diphtheria toxoid-containing vaccine. Subsequent routine Td boosters are recommended every 10 years.

3. **Haemophilus influenzae type b (Hib) conjugate vaccine.** Three Hib conjugate vaccines are licensed for infant use. If PRP-OMP (PedvaxHIB(r)or ComVax(r)[Merck]) is administered at ages 2 and 4 months, a dose at age 6 months is not required. DTaP/Hib combination products should not be used for primary immunization in infants at ages 2, 4 or 6 months, but can be used as boosters following any Hib vaccine.

4. **Measles, Mumps, and Rubella vaccine (MMR).** The second dose of MMR is recommended routinely at age 4-6 years but may be administered during any visit, provided at least 4 weeks have elapsed since the first dose and that both doses are administered beginning at or after age 12 months. Those who have not previously received the second dose should complete the schedule by the 11-/12-year-old visit.

8. **Influenza vaccine.** * Influenza vaccine is recommended annually only for children ages 6–24 months and children with certain risk factors (including but not limited to asthma, cardiac disease, sickle cell disease, renal failure, cystic fibrosis, HIV, and diabetes), and household members of persons in groups at high risk; (see MMWR 2002;51 (RR-3);1-31). Children aged ≤12 years should receive the vaccine in a dosage appropriate for their age (0.25 mL if age 6-35 months or 0.5 mL if age ≥3 years). Children age ≤8 years who are receiving the influenza vaccine for the first time should receive two doses separated by at least 4 weeks.

This schedule is approved by the Advisory Committee on Immunization Practices (www.cdc.gov/nip/acip), the American Academy of Pediatrics (www.aap.org), and the American Academy of Family Physicians (www.aafp.org).

For additional information about vaccines, including precautions and contraindications for immunization and vaccine shortages, please visit the National Immunization Program Web site at www.cdc.gov/nip/ or call the National Immunization Information Hotline at 1-800-232-2522 (English) or 1-800-232-0233 (Spanish).

5. **Varicella vaccine.** Varicella vaccine is recommended at any visit at or after age 12 months for susceptible children, i.e. those who lack a reliable history of chickenpox. Susceptible persons aged ≥13 years should receive two doses, given at least 4 weeks apart.

6. **Pneumococcal vaccine.** The heptavalent pneumococcal conjugate vaccine(PCV) is recommended for all children ages 2-23 months. It is also recommended for certain children ages 24-59 months. Pneumococcal polysaccharide vaccine (PPV) is recommended in addition to PCV for certain high-risk groups. See MMWR2000;49(RR-9);1-38.

7. **Hepatitis A vaccine.** Hepatitis A vaccine is recommended for children and adolescents in selected states and regions, and for certain high-risk groups; consult your local public health authority. Children and adolescents in these states, regions, and high-risk groups who have not been immunized against Hepatitis A can begin the Hepatitis A vaccination series during any visit. The two doses in the series should be administered at least 6 months apart. See MMWR1999;48(RR-12);1-37.

DTaP

The DTaP immunization provides protection against three different diseases:

- Diphtheria (a disease that attacks the throat and heart and that can lead to heart failure or death)

- Pertussis or whooping cough (a disease characterized by a severe cough that makes it difficult to breathe, eat, or drink and that can lead to pneumonia, convulsions, brain damage, and death)

- Tetanus (a disease that can lead to muscle spasms and death)

The Diphtheria and Tetanus portions of the vaccine may lead to pain and swelling at the injection site and—in rare cases—a skin rash that develops within 24 hours. The Pertussis portion of the vaccine may cause heat, redness, and tenderness at the site of the injection in about half of children receiving the vaccine. It may also cause fever and irritability and, in approximately 1 of 110,000 immunizations, inflammation of the brain may occur. (According to the American Academy of Pediatrics, because this complication is so rare, it is not known for certain whether the brain inflammation is caused by the vaccine itself or by some other substance or infection.)

Here's something else you need to know about the Pertussis portion of the vaccine. The newer acellular version of the pertussis vaccine (DTaP instead of DTP) has been proven to be every bit as effective as the earlier version, with substantially fewer side effects. Furthermore, administering acetaminophen at the time of injection and four and eight hours after the injection can help to decrease fevers and local reactions.

Polio

The polio vaccine provides protection against polio—a serious disease that can result in muscle pain and paralysis and death.

The vaccine used to be given either orally or by injection. The oral form provides slightly better protection than the injection form, but there is a slight risk (1 out of every 2.4 million doses of the vaccine) that the child or another family member could develop polio. This explains why the inactivated, injected form of the vaccine is now the only one in routine use in the United States.

Haemophilus influenza type B vaccine (Hib)

The Hib vaccine provides protection against Haemophilus influenza type b (Hib), a disease that can lead to meningitis, pneumonia, and a severe throat infection (epiglottitis) that can cause choking. Your child may develop a mild fever after having the injection. Note: Approximately 1 percent of children receiving the vaccine will experience some soreness, redness, or swelling around the injection site.

Measles, mumps, rubella (MMR) vaccine

This vaccine provides protection against three diseases:

- Measles (a disease that involves fever, rash, cough, runny nose, and watery eyes and that can cause ear infections, pneumonia, brain swelling, and even death)

- Mumps (a disease that can result in meningitis—the swelling of the coverings of the brain and spinal cord—and, in rare cases, testicular damage that may result in sterility)

- Rubella (a disease that can result in severe injury to or even the death of the fetus if it's contracted by a pregnant woman)

Although most children who have the MMR vaccine experience few, if any, side effects (for example, when such reactions occur, they tend to be limited to a rash or fever that develops 5 to 12 days after the immunization or a swelling of the glands in the neck), some children react to the vaccine by developing a high fever that may lead to convulsions. This type of reaction is more common in children who have reacted to a previous immunization or whose parents or siblings have experienced convulsions following an immunization. In rare cases, a child may develop meningitis (an infection of the fluid covering the brain and the spinal cord) or swelling of the testicles in response to the mumps portion of the vaccine. Be sure to warn your pediatrician ahead of time if reactions run in the family, or if your child has experienced a reaction to previous immunizations.

 NO KIDDING!

Your child should not receive the MMR vaccine if she

- has a disease or is taking a medication that affects the immune system
- has had a gamma globulin shot within the previous three months
- is allergic to an antibiotic called neomycin

Note: Because the current MMR vaccine no longer contains a significant amount of egg protein, an egg allergy is no longer a reason to avoid the vaccine. Still, it is a good idea to make sure that your child's doctor is aware of any egg allergies up front.

NO KIDDING!

Although there have been some reports in the media about a possible link between the MMR vaccine and autism, there's no hard evidence to back up this theory. So this is one worry you can strike off your immunization worry list right away.

About the chicken pox vaccine (Varivax)

Most American children are now immunized against chicken pox (varicella), a generally mild and nonlife-threatening disease that can, in some cases, lead to a number of potentially serious complications, including pneumonia (an infection of the lungs) and encephalitis (an infection of the brain).

The chicken pox vaccine can be given to your child shortly after her first birthday (at the same time that the MMR vaccine is administered but using a separate syringe and a different injection side). If you don't have the chicken pox vaccine given to your child at the same time, you'll have to wait for at least four more weeks before having the vaccine administered.

The chicken pox vaccine is not recommended for children who are allergic to any of the vaccine compounds (including gelatin and neomycin); who have a blood disorder or any type of cancer that affects the immune system; who are taking medications to suppress the immune system; who have active, untreated tuberculosis; or who have a fever.

The chicken pox vaccine is 98-percent effective against the severe forms of chicken pox and has only minor side effects: redness, stiffness, soreness, and/or swelling at the immunization site; fatigue; fussiness; fever; nausea; and, in 7 to 8 percent of cases, a temporary outbreak of small bumps or pimples at the immunization site approximately one month after the child has been immunized. Some children will develop a mild case of chicken pox (typically 50 spots or fewer as compared with the up-to-500 spots that can accompany a full-blown case of the chicken pox) one to two weeks after having the vaccine.

About the Pneumococcal vaccine for children

The pneumococcal vaccine provides protection against pneumococcal disease—a disease caused by the Streptococcus pneumoniae bacterium. This bacterium is the most frequent cause of pneumonia, blood infection, sinusitis, and ear infection in children under the age of five. The vaccine is recommended for children ages 2 to 23 months. It is also recommended for older children with certain types of health conditions (for example, sickle cell anemia, no spleen or a malfunctioning spleen, HIV infection, chronic disease, or immunodeficiencies).

MOTHER WISDOM

You can find out about all of the major childhood vaccinations by downloading a copy of the *Parents Guide to Childhood Immunization* (publication 00-5901) from the National Immunization Program Web page: www. cdc.gov/nip/publications/Parents-Guide/. You can also request a free copy of this publication by writing to the NIP Information/Distribution Center, 1600 Clifton Road, MS E-34, Atlanta, GA 30333. If you have immunization-related questions that the guide doesn't cover, you can call the National Immunization Program information hotline at 1-800-232-2522.

The side effects of the vaccine are relatively minor: 10 to 20 percent of infants under one year of age will experience pain and redness at the injection site as well as a fever; in children ages seven months to five years, up to 50 percent will experience pain and redness at the injection site and between 10 and 40 percent will experience a fever.

How to Tell When Your Child Is Sick

As you've no doubt discovered over the past few years, your "parent radar" is more highly developed than you might previously have believed. Mother Nature has programmed your child with a series of symptoms that are designed to tell you whether she's developed some sort of illness. (They're not unlike the error messages that show up on your computer screen from time to time, alerting you to the fact that your computer is anything but happy. But unlike that nice, neat little text box, child-related "error messages" tend to be a whole lot messier.)

You can expect your child to experience one or more of the symptoms outlined in Table 10.2 if she's doing battle with an illness.

TABLE 10.2

Common Symptoms of Illness in Children

Most children exhibit one or more of the following symptoms when they are ill:

Respiratory Symptoms

→ **Runny nose:** Your child's nose starts secreting clear, colorless mucus that may become thick and yellowish or greenish within a day or two. A runny nose is usually caused by a viral infection, such as the common cold, but it can also be caused by environmental or food allergies or chemical irritations. Your child should be checked by a doctor if her runny nose continues for longer than 10 days, in order to rule out these causes and to check for the presence of a sinus infection.

→ **Coughing:** Your child starts coughing because there's some sort of inflammation in the respiratory tract—anywhere from the nose to the lungs. Common causes of coughing include the common cold, allergies, chemical irritations (such as exposure to cigarette smoke), and cystic fibrosis and other chronic lung diseases, or because she has inhaled an object that's causing her to cough.

→ **Wheezing:** Your child makes wheezing sounds that are particularly noticeable when she's breathing out. Wheezing is caused by both the narrowing of the air passages in the lungs (caused, in turn, by both the constriction of the muscles surrounding the air passages and the swelling of the lining of those air passages) and the presence of excess mucus in those major airways (bronchi) or in the lungs, most often triggered by a viral infection. (The more rapid and labored your child's breathing, the more serious the infection.)

continued

Common Symptoms of Illness in Children *(continued)*

➜   **Croup:** Your child's breathing becomes very noisy when she breathes in (some children become very hoarse and develop a cough that sounds like a seal's bark), and, in severe cases, her windpipe may actually become obstructed. (The more labored and noisy your child's breathing, the more serious the airway obstruction.) Croup is caused by an inflammation of the windpipe below the vocal cords. See the section on treating croup in Table 10.3.

Gastrointestinal Symptoms

➜   **Diarrhea:** Your child's bowel movements become more frequent and/or their texture changes dramatically (that is, they become watery or unformed). Diarrhea is often accompanied by abdominal cramps or a stomach ache and is triggered when the bowel is stimulated or irritated (often by the presence of an infection). It can lead to dehydration if it's severe or continues for an extended period of time, so you'll want to monitor your child for any possible signs of dehydration. See the section on treating diarrhea in Table 10.3.

➜   **Dehydration:** Your child has a dry mouth, isn't drinking as much as usual, is urinating less often than usual, and doesn't shed any tears when she cries. She may also be experiencing vomiting and/or diarrhea. Dehydration is triggered by the loss of body fluids and results in reduced circulating blood volume. It can occur as a result of excessive or prolonged diarrhea, so you'll want to watch your child carefully if she's suffering from this problem—especially if she's also experiencing some vomiting. Signs that your child's dehydration may be severe include a weight loss of more than 5 percent of her weight; lethargic or irritable behavior; sunken eyes; a dry mouth; an absence of tears; pale, wrinkled skin; highly concentrated urine (urine that is dark yellow rather than pale in color); and infrequent urination.

➜   **Vomiting:** Your child begins vomiting. Vomiting is more common in children than in adults and tends to be less bothersome to children than adults (except, of course, the adults on clean-up patrol!). It can be caused by specific irritation to the stomach, or, more commonly,

Gastrointestinal Symptoms (continued)

it is simply a side effect of another illness. It's generally only worrisome if your child vomits often enough to become dehydrated or if she chokes and inhales vomit. See the section on managing vomiting in Table 10.3.

Skin Changes

➡ **Change in skin color:** Your child suddenly becomes pale or flushed, or the whites of her eyes take on a yellowish or pinkish hue. She may have developed some sort of an infection, whether it be a total body infection (such as stomach flu or jaundice) or an infection of the more localized variety (such as pink eye).

➡ **Rashes:** Your child develops some sort of skin rash. It could be the result of a viral or bacterial infection, or an allergic reaction to a food, medication, or other substance. See the section on skin conditions in Table 10.3.

Other Symptoms

➡ **Behavioral changes:** Your child becomes uncharacteristically fussy and irritable, or sleepy and lethargic. It's possible that some sort of illness or infection is responsible for these changes to her usual behavior.

➡ **Fever:** Your child's temperature is higher than normal, which often indicates the presence of an infection but that can also be caused by a reaction to an immunization or overdressing your child. Note: See the discussion about fever later in this chapter.

Although certain types of childhood illnesses require a trip to the doctor's office so that you can obtain the appropriate medication, many illnesses can be treated at home. (Note: Table 10.3 describes the causes, symptoms, and treatments for the most common types of childhood illnesses.) Of course, you'll want to seek medical attention for your child if she seems quite ill and you're simply not sure what type of illness you're dealing with. It's always best to err on the side of caution when your child's health is at stake.

Common Childhood Illnesses

There are hundreds of illnesses that can crop up during childhood. Due to space constraints, I had to limit myself to the more common ones—pediatric medicine's "greatest hits." If you want to find out about an illness that isn't listed here, I recommend that you visit one of the many excellent pediatric health Web sites listed in Appendix B.

Respiratory and Related Conditions

Condition	Allergies
Cause	Allergies can be caused by pollens, animal dander, molds, dust, and other substances.
Signs and Symptoms	A clear runny nose and watery eyes, sneezing fits, constant sniffing, nosebleeds, dark circles under the eyes, frequent colds or ear infections, a cough that is bothersome at night, a stuffy nose in the morning, and/or noisy breathing at night.
What You Can Do	• Eliminate or limit exposure to the substances that seem to trigger your child's allergies. • "Allergy-proof" your child's room by using allergy-proof zippered covers, purchasing nonallergenic bedding, removing stuffed animals from your child's room, removing all room deodorizers, vacuuming the mattress and washing all of your child's bedding at least once every two weeks, avoiding plush carpet (if possible), keeping your child's windows closed during allergy season, investing in a high-efficiency particulate remover (HEPA) filter, and vacuuming your child's room only when she's away from it (since vacuuming tends to stir up dust). One final tip: If you haven't done so already, make your home smoke-free. The last thing a child with allergies needs is to be exposed to smoke on a regular basis.

	• Keep your child comfortable by treating her symptoms (for example, using a nasal aspirator to clear her nose). You might want to ask your doctor whether your child would benefit from taking a decongestant or an antihistamine. A nasal steroid spray may be recommended for older children.
Condition	**Asthma** (a lung condition that affects the bronchial tubes)
Cause	Most commonly triggered after a viral respiratory infection inflames the lining of the bronchial tubes in the lungs. Asthma can also be caused by an irritant such as cigarette smoke or paint fumes; allergens such as pollens, mold spores, animal danders, house dust mites, and cockroaches; inhaling cold air; and certain cough medications. In some older children, exercise may also be a trigger for asthma.
Signs and Symptoms	Coughing and/or high-pitched wheezing or whistling as your child breathes. The cough typically gets worse at night or if your child comes into contact with an irritant such as cigarette smoke. In cases of severe asthma, your child's breathing may become very rapid, her heart rate may increase, and she may vomit; or she may become very tired and slow-moving and cough all the time (in which case she requires immediate medical attention). The majority of children with asthma develop symptoms by age five.
What You Can Do	• Try to eliminate anything that could be triggering your child's asthma problems, including such irritants as cigarette smoke and any allergens.
	• Work with your doctor to come up with a game plan for preventing and treating future asthma attacks through medication and/or lifestyle modifications.
	• Note: Some children suffer from exercise-induced asthma—asthma that is only triggered when a child exercises vigorously. If your child experiences these types of symptoms, your child's doctor is likely to recommend that your child use an inhaler about 10 minutes before exercising in order to prevent the onset of symptoms.

continued

Common Childhood Illnesses

Respiratory and Related Conditions (continued)

Condition	**Bronchiolitis** (an infection of the small breathing tubes of the lungs; not to be confused with bronchitis, which is an infection of the larger, more central airways)
Cause	Caused by a virus, most commonly the RSV or Respiratory Syncytial Virus (with an incubation period of 5–8 days), which results in swelling of the small bronchial tubes. It is typically picked up as a result of being exposed to someone with an upper respiratory tract illness. Bronchiolitis is most common in children under the age of two and is most likely to occur during the winter months. Note: According to the American Academy of Pediatrics, almost half of children who develop bronchiolitis will go on to develop asthma later in life.
Signs and Symptoms	It initially starts out like a normal cold with a runny nose and sneezing, but after a couple of days, a child with bronchiolitis starts coughing, wheezing, and having trouble breathing. Your child may also be irritable and may experience difficulty eating due to the coughing and breathing problems.
What You Can Do	• Watch for signs of rapid or labored breathing. • Keep your child comfortable by using a nasal aspirator or a vaporizer. (Just make sure that you clean the vaporizer on a regular basis—ideally once or twice a week—to prevent it from becoming a breeding ground for bacteria.) • Get in touch with your child's doctor to find out whether any additional treatment may be required. Some children who have a lot of difficulty breathing may require medication to open the bronchial tubes. A few also will need to be hospitalized so that oxygen and fluids may be administered until the child's breathing improves.

Condition	Common Cold
Cause	Spread from person to person via airborne droplets containing the cold virus or via contaminated hands and/or objects (for example, toys). It is most contagious from one day before to seven days after the onset of symptoms.
Signs and Symptoms	Runny nose, sore throat, cough, decreased appetite. May be accompanied by a fever, in which case, your child may also experience muscle aches and/or a headache. Although a cold typically lasts for five to seven days in an adult, children's colds tend to drag on a little longer.
What You Can Do	• Keep your child comfortable. You might want to clear out her runny nose by using a nasal aspirator or—if her nose is really stuffed up—by placing a vaporizer in her room. (Note: Be sure to clean the vaporizer frequently to prevent it from becoming a breeding ground for bacteria.)
	• Keep your child's face clean. Infections of the face can occur as a result of prolonged exposure to nasal secretions, and your child could end up with yellow pustules or wide, honey-colored scabs (impetigo).
	• Don't be surprised if your child's appetite decreases while she is ill. This is perfectly normal.
	• Get your doctor's go-ahead before administering any sort of cold medication to your child.
	• Get in touch with your child's doctor if she develops an earache or a fever; if she becomes exceptionally sleepy or if her night-time sleep is very disrupted; if she becomes overly cranky or fussy; if she develops a skin rash; if her breathing becomes rapid or labored, or if her cough becomes persistent or severe.

continued

Common Childhood Illnesses

Respiratory and Related Conditions (continued)

Condition	Croup or Laryngotracheitis (an inflammation of the voice box or larynx and windpipe or trachea)
Cause	Usually caused by a viral infection in or around the voice box. Children are most susceptible to croup between six months and three years of age. As children get older, their windpipe gets larger, so swelling to the larynx and trachea is less likely to result in breathing difficulties. There are two types of croup: spasmodic croup, which comes on suddenly and is caused by a mild upper respiratory infection or allergy, and viral croup, which results from a viral infection in the voice box and windpipe and that may be accompanied by noisy or labored breathing—a condition known as "stridor."
Signs and Symptoms	A cough that sounds similar to a seal-like bark and often accompanied by a hoarse voice. There may also be a fever.
What You Can Do	• Keep your child comfortable by using a cool-mist vaporizer in her room; by filling your bathroom with hot steam from the shower, and then letting her breathe in the moist vapors; or by taking her for a walk in the cool night air.
	• Get in touch with your doctor if the croup seems to be particularly severe or if your child shows the following types of symptoms: fever higher than 102°F; rapid or difficult breathing; severe sore throat; increased drooling; refusal to swallow; and/or discomfort when lying down. Note: Croup symptoms tend to be at their worst in the early hours of the morning when doctors' offices are closed. If you are concerned enough to call for advice at that time, it is best to take your child directly to the hospital for an assessment.

Condition	Ear Infections (otitis media)
Cause	Caused by a virus and/or bacteria and typically occur in the aftermath of a cold. Because a child's Eustachian tube (the tube that connects the middle ear to the back of the nose) is very short and very narrow, children are highly susceptible to ear infections. In fact, three-quarters of children will have at least one ear infection by the time they reach age three. Ear infections cannot be spread from one child to another.
Signs and Symptoms	Fussiness and irritability, difficulty sleeping (because lying down tends to increase ear pain), reduced appetite (because sucking and swallowing can result in painful pressure changes in the middle ear), difficulty hearing (for example, your child stops responding to certain types of sounds), fluid draining from your child's ear, and fever and cold symptoms. Note: If there is pus coming from your child's ear, this means that her eardrum has ruptured—something that will require treatment with antibiotic drops and/or oral antibiotics.
What You Can Do	• Keep your child comfortable by treating her fever and cold symptoms (see earlier sections of this chapter) and by offering her acetaminophen to treat her earache.
	• Get in touch with your doctor to arrange for your child's ears to be checked. Your doctor may want to prescribe an antibiotic to clear up the infection. Note: In most cases, there's no need to rush off to the emergency ward in the middle of the night to seek treatment for an ear infection. Simply treat your child's pain with acetaminophen during the night and then call your doctor's office in the morning to set up an appointment.
	• Even if your child's ear infection has already been diagnosed by a doctor, you should call your doctor's office again if she develops one or more of the following symptoms: an earache that worsens even after she's on antibiotics, a fever that's greater than 102°F 48–72 hours after treatment begins, excessive sleepiness, excessive crankiness or fussiness, a skin rash, rapid or difficult breathing, or hearing loss.

continued

Common Childhood Illnesses

Respiratory and Related Conditions (continued)

Ear Infections *(continued)*	• Your doctor may ask to have your child's ears rechecked after she's finished the antibiotic to ensure that there's no fluid remaining in her ear. (Fluid in the ear can lead to further infections and/or hearing problems down the road.)
What You Can Do	• If your child has recurrent problems with ear infections, your doctor may recommend either a preventive course of long-term antibiotics or surgery to insert ventilating tubes in her ears.

Condition	**Ear Infections—Swimmer's Ear**
Cause	Caused when frequent exposure to water allows bacteria and fungi to grow.
Signs and Symptoms	Occurs in the delicate skin of the outer ear canal. A child typically will experience itching followed by a swelling of the skin of the ear canal and then some drainage. A child with swimmer's ear will experience extreme pain when the ear lobe or other outside parts of the ear are touched.
What You Can Do	• The condition is treated with eardrops containing antibiotics and/or corticosteroids to help fight infection and reduce the amount of swelling in the ear canal. Your child's doctor may also recommend that you give her an over-the-counter pain relief medication to help relieve her discomfort.
	• Try to keep the child's ear as dry as possible during the healing process and try to avoid repeat infections by placing drops in your child's ear after she goes swimming. (A mixture of either 50/50 vinegar and water or 70/30 alcohol and water works well.) Also, make sure that you dry your child's ears after bathing or swimming.

Condition	Epiglottitis
Cause	A bacterial infection of the upper airway, caused by Haemophilus influenzae b, that results in inflammation of the epiglottis (the flap of skin that covers the upper airway when your child swallows).
Signs and Symptoms	Difficulty breathing in, difficulty swallowing, drooling (because of difficulty swallowing the saliva). A child with epiglottitis will typically sit upright and fight for every breath.
What You Can Do	• A child with epiglottitis requires emergency medical attention. Luckily, epiglottitis is now rarely encountered in the United States, as the vaccine Hib (given beginning at two months of age and hopefully completed by 15–18 months of age), protects your child from this potentially life-threatening disease.

Condition	Hay Fever (seasonal allergic rhinitis)
Cause	An allergic condition affecting the upper respiratory tract. Caused by exposure to hay (hence the name!) or other pollen-producing plants such as ragweed, grass, and trees, as well as some mold spores.
Signs and Symptoms	Sneezing, swollen nasal membranes, and a clear nasal discharge; dark circles under the eyes; red, watery eyes; itchiness inside the nose, inside the ears, and on the roof of the mouth. Note: If your child's symptoms continue year-round, your child suffers from perennial allergic rhinitis. More often than not, these symptoms are triggered by allergens such as house mites.

continued

Common Childhood Illnesses

Respiratory and Related Conditions (continued)

Hay Fever *(continued)*	• If you have air conditioning, close up the house at night so that your child can sleep without having to breathe in the allergens that are causing her so much misery.
What You Can Do	• If your child is having a hard time sleeping, ask your doctor to recommend an antihistamine to help control her runny nose, sneezing, and itchiness. Your doctor should be able to recommend an antihistamine that won't leave her feeling overly drowsy. For more severe cases, corticosteroid sprays and allergy shots may be recommended.
Condition	**Influenza**
Cause	Caused by a respiratory virus that is spread from person to person via droplets or contaminated objects.
Signs and Symptoms	Fever, chills, and shakes; extreme tiredness or fatigue; muscle aches and pains; and a dry, hacking cough. (It's different from the common cold in that a child with the common cold only has a fever, a runny nose, and a small amount of coughing.)
What You Can Do	• Keep your child comfortable by treating her fever and cold symptoms (see previous relevant sections).
Condition	**Pink Eye** (conjunctivitis)
Cause	Spread from person to person as a result of direct contact with secretions from the eye. It can also be triggered by excessive eye rubbing, allergies, or by viruses or bacteria.

Signs and Symptoms	Redness, itching, pain, and discharge from the eye.
What You Can Do	• Get in touch with your doctor to see whether antibiotic eye drops should be prescribed (for example, if your child's eye discharge is yellowish and thick).
	• Keep your child away from other people until the antibiotic eye drops have been used for at least one full day. Pink eye is contagious until 24 hours after antibiotic treatment has been started.
Condition	**Pneumonia** (infection of the lung)
Cause	Pneumonia can be caused by both viruses and bacterial infections.
Signs and Symptoms	Cough; fever, which is usually high; rapid or labored breathing; markedly decreased activity level and appetite.
What You Can Do	• Get in touch with your doctor so that the cause of the pneumonia can be determined and an appropriate course of treatment can be mapped out. Viral pneumonias typically are treated with acetaminophen (for fever) and bronchodilators (to minimize wheezing). Bacterial pneumonias, on the other hand, respond better to treatment that involves antibiotics, fluids, and humid air.
	• Monitor your child's symptoms carefully if she's being cared for at home and report any changes in her condition to her doctor. Your child may require emergency assistance if she's having difficulty breathing.

continued

Common Childhood Illnesses

Respiratory and Related Conditions (continued)

Condition	Sore Throat
Cause	Most sore throats are caused by viruses. In fact, they often accompany the common cold. Some more severe sore throats are caused by streptococcal bacteria (strep throat). See the following discussion. Note: Mononucleosis is caused by a virus and can result in a very sore throat with difficulty in swallowing.
Signs and Symptoms	Swelling and redness of the tissues in the throat; enlarged tonsils; fatigue; fever; pain ranging from mild soreness to extreme soreness, and difficulty swallowing. If your child is having extreme difficulty swallowing or difficulty breathing, you'll want to get in touch with your child's doctor or seek emergency attention for your child.
What You Can Do	• Have your child gargle with warm salt water or suck on candy or throat lozenges. • A cool-mist humidifier or vaporizer can also help to ease a sore throat by keeping your child's throat moist. • Acetaminophen can be used to control pain and manage any accompanying fever.

Condition	Strep Throat
Cause	Strep throat is a bacterial infection. It is transmitted via droplets or by touching contaminated objects and is contagious until 24 to 36 hours after the start of antibiotic treatment.
Signs and Symptoms	Sore throat, fever, swollen glands in the neck. Often a headache or stomach ache are also present with strep throat. Note: If a skin rash is also present, the condition is known as scarlet fever.

What You Can Do	• Get in touch with your child's doctor to arrange to have a throat swab taken to determine whether or not she has strep throat. If she does, an antibiotic will be prescribed to help kill off the strep germ. If left untreated, strep throat can result in kidney disease or rheumatic fever (a serious condition that can cause heart damage and joint swelling). It can also lead to skin infections, bloodstream infections, ear infections, and pneumonia.
	• Offer liquids and bland foods and watch for signs of dehydration.
Condition	**Sinusitis** (sinus infection)
Cause	The mucus in your child's sinuses becomes infected with bacteria, usually as the result of a lingering cold.
Signs and Symptoms	Persistent nasal discharge, fever, a cough that gets worse at night, tenderness in the face, dark circles under the eyes, puffy lower eyelids, bad breath, fatigue, poor appitite.
What You Can Do	• Get in touch with your child's doctor to talk about whether she should be on some sort of an antibiotic. (As a rule of thumb, most doctors will prescribe an antibiotic only if a child is experiencing both a nasal discharge and a cough that hasn't shown any sign of improvement after more than 10 to 14 days.) If your doctor does decide to prescribe an antibiotic, don't be surprised if she prescribes a three- to four-week supply! Sinus infections can be time-consuming to clear up.
	• Keep your child comfortable. (See the tips on treating the common cold given previously.)

continued

Common Childhood Illnesses

Respiratory and Related Conditions (continued)

Condition	Tonsillitis
Cause	Can be bacterial or viral in origin
Signs and Symptoms	Fever, swollen glands under the jaw, a very sore throat, cold symptoms, and abdominal pain.
What You Can Do	• Treat your child's fever and cold symptoms. (See previous discussion.) • Have your child examined by your doctor to find out whether an antibiotic should be prescribed.

Condition	Whooping Cough (pertussis)
Cause	Caused by the bacteria Bordatella pertussis. Pertussis is not common because children are vaccinated for it beginning at two months of age. For this reason, the very young infant (not yet vaccinated) is at highest risk for contracting the disease. The incubation period is seven to ten days.
Signs and Symptoms	Cold-like symptoms that linger. About two weeks into the illness, the cough suddenly worsens. When the child coughs, thick mucus is dislodged, causing her to gasp for her next breath (the "whoop" in whooping cough). She turns red in the face during the cough and then vomits afterwards. Whooping cough typically lasts for three to six weeks and is considered to be a serious illness in a child under age one.

What You Can Do

- Offer your child plenty of fluids.

- Find out whether a cool-mist vaporizer will help with your child's cough.

- Check with your doctor or pharmacist to find out whether an expectorant cough syrup would help.

- Seek immediate medical attention if your child becomes exhausted or is having difficulty breathing. Most children under one year of age end up being hospitalized so that they can be treated with oxygen (and antibiotics in the hope of preventing the illness from spreading).

(Note: Treatment with Erythromycin is generally recommended, if only to prevent the transmission and spread of this infection. If given early enough in the disease, Erythromycin may shorten the course of the illness, but usually it does not. Children with suspected or proven whooping cough can be released from quarantine after a week on Erythromycin.)

Skin and Scalp Conditions

Condition	Acne
Cause	Thought to be triggered by the hormonal changes associated with puberty. Girls tend to get acne at a younger age than boys, but boys typically develop more severe cases of acne.
Signs and Symptoms	The appearance of blackheads, whiteheads, pimples, and cysts that typically appear on the face, back, neck, chest, and shoulders. Acne can be itchy or painful. Scarring may result in severe cases.

continued

Common Childhood Illnesses

Skin and Scalp Conditions (continued)

Acne *(continued)*	
What You Can Do	• There's no need to treat minor acne flare-ups, but more severe breakouts can be treated with benzoyl peroxide, antibiotic creams, exfoliating creams like tretinoin and salicylic acid, oral antibiotics, and, in particularly severe cases, Isotretinoin (Accutane). Note: Accutane can cause major birth defects, so it's important to caution your child against sharing his or her medication with anyone. If it were to be used by a teenaged friend who subsequently became pregnant, that friend could end up giving birth to a baby with serious birth defects.
Condition	**Boils**
Cause	Usually caused by staphylococcus bacteria from an infected pimple.
Signs and Symptoms	Raised red, tender, warm swellings on the skin. Most commonly found on the buttocks.
What You Can Do	• Apply hot compresses to the boils 10 times daily in order to bring them to a head and then continue applying them for a few days after the boils pop and drain. Avoid picking at or squeezing at your child's boils, as this may result in scarring and spreading.
	• Get in touch with your child's doctor. If the boils don't drain on their own, they may need to be incised and drained by your doctor. A topical antibiotic or oral antibiotic may also be required.

Condition	Cellulitis
Cause	Usually caused by a bacterial infection such as staphylococcus or streptococcus
Signs and Symptoms	Swollen, red, tender, warm areas of skin that are usually found on the extremities or the buttocks. They often start out as a boil or a puncture wound but then become infected. They're typically accompanied by a fever and swollen and tender lymph glands.
What You Can Do	• Apply hot compresses for a few minutes every two hours. • Elevate the affected area. • Give your child acetaminophen to help control the fever and pain. • Contact your child's doctor. This condition will need to be treated with antibiotics (oral, injected, or intravenous, depending on the severity of the case).

Condition	Chicken pox
Cause	Caused by a viral infection that is spread from person to person. The incubation period is two to three weeks. It is very difficult to control the spread of chicken pox because it can be transmitted through direct contact with an infected person (usually via fluid from broken blisters), through the air when an infected person coughs or sneezes, and through direct contact with lesions (sores) from a person with shingles (a possible complication of chicken pox). Outbreaks are most common in winter and in early spring.

continued

Common Childhood Illnesses

Skin and Scalp Conditions (continued)

Chicken Pox (continued)

Signs and Symptoms A rash with small blisters that develops on the scalp and thorax and then spreads to the face, arms, and legs over a period of three to four days. A child can end up with anywhere from less than a dozen to more than 500 itchy blisters that dry up and turn into scabs two to four days later. Other symptoms of chicken pox include coughing, fussiness, loss of appetite, and headaches. A fever usually accompanies chicken pox. Chicken pox is contagious from two days before to five days after the rash appears.

What You Can Do
- Try to minimize the amount of itching your child experiences by giving her oatmeal or baking soda baths or by dabbing calamine lotion on her spots. Note: Don't apply calamine lotion to the spots in her mouth. Calamine lotion is for external use only.

- Give your child acetaminophen to help bring down her fever and eliminate some of her discomfort. Note: Do not give children aspirin or drugs containing salicylate at any time, because aspirin use during certain illnesses, including chicken pox, has been linked to Reye's syndrome—a potentially fatal disease that affects the liver and the brain. Note: A highly disputed and controversial issue is whether or not you should also avoid giving your child ibuprofen while she has the chicken pox, and whether there is a possible link between ibuprofen use during outbreaks of the chicken pox and severe soft tissue super-infections (flesh-eating disease).

- Be sure to get in touch with your doctor if your child's fever lasts longer than four days; if it remains high after the third day after the spots appear; if your child shows signs of becoming dehydrated; or if your child's rash becomes warm, red, or tender.

Condition	Cold Sores
Cause	Caused by the herpes simplex virus, a virus that is passed through saliva.
Signs and Symptoms	Oozing blisters that can erupt on any part of the body, but that occur most often on or near the lips or inside the mouth.
What You Can Do	• Lip balm helps to relieve the discomfort of cold sores by keeping cold sores moist until they've had a chance to run their course, form scabs, and heal—a process that typically takes about 14 days.
	• Children with compromised immune systems and/or who experience severe outbreaks can be treated with antiviral drugs that help to relieve symptoms and shorten the duration of the illness.

Condition	Eczema
Cause	Unknown, but it tends to be worse in winter when your child's skin is driest. Eczema is no longer believed to be triggered by allergies. It is not contagious.
Signs and Symptoms	Excessively dry, scaly, or rough skin, often occurring in patches that become red and inflamed. It typically itches and can cause an uncomfortable, burning sensation.

• Although uncommon, occasionally doctors might choose to prescribe an antiviral medicine to make the chicken pox less severe, but, in order to be effective, this medication must be administered within the first 24 hours of the onset of chicken pox. Your child's doctor may suggest that your child receive a dose of a special immune globulin (VZIG) that can help to prevent chicken pox.

Note: The chicken pox vaccine can also help to prevent chicken pox. See the section on vaccinations elsewhere in this chapter for more about this vaccine.

continued

Common Childhood Illnesses

Skin and Scalp Conditions (continued)

Eczema (continued) **What You Can Do**	• Keep your child's skin well moisturized by applying a nonallergenic moisturizing lotion a couple of times each day and dress your child in cotton and other breathable fabrics.
	• Keep your child's nails trimmed so that she'll be less likely to infect her skin through scratching.
	• Give your child an oatmeal bath. (Don't open the cereal cupboard; you need colloidal oatmeal, a product that can be purchased in the drugstore.)
	• Your doctor may prescribe a steroid cream if your child's eczema is particularly severe, but she'll recommend that you use it sparingly. Non-steroid creams can be used to prevent eczema flare ups.
Condition	**Fifth Disease** (erythema infectiosum)
Cause	Caused by a virus known as parvovirus B19. After the rash appears, the disease is no longer likely to spread.
Signs and Symptoms	A "slapped cheek" rash on the face accompanied by a red lace-like rash on the trunk and extremities. The child may also have a fever and sore joints. This illness is more common in school-aged children than in younger children.
What You Can Do	• Get in touch with your child's doctor as soon as possible if your child has sickle-cell anemia or some other form of chronic anemia. Fifth disease may heighten anemia in children who are already anemic.
	• There is no treatment for fifth disease, nor is there any vaccine available. This is one of those diseases that you simply have to "wait out."

	• It's important to keep your child away from pregnant women—or women who could potentially be pregnant—while your child is experiencing an outbreak of Fifth Disease. Parvovirus B19 infection during pregnancy has been associated with a fetal death rate of 2% to 6%. It's particularly risky to the developing baby if such exposure occurs during the first half of pregnancy.
Condition	**Hand, Foot, and Mouth Disease**
Cause	Caused by the Coxsackie virus—a contagious virus with an incubation period of three to six days.
Signs and Symptoms	Tiny blister-like sores in the mouth, on the palms of the hands, and on the soles of the feet that are accompanied by a mild fever, a sore throat, and painful swallowing. Lasts approximately seven to ten days and is contagious from one day before until one day after the blisters appear.
What You Can Do	• Give your child plenty of liquids and, if she's old enough, soft foods as well. Note: Frozen treats, such as popsicles, can ease some of the discomfort of the sores in the mouth while ensuring that your child remains well hydrated.
	• Keep your child comfortable by treating her with acetaminophen until her symptoms start to subside.
Condition	**Herpangina** (inflammation of the inside of the mouth)
Cause	Caused by the Coxsackie virus (the same virus responsible for hand, foot, and mouth disease), a contagious virus that has an incubation period of three to six days.
Signs and Symptoms	Numerous painful grayish-white ulcers on the child's tongue and on the roof of the child's mouth toward the back, painful swallowing, a fever of 102 to 104°F (38.9 to 40°C), diarrhea, and a pink rash on the trunk. The symptoms last about seven days, and the illness is highly contagious until the ulcers are gone.

continued

Common Childhood Illnesses

Skin and Scalp Conditions (continued)

Herpangina *(continued)*	• Take your child to the doctor to have the diagnosis confirmed.
What You Can Do	• Give your child plenty of fluids but avoid giving your child acidic juices that may make her mouth ulcers sting. If your child refuses to eat, offer soft food and liquids to prevent dehydration.
	• Give your child acetaminophen to help bring down her fever and to help reduce the pain associated with the mouth ulcers.
Condition	Hives *(urticaria)*
Cause	Triggered by a recent viral illness, allergies to foods, insect bites, or antibiotics. In many cases, it is impossible to pinpoint the trigger behind a particular outbreak of hives.
Signs and Symptoms	Severe itching accompanied by a raised, pink rash or skin lesions. In severe cases, your child may have difficulty speaking or swallowing, due to swelling in the mouth. In such a situation, you will need to seek emergency assistance for your child.
What You Can Do	• It's not unusual for a child to have an isolated outbreak of hives. Hives typically go away on their own within three to four days. In the meantime, your child's doctor may recommend that you give her an oral antihistamine to help reduce the itchiness. Cool baths and cold compresses can also be quite soothing.

Condition	Impetigo (an infection of the skin)
Cause	Caused by a bacterial infection
Signs and Symptoms	A rash featuring oozing, blister-like, honey-colored crusts that may be as small as pimples or as large as coins. Outbreaks of impetigo typically occur below the nose or on the buttocks or at the site of an insect bite or a scrape.
What you can do	• Have your child seen by a doctor so that the rash can be diagnosed and an antibacterial ointment and/or an oral antibiotic can be prescribed.
	• Trim your child's nails to prevent her from scratching the rash and keep the sores covered to minimize the chance that they'll spread to other parts of the body and other people.

Condition	Lice (pediculosis)
Cause	Lice infestation occurs when lice—crawling insects—make their home in human hair, feeding on blood from the scalp. They are transmitted through direct contact between children.
Signs and Symptoms	An itchy scalp that may be accompanied by reddened, rash-like areas where your child has been bitten by adult lice. You are also likely to find tiny white eggs (called nits) in your child's hair. These white eggs look like dandruff, but can't be shaken or brushed off: they stubbornly attach themselves to the hair shaft and have to be painstakingly removed—a tedious and frustrating process for parents and kids alike.

continued

Common Childhood Illnesses

Skin and Scalp Conditions (continued)

Lice (continued)	
What you can do	• Do period spot checks of your child's head, particularly if you know that your child has been in contact with another child with head lice. Be sure to focus on the area close to the scalp, behind the ears, toward the back of the neck, and on the top of the head. Mature insects (one-millimeter-long, dark-colored insects) are more difficult to spot than nits (grayish-white ovals that resemble dandruff).
	• If you detect head lice, treat your child with an insecticide that kills lice. According to the American Academy of Pediatrics, this is the only effective method of treating head lice. Because products designed to treat head lice contain highly toxic chemicals, you should only use these products if you are sure your child has actually been infected with head lice. Note: You may, however, also want to treat any siblings who share the same bed as an infected child.
	• After you've finished treating the nits, you can remove any remaining nits by either applying a damp towel to your child's scalp for 30 to 60 minutes, soaking her hair with a solution made up of equal parts of vinegar and water and then applying a towel soaked in the same solution for 15 minutes, or washing your child's hair and then applying cream rinse containing 8 percent formic acid (a substance that helps to dissolve the "glue" that binds the nit to the hair shaft).
	• At this point, you can then comb the nits off your child's hair by using a fine-toothed nit comb or by scraping the nits off using your thumbnail. Note: You're only removing the nits for cosmetic reasons, so don't' feel that you have to remove every single nit.

- Wash all of your child's bed linens and stuffed animals in hot water and put in hot dryer for at least 20 minutes. Any stuffed animals that aren't fully washable should be placed in "quarantine" for 10 days. Combs and brushes should be soaked in hot water for 20 minutes or washed with a pediculicide shampoo.

- All head-lice treatments require a second treatment seven to ten days after the first treatment. Nits that were not killed by the first round of treatment can hatch and start the infestation cycle all over again.

Condition	Measles (rubeola)
Cause	Spread by a virus that has an incubation period of 8 to 12 days
Signs and Symptoms	Cold, high fever (104°F), cough, bloodshot eyes that are sensitive to light. Around the fourth day of illness, a bright red rash erupts on the face and spreads all over the body. (Even the inner cheeks will have spots, which will be white in color.) At around the time that the spots break out, the child starts feeling quite ill. The infectious period lasts from three to five days before the rash appears until after the rash disappears (typically four days after the rash appears).
What You Can Do	• Have your child seen by your doctor so that the illness can be properly diagnosed and any complications (pneumonia, encephalitis, ear infections, and so on) can be treated.
	• Give your child acetaminophen to manage her fever and plenty of fluids to keep her well hydrated.

continued

Common Childhood Illnesses

Skin and Scalp Conditions (continued)

Condition	Poison Ivy
Cause	Caused by exposure to poison ivy or poison oak. It is not contagious from person to person.
Signs and Symptoms	An itchy, unsightly rash that can last up to two weeks. If your child has an allergic reaction to the poison ivy or oak, her skin will become reddened, swollen, and blistered. Children experiencing such a reaction report severe itching and burning sensations.
What You Can Do	• Soak the affected area in cool water for a few minutes at a time to help to relieve some of the itching and oozing from the affected areas.
	• Topical steroid creams can help to discourage scratching, as can an antihistamine taken orally. (If your child has a tendency to scratch, you may need to keep her nails well trimmed.) Note: Oral steroid therapy may be an option.
	• If your child seems particularly uncomfortable, the rash is particularly severe or shows signs of infection, or the rash has erupted on your child's face or groin, you will want to seek medical advice.

Condition	Ringworm
Cause	Caused by a fungus that is spread from person to person through touch.
Signs and Symptoms	An itchy and flaky rash that may be ring-shaped and have a raised, red edge, usually with a white or lighter-colored center. When the scalp is affected, a bald area may develop. Ringworm is highly contagious until treatment has commenced.

What You Can Do	• Take your child to see the doctor so that oral medications and/or topical ointments or creams may be prescribed to treat the outbreak.
Condition	**Roseola**
Cause	Caused by a virus with an incubation period of five to ten days. Roseola is very common in 6- to 24-month-old children, less common in 3- and 4-year-olds, are very rare in children over the age of 4.
Signs and Symptoms	High fever that arises suddenly in a previously well child, and which may result in febrile convulsions. The fever breaks on the third day and is then followed by a faint pink rash that appears on the trunk and the extremities and lasts for one day.
What You Can Do	• Treat your child's fever and give her plenty of fluids to prevent dehydration.
Condition	**Rubella** (German measles)
Cause	Caused by the rubella virus—a virus that has an incubation period of 14 to 21 days and that is contagious from a few days before until seven days after the rash appears.
Signs and Symptoms	A low-grade fever, flu-like symptoms, a slight cold, and a pinkish red, spotted rash that starts on the face, spreads rapidly to the trunk, and disappears by the third day. Also accompanied by swollen glands behind the ears and in the nape of the neck.

continued

Common Childhood Illnesses

Skin and Scalp Conditions (*continued*)

Rubella (*continued*) What You Can Do	• Have your child examined by a doctor to confirm that she has developed rubella. Sometimes only a blood test can confirm that the rash and other symptoms have been caused by rubella as opposed to some other illness. • Keep your child away from women who are or could be pregnant. Rubella can be very dangerous to the developing fetus.
Condition	**Scabies**
Cause	Caused by tiny insects called mites, which burrow into the upper layer of the skin, causing severe itching.
Signs and Symptoms	Severe itching, red bumps, and, in some cases, pus-filled sores.
What You Can Do	• Itching can be eased through cool baths or compresses and through the use of medications containing permethrin (such as Kwellada-P). • Scabies is contagious, so you will need to keep your child home until treatment has been completed.
Condition	**Scarlet Fever**
Cause	Caused by streptococcus bacteria; has an incubation period of two to five days.
Signs and Symptoms	Sunburn-like rash over face, trunk, and extremities; sandpaper-like skin; fever; sore throat, abdominal pain and or vomiting; headache. The rash usually disappears in five days. Despite its scary name, it's usually no more serious than strep throat, but it's contagious until one to two days after antibiotic treatment has begun. It's more common in school-aged children than in younger children.

What You Can Do	• Have your child seen by your doctor so that antibiotic treatment can be started.
	• Offer liquids and bland foods and watch for signs of dehydration.
Condition	**Shingles**
Cause	Caused by the zoster virus—the same virus that is responsible for the chicken pox.
Signs and Symptoms	A rash with small blisters that begin to crust over; intense itching. Shingles is very contagious while the rash is present; it's possible to spread the disease to anyone who has not had the chicken pox. They won't become infected with shingles; however, what you risk passing along is a case of the chicken pox.
What You Can Do	• Follow the guidelines for treating the chicken pox. (See previous discussion.)
Condition	**Warts**
Cause	Caused by viruses
Signs and Symptoms	Can be uncomfortable, especially if they occur on the soles of the feet, but they are generally harmless.
What You Can Do	• If your child's warts are uncomfortable, infected, or bleeding, talk to your child's doctor about what options may be available for treating and removing them. Warts can be removed through the daily application of salicylic and lactic acid solution (a process that can take months) or by surgery, freezing, or electrical cauterization.

continued

Common Childhood Illnesses

Gastrointestinal Conditions

Condition	**Campylobacter**
Cause	Source of infection may be poultry, beef, unpasteurized milk, or other food. The germ that causes this condition is excreted in the stool, so your child is infectious while she has symptoms.
Signs and Symptoms	Fever, diarrhea, blood in stool, cramps.
What You Can Do	• Get in touch with your child's doctor to see whether a stool sample is required in order to confirm that your child has been infected with campylobacter.
	• Keep your child away from other children while you treat the illness.
	• Give your child acetaminophen to reduce her discomfort and treat her fever. Also, see tips under diarrhea (later in this chapter) for advice on managing your child's diarrhea.

Condition	**Constipation**
Cause	Too little water in the intestines and/or poor muscle tone in the lower intestines and rectum. The problem can also be caused by a diet low in fiber, and/or high in dairy and refined carbohydrates.
Signs and Symptoms	Abdominal discomfort and hard, dry stools that may be painful for your child to pass and that may be streaked with blood when they finally emerge.
What You Can Do	• Up your child's intake of water, prune juice, prunes, pears, plums, and peaches—nature's stool softeners! If they aren't effective, ask your doctor about the pros and cons of using mineral oil, nonprescription stool softeners, or laxative suppositories.

- Limit the number and quantities of constipating foods that your child eats (for example, white rice, rice cereal, bananas, apples, cooked carrots, milk, and cheese) while adding fiber to your child's diet. (Good sources of fiber for children include bran cereals, whole grain breads and crackers, and fiber-rich vegetables such as peas and beans.)

Condition	Diarrhea
Cause	Caused by gastrointestinal infections (most of which are viral in nature), food intolerances, and antibiotic treatments.
Signs and Symptoms	Frequent watery, green, mucusy, foul-smelling, explosive, and occasionally blood-tinged stools. Diarrhea is frequently accompanied by a bright red rash around the anus. A child with diarrhea can also be expected to show other signs of a viral infection. Note: Because each child's pattern of bowel movements is different, what you're looking for is a change in the consistency of your child's bowel movements.
What You Can Do	• Start tracking the frequency and quality of your child's stools and note whether she's vomiting or not, how much food and liquid she's been taking in, and how ill she seems. This information will help your doctor assess whether your child is at risk of becoming dehydrated.
	• Assess the severity of the diarrhea and watch for any signs of dehydration, particularly if your child is also experiencing a lot of vomiting. Diarrhea can throw your child's balance of salts (called electrolytes) and water out of whack—something that can affect the functioning of her organs.
	• Try to figure out what has triggered the diarrhea: illness, a change in diet (for example, too much fruit juice), or the result of antibiotic treatment for an ear infection, for example.

continued

Common Childhood Illnesses

Gastrointestinal Conditions (continued)

Diarrhea *(continued)* **What You Can Do**	• Give your child an oral electrolyte solution. While mothers a generation ago were told to treat diarrhea by giving their children ginger ale, juice, and sugar water, doctors no longer recommend that these beverages be given because their salt content is too low and their sugar content too high—something that can actually aggravate the child's diarrhea. Add to this the fact that certain types of fruit juices can have a laxative effect—the last thing your child needs when she's battling diarrhea!—and that many types of soda pop contain caffeine (a diuretic that can cause your child to become dehydrated), and you can see why oral electrolyte solutions (also known as oral rehydration solutions) are becoming the first-line defense against diarrhea. Believe it or not, even plain water isn't recommended for a child who is becoming dehydrated because it can result in a lowering in the amount of salt or sugar in the blood.
	• Don't give your child any diarrhea medication unless you're specifically advised to do so by your doctor. These medications, which slow down the action of the intestines, can actually worsen diarrhea by allowing the germs and infected fluid to stagnate in the gut.
	• Once the vomiting stops, reintroduce your child's usual formula or whole milk, or offer small quantities of non-irritating foods throughout the day. (Do not offer fruit juices or sweetened desserts until the diarrhea has stopped, or it may worsen again.)
	• Don't be alarmed if your child has more frequent bowel movements after you reintroduce these foods. It may take seven to ten days or even longer for her stools to go back to normal again. The bowel is relatively slow to heal.

- If you notice the diarrhea starting up again, you might want to back off and stick to foods that you know she can tolerate well. If the diarrhea continues to be a problem, get in touch with your doctor. She may want to order stool cultures to see whether there's a parasite such as giardia triggering the diarrhea.

- Call your child's doctor or go to the hospital immediately if your child is having bloody or black stools, has been vomiting for more than six to twelve hours, has a relatively high fever (over 102.5°F), or is showing some signs of dehydration. (See the section on dehydration earlier in this chapter.)

Condition	**Escherichia coli** (E. coli) Gastroenteritis
Cause	Can be picked up from poultry, beef, unpasteurized milk, or other food sources.
Signs and Symptoms	Fever, diarrhea, blood in stool, cramps. The germ that causes this condition is excreted in the stool, so your child is infectious while she has symptoms.
What You Can Do	• Get in touch with your child's doctor to see whether a stool sample is required to attempt to confirm that your child has been infected with E. coli.
	• Keep your child away from other children while you treat the illness.
	• Give your child acetaminophen to reduce her discomfort and treat her fever. Also, see tips under diarrhea (previously) for advice on how to manage your child's diarrhea.

continued

Common Childhood Illnesses

Gastrointestinal Conditions (continued)

Condition	Food Poisoning
Cause	Caused by eating contaminated food.
Signs and Symptoms	Nausea, vomiting, cramps, diarrhea. Not infectious, but symptoms may be shared by all members of the family who ate the same food.
What You Can Do	• Contact your child's doctor if your child's symptoms are severe. Otherwise, offer plenty of fluids and follow the tips on treating vomiting and diarrhea.
Condition	**Giardia** (a parasite in the stool that causes bowel infections)
Cause	Spread from person to person (quite common in childcare or preschool settings).
Signs and Symptoms	Most children have no symptoms, but some may experience loss of appetite, vomiting, cramps, diarrhea, very soft stools, and excessive gas. This condition is infectious until cured.
What You Can Do	• Get in touch with your child's doctor to see whether a stool sample is required to attempt to confirm that your child has been infected with giardia.
	• Keep your child away from other children while you treat the illness.
	• Give your child acetaminophen to reduce her discomfort and treat her fever. Also, see tips under diarrhea (previously) for advice on how to manage your child's diarrhea.

Condition	**Hepatitis A** (a liver infection)
Cause	A virus in the stool that can be spread from person to person or via food or water.
Signs and Symptoms	Most children exhibit few symptoms. Where symptoms are present, they include fever, reduced appetite, nausea, vomiting, and jaundice (a yellowish tinge to skin and eyes). Hepatitis A is infectious from two weeks before to one week after the onset of jaundice.
What You Can Do	• Get in touch with your child's doctor. She may want to order an immune globulin vaccine for all members of your family, including your child.
Condition	**Norwalk Virus**
Cause	Spread from person to person via the air.
Signs and Symptoms	Vomiting for one to two days. Contagious for the duration of the illness.
What You Can Do	• Get in touch with your child's doctor to see whether a stool sample is required to attempt to confirm that your child has been infected with Norwalk Virus.
	• Keep your child away from other children while you treat the illness.
	• Give your child acetaminophen to reduce her discomfort and treat her fever. Also, see tips under diarrhea (previously) for advice on how to manage your child's diarrhea.
Condition	**Rotavirus** (Gastroenteritis)
Cause	Caused by a virus in the stool that is spread through person-to-person contact. Rotavirus is the most common cause of diarrhea outbreaks in child-care centers.

continued

Common Childhood Illnesses

Gastrointestinal Conditions (continued)

Rotavirus *(continued)*	
Signs and Symptoms	Fever and vomiting followed by watery diarrhea. Can lead to rapid dehydration in infants. Contagious for duration of illness.
What You Can Do	• Get in touch with your child's doctor to see whether a stool sample is required to attempt to confirm that your child has been infected with rotavirus. • Keep your child away from other children while you treat the illness. • Give your child acetaminophen to reduce her discomfort and treat her fever. Also, see diarrhea section (previously) for managing your child's diarrhea.
Condition	**Salmonella** (Enteritis)
Cause	Acquired mainly by eating food that has been contaminated with salmonella. Such foods typically include eggs, egg products, beef, poultry, and unpasteurized milk.
Signs and Symptoms	Diarrhea, fever, blood in stool. Infectious while symptoms persist.
What You Can Do	• Contact your child's doctor when your child's symptoms are severe. Otherwise, offer plenty of fluids and follow the tips on treating vomiting and diarrhea.
Condition	**Shigella** (Enteritis)
Cause	Caused by a virus in the stool that can be spread from person to person.
Signs and Symptoms	Diarrhea, fever, blood and/or mucus in stool, cramps. Highly contagious for the duration of the illness.

What You Can Do	• Get in touch with your child's doctor to see if a stool sample is required to attempt to confirm that your child has been infected with shigella.
	• Keep your child away from other children while you treat the illness.
	• Give your child acetaminophen to reduce her discomfort and treat her fever. Also, see tips under diarrhea (previously) for advice on how to manage your child's diarrhea.
Condition	**Vomiting**
Cause	Vomiting can be caused by a viral infection, food poisoning, or by a medical condition such as pyloric stenosis (projectile vomiting caused by a partial or complete intestinal blockage that requires surgical correction) or gastroesophageal reflux (a condition in which stomach acids are regurgitated into the esophagus, frequently resulting in forceful regurgitation through the nose).
Signs and Symptoms	Vomiting can be accompanied by diarrhea or other symptoms, depending on the underlying cause.
What You Can Do	• Offer small, frequent servings of fluid to prevent dehydration. If your child is old enough to eat a popsicle, you might want to try making popsicles out of the oral electrolyte solution to see if this makes it easier for her to keep the fluid down. Notify your child's doctor if the vomiting continues for longer than six to twelve hours or if abdominal pain and fever are also present.
	• If your child is hungry and seems able to keep some foods down, offer "stomach-friendly" foods such as toast, bananas, oatmeal, cooked rice, and crackers.

continued

Common Childhood Illnesses

Genitourinary Tract Infections

Condition	**Balanoposthitis** (an infection of the penis)
Cause	An infection that can occur in uncircumcised boys. It can be caused by forcing back a foreskin that doesn't retract easily (something that results in irritation to the membranes and/or painful urination). Note: A related condition, paraphimosis (when a foreskin with a relatively tight opening is retracted and becomes trapped around the base of the penis) can become extremely painful and requires immediate medical attention.
Signs and Symptoms	Pain and swelling of the tip of the penis (the glans) as well as the membranes of the foreskin. White or gray discharge may be present if the inflammation is due to infection.
What You Can Do	• Your son's doctor will likely prescribe antibiotics to treat his balanoposthitis. If urination continues to be painful while you're waiting for the antibiotics to start to work, encourage your son to take frequent tepid warm-water baths and to urinate while sitting in the tub, if that's the only way to urinate without experiencing extreme discomfort.
Condition	**Urinary Tract Infections**
Cause	The usual cause is bacteria, normally found in stool, which inadvertently contaminate the urethra and bladder. This often occurs in the newly toilet-trained age group where children begin wiping themselves after using the restroom. However, in the young infant, the cause is much more likely to be related to a condition known as reflux (where the bladder contracts, sending urine both forward and backward toward the kidneys, often not emptying out all the of the urine.) Overall, urinary tract infections are more common in girls than in boys.
Signs and symptoms	Painful and frequent urination, urgency to urinate, dribbling or wetting the underpants, foul odor to the urine, fever, abdominal pain, and vomiting

What You Can Do	• Get in touch with your child's doctor so that the urinary tract infection can be diagnosed and antibiotic treatment can be started. Note: Children who have problems with recurrent urinary tract infections often benefit from longer-term daily antibiotic treatment.
	• If your child suffers from recurrent urinary tract infections, your doctor may order an ultrasound and x-ray or some other type of test to make sure that your child's kidneys are functioning properly and/or to see whether there is a correctable reason for the infections.
Condition	**Vulvitis** (if just the vulva is involved) or vulvovaginitis (if both the vulva and the vagina are involved)
Cause	Irritants and moisture can become trapped in the vulva, causing infection. Other common causes include sensitivity to soaps and perfumes, improper wiping, and tight clothing that traps moisture. Sometimes vulvitis is caused by a yeast infection or a group A strep infection.
Signs and Symptoms	The vulva and the vagina become red and sore to touch. There may be a discharge. Itching and burning may be particularly intense at the time of urination but may persist in between urinations. Note: Chronic vulvitis can cause the labia minora (the thin flaps of tissue on either side of the urethral and vaginal openings) to stick together. This condition—which is known as labial adhesion—can be treated.
What You Can Do	• If vulvitis is a problem for your daughter, you will want to limit her use of bubble baths and avoid applying soap directly to the membranes of her vulva.
	• When she is experiencing a flare-up, she may find it soothing to soak in a tepid, plain-water tub. After she gets out of the tub, pat her vulva area with a towel gently without rubbing and then allow her vulva to finish air-drying before she gets dressed.

continued

Common Childhood Illnesses

Genitourinary Tract Infections *(continued)*

Vulvitis *(continued)*	
What You Can Do	• Encourage your daughter to wear loose-fitting clothing that allows air circulation around the vulva.
	• Make sure your daughter is using proper wiping techniques after she uses the toilet (e.g., wiping from front to back).
	• If the vulvitis is severe or is accompanied by a discharge, the doctor may wish to order a few tests to try to figure out what's triggering the vulvitis and to prescribe some antibiotics to try to clear up the problem. Note: Antibiotics won't help with run-of-the-mill vulvitis and vulvovaginitis, but they can help if group A strep, yeast, or pinworms are triggering the outbreak.
	• If there's any possibility that your daughter may have been sexually assaulted or involved in voluntary sexual activity, she should be screened for sexually transmitted diseases and counseled on pregnancy prevention.

Other Conditions

Condition	Meningitis
Cause	Can be bacterial or viral in origin. Meningitis can be fatal. The incubation period is usually 10 to 14 days. Fortunately, bacterial meningitis—the most serious kind—is very rare in preschool children over the age of six weeks who have been fully immunized. Bacterial meningitis may be caused by haemophilus influenza, pneumoccal bacteria, or meningococcal bacteria. The first two are most common during infancy.
Signs and Symptoms	Bacterial meningitis (spinal meningitis) may begin like a cold, flu, or ear infection, but the child becomes increasingly ill and very lethargic; develops a fever of 102 to 105°F. The child typically has a headache and/or stiff neck. With viral meningitis, the child exhibits similar symptoms but isn't quite as ill.

What You Can Do	• Contact your doctor immediately. She'll want to do a spinal tap to determine whether the meningitis is bacterial or viral in origin. The sooner the illness is diagnosed and treated, the better the outcome.
	• If the meningitis turns out to be bacterial in origin, your doctor will want to treat the illness with intravenous antibiotics for at least seven days.
	• If it turns out to be viral in origin, the illness will be treated like the flu.
	• Prevnar vaccine is designed to prevent pneumococcal infections. Because pneumococcal meningitis predominates in infancy, it is best not to delay the administration of this vaccine beyond the first year of life. Note: The HIB vaccine is designed to prevent haemophilus infections. The Menomune vaccine is designed to prevent meningococcal disease.
Condition	**Mumps**
Cause	Spread by a virus that has an incubation period of seven to ten days.
Signs and Symptoms	Flu-like symptoms and an upset stomach initially; then tender swollen glands beneath the ear lobes two or three days later. Your child may look as if she has "chipmunk cheeks" and may find it painful to open her jaw. She may also have a low-grade fever. Mumps typically last for seven to ten days, and the illness is contagious until the swelling is gone.
What You Can Do	• Feed your child liquids and soft foods.
	• Apply cool compresses to the neck.
	• Administer acetaminophen to relieve discomfort and pain.
	• Call your doctor's office immediately if your child becomes drowsy, starts vomiting repeatedly, becomes dehydrated, or develops a stiff neck.

Antibiotic Alert

Antibiotics are powerful medications that can be used to treat life-threatening illnesses, such as meningitis, as well as less serious infections, such as impetigo. Because they are so effective, they tend to be used widely—something that has unfortunately led to the emergence of antibiotic-resistant strains of bacteria.

According to the American Academy of Pediatrics, you can do your bit to prevent antibiotic-resistant strains of bacteria from becoming more of a problem by:

- seeking antibiotic treatment for your child only in situations where their use is warranted (for example, children with colds should not be treated with antibiotics)

- ensuring that you follow your doctor's instructions for antibiotic use carefully (that is, the prescribed dose is given and the antibiotics are taken for the recommended length of time)

- seeing that your child doesn't take any antibiotics that have been prescribed for anyone else

- ensuring that your child doesn't use any antibiotics that are left over from an unfinished prescription

You can find out more about the American Academy of Pediatric's position on the safe use of antibiotics by visiting the AAP's Web site at www.aap.org.

MOTHER WISDOM

Don't be surprised if your child's temperature remains high for the first day or two after she starts antibiotic treatment. It takes time for the antibiotics to start working their magic.

MOTHER WISDOM

Here are some important questions to ask your doctor or pharmacist when your doctor prescribes a medication for your child for the very first time:

- How will this medication help my child?
- What is the correct dosage?
- Do I need to shake the bottle before administering the medication to my child?
- How often do I give my child the medication? Does it have to be administered at a particular time of day?
- How long does my child have to take the medication? Will the prescription be repeated, or is this a "one-shot" deal?
- Should the medication be taken on a full or empty stomach?
- Are there any foods or drinks my child needs to avoid while taking this medication?
- Should the medication be stored in the refrigerator or at room temperature?
- Is it necessary to wake my child up in the night to administer this medication?
- Are there any side effects to this medication that I need to know about?
- Is there any chance that my child could have an allergic reaction to this medication? If so, what warning signs should I watch out for?

More About Fever

Before we move on to our discussion of the most common types of childhood illnesses, let's take a moment to talk about children and fevers—a perennial cause of concern to parents.

Fever Isn't the Bad Guy; the Illness Is

The first thing you need to know about fevers is that fever in and of itself is rarely dangerous. Contrary to popular belief, brain damage due to a high temperature is extremely rare. In order for brain damage to occur, your child's temperature would have to shoot to about 107.6º F (42º C) for an extended period of time. Fevers that are caused by an infection rarely manage to climb above 105º F (40.5º C) unless a child is overdressed or in an extremely hot environment. That's one fever-related worry you can strike off your list relatively easily.

Fever can, in fact, be a *good* thing, even though it can make your child (and consequently you) feel downright miserable for a while. The presence of a fever is usually a sign that your child's body is hard at work fighting off an infection (typically a common illness such as a cold, a sore throat, or an ear infection, but possibly something more serious). Most of the bacteria and viruses that cause infections in humans thrive at our normal body temperature, so one of the body's key strategies for defending itself is to elevate its temperature by a couple of degrees. Add the fact that fever helps to activate the immune system, boosting the production of white blood cells, antibodies, and many other infection-fighting agents, and you'll see that there's no need to sweat it when your child gets a fever. (Sorry, I couldn't resist that particular pun!)

This does not compute

Something else you need to know is that the height of the fever is not necessarily directly related to the severity of your child's illness. In other words, even though your child may have a relatively high fever, it's possible that she's only mildly ill. On the other hand, a child with a relatively low fever can, in fact, be quite ill, which is why it's important to pay attention to her other symptoms. Instead of getting hung up on the number on the thermometer—an easy trap to fall into, by the way—concentrate on how sick your child is acting and look for symptoms of any underlying infection. (See Table 10.4.)

NO KIDDING!

The most common causes of fever in children under the age of six are viral infections, strep throat, ear infections, bronchitis, gastrointestinal infections, and urinary-tract infections.

The most common causes of fever in school-aged kids are viral respiratory-tract infections, strep throat, and urinary-tract infections, which tend to be particularly common in girls.

TABLE 10.4

Common Illnesses That Can Cause a Fever

Symptoms	What Could Be Causing These Symptoms
Fever, cough, runny nose, trouble breathing, sore throat, sore muscles	Common cold, influenza, other respiratory infections
Fever, rash, sore throat, and/or swollen glands	Chicken pox or viral illness such as stomach flu
Fever, earache, discharge from ears, dizziness from pain	Ear infection
Fever, swollen glands, sore throat	Tonsillitis, streptococcal or viral infection, mononucleosis
Fever, nausea, vomiting, diarrhea, and/or cramps	Infectious gastroenteritis (viral or bacterial)

What type of thermometer to use

If you've checked out the thermometer aisle at your local drugstore lately, you already know that there are dozens of different models on the market today—everything from old-fashioned glass thermometers (the Chevys of the thermometer world) to state-of-the-art ear thermometers (the undisputed Cadillacs—at least when it comes to price!). Fortunately, the decision about which thermometer to buy is relatively simple: it's best to stick to using digital rather than glass thermometers, due to the risk of breakage. Besides, today's digital thermometers are every bit as accurate as the glass thermometers of yesteryear (the traditional gold standard). What's more, they offer a few additional advantages: they're faster to use; they beep when the maximum temperature has been reached; they're easier to read; and the same thermometer can be used for both oral and rectal temperatures, (provided they're cleaned thoroughly between uses!).

How to take your child's temperature

You have two basic choices when it comes to taking the temperature of a preschooler: taking it rectally or taking an axillary temperature (under the armpit). Temperatures of children under four years of age should not be taken orally.

Rectal temperature-taking

Rectal temperatures tend to be the most accurate, but they aren't exactly the temperature-taking method of choice for either parents or children. Here's what's involved in taking your child's temperature rectally:

- Place your child on her back with her knees bent over her abdomen.

- Coat the tip of the thermometer with water-soluble jelly and insert it about 1 inch into your child's rectum.

- Hold the thermometer in place until the digital thermometer beeps to indicate that the final temperature reading has been obtained—something that typically takes about two minutes.

- Clean the thermometer thoroughly using soap and warm water.

- Keep in mind that rectal temperature readings tend to be about 1°F higher than temperatures taken orally; a "normal" range for a rectal temperature is 97.9° F to 101° F.

Note: Rectal temperatures can also be taken on older children when a child's nose is so congested that it's impossible for her to keep her mouth closed with a thermometer in place, or in other extenuating circumstances.

Axillary temperature-taking

Axillary temperatures (temperatures that are taken under the armpit) tend to be slightly less accurate, but they're much easier to take. Here's what's involved:

- Place the bulb of the thermometer under your child's arm so that it's nestled in her armpit, and then hold her arm against her body so that the bulb is thoroughly covered.

- Hold the thermometer in place until it beeps to indicate that the final temperature reading has been obtained—something that typically takes about two minutes.

- Clean the thermometer thoroughly using soap and warm water.

- Keep in mind that axillary temperature readings tend to be about 0.5° F lower than temperatures taken orally; a "normal" range for an axillary temperature is 94.5° F to 99.1° F.

Oral temperature-taking

If your child is age four or older, you'll want to take your child's temperature orally. Here's how to proceed:

- Make sure that the thermometer is clean. (Ideally, it should be cleaned after each use so that it's always ready to go; if you're not sure whether it was cleaned properly the last time it was used, clean it with soap and water first.)

- Place the thermometer under your child's tongue and have her close her lips to help hold the thermometer in place. She should keep the thermometer in her mouth until it beeps to indicate that the final temperature reading has been obtained—something that typically takes about two minutes.

- Clean the thermometer thoroughly using soap and warm water.

- A normal oral temperature is 98.6° F, but anything between 97.0° F and 100.0° F is considered to be within the normal range.

What you need to know about febrile convulsions

Febrile convulsions (seizures) tend to occur when a child's temperature shoots up very suddenly. They are more common in infants than in older children (most children outgrow them by age four or five), and are more likely to occur in families with a history of febrile convulsions. They occur in approximately 4 percent of children.

Although febrile convulsions are relatively common and generally quite harmless, they can be extremely frightening to watch. If your child has a febrile convulsion, she may breathe heavily, drool, turn dusky or pale in color, roll her eyes back in her head, and/or shake her arms and legs uncontrollably.

If your child has a febrile convulsion, you should lay her on her back or side (ensuring that she's far away from anything she could hurt herself on) and then gently turn her head to one side so that any vomit or saliva can drain easily. You should note how long the convulsion lasts—anywhere from ten seconds to three to four minutes is common. After the convulsion is over, it is fine to administer acetaminophen to bring down your child's temperature. (See the tips on treating your child's fever later in this chapter.)

When to call the doctor

Although most fevers are harmless, you should plan to get in touch with your child's doctor if:

- your child's fever is very high (over 102° F)

- your child is acting very sick

- your child has had a fever for a couple of days and/or her temperature is not coming down

- she's crying inconsolably, seems cranky or irritable, or is whimpering and seems weak

- she's having difficulty waking up or seems listless and confused

- she's limp

- she's having convulsions (if she turned blue during the seizure, had convulsions that lasted more than a few minutes, had difficulty breathing after the seizure passed, or still seems drowsy or lethargic an hour later, seek emergency medical assistance)

- she appears to have a stiff neck or an ususually severe headache

- she's experiencing stomach pain

- she has purple (not red) spots on the skin or large purple blotches (possible signs of meningitis, an infection of the brain)

- she's having difficulty breathing (a possible sign of asthma or pneumonia)

- she has constant vomiting or diarrhea

- she is becoming dehydrated

- she's unable to swallow and is drooling excessively (a possible sign of epiglottitis, a life-threatening infection that causes swelling in the back of the throat)

- you know that she has a weakened immune system

 NO KIDDING!

Don't expect your doctor to prescribe an antibiotic to ward off your child's fever unless there's a specific underlying infection that requires treatment. The vast majority of children with fevers have nonbacterial (viral) upper respiratory infections that don't require antibiotics. That means your first line of defense against fever is likely to be none other than acetaminophen.

Treating a fever

Of course, it's not necessary to rush off to the emergency department every time your child's temperature shoots up by a degree or two. The majority of fevers can be managed at home. Here's what you need to know:

- The best way to treat a fever—assuming, of course, that it actually needs to be treated at all—is by administering acetaminophen—an analgesic that helps to bring down your child's fever while relieving some of her discomfort. (See Table 10.5 for a complete list of items that should be in the family medicine chest while you have children in your family.) You'll also want to find out whether any of the other cough or cold medications that your child is taking contain acetaminophen. If she's receiving acetaminophen in both a cold medicine and a pain medication, she may be receiving more than the recommended dose of acetaminophen—something that can be potentially serious or life threatening.

Note: You can find some other helpful tips on administering medication to a child in Table 10.6.

- Avoid overdressing your child. Dressing her in loose, light-weight cotton clothing with only a sheet or light blanket for covering will help to bring down her fever naturally.

- Give your child plenty of fluids in order to help bring her body temperature down and help protect against dehydration.

 NO KIDDING!

Studies have shown that giving a child twice the recommended dose of acetaminophen over a period of days can be toxic. If your child becomes nauseated, starts vomiting, and experiences abdominal pain, you should try to determine if she has received too much acetaminophen.

 NO KIDDING!

A study reported in the *Archives of Pediatrics & Adolescent Medicine* found that 43 percent of parents and caregivers had given the children in their care the wrong dose of acetaminophen—either too much or too little.

- Keep your child's room cool, but not cold. If she gets too cold, her body will start shivering, which will cause her body temperature to rise.

- You can also try to lower your child's temperature by sponging her down with lukewarm water (a sponge bath) or giving her a lukewarm bath. (Don't use cold water or she'll start shivering—something that can prove counterproductive.) Then, instead of drying your child off, let the water evaporate from her skin. This will help to cool her down. Whatever you do, don't add alcohol to the water in the mistaken belief that this will somehow help to bring down your child's temperature. Doing so could lead to serious—even life-threatening—complications.

TABLE 10.5

Medicine Chest Essentials

Make a point of keeping your family medicine cabinet stocked with the following items so that you'll have what you need on hand to handle most common illnesses and injuries:

→ acetaminophen

→ adhesive tape

→ antibiotic ointment

→ antiseptic solution

→ bandages

→ calamine lotion (to relieve itching from insect bites and rashes)

→ cotton balls

→ cotton-tipped swabs (Q-Tips)

→ decongestant (children's-strength liquid formulation approved by your child's doctor)

→ flashlight

→ gauze (rolls and pads)

→ hydrogen peroxide

→ ice packs (the instant type that don't require refrigeration)

→ infant dropper or medicine syringe

→ insect repellant (child-safe)

→ poison control hotline phone number

→ activated charcoal (to induce vomiting if that course of action is recommended by the poison control center staff)

→ lubricant (water-based), to lubricate rectal thermometer

→ medicine dropper, oral syringe, and/or calibrated cup or spoon for administering medications

→ nail clippers (child-safe type)

→ nasal aspirator

→ nose drops (saline)

→ oral electrolyte solution (to prevent dehydration)

→ rubbing alcohol (for sterilizing thermometers, tweezers, and scissors)

→ scissors (blunt-ended)

→ sunscreen

→ thermometer (digital)

→ tweezers

TABLE 10.6

Administering Medication to a Child

Forget about the spoonful of sugar: what it really takes to get the medicine down is proper technique. Here are tips on administering some of the types of medication that your doctor may prescribe for your child:

Oral Medications
→ Use a syringe or an oral dropper to administer an accurate dose of medication to young children. (Note: Avoid squirting the medication into the back of your child's throat, or you'll trigger her gag reflex. Try to avoid hitting the taste buds at the front and center of your child's tongue.)

continued

Administering Medication to a Child *continued*

Oral Medications continued

➡   Avoid adding any sort of medication to a glass of milk or bowl of cereal. If your child wants only part of her milk or her cereal, she'll miss out on some of the medication. If you absolutely have to mix it with some sort of food because she refuses to take it any other way, make sure to use a very small amount of food or liquid—a quantity that you know your child will have no trouble eating or drinking.

➡   Let your doctor know if your child vomits repeatedly after taking a particular medication or if she has a stomach flu that makes it impossible for her to keep anything down. Your doctor may decide to prescribe an injection or suppository instead.

➡   If you miss a dose, administer the next dose as soon as you remember. Then add the missed dose to the end of the course of medication. Don't double up on doses unless your doctor specifically tells you to do so and be sure to get in touch with your doctor if your child ends up missing an entire day's worth of medication.

Ear Drops

➡   Lay your child down.

➡   Remove any medication that may have built up on the outer ear as a result of past treatments before you administer the next dose.

➡   Turn your child's head to one side and gently pull the middle of the outer ear back slightly. This will allow fluid to enter the ear canal more readily.

Eye Drops or Ointments

➡   Gently pull down the lower lid of your child's eye and apply the ointment or administer the drops. Don't allow the dropper or the tube to touch your child's eye, or it may become contaminated. (Just to be on the safe side, wipe the dropper or the tube with a tissue after you're finished doing the treatment.)

Skin Ointments or Creams

→ Apply some of the ointment or cream to a tissue.

→ Using the tissue or a clean finger, apply the ointment or cream to your child's skin. To reduce the chance of contaminating the ointment or cream, discard the used tissue and use a fresh one if more ointment or cream is required, or make a point of rewashing your hands between applications.

Your Top Pediatric Health Questions Answered

Up until now, I've focused on illnesses and fevers. This section tackles some other important pediatric health topics by zeroing in on some of the most commonly asked questions about children's health.

Just one important note before I get down to business. Obviously, it's simply not possible for me to address every conceivable child health topic in one chapter (as it is, it's already the heftiest chapter in the book!). If your question isn't addressed here, I encourage you to flip to the index (to find out whether I've answered your question in one of the other health-related chapters in the book) or the appendices (to learn about pediatric health organizations and Web sites that may be helpful to you in your search for reliable health information).

My seven-year-old sometimes wakes up in the night complaining of pains in his legs. Are these "growing pains"?

It's quite possible that the middle-of-the-night pains that are causing your child so much discomfort are just that: growing pains. But because aches and pains in the legs can be caused by everything from bumping into a coffee table to falling off a bike, you'll want to look for a few more clues before you decide that's what to blame. Here's what to look for:

- pain that occurs in both legs, rather than just one (Note: sometimes kids report that one leg seems to hurt more than the other or that one leg hurts some nights while the other leg hurts other nights).

- pain that occurs when the legs are motionless (pain that occurs when your child is motionless—even sleeping—is characteristic of growing pains)

- pain that is centered in the calves and shins but may be felt in the foot, ankle, knee, or thigh

- pain that gets worse, not better, when you massage the affected area (again, this can be a clue that he's dealing with growing pains rather than some other type of problem)

- pain that eases up in the morning (growing pains tend to be worse at night, so if your child seems to be as good as new in the morning—for example, he's not limping around or otherwise in pain—you can probably pin the blame for his nocturnal discomfort on growing pains)

Growing pains are most common in children between the ages of 2 and 5 (more common in boys), and, while they last, they can be quite painful. Don't make the mistake of assuming that your child's growing pains are all in his head; they're very real indeed.

My 10-year-old has recurrent stomach aches. What are some of the more common causes of stomach aches in young children?

Although it's easy to assume the worst when abdominal pain is involved, in 95 percent of cases, there's something relatively innocuous to blame, such as worry or anxiety, constipation, or food intolerances. There's generally more cause for concern if:

- the pain is particularly sudden (that is, it's severe enough to wake your child from a deep sleep in the middle of the night)

- your child's symptoms last for more than 2 hours (especially if the pain ebbs and flows for a period longer than 12 hours)

- your child is vomiting blood or green bile

- your child has an extremely high fever

- your child has blood in her stool

Getting a handle on what's causing your child's stomach aches can be a challenge for parents and doctors alike. You'll be able to pick up a few clues as to what may be going on if you're able to get your child to describe her symptoms in a little more detail. Does she feel like throwing up? Does she feel like she has to go to the bathroom? Does her stomach feel overly full and bloated, kind of like she ate too much?

 NO KIDDING!

You should assume that your child is experiencing an appendicitis attack if the pain in your child's stomach is centered in her navel initially, but then starts to move to the lower right part of her abdomen (an area that may be extremely tender to the touch). She is likely to have a fever, too, and she may experience some vomiting. Often these children have difficulty walking because of the pain. It's important to seek medical attention immediately if you think your child may have appendicitis because appendicitis can quickly progress into a medical emergency. You want to have your child treated before her appendix ruptures, if at all possible, to minimize both the amount of pain she experiences and to avoid dangerous complications.

Here are some common causes of stomach aches in children:

- **Constipation:** If your child doesn't have bowel movements frequently enough or is in the habit of withholding bowel movements (stool withholding), your child may experience a lot of cramping and abdominal pain. (See more on stool withholding in the section on encopresis that follows.)

- **Gastroesophageal reflux:** Gastroesophageal reflux—a condition in which acid from the stomach is regurgitated—can lead to heartburn-like symptoms.

- **H. pylori infection:** H. pylori infection refers to ulceration and inflammation caused by a bacterium that lives in the stomach. Note: Sometimes this condition occurs without any accompanying sensations of pain.

- **Intestinal and urinary tract infections:** Intestinal and urinary tract infections can also lead to abdominal discomfort. (See Table 10.2 for more about some of the specific gastrointestinal conditions that may be to blame.)

- **Irritable bowel syndrome:** Irritable bowel syndrome (a group of symptoms in which abdominal pain or discomfort is associated with a change in bowel patterns, such as loose or more frequent bowel movements, diarrhea, and/or constipation) is one of the most common causes of abdominal pain in children.

- **Lactose intolerance:** Lactose intolerance—the inability to digest the sugar found in milk and dairy products—can lead to gas, cramps, and, in some children, diarrhea.

- **Other food intolerances:** Other types of food intolerances, such as wheat allergies, can also trigger similar symptoms—gas, cramps, and diarrhea.

- **Stress:** Stress can also trigger stomach aches in young children. (See the section on anxiety disorders at the end of this chapter.)

If you feel reasonably certain that whatever it is that's causing the discomfort doesn't pose any immediate threat to your child's health, you'll want to focus on making her comfortable. She may find it soothing to use a heating pad, for example. If she's hungry, offer her clear fluids until you figure out what's going on. (If you offer her solid foods, she's likely to feel worse.)

My 10-year-old keeps soiling his underwear. I'm not sure if he's being lazy about going to the bathroom or whether there's an underlying medical problem.

Soiling (encopresis) affects approximately 1.5 percent of children. It is six times as common in boys as it is in girls.

There are two types of encopresis:

- **primary encopresis** (when children have always had problems with soiling their underwear).

- **secondary encopresis** (when a child suddenly starts soiling his underwear after a period of being toilet-trained).

Soiling tends to occur in kids who are chronically constipated, particularly those who are not in the habit of responding promptly to the urge to produce a bowel movement. Delaying this urge can cause the intestinal walls and nerves contained within the intestinal walls to stretch. This causes the intestines to become less efficient at contracting and squeezing stool out and the nerves to become less effective at triggering the urge to defecate. Over time, the retained mass of stool becomes larger, harder, and more difficult to pass, which can lead the child to become even more constipated in an attempt to avoid a potentially painful bowel movement (stool withholding)—something that can, in turn, lead to cramping and abdominal pain. Eventually, the sphincter muscles are no longer able to retain the stool. Liquid stool begins seeping around the impacted mass, staining the underwear, and, in some cases, the child may pass semi-formed stools or have partial bowel movements.

Because of the decreased sensation in his intestinal system, the child may not even be aware that he has passed some stool. Over time, he may get used to the odor of stool, so he may eventually lose all awareness of the fact that he has soiled himself—something that can have rather unfortunate social implications for the child.

The first step in treating this condition is to use medications to clean out the intestinal tract. Enemas, laxatives, and/or suppositories may be required to get rid of all the retained stool so that the intestinal tract can begin to shrink back to a more normal size. (Note: You'll want to get some guidance from your child's doctor on how to deal with this problem.)

 MOM'S THE WORD

"We've stopped bugging our four-year-old about his stool-withholding problem. The bigger the scene we make, the less likely he will go on his own. He actually has this dance he does around the house that we call the 'poop dance.' This combo of hopping and swaggering and pressing on his stomach allows him to successfully hold in a bowel movement for days. If we don't say anything to him, he'll eventually go on his own. I have to say, this is one of our all-time biggest parenting challenges."

—*Shelly, 32, mother of three*

After your child has eliminated this mass of stool, you'll want to encourage him to have bowel movements more regularly by ensuring that his diet contains plenty of fluids and high-fiber foods. You may also want to supplement these dietary measures by administering medications recommended by your child's doctor. The goal is to keep your child's intestinal system functioning fairly regularly for at least three to six months, so that his intestinal tract can shrink back to its normal size, and he can avoid the soiling problem in the future.

Relapses are common with this condition, so don't be surprised if you find yourself in for a few frustrating bouts of treatment (to say nothing of a lot of soiled laundry). Rome wasn't built in a day, and encopresis isn't cured overnight.

My preteen gets a lot of headaches. Is it possible that she could be prone to migraines?

Although it is possible for even very young children to develop migraines, more often than not, when kids experience headaches, garden-variety tension headaches are to blame. Tension headaches are characterized by a tight feeling in the head, particularly around the temples and in the neck muscles. This type of headache is caused by a contraction of the muscles in the neck.

MOTHER WISDOM

Sudden, severe headaches require immediate medical attention because they may indicate a more serious medical problem. If you're having difficulty differentiating between a severe headache and a migraine, seek medical attention for your child. Better safe than sorry.

A child who develops a migraine can expect to experience nausea, vomiting, and visual disturbances in addition to a headache. Some children who are prone to migraines complain that they feel a burning, tingling, aching, or squeezing sensation in their heads—sensations that are triggered by the effects of various brain chemicals on the blood vessels in the brain. Migraines typically last for a couple of hours or even overnight.

A child who is experiencing a migraine will be most comfortable if allowed to rest in a quiet, darkened room. If a child experiences migraines more than two to three times per month, oral or nasal medications may be recommended to reduce the frequency of the child's migraine attacks.

Because migraines tend to run in the family, some children are predisposed to developing them. So, if you or your partner has struggled with migraines for much of your life, your child may very well follow in your footsteps.

What is the difference between a nightmare and a night terror?

Although some parents use the terms *night terror* and *nightmare* interchangeably, they're actually two entirely different things.

Nightmares occur during a period of light sleep (dream sleep). When a child is having a nightmare, she may be crying and screaming, but she can be easily awakened. All that may be required to get her back to sleep is a bit of reassurance that what happened in her dream wasn't real. (Young children often find it difficult to tell what's real and what's a dream.)

Night terrors, on the other hand, occur when a child is moving from a deep stage of sleep to a lighter stage of sleep. A child who is experiencing a night terror may let out a blood-curdling scream and then sit bolt upright in bed with her heart pounding, her body dripping with sweat, and her eyes wide open in a zombie-like state. She will be completely unaware of her surroundings and—despite the fact that the episode may last as long as half an hour—she will have no memory of it in the morning. It's impossible to wake a child who is experiencing night terrors—nor would you want to; waking your child will only serve to prolong the episode. One thing you will want to do, however, is to stay with your child to prevent her from accidentally injuring herself.

Although night terrors are quite common in three- to six-year-olds (1 to 5 percent of children experience them), most children outgrow night terrors by four years of age. During this period, the night terrors will come and go, appearing most often when a child is overtired or agitated. They tend to happen in clusters: a child may have none at all for a long period of time, and then one or two a week for a couple of months. They also tend to run in the family. If you experienced them in your own growing-up years, your child may very well experience them, too.

MOM'S THE WORD

"My youngest child went through about a six-month period where he thought there was a 'bad guy' in his room. We eliminated all movies with scary things in them, any kids' TV shows with scary stories or characters, and scary games like hide and seek. Things improved dramatically."

—*Mary, 37, mother of three*

You don't have to worry that night terrors indicate any sort of underlying mental health problem. They are just one of those strange things that some kids experience en route to adulthood.

Lately, my 11-year-old has started sleepwalking. Is it true that sleepwalking is fairly common amongst preteens?

Yes. Although sleepwalking is relatively common in children of all ages (15 percent of kids between the ages of 5 and 12 have experienced at least one sleepwalking episode), sleepwalking reaches its peak during the preteen years. Sleepwalking is more common with boys than with girls and is more likely to occur if a child tends to have problems with bedwetting. It also tends to run in the family.

Children who sleepwalk tend to get out of bed, wander around aimlessly with a blank look on their face, and talk incoherently. They typically have no memory of these episodes in the morning. Because sleepwalkers are totally unaware of danger, you'll want to ensure that you keep your doors and windows locked if you have a child who sleepwalks.

Studies have shown that sleepwalking can be avoided if parents get in the habit of waking up their child approximately 15 minutes before the time of night when sleepwalking tends to occur and then keep their child awake for 5 minutes. This will prevent sleepwalking 80 percent of the time.

Although medication can be used to treat sleepwalking, it is typically reserved for those situations where sleepwalking is happening very frequently and/or where the sleepwalker gets into a lot of trouble or repeatedly injures himself while sleepwalking.

My daughter was just diagnosed with sleep apnea. What can be done to treat this condition?

Approximately 1 to 3 percent of children suffer from obstructive sleep apnea syndrome, a condition that causes them to stop breathing for short periods of time. (The child's breathing is interrupted due to an obstruction in the respiratory tract—typically the result of enlarged tonsils, enlarged adenoids, or obesity.)

The symptoms of obstructive sleep apnea syndrome include snoring, difficulty breathing or cessation of breathing during sleep, mouth breathing during sleep, sleeping in unusual positions, a change in color while sleeping, and chronic sleepiness or tiredness during the day.

Fortunately, a range of treatment options is available. The surgical removal of the tonsils and adenoids cures 95 percent of cases of sleep apnea. It's important to seek treatment for your child. If left untreated, this condition can lead to neurological or behavioral problems, poor growth, and—in the most severe cases—heart damage.

Should I be concerned about my child's snoring?

Up until quite recently, the experts would have told you that there was no reason to be unduly concerned about snoring, but now doctors are recommending that parents report incidences of snoring in children so that snorers can be screened for sleep apnea. Between 3 and 12 percent of children snore, and approximately 2 percent of kids have sleep apnea. Because virtually all kids with sleep apnea are snorers, snoring can serve as a convenient red flag in screening for potential cases of sleep apnea.

My three-year-old likes to rock himself to sleep. Should I try to break him of this habit?

Some kids get in the habit of rocking themselves to sleep (and, in some cases, repeatedly banging their heads against the crib or the wall) during infancy. This particular habit, which is more common in boys than in girls and more likely to occur in children with neurological problems such as autism and mental retardation, typically disappears by age one, but, in some children, the behavior continues until a child is four or five. Children who like to rock themselves to sleep typically do so because they find it soothing.

Most kids break themselves of this habit by the time they start school, but if it's still a problem for your child by the time your child turns five, you'll want to talk to your child's doctor about having him assessed for any underlying health or emotional problems. In the meantime, your best bet is to ignore the behavior. Not only do you want to avoid reinforcing the behavior by drawing undue attention to it, but also it's pretty much out of your control anyway.

How much sleep do kids need? Getting my daughter to go to sleep is a huge battle, and she's an early riser, too. Sometimes I think I need more sleep than she does!

Research has shown that an average child between the ages of 5 and 12 sleeps between eight and ten hours per day. Of course, because we're talking averages, this means that some kids require more than 10 hours sleep each night, while others require less than eight. Perhaps your daughter falls into the latter category!

It's also worth pointing out that how much sleep kids *need* and how much sleep kids get can be two entirely different matters. Some pediatric health experts have made the case that today's generation of kids—like their parents—is running a chronic sleep deficit. They simply aren't getting the sleep they need to function at their best.

MOM'S THE WORD

"I think kids in general do not get enough sleep these days. There are so many demands on their time between school clubs, sports, and other activities; homework; video games; and the computer that it is hard for them to do everything they want to do and still get a decent amount of sleep. I feel that for children in general the pace of life is too fast."

—*Kerri, 37, mother of six*

Children are sometimes reluctant to go to bed because they're eager to spend more time with their parents—sometimes because the family is on a busy schedule and they haven't had much chance to spend time with their parents that day. Other kids rebel at bedtime because their bedtime is either too early for them and they aren't physically tired yet, or they have a medical condition such as attention deficit hyperactivity disorder that makes it difficult for them to settle down to sleep at the end of the day. The vast majority of children who resist going to bed do so for a much less complicated reason; they simply don't want to!

Here are a few tips on making bedtime less of a battle between you and your kids:

- **Make sure that the bedtime that you've chosen for your child is realistic.** You can't force your child to be tired just because you're tired. ("You can lead a kid to bed, but you

can't make him rest!" insists Jennifer, a 35-year-old mother
of two.)

- **Aim for as much consistency as possible.** Although you
  don't want to turn bedtime into a boot-camp-like experience, children tend to respond well to routine, so you may
  as well put that basic fact of child psychology to work for
  you. If you stick with a relatively consistent bedtime, over
  time your child will learn that you mean business. It's when
  you don't follow your own rules that you can run into trouble, admits Tara, a 32-year-old mother of two: "If I stop
  being consistent and allow exceptions to the rules, then
  things quickly spin out of control for me."

- **Don't be overly rigid about the lights-out rule.** Sometimes
  a little night light can help to alleviate a big sleep problem.
  "The girls are afraid of the dark, so I leave either a hall light
  or a bathroom light on until I go to bed," explains Ed, a 36-
  year-old father of two. "Once they are asleep they are fine.
  I also find that those small night lights work great: the
  bogeyman doesn't visit the girls!"

- **Help your child chase the monsters away.** If nightmares
  are preventing your child (and you!) from getting a good
  night's sleep, come up with some creative ways of dealing
  with the problem. "My son had a brief fear of monsters until
  we put his active imagination to work," recalls Jennifer, a 35-
  year-old mother of two. "We asked him to describe the monster (it was a big, blue monster that spit) and then we asked
  him to describe what he could do about the monster. In the
  end, he decided he could talk to the monster and that the
  monster would be friendly." This talking-things-through
  strategy has also worked well for Marjory, a 38-year-old
  mother of two and child psychologist: "Sometimes I have
  kids rewrite the ending to their nightmare before they fall

asleep. For example, kids may come up with special powers or magical spells that will help ward off the bad guys in recurring dreams."

- **Come up with some strategies for dealing with the early risers in your family.** If your children are preschoolers, you may want to have a rule that says that your kids have to play in their room until a grown-up is ready to get up. If they're a little older, you may be willing to allow them to get up on their own while you grab a bit of extra shut-eye. "All three of my children are early risers," explains Chonee, a 39-year-old mother of three. "I am not. The deal is that they have to check in with me first thing in the morning so that I know they are up. They can then get up and get dressed (on weekdays) or stay in their PJs (on weekends) and are allowed to play in their rooms or go down into the family room and watch TV or play until we get up. They know they must be quiet: no rough-housing or yelling is allowed. And, I always make a point of leaving juice boxes, cereal, and/or cereal bars and fresh fruit on the table for them to nibble on so that they aren't eating junk food. It works out just fine. We've never once had a problem."

My six-year-old wets her bed most nights. When is she finally going to be able to stay dry through the night?

Although you may feel like you're the only parent in town with a six-year-old who is still wetting the bed, bed-wetting statistics indicate otherwise. Studies have shown that approximately 1 in 10 six-year-olds has difficulty staying dry at night. If you're wondering what percentage of children of other ages have problems with bedwetting, here are the numbers: 40 percent of three-year-olds; 20 percent of five-year-olds; 10 percent of six-year-olds; and 3 percent of 12-year-olds wet the bed on a regular basis.

NO KIDDING!

If you and your partner each had problems with bedwetting when you were growing up, your child has a 70-percent chance of being a bedwetter, too.

In 1 percent of cases, some underlying medical problem, such as a kidney or bladder infection, diabetes, or a congenital defect of the urinary tract system, is to blame, but, in most cases, it's neurodevelopmental immaturity that's responsible for the bedwetting.

Because bedwetting is almost always beyond the child's control, it's important not to pressure your child to stay dry before she's ready (even if you're fed up with doing laundry every morning). This will only add to her stress level and increase the likelihood that bedwetting will occur. (Bedwetting is more likely to occur during times of stress.)

It's also important to reassure your child that night-time dryness will come with time: approximately 15 percent of children who are bedwetters stop wetting the bed with each passing birthday. In the meantime, your child can practice bladder-stretching exercises during the day that are aimed at increasing her bladder capacity and improving bladder control and can use a bedwetting alarm system at night (assuming, of course, that you and your child's doctor support this method of dealing with bedwetting—not everyone's a fan of this particular approach).

You may also want to talk to your child's doctor about prescribing desmopressin acetate (DDAVP) for your child (a hormone that helps to reduce the amount of urine in your child's kidneys and, therefore, helps to reduce the likelihood of bedwetting). Bedwetting can be extremely embarrassing for older children, causing them to voluntarily opt out of any overnight experience that may expose their painful "secret." Never punish your child or withhold privileges because of their bedwetting. The problem isn't something that they can control.

MOM'S THE WORD

"My son's bedwetting increased when his teacher was off on sick leave for a couple of months. It was difficult because nothing we did seemed to help. We tried to keep him happy by giving him a picture of his teacher, and we made her get-well cards together. This helped a little, but he was still stressed out about it. We talked about her and all the things they'd done together, but he was very concerned that she wasn't ever coming back. A letter from the school announcing her return made him feel much better."

—*Mary, 37, mother of three*

My four-year-old is afraid of so many things that he's having difficulty sleeping at night. What can I do to help to ease his fears?

Fears are very common in children of all ages.

Young children often fear imaginary dangers—the much-talked-about monster in the closet—because they have a hard time telling what's real and what's not.

Slightly older children are more likely to fear something a little more rooted in reality—storms, fires, or personal injury, for example—but they may have an unrealistic idea about the odds of disaster striking them or someone they love.

Of course, a child who has had a negative experience with an animal or who has seen a parent react with extreme fear to a spider or a mouse may exhibit the same fears.

Here are some tips on helping your child to manage her fears so that she's less afraid both during the daytime and at night:

- **Don't trivialize your child's fears.** You may know that the man inside the clown suit is actually the nice man next door, but your two-year-old doesn't know that. All she knows is that some strange man with a painted-on face and a bicycle horn keeps trying to shove balloons in her face.

Wouldn't you be scared if you didn't understand what was going on?

- **Don't force your child to "face his fears" by forcing him into a situation in which he is genuinely afraid.** If your child is deathly afraid of cats, being forced to pet one isn't going to make him any less afraid. It'll simply make him more anxious about going outside to play. He'll constantly be wondering when you're going to make him pet another cat—and if lions, tigers, and cheetahs are next on your list of "nice kittys"!

- **Come up with creative—but non-threatening—ways of helping your child to confront her fears.** Try to find ways to desensitize your child by introducing her to less scary versions of the real thing, such as a stuffed cat rather than a real cat, or a book about cats.

- **Show your child how to manage her physical reactions to fear.** Teach her to take a slow, deep breath when the "fight or flight" reaction strikes. Show her how to lie down on her bed, put her hands on her belly just below her belly button and pretend she's trying to breathe in deeply enough to fill up a balloon in her belly and then breathe out slowly enough to gradually let the air out. (Note: You can find additional tips on teaching relaxation techniques to kids at www.kidshavestresstoo.org.)

- **Encourage your child to talk about her fears.** If she is too young to put her feelings into words, try to find storybooks that talk about thunderstorms, doctor's visits, or whatever else it is that she finds so scary. Helping your child to act out situations that she finds frightening or to draw a picture depicting her fears can also help to get the dialogue started.

MOM'S THE WORD

"My oldest son is very afraid of clowns. We try to explain that we wouldn't let the clowns hurt him, but he does not even want to go to a birthday party where there are clowns."

—*Olivia, 31, mother of three*

MOM'S THE WORD

"We had a very bad time with our son when he was about three-and-a-half years old. It was around Christmas time and he suddenly refused to go to nursery school, skating, or shopping. He just wanted to stay home. I suddenly realized those were all the places he had seen Santa. He even made a point of hanging his stocking on the bathroom door so that Santa wouldn't go near his room. Once I figured out what the problem was, I was able to explain that Christmas was over and Santa was too busy sleeping and resting after all his hard work to be shopping or anywhere else. It took a bit of convincing on my part, mind you!"

—*Olivia, 31, mother of three*

- **See whether you can figure out what's at the root of your child's fear.** If your preschooler has a fear of the self-flushing toilets that are found in public washrooms, it could be because they flush unexpectedly or because they make such a loud noise when they flush. If it's the timing issue that's bothering your child, you may be able to deal with this problem by triggering the toilet to flush before your child sits down to use the toilet, knowing that doing so will buy you at least a couple of flush-free minutes! The noise issue is a little trickier. You may want to offer to cover your child's ears for her if the toilet starts to flush unexpectedly.

- **Eliminate as much of the unexpected as possible.** Sometimes what children are really fearing is the unknown. They don't want to go to a birthday party because they don't know what to expect. If you can give them a crash course in what birthdays are all about or offer to stick around at this one until your child is certain she's ready to go solo on the birthday party front, your child may be less fearful.

- **Encourage older children to get their worries and fears down on paper.** Let your child know that you will respect her privacy if she wants to jot down some of her fears—that you'll leave it up to her to decide whether she wants to share anything in her private notebook with you.

What types of events can trigger post-traumatic stress disorder in children?

Post-traumatic stress disorder can occur following a terrifying event in which physical harm was threatened, witnessed, or actually experienced by a child. A child who is suffering from post-traumatic stress disorder experiences intense fear, helplessness, or horror in response to this event. The event triggering the trauma could be a physical or sexual assault, a violent incident at home or at school, a car accident, or some other traumatic event.

Children with post-traumatic stress disorder can experience a sudden and dramatic onset of symptoms, or their symptoms may come on gradually. Typical symptoms include headaches, dizziness, gastrointestinal symptoms, sleep problems, nightmares, irritability, agitation, difficulty concentrating, feeling numb or detached, no longer enjoying activities that once brought the child great pleasure, feeling helpless or like her life is out of control, difficulty getting along with other people, paranoia and distrust, feeling guilty for surviving a tragedy that others may not have survived, intense preoccupation with the events of the tragedy and/or an unwillingness to talk about the traumatic incident, and suicidal thoughts and gestures. Some behavior problems that can arise as a result of post-traumatic stress disorder but that are not part of the criteria for diagnosing the disorder include disruptive behavior disorders, eating disorders, sexual acting-out, depression, anxiety disorders, dissociation, difficulty concentrating, and extreme moodiness.

If you suspect that your child is suffering from post-traumatic stress disorder, don't just wait for the problem to go away on its own. Arrange for your child to be evaluated by a doctor so that treatment (typically therapy combined with medication) can be started as soon as possible and your child can begin to get some relief from his troubling symptoms.

MOTHER WISDOM

Wondering how to help kids cope with frightening events in the news? Here are a few tips:

- Don't assume that kids aren't aware of scary stories in the news. They may have overheard other children or adults talking about these events.
- Don't overexpose kids to media coverage of upsetting events. Having traumatic events replayed over and over again may heighten a child's fear by making her think that the events are happening over and over again.
- Make sure that your kids know that they are safe. They need to know that as scary as these events in the news may be, they themselves are in no immediate danger.
- Give your child plenty of opportunity to talk about these events so that you'll get a clearer idea of how she's reacting to the tragedy. That way, you can address any specific fears or misconceptions.
- Stick with your child's normal routines as much as possible. Routines help maintain a semblance of normalcy when the world seems anything but normal and can help your child to stick with her usual eating and sleeping habits—something that will leave her feeling less out of balance.
- Realize that your child is likely to be more anxious than other children if she's already dealing with another upsetting event in her life at the same time, such as the death of a much loved pet or her best friend's recent move.
- Help older children to analyze media coverage and to be alert to unnecessary sensationalism during times of tragedy and trauma. They need to know that TV news is a business and that building audience share is the name of the game. You may want to show your kids how members of the alternative media have handled reporting of news events as opposed to

members of the mainstream media. And you may also want to take your kids online so that they can compare how media in different countries handle the same international news story.

- Reinforce the fact that revenge isn't the answer, even if the event was a terrorist act. It's important to teach kids about empathy and tolerance, even during troubled times.

- If your child expresses a strong desire to do something about the tragedy, help her to come up with a plan—perhaps organizing a clothing drive for victims of a flood or organizing a fundraiser to help victims of some other sort of disaster.

- Stress the fact that good can come out of any tragedy. The grief that tends to be expressed in the aftermath of a tragedy can lead to actions that make the world a better place and cause everyone to pause and think about what really matters most—family members and friends.

My six-year-old doesn't do a very good job of brushing her teeth. What can I do to encourage her to take care of her teeth until she starts taking greater interest in her own dental hygiene?

You're wise to pay careful attention to dental hygiene, even though your child is still likely to have mostly baby teeth. If your child were to lose her baby teeth early as a result of dental decay, her permanent teeth may erupt prematurely and come in crooked because her jaw would not yet be big enough to accommodate them. Believe it or not, orthodontists estimate that 30 percent of their business results from the premature loss of baby teeth, whether due to decay or injury!

Of course, getting a reluctant brusher to get with the program can be a challenge for any parent—particularly after your child reaches the age at which she will no longer allow you to co-pilot the toothbrush. That being said, here are a few tooth-brushing tricks of the trade:

- **Start with the right tools.** Make sure that your child is using an appropriately sized soft nylon-bristle toothbrush.

If the toothbrush is too large for her mouth, she'll have a hard time cleaning her teeth with it. She may also be reluctant to brush if the toothbrush causes her to gag—a common problem if the toothbrush is simply too big for her.

- **Check your position.** If your child has a habit of wriggling away while you're brushing her teeth, stand behind her and lean her head back against your stomach. Not only will this position make it more difficult for her to run away, but also it'll feel more natural to you because it's similar to the position you use when you're brushing your own teeth.

- **Keep it clean.** (The toothbrush, that is.) To minimize bacteria growth, rinse your child's toothbrush thoroughly before you put it away. And make a point of replacing the toothbrush at least twice a year—more often than that if the bristles start to look flattened and worn.

- **Introduce flossing early.** Ideally, you should encourage (or help!) your child to floss her teeth at least once a day. And, if you're still playing a hands-on role in tooth brushing (something you're likely to be doing until your child is at least seven years old), try to give your child's tongue a scrub from time to time in order to remove some of the bacteria that lives on the tongue.

- **Pay careful attention to safety.** Don't allow your child to run around while she's carrying her toothbrush. A child can be seriously injured as a result of falling with a toothbrush in her mouth.

While we're talking healthy teeth, here are a few other things you can do to promote your child's oral health:

- **Ensure that your child is eating a balanced diet made up of a variety of healthy foods.** Ideally, you want to encourage your child to eat a series of meals and snacks, rather than grazing from morning until night. Not only is this better for her teeth, but also you'll be promoting healthy eating habits at the same time. Note: See Chapter 12 for more on kids and nutrition.

- **Offer alternatives to sticky, sugary-sweet snacks.** Sugar promotes tooth decay, so it's best to limit your child's consumptions of super-sugary, super-sticky foods. However, these types of foods (including raisins and other dried fruits) won't do quite as much harm to your child's teeth if they're eaten as part of a meal rather than on their own, so if you choose to include these foods in your child's diet, make sure they're served along with other foods.

 NO KIDDING!

Here's another reason to kick your smoking habit. Children exposed to second-hand smoke may be more susceptible to cavities than kids from smoke-free homes. Researchers from the University of Rochester and the American Academy of Pediatrics' Center for Child Health Research found that children whose parents smoked face double the risk of developing cavities in their primary teeth as children from smoke-free homes.

- **Encourage your child to brush her teeth within 5 to 10 minutes of eating.** The longer the food sits on your child's teeth, the greater the opportunity it has to do damage.

- **Ensure that your child visits the dentist regularly.** Twice-yearly visits are the ideal so that your child's teeth can be cleaned regularly, and her overall oral health can be monitored on an ongoing basis. Depending on the condition of your child's teeth, she may benefit from fluoride treatments and/or the application of sealants to help "cavity-proof" any grooves in her molars. Studies have shown that fluoride treatments plus the use of sealants can reduce the incidence of cavities by 90 percent.

When can I expect my six-year-old to start losing his teeth?

Most children start losing their teeth at around age seven when the lower central incisors—the middle front teeth on the lower jaw—start falling out (see Table 10.7). Fortunately, the process of losing a tooth is relatively painless in most cases. By the time one of your child's baby teeth starts to become wiggly, the roots of the tooth have been reabsorbed by your child's body, and the only thing holding the tooth in place is a tiny bit of tissue.

How can I tell if my child has a vision problem?

Although your child's doctor will give her a thorough eye examination before she starts school and will continue to look for possible vision problems when she goes for her annual checkups, it's important for you to be on the lookout in between checkups for any indications that she may be experiencing some vision problems, for example:

- poor focusing

- abnormal alignment or movement of the eyes (such as crossed eyes or a wandering eye)

- constant eye-rubbing

- extreme light sensitivity

- redness or cloudiness of the eyes

- chronic tearing of the eyes

When you take your child for an eye checkup, the doctor will:

- ask your child to identify letters or shapes on an eye chart

- examine the exterior and interior of your child's eyes

- check the coordination of your child's eye muscles and check for any tracking or coordination problems, such as misaligned eyes (strabismus) or lazy eye (amblyopia)

- screen for focusing problems

- check your child's color vision

- assess your child's depth perception

- look for any signs of glaucoma and other eye diseases

Myopia (nearsightedness) is the most common type of vision problem among school-aged children. It is typically diagnosed at some point between age six and adolescence. A child who is nearsighted will have difficulty seeing objects that are far away. (Children with hyperopia—farsightedness—have the opposite problem. They have difficulty seeing objects that are close to them.)

Both myopia and hyperopia can be managed with glasses. Opthamologists generally recommend glasses with plastic lenses for kids, to minimize the risk of injury in the event of breakage. Contact lenses are not generally recommended before a child reaches adolescence.

MOTHER WISDOM

Don't wait for your child to tell you that she thinks she may have a vision problem. What she sees is likely to feel "normal" to her, even if it would be anything but normal to anyone else. That explains why it's not unusual for vision problems to become apparent for the first time during the early grade-school years. It may suddenly become obvious to your child's teacher that she's having difficulty seeing the blackboard or reading her schoolbooks.

How can I tell if my child has a hearing problem?

You should consider the possibility that your child may have a hearing problem if:

- she appears to be able to hear only certain types of sounds

- she doesn't respond when she is spoken to unless she happens to be looking at you directly when you are speaking

- she is often inattentive or prone to daydreaming

- she talks too loudly and watches the TV with the volume turned up too high

- her school marks are mediocre and/or in decline because she is having difficulty hearing the teacher

- she keeps complaining of a ringing sound in her ears (tinnitus)

- she mispronounces words

If your doctor agrees that there could be a problem, he will likely order some additional hearing tests beyond what he is capable of doing in his office: for example, an auditory brainstem response test, which measures brain activity in response to sound, and/or an audiometer test (a test with a machine that produces sounds like beeps and whistles that can be used to assess the degree of hearing loss).

The type of treatment that will be recommended will depend on the nature of the hearing loss:

- If your child's hearing loss is believed to be caused by a fluid buildup in the ear caused by infections, the doctor may order antibiotics in an attempt to clear up the infection.

- If the hearing loss appears to be caused by a wax buildup or some sort of foreign object that your child has inserted in his ear (hey, it happens!), the doctor will attempt to remove the wax buildup or the object.

- If your child is experiencing a more permanent hearing loss, the doctor may recommend hearing aids to amplify the sound (or a cochlear implant, in the event of severe or profound hearing loss); vibrotactile aids, which translate sound into vibrations that can be felt through the skin; and/or speech therapy.

See the section that follows on dealing with a child with a chronic medical condition. Be sure to check out Appendix A for leads on organizations of interest to parents with hearing-impaired children.

 NO KIDDING!

Your child faces an above-average risk of having a hearing problem if:

- there is a history of childhood hearing loss in your family
- you contracted either rubella (German measles) or CMV (cytomegalovirus) infection during pregnancy
- your child was born prematurely or experienced severe medical problems at birth
- your child has had a series of ear infections
- your child has had meningitis (an infection of the tissues covering the brain) or was born with certain birth defects involving the ears, face, skull, or brain

---

My three-year-old has started stuttering recently. Should I be concerned?

Most children—90 percent, in fact—go through a period of stuttering at some point during the toddler or preschool years. Psychologists believe this may occur at this stage of a child's development when the child's thoughts and ideas may be racing miles ahead of her ability to put those thoughts and ideas into words.

Although it can be frustrating to see your child struggling with her speech (a child who stutters will repeat sounds or entire words, disrupting the flow of communication), there is generally little cause for concern in children this age. The best way to handle the problem is to ignore it. Stuttering usually goes away on its own after a couple of months.

Stuttering sometimes occurs in older children during periods of severe stress. Drawing attention to your child's stuttering will only add to her stress level, and, therefore, makes the stuttering worse, so, again, your best bet is to ignore the stuttering and to deal with the underlying problem that is causing your child so much stress. Typically, when the source of stress is removed, the stuttering disappears on its own.

MOTHER WISDOM

If your child is having difficulty with stuttering, resist the temptation to correct your child's speech, interrupt your child when she is speaking, finish her sentences for her, ask her to practice certain words or sounds, or ask her to repeat back certain sentences or phrases to you. Rather than helping to solve the problem, these techniques tend to backfire by making the child even more self-conscious about her speech—something that serves to increase her stress level and increase the likelihood that the stuttering will continue.

Only 1 percent of school-aged children experience true stuttering. Unlike other forms of stuttering, this type of stuttering tends to become worse over time. You can differentiate between this type of stuttering and the less worrying type of stuttering that tends to occur in younger children by paying attention to the types of speech errors that occur when your child is stuttering and noting any accompanying behaviors. A child who is struggling with true stuttering makes speech errors that are consistent (for example, she struggles with the same words or sounds from one day to the next), and may exhibit some related behaviors such as knee-slapping, foot-tapping, or other repetitive behaviors (such as tics). If your child is struggling with this form of stuttering, your doctor will likely refer her to a speech and language pathologist for speech therapy and/or a child therapist so that she will learn ways of coping with this frustrating and sometimes embarrassing speech problem while she waits to outgrow it. (Approximately 80 percent of children who stutter outgrow their stuttering by the time they reach the teen years.)

Note: You can find leads on resources of interest to parents of children with speech difficulties in Appendix A.

My child is thirsty all the time. I am starting to worry that he could be diabetic. Other than extreme thirst, what are some of the other key warning signs of diabetes in children?

In addition to feeling extremely thirsty, a child with untreated diabetes is likely to be urinating frequently, to have an increased appetite, to be tired all the time, and to be losing weight. If these symptoms are not detected quickly, the child may need to be hospitalized so that his diabetes can be brought under control. (If not properly managed, diabetes can lead to heart, kidney, blood vessel, and neurological system damage and a progressive loss of vision over time.)

Diabetes is a metabolic disorder that prevents the normal breakdown of food. In children, it is caused by insufficient insulin production. The child's body can't metabolize sugars properly, so they build up in the blood stream and are excreted through the urine. The peak periods of onset in children are around age 5 or 6 and then again from ages 11 to 13.

A strict regime of insulin injections, dietary modifications, and exercise will generally allow a diabetic child to keep her diabetes under control and to enjoy an excellent quality of life. Although you'll want to oversee her diabetes management carefully while she's young, as your child enters the preteen years, you'll gradually want to allow your child to start assuming responsibility for managing her diabetes, both by checking her blood sugars and by giving herself injections. Of course, you'll need to supervise her carefully until you're sure she's got the hang of things: having too much insulin in her system can put a child into insulin shock (the child will feel clammy, start trembling, experience a rapid heartbeat, and eventually lose consciousness) and having too little insulin in her system will cause your child's diabetes symptoms to worsen, potentially resulting in damage to her body systems.

Note: See the section that follows for tips on coping with a child's chronic medical condition.

My eight-year-old bites her nails until her fingers bleed. What can I do to get her to stop?

Nail-biting, hair-twirling, and other nervous habits are ways of relieving boredom and tension. A child who engages in these types of behaviors is often unaware of what she's doing. (Despite what you might think, it's not a deliberate attempt to drive you crazy!)

These types of behaviors tend to disappear on their own over time. Your best strategy is simply to ignore them. If you draw attention to them, you risk reinforcing the problem behavior—something that can cause it to become more frequent or more entrenched.

 NO KIDDING!

Another nervous habit besides nail-biting is thumb-sucking. Thumb-sucking usually disappears between the ages six and eight. Not only do kids this age develop other techniques for soothing themselves in times of stress, but also peer pressure makes it painfully obvious that thumb-sucking is not socially acceptable behavior when you're a "big kid."

What causes tics?

Tics—rapid and repeated involuntary movements—frequently occur during times of stress. They are often centered in the face and the neck and may include such behaviors as eye blinking, shoulder shrugging, facial grimaces, neck twisting, throat clearing, sniffing, and coughing (when there's no physical trigger for the cough). Tics occur in approximately 20 percent of school-aged kids and are more likely to be a problem for a child if other members of her family also have trouble with tics.

If your child develops a tic, it's important to remember that her behaviors are involuntary. Pressing the child to stop acting this way will only make the problem worse. Rather than badgering your child about the problem behavior, focus on relieving any underlying causes of stress that may be making the problem worse and helping her to come up with strategies to explain her tics to her friends.

My six-year-old is in the habit of picking her nose. I've tried to convince her to use a tissue, but every time I turn around, she seems to have her finger up her nose again. Help! She's driving me crazy.

Many children get in the habit of picking their nose, either because they're curious about what's inside the nasal cavity, because they are looking for relief from cold or allergy symptoms, or because their nasal passages are dry and itchy.

The best way to handle the problem is to try to get at the root cause.

- If you suspect that an overly dry home environment is making your child's nasal passages dry and itchy, you may want to run a room humidifier or squirt a blast or two of saline nasal spray up each of your child's nostrils.

- If you suspect that your child is bothered by a runny nose, hand her a box of tissues and teach her how to use them to wipe or blow her nose.

- If you suspect that your child is picking her nose as a result of either curiosity or boredom, you may want to give her something else to do with her hands.

Don't get into a power struggle with your child over nose-picking, or you could make the problem worse. Rather than trying to kick her of this annoying bad habit right now, simply remind yourself that it's unlikely that you'll catch her picking her nose a decade or two from now as she marches across the stage to pick up her university diploma. Chances are she'll abandon the habit as soon as she starts getting social pressure to stop. (This is one of those times when peer pressure can actually work in a parent's favor!)

It's a battle getting my 10-year-old to take a shower, and, when she does, half the time she fails to use soap! As a result, she's developed a strong body odor that can be pretty overwhelming at times. Any advice on getting her to pay greater attention to personal hygiene?

Sometimes school-aged kids simply don't want to take the time to have baths or attend to other personal hygiene tasks such as combing their hair, washing their faces, brushing their teeth, and so on. They've got places to go and people to see. Personal hygiene simply isn't a priority for them at this stage of their lives—something that tends to drive their parents completely up the wall!

Preteens can also be lackadaisical about personal hygiene, even if they're developing a rather overpowering odor that makes them less-than-pleasant companions. They may not realize that their soap-phobia doesn't mesh well with the increasing sweat gland and oil gland production of puberty. You may have to give your preteen a little coaching on the art of personal hygiene until she gets the basics right. (My husband and I had to explain to one of our kids that deodorant is a supplement to—not a replacement for!—soap.)

I think my preteen may be depressed. Until it happened to my own child, I didn't think that children this age could suffer from depression. How common is childhood depression?

The jury's still out as to whether childhood depression is starting to occur earlier in kids than it did in generations past or whether mental health experts are simply doing a better job of diagnosing depression in children. What we do know, however, is that there are increasing numbers of kids being diagnosed with depressive disorders and that those diagnoses are being made earlier on in life; the rate of depression is currently pegged at around 3 to 5 percent of preteens.

The symptoms of depression in a preteen are often quite different from the symptoms we would expect to see in a teenager or an adult. The most common symptoms in preteens are headaches, stomach aches, irritability, social withdrawal, and general sadness. To meet the clinical definition of depression, a child must exhibit at least five of the following symptoms over a two-week period:

- depressed or irritable mood

- diminished pleasure or a complete loss of pleasure in activities the child previously enjoyed

- sleep disturbances

- weight changes or appetite disturbances (in children, this can also be a failure to achieve desired weight gain)

- decreased concentration

- indecisiveness

- suicidal thoughts

- restlessness or lethargy

- fatigue or loss of energy

- feelings of worthlessness

- inappropriate guilt

After a child has been diagnosed with depression, treatment options include therapy or medication or both. It may take time to pinpoint the medication or combination of medications that will help to relieve a particular child's symptoms, and, what's more, it can take time for many of these medications to start working, so don't expect to see a huge change in your child's mood overnight.

Here's another important point to keep in mind: although medication can make a world of difference in helping to offset any biochemical imbalances that could be contributing to your child's depression, she'll need to deal with any psychological or emotional issues that are troubling her, too, in order to experience a lasting lift in mood. Medication isn't a fix-all; it's simply one piece in the treatment puzzle.

Note: Like other mood disorders, depression tends to run in the family, so if there is a history of depression in your family, your child faces a higher-than-average risk of experiencing depression problems during her lifetime.

What other types of psychiatric conditions can occur in young children?

Children can experience many of the same psychiatric disorders as adults. Here's what you need to know about a few of the more common disorders:

- **Bipolar disorder:** Bipolar disorder (sometimes called manic depression) is a mood disorder that is characterized by periods of both depression and either mania (an elevated mood that lasts for at least a week and that is characterized by a decreased need for sleep, racing thoughts, rapid speech, goal-directed activities and projects, reckless behaviors, risk-taking, and delusions of grandeur) or hypomania (a less severe form of mania in which there is no psychotic or delusional thinking involved). Bipolar disorder can be challenging to diagnose in children because such common childhood behaviors as irritability, tantrums, physical aggression, and behavioral problems may also be symptoms of attention deficit hyperactivity disorder (ADHD). To muddy the waters further, children with bipolar disorder often have ADHD as well and, in some kids with ADHD, a bipolar disorder diagnosis may be missed because it can be difficult to distinguish between ADHD and bipolar symptoms. Bipolar disorder is typically diagnosed in 0.2 to 0.4 percent of children and 1 percent of adolescents. Like depression, it tends to run in the family. This condition can be treated with a combination of medication and therapy.

 NO KIDDING!

It's important to pay careful attention to your child's behavior and to seek treatment for bipolar disorder if you suspect your child has a problem: children and adolescents with bipolar disorder are three times as likely to abuse alcohol and drugs as other kids, and they face an elevated risk of suicide.

- **Schizophrenia:** Schizophrenia is another major type of mental illness—one that is believed to be triggered by a complex cocktail of genetic, biochemical, and environmental factors. Children with schizophrenia typically exhibit the following types of behaviors: seeing things and hearing voices that are not real, exhibiting odd or eccentric behavior or speech, having unusual or bizarre thoughts and ideas, being unable to distinguish between fantasy and reality, confused thinking, extreme moodiness, paranoia, acting younger than they are, severe anxiety and fearfulness, difficulty making and keeping friends, social isolation, and a decline in personal hygiene. Schizophrenia can be controlled, but not cured, through a combination of medication and therapy.

- **Anxiety disorders:** The 2.9 to 4.6 percent of children and preteens who suffer from anxiety disorders generally worry more often and more intensely than other children; and their worries are likely to be more persistent and more overblown than those of an average child. They have a hard time "turning off" these worries, so their heightened anxiety levels can interfere with their ability to concentrate on their schoolwork and go about their day-to-day lives. They may be hypercritical of themselves and/or highly perfectionist. They may also experience a lot of physical symptoms of anxiety: stomach aches, headaches, shortness of breath, a rapid heartbeat, sweating, nausea, diarrhea, frequent urination, cold and clammy hands, difficulty swallowing, muscle soreness and aches, trembling, and twitching. Anxiety disorders are more common in adolescents than in younger children, and such disorders tend to run in the family. Some children with anxiety disorders are diagnosed with generalized anxiety disorder (they are generally anxious), while others are diagnosed with more specific types of anxiety disorders: for example, specific phobias (fear of a specific object or situation that presents little or no threat in real life), social phobias (social anxiety disorder—a fear of school or performance situations in which embarrassment may occur), and panic disorder (an anxiety disorder that is accompanied by full-blown panic attacks). Medication, behavioral therapy, and stress management training can help kids learn to manage their anxiety disorders. Note: Kids who are highly anxious during childhood face a higher-than-average risk of developing full-blown depression during adolescence, so it's important to be on the lookout for the early warning signs of depression if you have a highly anxious child.

- **Obsessive compulsive disorder:** The 2 percent of children who struggle with obsessive compulsive disorder are preoccupied with repetitive thoughts or actions that seem strange or illogical to other people: for example, an obsession with dirt, disease, death, or violence or an obsessive need to repeat the same behaviors (such as looking in their backpack 10 times to make sure that their math homework is really there). To meet the clinical definition of obsessive compulsive disorder, these obsessive behaviors or compulsions must be present for at least an hour a day and must significantly interfere with the child's schoolwork, social activities, or family relationships. Like most other types of mental health problems, obsessive compulsive disorder tends to run in the family. They are most likely to be picked up prior to adolescence in boys and during adolescence in girls. Children with obsessive compulsive disorder face a high risk of suicide: 10 percent will make a suicide attempt during their teen years. Fortunately, behavioral therapy can be very successful with kids with obsessive compulsive disorder. It may help to desensitize them to something that they find very frightening or help them to develop new ways of coping with situations that they find overwhelming, something that can help to bring them considerable peace of mind.

Note: Eating disorders are generally included in the list of psychiatric conditions affecting children. You will find a detailed discussion of eating disorders in Chapter 12.

Caring for a Child with a Chronic Medical Condition

Approximately 10 to 20 percent of kids have some sort of long-term illness, disability, or other health problem; and approximately 2 percent of children have chronic illnesses that impact their lives—and consequently their families' lives—in a major way.

If your child has just been diagnosed with a chronic medical condition, you may feel overwhelmed and scared. You may wonder what the future will hold for you and your child and question whether you have the skills needed to help your child to deal with the challenges that she will face during the months and years ahead.

Most parents who have been through the experience of having a child diagnosed with a major illness or chronic medical condition find that they are better able to cope with the situation once they have a clearer idea about what they're dealing with. That's why it's a good idea to gather as much information as possible about your child's illness or medical condition at the time of diagnosis.

If you're too upset to absorb this information initially, you may want to ask a friend or family member to accompany you to your child's doctor's appointment so that they can help you to remember some of the key details. Or you may want to schedule a follow-up visit with your child's doctor to review what he said earlier and to ask some more detailed questions once the news has had a chance to settle in. Here are some of the types of questions you may want to ask:

- Is this health problem something that my child is likely to outgrow or is it likely to be a chronic health problem?

- What should our family expect in terms of the overall course of the illness or medical condition? Will my child's symptoms become progressively worse over time or remain relatively stable? If it's the kind of illness where symptoms become progressively worse, is this progression likely to happen quickly or at a relatively slow pace?

- How is the medical condition likely to affect my child's day-to-day life?

- What treatment options are available to my child? What are the pros, cons, and expected outcomes for each treatment option?

- Will you be exclusively responsible for managing my child's care, or will there be an entire team of specialists working on her case?

- What do I need to know about managing my child's illness and/or symptoms?

- Are there any resource materials available that would assist me in explaining my child's medical condition to her?

- Are there any resources that would be helpful to me in researching my child's medical condition further?

- Can you recommend any support groups for parents and/or children living with this medical condition?

After you've done your homework, you'll want to explain what's going on to your child. It's important to provide your child with age-appropriate information about her illness and to let her know what she can expect in terms of treatment. Of course, you'll want to keep adding to your child's knowledge of her medical condition as she gets older and becomes better able to grasp information about her condition and her treatment plan. Note: If your child seems to having a great deal of difficulty dealing with any limitations posed by her medical condition or if she's rebelling against aspects of her treatment plan, you may want to see if your child's doctor can recommend a counselor who could help her to deal with her feelings about her medical condition.

You'll also want to try to find ways to keep your child's life as normal as possible—something that is obviously easier said than done if your child's medical condition requires lengthy hospital stays or a weekly barrage of doctor's appointments. But challenging as it may be, it's important to encourage your child to try as much as possible to go to school, keep in contact with her friends, and engage in a range of age-appropriate activities. (Note: You may have to advocate for your child within the school system, to ensure that she receives any academic support to which she is entitled as a result of her medical condition. You also may need to help your child to educate her peers about her medical condition so that they she won't find herself getting ditched by a group of her former friends who suddenly became fearful that they might "catch" her leukemia.)

It's easy to become overly protective when your child has a chronic medical condition, so you may have to constantly challenge yourself to encourage your child to venture out into the world and to come up with creative solutions for dealing with any problems that may arise while she's away from you: for example, ensuring that your child's friends' parents know what to do if your child has an epileptic seizure while playing at their house. It can be scary to allow your child some of the usual freedoms of childhood, but it's important to provide her with as normal a growing-up experience as possible.

If you have other children, you'll also want to keep an eye on how they react to their sibling's diagnosis. It's not unusual for siblings to act up, become withdrawn, or to become angry if they feel like they're being ignored or being asked to do more than their fair share of chores while your other child is in hospital. It's important to ensure that their needs are met, too—something that may leave you feeling totally stretched to the limit in terms of your parental resources.

And if you have a partner, you'll want to remember to invest in your relationship with your partner, too. It's easy for couples to grow apart if a child's illness or chronic medical condition is allowed to become the sole focus of their relationship.

Finally, don't forget to reinvest in yourself—to take breaks from the parenting trenches so that you'll come back feeling renewed, refreshed, and better able to face another day of parenting. Dealing with a child with a serious illness or chronic medical condition can be physically and emotionally draining, and as the parent of such a child, you face a higher-than-average risk of parent burnout. No matter how many other demands there may be on your time and energies, you have to make taking care of your own needs a priority. You can't be a good parent if you're constantly running on empty. (See Chapter 1 for more on preventing parent burnout.)

CHAPTER 11

The Worry Zone

*"Every mother has a certain amount of 'worry energy' to
disperse into the world, and a child is an excellent,
almost unavoidable, lightning rod for it."*
—*Harriet Lerner,* The Mother Dance: How
Children Change Your Life

Although you can ask other people to help out with a lot
of the other tasks associated with being a parent, there's
one job that can't be easily delegated to someone else:
responsibility for worrying about your child. (Like it or not,
you're pretty much destined to be the Worrier-in-Chief for the
next 18 years and beyond!)

In this chapter, I talk about what's involved in coming to
terms with the 24-hour-a-day worry that goes along with being
a parent: how to balance off your desire to keep your child safe
against the need to allow him to spread his wings in an age-
appropriate manner. After I take you on a quick tour of the
worry zone, I talk about what you can do to keep your child safe.
I start out by talking about the most common types of pediatric
injuries and how to avoid them (and what to do if, despite your
best efforts, your child does end up being injured and in need of
first aid). Finally, I wrap up the chapter by talking about the ins
and outs of streetproofing kids so that they're alert to (but not
petrified by) the dangers they may face in the world around

them. Hopefully, by the time you're finished reading this chapter, you'll feel a little less overwhelmed about what's involved in keeping your child safe during his growing-up years.

 MOM'S THE WORD

"Worry is just something you have to learn to live with. I'm always finding myself saying 'Be careful' about something, to which my daughter's response is usually, 'Don't worry, Mom. I'm okay.'"

—*Janice, 40, mother of one*

Coping with the Worry That Goes Along with Being a Parent

The needle on your worry-o-meter started dancing around the moment your child was born. Suddenly the world seemed like a much more dangerous place. "How can I possibly keep this tiny infant safe?" you wondered.

Although you're probably not worrying about your child quite as intensely as you did during his baby days, if you're like most parents, you're probably still giving the worry-o-meter a workout on a regular basis. Whether it's worry about whether your four-year-old is really old enough to step on board that huge school bus and make the journey off to kindergarten on his own, whether your 10-year-old is going to get roughed up by that tough new kid on his hockey team, or whether there really is going to be a parent home during the co-ed birthday bash your 12-year-old is so keen to attend, there always seems to be something new to worry about.

Sometimes, it's tempting to micromanage every conceivable aspect of our children's lives in order to safeguard them against whatever real and imagined dangers may be lurking beyond the front door. Although we may think we're doing our kids a favor by switching into Super Vigilant Parent Mode, we may actually be doing them a huge disservice, warns Jennifer, a 35-year-old mother of two. "Round-the-clock insulation does not give a child the skills and experience he needs to become a well-rounded, productive, healthy, and happy adult," she cautions.

Karen, a 35-year-old mother of three, agrees: "We are protecting our children, but I believe we are spoiling our children and not teaching them how to be self-sufficient. By over-protecting our kids, I think we are smothering their natural instincts to sense danger and are sending them out into the world unprepared."

"I think as parents we have to deal with our own 'stuff' and ensure we don't project it on to our kids," says Angela, a 37-year-old mother of two. "I don't worry about my kids 24 hours a day. I have learned to trust the process and enjoy the moment."

The key to cutting back on the amount of time you spend worrying about your child is to accept the fact that some things are beyond your control as a parent. Although it's a difficult fact to accept (particularly for card-carrying control freaks like me), some things in life are quite simply beyond our control. We can't keep our kids safe 24 hours a day, even if we bankrupt ourselves by buying every possible piece of childproof hardware and child protective gear. Stuff happens—and it is going to happen to your kid, despite your best efforts to protect him. As long as you weren't deliberately negligent (that is, you didn't allow your three-year-old to play in traffic or allow your five-year-old to juggle flaming torches!), then there's probably no point in beating yourself up about what happened. Simply focus your energies on trying to teach your child how to avoid similar situations in the future so that he can start to assume greater responsibility for his own safety over time—something that is good for him and that will help to take some of the heat off of you. (Who knows? Pretty soon you may have cut your worrying time to a positively leisurely 22 hours per day!)

MOM'S THE WORD

"Teaching children to fear everyone and everything new creates paranoid, stressed, miserable people, which, in my mind, is far more damaging than any danger that could befall children in the world."

—*Jennifer, 35, mother of two*

The Most Common Types of Pediatric Injuries and How to Avoid Them

Accidents happen—and they happen fast when kids are involved. Even though it's impossible to protect your child from every bump and bruise, you want to take steps to reduce the likelihood of more serious injuries occurring. Here's what you need to know in order to avoid some of the most common types of childhood injuries:

- **Injuries in the home:** Although injuries in the home are far less common after your child heads into the preschool years than they were when he was a baby or a toddler, you'll still want to keep an eye out for any possible hazards in the home, such as anything that could lead to falls, burns, choking, suffocation, or other types of injuries. (See the National Safe Kids Campaign Web site at www.safekids.org for tips on preventing injuries and accidents in the home.)

MOTHER WISDOM

Garages play host to some of the most hazardous items in our homes: gasoline, antifreeze, paints, solvents, pesticides, power tools, lawnmowers, and so on. That's why it's a good idea to designate garages as kid-free zones and to store bicycles and other outdoor play equipment in a shed or other location.

- **Bike safety:** According to the National Safe Kids Campaign, 168 children ages 14 and under were killed in bicycle-related crashes in 2000 and nearly 314,600 were treated in hospital emergency rooms for bicycle-related injuries the following year. Most of the more serious injuries could have been prevented by the use of bicycle helmets, which is required by law in many states. Still, despite widespread knowledge about the benefits of helmet use, the 2001 Centers for Disease Control and Prevention Youth Risk Behavior Surveillance Survey found that 84.7 percent of the 65.1 percent of high school students who had ridden a bicycle during the previous six months admitted to "rarely" or "never" wearing a helmet.

You can do your bit to help keep your child safe by insisting that your child wear his helmet every time he hops on his bike, whether he considers it cool or not, and ensuring that the bicycle (not hockey!) helmet that you purchased for your child is in good condition and that it fits properly (it should be snug but not uncomfortable). While you're sizing up your child's helmet, size up his bike, too; he should be able to place his feet flat on the ground while he's sitting on the bicycle seat.

- **Playground injuries:** More than 205,860 preschool and elementary children are injured on playgrounds each year. Three-quarters of these injuries occur on public playground equipment, and the remaining one-quarter of injuries occur on home playground equipment. Because the majority of injuries result from falls, it's a good idea to remember the rule of five (keep children under age 5 off any piece of equipment that's higher than 5 feet). It's also important to check playground equipment for signs of wear and to ensure that such equipment conforms with current safety standards. See the U.S. Consumer Product Safety Commission Web site (www.cpsc.gov/cpscpub/pubs/playpubs.html) for additional information on playground safety, including checklists on what constitutes safe playground equipment for backyard and public playgrounds. If you don't have access to the Internet, you can call or write to the CPSC instead. See Appendix A for the organization's contact information.

- **Sports injuries:** More than 3.5 million children require medical treatment for sports-related injuries each year. According to the National Safe Kids Campaign, nearly half of all sports- and recreation-related injuries occur while children are bicycling, skating, or skateboarding.

MOTHER WISDOM

If your child is taking up a new sport, you'll want to ensure that he has the strength, coordination, and skills needed to play and that you've provided him with all the appropriate protective equipment. Newcomers to a particular sport face a greater risk of injury than the veterans. You'll also want to encourage proper fitness and conditioning in addition to the time actually spent playing a sport; sports physiologists recommend that children who participate in sports such as hockey be active an additional 30 to 60 minutes per day.

- **Other recreational injuries:** Two of the key sources of injuries involving children are rollerblades and unpowered scooters. Once again, you'll want to make sure that your child has the know-how to use this equipment and that he has the necessary protective gear. You'll also want to set limits on where he can use these pieces of equipment (the driveway versus the road) and remind him that listening to music on headphones while using rollerblades or a scooter is a definite no-no.

- **Drowning:** Two-thirds of drowning deaths involving children under the age of 15 occur between May and August, so you'll want to be particularly conscious of this particular hazard when the kids are out of school. In addition to taking appropriate precautions with your own backyard pool—using pool alarms and ensuring that the pool area is enclosed inside a 4-foot-high fence with a self-closing, self-latching gate—you'll want to give some thought to other water hazards near your home: ponds, your neighbor's backyard hot tub, undrained wading pools, and so on. Of course, that doesn't mean that you can afford to be complacent at other times of the year. Children can drown in any body of water—indoor or outdoor—year-round.

MOTHER WISDOM

Encourage your child to play a variety of different types of sports at different times of the year. Children who stick with a particular sport year-round are more likely to develop repetitive-stress injuries than children who rotate sports from season to season.

MOTHER WISDOM

If your preschooler falls and knocks out one of his teeth, remove the tooth from your child's mouth (to prevent your child from accidentally swallowing or choking on the tooth) and seek emergency dental care (either through your dentist's office or your hospital emergency room). Store the tooth in saline solution or milk "as is." Do not attempt to clean it.

If your child is slightly older and you feel confident that he won't swallow the tooth that has been knocked out, place the tooth back in its socket and cover it with a piece of gauze. Then have your child gently bite down on the piece of gauze to hold the tooth in place. Note: You should not try to put the tooth back in your child's mouth if he is crying or upset because he could accidentally swallow the tooth.

- **Dog bites:** Even though dogs may be man's best friend, some dogs are anything but friendly toward children. Although nearly half of dog bites are caused by the child's own pet, it's important to teach your child how to behave around other people's dogs and to supervise all children under five whenever they're around animals. You'll also want to teach your child to be gentle when handling or stroking animals; to avoid any sudden movements or loud noises that could frighten or anger an animal; to respect an animal's need for privacy (for example, if a cat hides underneath someone's porch, chances are it wants to be left alone!); and to proceed with caution when he encounters a strange animal. You don't want to make your child totally paranoid when he's around animals; however, he needs to know that it's unwise to approach or pet someone else's pet unless the owner has given him the go-ahead. Some pets don't react well to children. You don't want your child to learn that lesson the hard way.

MOTHER WISDOM

If your family is in the market for a pet, you'll want to choose the type and breed of pet with care. Some types of animals are completely unsuitable for families with young children. Ferrets and vicious dogs are a poor choice, due to the risk of a child being attacked; and reptiles are not recommended because they're a source of the potentially deadly bacteria salmonella—a bacterium that will contaminate the cage and any other surface with which the reptile comes into contact.

The National Center for Infectious Diseases has prepared a Web site that summarizes the key diseases that various types of animals can transmit to humans. You can find it at www.cdc.gov/healthypets/index.htm.

While you're surfing the Web in search of pet-related information, you may want to head over to the American Veterinary Medical Association's Web site: www.avma.org/careforanimals. You'll find practical tips on preparing your child for the responsibilities that go along with pet ownership and helping your child to interact safely with the newest member of the family.

- **Pedestrian accidents:** According to the National Safe Kids Campaign, more than 47,300 children were treated in U.S.

hospital emergency rooms in 2001 for pedestrian-related injuries. In many cases, the root cause of these accidents was a lack of judgment on the child's part. Studies have shown that children under the age of nine are not developmentally capable of making safe traffic decisions on their own, even after they have had road safety rules explained to them, which is why child safety experts recommend that children this age be accompanied by an adult or an older child whenever they are crossing the street. Because the peripheral vision in children this age is not fully developed, they have difficulty judging the speed of objects and the distance between themselves and an approaching vehicle, and they tend to underestimate the risks and consequences of collisions. It's also important to review other key safety rules with children of all ages; for example, they need to:

- wear bright or reflective clothing so that they're more visible to drivers, particularly at night

- stay on sidewalks as much as possible

- stay away from parked cars when crossing the street

- cross only at corners or pedestrian crosswalks

- use extra caution when crossing at an intersection without lights

- use pedestrian crossing signals where they are available (but not to proceed into the intersection until they've made eye contact with the driver, and they are sure the driver is going to stop)

- **Car accidents:** According to the National Center for Injury Prevention and Control, motor vehicle injuries are the leading cause of death among children of every age after the age of one. In 2000, 1,471 children up to the age of 14 died in motor vehicle accidents in the United States and an additional 250,000 suffered injuries serious enough to require treatment in a hospital emergency department. Despite the fact that booster seats have been proven to reduce the risk of a car accident fatality by an astonishing 86 percent, fewer than 10 percent of 5- to 8-year-olds are placed in this type of child safety seat by their parents. Here's what you need to know about the use of booster seats: A child is only ready to sit in a regular vehicle seat when the lap belt can be correctly positioned across his thighs and the shoulder belt can be comfortably positioned across his chest. If he's too small for a regular seat, he risks being ejected from the vehicle or suffering severe abdominal injuries in the event of a crash. The key car safety issue for older kids is seatbelt use: according to a study of California high school students conducted by the Insurance Institute for Highway Safety, teenagers don't buckle up as often as they should. The researchers found that when teens were dropped off at school by their parents in the morning, nearly half of the teens (46 percent) weren't wearing their seat belts.

NO KIDDING!

Auto manufacturers are in the process of phasing in a new generation of "smart" air bags that are capable of taking into account a passenger's size, but safety experts say that drivers should still err on the side of caution by insisting that smaller passengers—including children—ride in the backseat. While the number of airbag-related deaths has been on the wane in recent years, the National Highway Traffic Safety Administration has continued to spread the word that it's unsafe for children and other small passengers to ride in the front seat. A NHTSA study in 2002 found that a significant number of children are still riding up front. NHTSA researchers found that 15 percent of infants, 10 percent of 1- to 3-year-olds, and 29 percent of 4- to 7-year-olds are allowed to ride in the front seat.

- **Travel safety:** Don't forget to pay attention to safety when you're visiting other people's homes. You don't want to find out the hard way that medications and other hazardous products were left in your child's reach—perhaps in Grandma's purse. You should also give some thought to the types of items that may be stashed away in your own suitcase while you're traveling: pain relief medications, birth control pills, and so on. Of course, you'll want to be particularly careful about safety if the people you are visiting have a hot tub or swimming pool or if they live on a busy street. (If they don't have young children of their own, they may not be tuned in to what constitutes a risk to visiting children.)

All-Seasons Safety

Depending on where you live, you may need to know how to keep your kids safe and healthy despite extremes of heat and cold. Here's the lowdown on preventing frostbite in winter and excessive sun exposure in summer.

Preventing frostbite

Skin that is exposed to extreme temperatures will freeze quickly if it's left exposed, so you'll want to make a point of encouraging your child to bundle up during cold weather, even if he tries to convince you that it's "uncool" to zip up or wear a winter coat. Your child is more likely to stay warm if he dresses in layers or warm clothing and makes sure that his extremities are covered. That means wearing a coat, warm winter hat (not a baseball cap!), boots, and mittens, whether they're cool or uncool. A child's cheeks, ears, nose, hands, and feet are most vulnerable to frostbite in cold weather.

Wondering about the warning signs of frostbite? Here's what to look out for: Initially, the affected skin becomes red and swollen and feels like it's stinging or burning. If the skin continues to be exposed to the cold, it will tingle, turn grayish, and then turn shiny and white and lose all sensation.

If your child comes in from the cold complaining of a sore body part—the key warning sign of frostbite—you should help him remove any clothing that's covering the frostbitten area and slowly re-warm the area using body heat. Don't massage or rub snow onto the frostbitten skin or use heat or warm water to "defrost" the frozen skin. Instead, call your child's doctor to discuss treatment.

 NO KIDDING!

Don't forget the sunscreen during the winter months. Ultraviolet rays from the sun can pose a threat to children's health on even the frostiest of winter days.

Playing it safe in the summer

To prevent your child from overheating or receiving skin or eye damage from ultraviolet rays, you should encourage your child to wear light-colored, loose-fitting clothing that allows the sweat to evaporate; wear a wide-brimmed hat that is generously enough sized to allow for plenty of air flow; avoid a lot of activity or stay in the shade during the hottest time of the day (between 10 A.M. and 2 P.M.); avoid lengthy exposure to the sun; wear a sunscreen that is SPF 30 or higher anytime they are in direct sunlight (don't use sunscreen on any child younger than six months of age); wear sunglasses that are UVA/UVB CSA certified; and to drink plenty of water.

NO KIDDING!

If you're living in an area where the West Nile virus is a problem, you'll want to look for long-sleeved garments that cover up as much of your child's skin as possible. It's important to use an insect repellent containing DEET. (The American Academy of Pediatrics recommends products with up to 30 percent for children under 12, provided that the product instructions are followed carefully, and that you use DEET sparingly on exposed skin; avoid using it under clothing; do not use it on the hands of young children; avoid applying it to areas around the eyes and the mouth; avoid applying it to cuts, wounds, or irritated skin; do not use it near food; and avoid spraying it in enclosed areas.) Note: You can obtain updates on the West Nile Virus situation by searching on "West Nile" at http://aapnews.aappublications.org/.

First Aid Essentials: What to Do When Your Child Is Injured

Every parent should make a point of taking a first-aid and cardiopulmonary resuscitation (CPR) course. Even if you have taken appropriate training in emergency first aid, it can be easy to draw a blank when your child starts choking or gets a bad burn. That's why I've included a quick reference chart outlining some basic first-aid procedures (see Table 11.1).

Please note that I was barely able to scratch the surface here, due to space constraints, so don't make the mistake of considering this chart as a substitute for proper training in first aid and CPR or emergency medical assistance. You still need hands-on training to perform chest compressions and other life-saving maneuvers safety and effectively.

TABLE 11.1

Emergency First-Aid Procedures

Type of Emergency	What to Do
Allergic reaction	• If your child is exhibiting the symptoms of an allergic reaction (for example, swollen hands and eyelids, wheezing, and a hive-like rash), take him to your doctor's office or the hospital emergency ward immediately. • Talk to your doctor about how to handle future allergic reactions, which, by the way, are likely to be more severe. You may want to carry a kit with injectable adrenalin in order to buy your child enough time to get to the hospital for emergency treatment.
Bleeding	• If your child starts bleeding and the cut appears to be fairly deep, place a clean piece of gauze or cloth over the site of the bleeding and apply firm pressure for two minutes. If that stops the bleeding, you should attempt to clean the wound by running it under cold water. If the bleeding continues, apply more gauze and wrap tape around the cut to keep pressure on the bleeding. • Position your child so that the area that is bleeding is above the level of his heart. This will help to reduce the amount of bleeding. • If the bleeding still won't stop, the wound is gaping, and the cut appears to be quite deep, you'll need to take your child to the hospital or your doctor's office for stitches. You'll also need to seek medical attention for your child if the cut has dirt in it that won't come out; the cut becomes inflamed; your child starts running a fever; the cut begins oozing a thick, creamy, greyish fluid; red streaks form near the wound; or the wound is caused by a human or animal bite.

Type of Emergency	What to Do
Breathing, cessation of	• Try to figure out why your child isn't breathing if you discover that he's pale or turning blue. Turn him onto one side to look for any foreign objects in the mouth and clear out any vomit, mucus, or fluid that could be making it difficult for him to breathe. If you suspect that he's choking, follow the steps outlined later in this table on dealing with a choking emergency and call for help. If you're on your own, call for help as soon as it's practical—within a minute or two of starting CPR.
	• Place your child on his back. Push down on the back of his head and up on his chin in order to clear the tongue away from the back of his throat. Don't push his head too far back, however, or you may end up obstructing the airway. If you roll a towel and slide it under your child's neck, he'll probably end up in the correct position.
	• Give your child mouth-to-mouth resuscitation. Make a seal around your child's mouth and give two quick breaths. If his chest rises with each breath, the airway is clear, and you should continue administering mouth-to-mouth resuscitation until help arrives or your child starts breathing on his own. If he still isn't breathing, follow the procedures outlined later in this table for dealing with choking.
	• Check your child's pulse to find out whether his heart is beating. If it's not, you'll need to begin chest compressions (rhythmic thrusts with one hand only on your child's breastbone at a rate of at least 100 thrusts per minute), pausing to give him a puff of air through mouth-to-mouth resuscitation after every fifth heart compression.

continued

Emergency First-Aid Procedures *(continued)*

Type of Emergency	*What to Do*
Breathing, cessation of *(continued)*	Note: CPR should not be attempted without training, so make sure that you sign up for a CPR course, if you haven't received such training already.
Burns	• Assess the severity of the burn. First-degree burns (such as sunburns) cause redness and minor soreness and can be treated with cool water and some soothing ointment. Second-degree burns cause blistering, swelling, and peeling; are very painful; and may require medical treatment. Third-degree burns damage the underlying layers of the skin and can lead to permanent damage; medical treatment is a must. • Submerge the burned area in cool water for at least 20 minutes (or, in the case of a burn to the face, apply a cool, water-soaked face cloth to the burn). This will help to ease your child's pain as well as lessening the amount of skin damage. Do not apply ice to a burn, as this can cause damage to the tissues. • If the skin becomes blistered, white, or charred, apply an antiseptic ointment and cover the wound before heading to your doctor's office or the hospital. Note: You'll also want to give your child a dose of acetaminophen to help control the pain. • If your child gets a chemical burn as a result of coming into contact with a caustic substance, immerse the burned area under cool, running water for 20 minutes. Gently wash the affected area with soap. (Vigorous scrubbing will cause more of the poison to be absorbed into the skin.) If the substance was also inhaled or swallowed, get in touch with your local poison control center

Type of Emergency	*What to Do*
	immediately. If a caustic substance was splashed into your child's eyes, flush the area for 20 minutes. (If your child is still quite young, try wrapping him in a towel to keep his arms out of the way and laying him on his side. Then pour water into his eye and onto a towel below. If your child closes his eyes tightly, pull down on the lower lid or put your index finger on the upper lid just below the eyebrow and gently pry your child's eyes open. When you've finished flushing your child's eyes, call for medical advice.)
Choking	• Quickly determine whether or not your child is able to breathe. If your child can cough, cry, or speak, the airway is not obstructed, and your child's built-in gag and cough reflex will help to dislodge the object. In this case, your best bet is to do nothing other than to reassure your child that he's going to be all right.
	• If your child does not appear to be breathing, he will likely be gasping for air or turning blue, losing consciousness, and/or looking panicked (wide eyes and mouth wide open). In this case, you should straddle the child along your forearm so that his head is lower than his feet and his face is pointing toward the floor and then apply four quick, forceful blows between your child's shoulder blades using the heel of your hand. If you are in a public place, shout for help; if you're at home alone, run with the child to the phone and dial 911 while you attempt to resuscitate him.

continued

Emergency First-Aid Procedures *(continued)*

Type of Emergency	What to Do
Choking *(continued)*	• If the back blows don't dislodge the object and your child still isn't breathing, immediately flip your child over and deal four quick, forceful chest thrusts to the child's breastbone (about one finger's width below the level of the child's nipples, in the middle of the chest). To administer a chest thrust, you quickly depress the breastbone to a depth of 1.5 to 2.5 centimeters. You keep your fingers in the same position between thrusts but allow the breastbone to return to its normal position.
	• If your child is still not breathing, hold his tongue down with your thumb and forefinger, lift the jaw open, and try to see the object that's causing the blockage. (The mere act of holding your child's tongue away from the back of his throat may relieve the obstruction.) If you see the object, carefully sweep it out. If you can't see it, don't poke your finger down your child's throat or you may accidentally cause an object that's out of sight to become further lodged in your child's throat.
	• If the tongue-jaw lift doesn't work, begin mouth-to-mouth resuscitation on your child. Make a seal around his mouth and nose and give two quick breaths. If your child's chest rises with each breath and the airway is clear, you should continue administering mouth-to-mouth resuscitation until help arrives or your child starts breathing on his own.
	• If your child still isn't breathing, repeat all of these steps until help arrives.

Type of Emergency	What to Do
Convulsions (seizures)	• Assess the severity of the convulsion. Convulsions can range from localized muscle shakes to full-body shakes (*grand mal* seizures), which may involve falling and writhing on the ground, the rolling back of the eyes, frothing at the mouth, tongue biting, and a temporary loss of consciousness.
	• Take steps to ensure that your child's tongue or secretions do not block his airway. Place him safely on the floor, either face down or on his side to allow the tongue to come forward. This will also help to drain secretions from the mouth.
	• Keep your child away from furniture so that he won't injure himself during the convulsion.
	• Don't give your child any food or drink during or immediately after a convulsion.
	• If your child's lips start to turn blue or he stops breathing, clear his airway and give mouth-to-mouth resuscitation. Make a seal around his mouth and nose and give two quick breaths. If his chest rises with each breath, the airway is clear and you should continue administering mouth-to-mouth resuscitation until help arrives or your child starts breathing on his own.
	• If your child has a fever, treat the fever to try to prevent any subsequent seizures. (See Chapter 10 for tips on treating a fever.)
	• Have your child seen by a doctor.
Head injury	• Try to assess the seriousness of the situation. If your child is unconscious but is still breathing and pinkish in color rather than blue, lay him on a flat surface and call for emergency assistance. Do not attempt to move him if you suspect that his neck may be injured.

continued

Emergency First-Aid Procedures *(continued)*

Type of Emergency	What to Do
Head injury *(continued)*	• If he's not breathing, follow the steps outlined previously on dealing with a child who isn't breathing.
	• If he's having a convulsion, keep his airway clear by placing him on his back and pushing down on the back of his head and up on his chin in order to clear the tongue away from the back of his throat. Don't push his head too far back, however, or you may end up obstructing the airway. If you roll a towel and slide it under your child's neck, he'll probably end up in the correct position.
	• If your child is acting like himself (that is, he's alert and conscious and seems to be behaving normally), apply an ice pack (wrapped in a sock or face cloth) or a bag of frozen vegetables to the cut or bump and monitor your child closely over the next 24 hours—checking him every two hours around the clock to see that his color is still normal (pink rather than pale or blue), that he's breathing normally (there may be cause for concern if your child's breathing becomes shallow, irregular, he's gasping for air, or he periodically stops breathing altogether), and to make sure that he's not twitching on one side (a sign of a possible brain injury). If he seems well, you can let him continue sleeping. If you're concerned that there could be a problem, sit or stand your child up and then lie him back down again. Normally, this will cause the child to react. If you don't get a suitable reaction, seek medical attention immediately.

Type of Emergency	What to Do
	• You should seek medical attention immediately if you notice any signs of disorientation, crossed eyes, pupils that are unequal sizes, persistent vomiting (as opposed to just a one-time occurrence), oozing of blood or watery fluid from the ear canal, convulsions, or any signs that your child's sense of balance has been thrown off.
Poisoning	• Seek emergency medical attention if your child seems to be exhibiting any signs of severe poisoning-related distress (such as severe throat pain, excessive drooling, difficulty breathing, convulsions, and/or excessive drowsiness). • If the situation seems to be less urgent, call your local poison control center for advice. The person handling the call will want to know the name of the product that was ingested and what its ingredients are, so be sure to have this information handy. You'll also be asked the time of the poisoning and approximately how much of the poison your child ingested, the age and weight of your child, and whether he's exhibiting any symptoms (such as vomiting, coughing, behavioral changes, and so on). • Do not attempt to induce vomiting unless the poison control center staff member specifically instructs you to do so. Inducing vomiting under the wrong circumstances (for example, if a caustic substance was ingested) could lead to severe tissue damage. In some cases, you'll be instructed to give your child a particular antidote—sometimes something as simple as a couple of glasses of water or a glass of milk.

continued

Emergency First-Aid Procedures *(continued)*

Type of Emergency	What to Do
Poisoning *(continued)*	• If you're told to induce vomiting, give your child one tablespoon of syrup of ipecac followed by one cup of water or non-carbonated fruit juice. Then gently bounce him on your knee. Vomiting should occur within 20 minutes. If it does not, repeat the dose. When your child starts vomiting, hold him face down so that his head is lower than his body. Have your child vomit into a basin rather than the toilet so that the vomit can be analyzed to determine how much and what type(s) of poison he consumed. Be sure to observe your child closely for the next couple of hours and seek medical attention if warranted.

Stranger Danger: Streetproofing in the Real World

Although you don't want to make your child totally paranoid about the dangers that may be lurking on the other side of your front door, it's important to teach kids the skills they need to stay safe. Here's what you need to know about real-world streetproofing.

Streetproofing kids is all about teaching kids to pay attention to their instincts—the voice inside them that's telling them that something's not right or not safe. It's also about keeping the lines of communication open so that your child feels comfortable talking to you about any situation that he may happen to encounter and feels uneasy about. You'll also want to teach your child from a very young age what a stranger is and why he should never go anywhere with any adult without your permission, whether that person is a stranger or a friend.

Here are some other key pieces of information that you'll want to convey to your child:

- **Strangers shouldn't ask kids for help.** Your child needs to know that it's unusual for adults to ask children for help or for directions (a common ploy in abduction attempts). You also need to explain what to do in such a situation. Your child should run for help and scream, kick, make a lot of noise, and keep yelling, "You're not my mother" or "You're not my father" if the stranger attempts to grab him.

- **Your child shouldn't go with any adult unless that adult knows your secret family password.** To leave your child less vulnerable to adults who may pretend that you've asked them to pick your child up on your behalf because you're supposedly sick or injured (another common ploy among child abductors), you may want to come up with a secret family password that you can pass along to selected adults who have your permission to pick up your child. You can tell your child that he only has your permission to go with adults who know the secret password.

MOM'S THE WORD

"I think kids today are safer than we were when we were growing up. We now have seat belts, scheduled play dates, smoke-free spaces, and so on. However, we still can't help but worry."

—*Christine, 39, mother of four*

It's also a good idea to keep an up-to-date child identification kit for your child. Such a kit usually includes an up-to-date photograph of your child plus at least one per year from when he was younger, a set of your child's fingerprints (many police departments will do this for you at an annual child identification clinic; call to see whether this service is provided in your community), and a medical and dental history for your child. It's one of those things that you hope you'll never have to use, but that could prove invaluable to police in the event that your child were to go missing.

Note: You can learn more about streetproofing children by visiting the National Crime Prevention Council's main Web site at www.ncpc.org and the grown-ups' pages of their kids' "McGruff" Web site: http://www.mcgruff.org/grownups.htm.

CHAPTER 12

Healthy Lifestyles, Healthy Kids

The latest figures from the Surgeon General paint an anything-but-rosy picture of the health of American kids: an estimated 15 percent of children and teens are overweight, nearly three times as many as a generation ago.

The question, of course, is what to do about the problem. Although we all know that teaching kids to make healthier food choices and to fit more physical activity into their increasingly sedentary lives is what's required to do battle with the growing problem of childhood obesity, it can be challenging to motivate kids to turn off the video game console, to hop on their bikes, and to "just say no" to those oh-so-seductive advertising messages pitching everything from super-sized snacks to fast food.

In this chapter, I offer practical tips on promoting healthy nutrition, active living, and positive body image within the family—the three key ingredients for raising healthy, active kids. Not every strategy is going to work for every kid, so this is one of those areas where you're going to have to let your knowledge of your child be your guide. But, hopefully, by the time you have finished reading this part of the book, you will have picked up at least a few new ideas that will help you to encourage your kids to get with the healthy living program.

Nutrition on the Run: Nutrition Tips for Busy Families

Kids learn their most important nutrition lessons around the family dinner table, so make sure that the lessons that your kids are learning are ones that will serve them well through their growing-up years and beyond. Here are some key points to keep in mind when teaching kids about healthy eating:

- **Make family mealtimes a priority.** Try to provide a relaxed, unhurried setting that is as distraction-free as possible. (Hint: Turn off the TV!) Although there will undoubtedly be times when dinner consists of a quick trip to the nearest drive-thru, these sorts of "meals on the run" should be the exception rather than the rule.

- **Teach your kids to view food as fuel.** Make sure that your kids understand that food is the fuel that allows our bodies to function properly, and that the quality of the fuel that we give our bodies will determine how well our bodies are able to function. (If your kids are having a hard time understanding what you're talking about, ask them to remember how they felt the last time they tried to go for a lengthy bike ride after eating only a doughnut for breakfast!)

- **Remind your kids that variety is the spice of life.** Kids need to know that our bodies need a variety of healthy foods in order to function well; despite what some advertisers would have you believe, there's no one "perfect food" that can meet all our bodies' nutritional needs.

- **Aim to include at least one serving from each of the five food groups at each meal.** Not only do meals drawn from all five food groups (see Table 12.1) provide an important cross-section of nutrients, but they're also likely to provide a variety of tastes, textures, and colors—something that's likely to make mealtime more enjoyable for the entire family, including your kids. (Snacks should provide servings from at least two of the five food groups. If one of the foods chosen is a good source of protein, such as celery with peanut butter, the snack will have more staying power.)

- **Don't become overly concerned if your child ignores some food groups entirely for a day or two.** Rather than analyzing your child's nutrient intake from meal to meal (or even from day to day), look at her food choices over the course of a week or two. It is the overall pattern of foods eaten over time that determines good health, not what is eaten at a particular meal or over the course of a particular day. So, there's no need to panic if your child is on a short-term veggie boycott—or if your child has eaten the identical breakfast and lunch every day this week. Odds are her food choices will balance out over time.

- **Help your kids to become "food literate."** Although most kids quickly grasp the concept of the five food groups—they're able to tell you that an apple falls into the fruits group and that a bagel falls into the bread, cereal, rice, and pasta group—they have a bit more difficulty sizing up the various food choices within each food group. They'll need a bit of coaching from you to understand that an apple, a container of apple punch, and a slice of apple pie are not all created equal—at least not from a nutritional standpoint.

MOTHER WISDOM

If the foods that are offered in the vending machines or cafeteria at your children's school are less than inspiring from a nutritional standpoint, suggest that the school reconsider its food choices. Ditto for any chocolate-bar sale fundraisers: why not suggest a bike-a-thon instead?

NO KIDDING!

Don't automatically assume that your child needs a vitamin just because the drugstore shelves are lined with these products. According to the American Academy of Pediatrics, vitamin and mineral supplements are rarely necessary if a child is eating a variety of foods, is growing well, and is in good health. If you do decide to give your child a pediatric vitamin supplement, make sure that you keep the vitamin jar well out of her reach. Ingesting large quantities of vitamins can be harmful to a child.

- **Refuse to take on the role of food cop.** Instead of trying to direct "food traffic" at the dinner table by trying to tell your kids how much or how little they need to eat, encourage your kids to listen to their own bodies. The amount of the food and the number of servings each child needs is determined by such factors as the child's body size, how physically active she is, and how quickly she is growing. When kids are healthy and active, their appetite is the best indicator of how much food they need, so it's best to encourage them to go with their gut instinct—literally.

- **Don't fall into the trap of categorizing foods as "healthy" and "unhealthy."** Labeling foods as "healthy" and "unhealthy" (or "good" and "bad") will only encourage your child to gravitate toward the less healthy choices. Instead, reinforce the idea that *all* foods have a place in our diets (even junk food) and try to teach your child to think about foods as "everyday foods" and "sometimes foods." We may not eat ice cream and doughnuts every day, but it's okay to enjoy them sometimes.

- **Sell your kids on the merits of eating breakfast.** If your kids are in the habit of skipping breakfast, get them involved in brainstorming some breakfast ideas. If you put your heads together, you should be able to come up with some ideas for breakfast foods that are nutritious, tasty, and suitable for eating on the run. Hint: Fruit and yogurt smoothies tend to be a particular hit with older kids who like to sleep in until the last possible second.

- **Don't go condiment crazy.** Encourage your child to develop an appreciation for the natural flavors of foods rather than automatically adding salt, salad dressings, butter, or margarine to whatever happens to be on her plate.

- **Sing the praises of H$_2$O.** Encourage your child to develop a taste for water so that she'll be more inclined to hit the water cooler than the soda pop machine on a blistering hot day. Although kids may tend to reach for soda pop or fruit-flavored drinks, these beverages deliver little in terms of nutrients and are loaded with sugar. Here's something else to consider on the beverage front: kids—like adults—need be taught to use caffeine in moderation. That means limiting the consumption of caffeine-containing beverages such as colas, hot chocolate, and chocolate milk.

- **Try some new recipes if you feel like you're getting into a dinnertime rut.** You'll get more buy-in from other family members if you let them know that the recipe you're trying is an experiment and that you're eager to find out whether they like it or not. "Sometimes I try new recipes and ask everyone's opinion about whether they would like me to make that dinner again," explains Rita, a 38-year-old mother of two. "If the majority didn't like it, it's off the list. I think this helps to give the kids a say in what the family eats, which helps."

- **Find a cookbook with recipes that appeal to both parents and kids alike.** After you've cooked your way through that particular cookbook, expand your recipe repertoire by finding out whether that particular cookbook author has written any other cookbooks that may appeal to your family, or by asking your local bookseller to recommend other cookbooks that feature a similar style of cooking. (You may want to swap cookbook recommendations with other moms by visiting some of the growing number of health-oriented parenting Web sites. Visit www.wherethemomsare.com for leads on message boards specifically devoted to cooking and family nutrition.)

MOTHER WISDOM

Wondering how much food to send to school in your child's lunch?

Most school-aged kids require two servings of breads, cereals, or other grain products; two servings of vegetables and fruit; one to two servings of milk products; one to two servings of meat and alternatives such as hard-boiled eggs and chili (either meat- or bean-based).

Here are some lunch-friendly ideas that fall within each of these categories:

- *Breads, cereals, and grain products:* breads and buns, bread sticks, pita bread, bagels, English muffins, crackers, tortillas, pretzels, plain popcorn, plain granola bars, muffins, banana loaf, fig bars, dry cereal.
- *Vegetables and fruit:* Apples, bananas, oranges, clementines, pears, peaches, plums, pineapple, melons (cantaloupe, honeydew melon, watermelon, and so on), kiwi, raisins, apple sauce, fruit cup, fruit juice (sugar-free), salad, vegetable sticks.
- *Milk products:* White milk, chocolate milk, yogurt, cheese, milk pudding, soup made with milk, hot chocolate made with milk, yogurt drinks.
- *Meats and alternatives:* Hard-boiled eggs, tuna, salmon, cold meats (ham, turkey, chicken, roast beef), sunflower seeds, hummus, beef stew, chili (either meat- or bean-based).

You'll probably find that you'll need to increase or decrease the number of servings from time to time as your child passes through growth spurts or increases or decreases her activity level. If you notice that your child is consistently eating everything in her lunch bag and coming home totally ravenous after school, you may want to send an extra serving or two of food with her to school. If, on the other hand, she's barely eating half of the food she's been given, you may want to consider cutting back on the number of servings for a while. (Of course, you'll also want to find out if there's another explanation for her less-than-enthusiastic appetite at lunch; perhaps she's using her allowance money to buy chocolate bars from the vending machine in the school cafeteria—something that could very well kill her appetite for the broccoli you so painstakingly wrapped up the night before!)

NO KIDDING!

Try to get in the habit of eating together as a family as often as possible. Research has shown that teenagers are more likely to eat fruits, vegetables, grains, and dairy products, and to consume fewer soft drinks, if meals are eaten as a family, so you may as well tilt the nutritional roulette wheel in your child's favor by getting your child in the family mealtime habit right from day one.

Winning at Food Group Roulette

Of course, it's one thing to see the *Food Guide Pyramid* neatly mapped out on a piece of paper. It's quite another to actually convince your child to get friendly with the five major food groups every now and again (see Table 12.1). Here are some relatively pain-free ways to encourage your kids to gravitate toward some of the healthier foods within each of the five major food groups.

Food Guide Pyramid
A Guide to Daily Food Choices

Fats, Oils, & Sweets
USE SPARINGLY

KEY
∘ Fat (naturally occurring and added)
▾ Sugars (added)
These symbols show fat and added sugars in foods.

Milk, Yogurt,
& Cheese
Group
2-3 SERVINGS

Meat, Poultry, Fish,
Dry Beans, Eggs,
& Nuts Group
2-3 SERVINGS

Vegetable
Group
3-5 SERVINGS

Fruit
Group
2-4 SERVINGS

Bread, Cereal,
Rice, & Pasta
Group
**6-11
SERVINGS**

Source: U.S. Department of Agriculture/U.S. Department of Health and Human Services, August 1992

TABLE 12.1

Food Guide Pyramid: The Foods Kids Need

The number of food servings that a child requires varies from child to child and from day to day. Younger children may not even be able to manage to eat the minimum number of servings recommended for each food group. As long as a child is full of energy, continuing to grow at a healthy rate, and eating a variety of healthy foods from each of the five major food groups, however, you can feel confident that your child's food intake is adequate.

Food Group	Why Your Child Needs Them	Number of Servings	What Constitutes a Serving	What Else You Need to Know
Bread, cereal, rice, and pasta group	Foods from this group are critical for converting food to energy and for maintaining a healthy nervous system. They're also an excellent source of B vitamins, minerals (especially iron), and fiber (if whole-grain products are served).	8 to 11 servings/day.	One serving: • 1 slice of bread • 1 ounce of ready-to-eat cereal • 1/2 cup of cooked cereal, rice, or pasta	Make a point of including whole grain and enriched products in your child's diet.

Vegetable group	Vegetables are a good source of fiber and an excellent source of vitamin C as well as disease-fighting compounds called phytochemicals. Vegetables are also an excellent source of vitamin A, folacin, and iron.	3 to 5 servings/day	• 1 cup of raw, leafy vegetables • 1/2 cup of other vegetables, cooked or chopped, raw • 3/4 cup of vegetable juice	Make a point of including dark green and orange vegetables in your child's diet on a regular basis.
Fruit group	Fruit is a good source of fiber and an excellent source of vitamin C as well as hundreds of disease-fighting compounds called phytochemicals.	2 to 4 servings/day	• 1 medium-sized apple, banana, or orange • 1/2 cup of chopped, cooked, or canned fruit • 3/4 cup fruit juice	Make a point of including orange fruit in your child's diet on a regular basis.

continued

Food Guide Pyramid: The Foods Kids Need *(continued)*

Food Group	Why Your Child Needs Them	Number of Servings	What Constitutes a Serving	What Else You Need to Know
Milk yogurt, and cheese group	Milk products are an excellent source of protein, calcium (the mineral responsible for keeping bones healthy and strong), and vitamins D, A, and B12.	3 to 5 servings/day	• 1 cup milk or yogurt • 1 1/2 ounces of natural cheese • 2 slices of processed cheese	Cottage cheese is lower in calcium than most cheeses. One cup of cottage cheese counts as only 1/2 serving of milk.
Meat, poultry, fish, dry beans, eggs, and nuts group	The foods in this group are an important source of proteins and B vitamins and minerals (particularly iron). Protein helps to build and repair body tissues, including muscle, bone, and blood, and to manufacture the antibodies needed to fight infection.	2 to 3 servings/day	• 3 ounces of cooked lean meat, poultry, or fish • 1/2 cup of cooked dry beans or 1 egg counts as 1 ounce of lean meat. • 2 tablespoons of peanut butter or 1/3 cup of nuts counts as 1 ounce of meat.	Make a point of including poultry, and fish, as well as dried peas, beans, and lentils more often.

Note: The Food Guide Pyramid also includes fats, oils, and sweets. These are foods such as salad dressings and oils, cream, butter, margarine, sugars, soft drinks, candies, and sweet desserts. These foods provide calories and little else nutritionally. Most people should use them sparingly.

Bread, Cereal, Rice, and Pasta Group

Here are some tips on making the foods you serve from the bread, cereal, rice, and pasta group kid-friendly and nutritious, too:

- Make a point of serving whole-grain breads and cereals, brown rice, and whole wheat pasta at home so that your child develops a taste for these healthy grains and cereals right from day one.

- When you're baking, use a mixture of whole wheat flour and white flour. The baked goods you put on the table will be tastier and more nutritious.

- Add fresh or dried fruits to cereals, pancakes, and muffins rather than sweetening these foods with syrups or sugars.

- Try cutting back on the amount of sugar in muffin recipes where sugar is required.

Vegetable Group

Looking for some tips on squeezing more vegetables into your child's diet? Here are some strategies that have worked for other parents.

- Offer your child a variety of different vegetables. You want to expose her to as many different tastes as possible. If your child claims to hate all vegetables, see whether you can win her over by serving her one of the veggies that kids like best: corn, peas, carrots, beans, and sweet potatoes.

- Prepare fruits and vegetables in a variety of different ways: raw (perhaps some from your own garden!), cooked, *au naturel,* or sprinkled with cheese or herbs and spices.

- Don't be surprised if your preschooler prefers raw veggies to cooked ones. Most vegetables acquire a stronger, more bitter taste when they're cooked—something that turns young children (and some adults!) off.

- Serve your child veggies and dip (yogurt, hummus, black bean, and guacamole dips tend to be perennial favorites with kids). Not only will your child be more likely to munch her way through that plate of veggies if she's got some dip to play around with, but the fat in the dip will also make it easier for her body to absorb the vitamin A and beta carotene in the veggies.

- When you're planning your child's meals, try to zero in on fruits and vegetables that are rich in vitamin A (carrots, spinach, cantaloupe, and apricots) and vitamin C (tomatoes, green peppers, oranges, and strawberries). Fruits and vegetables are important sources of these two vital vitamins.

- If your child is a card-carrying veggie-o-phobe, you may have to find creative ways to include vegetables in foods she already likes. Try puréeing vegetables and including them in spaghetti sauces, soups, or stews; adding finely chopped spinach, mushroom, or green pepper to omelets; making vegetable lasagna, pizza with vegetable toppings, or meatloaf with lots of built-in veggies; pumping up the vegetable content of family favorites such as shepherd's pie or tuna casserole; or whipping up a batch of pumpkin, carrot, or zucchini muffins. If all else fails, up her fruit intake instead. That will help to make up for some of the nutrients she's missing on the veggie front.

Fruit Group

While most kids tend to like fruit, it can still be a challenge to ensure that your kids are working enough servings of fruit into their diet, and that they aren't overdoing it in the juice department. Here are a few points to keep in mind.

- If you have a child who doesn't like fruit, you may want to get in the habit of serving breakfast or bedtime smoothies made from yogurt, bananas, pineapple, berries, or other blender-friendly fruits. You can also pack a lot of fruit (and certain types of veggies) into muffins and low-fat snack breads. All you need is a good cookbook and a great food grater.

- Try to discourage your child from drinking too much fruit juice. Some kids fill up on juice and don't eat properly at mealtimes. Others drink a lot of juice on top of their regular meals and snacks, something that can lead to excess weight gain over time. (Juice is naturally high in sugar and, consequently, high in calories, too.) Besides, if your child gets her fruit servings via fruit juice rather than fruit, she'll miss out on a lot of the fiber.

Milk, Yogurt, and Cheese Group

Dairy products have an important role to play in the diet of a growing kid. Here's what you need to know in order to ensure that your child receives the recommended number of servings from the milk, yogurt, and cheese group on a regular basis:

- Milk is an excellent source of vitamin D and calcium—the nutrients needed to build healthy bones and strong teeth. Although vitamin D can be obtained through sun exposure, increased use of sunscreens limits the amount of vitamin D that can be obtained from the sun. Consequently, it's more important than ever to ensure that your child's diet contains vitamin D–rich foods, especially milk.

- Although it's okay to offer your child chocolate milk on occasion, don't let it replace the regular milk in her diet. Chocolate milk is much higher in sugar than regular milk. If your child really enjoys her chocolate milk, dilute it with regular milk so that she's not getting quite as much sugar.

Chocolate milk is much more nutritious than soda pop, however, so if you want to give her the choice of ordering something other than regular milk at a fast-food restaurant, chocolate milk is a healthy choice. (Just bear in mind that chocolate milk has caffeine, so it might not be the ideal pre-bedtime beverage!)

- Limit your child's use of processed cheese slices and spreads, as these products are much higher in salt than natural cheeses. Don't get in the habit of serving ice cream and frozen yogurt on a regular basis because they tend to contain a lot of fat and sugar.

- Don't go crazy with flavored yogurts, as they tend to be quite high in sugar. You can get a lot of mileage out of a small serving of flavored yogurt by letting your child use it as dip for fruit slices. Or, if you prefer, buy plain yogurt and add your own flavoring, such as some fresh fruit, vanilla flavoring, and so on.

Meat and alternatives

Whether you've got a child who hates meat or who would live on hotdogs alone if she had her way, here are a few points to keep in mind when you're offering your child foods from the meat and alternatives group.

- Get in the habit of trimming visible fat from meats before cooking and removing skin from poultry before you serve it to your child. Although kids need a certain amount of fat in their diets, it's a good idea to introduce kids to lower fat meat products earlier on in life so that they can begin to develop a taste for lower fat foods.

- If you serve luncheon meats to your child, stick with lower sodium, lower fat varieties. Try to find alternatives to frying and deep-frying meat, fish, and poultry, such as barbecuing or grilling instead.

• If you're serving a vegetarian entrée, make a point of including a source of vitamin C with the meal. The iron in meat, poultry, and fish is absorbed at a much higher rate than the iron in legumes, seeds, and nuts—roughly 20 percent versus 8 percent—but combining these vegetarian sources of protein with vitamin C boosts the absorption rate considerably.

No More Food Fights! De-stressing Family Mealtimes

Most of us have been involved in at least one parent-child food fight—either as the parent, the child, or as a spectator. (Who knows? Maybe you were lucky enough to have a sibling who could be counted on to provide the mealtime entertainment each night, challenging Mom or Dad to just try to make him eat a single bit of the mystery casserole *du jour!*)

If you've been embroiled in a parent-child tug-of-war over a piece of broccoli, you already know what it's taken child development experts decades of study to figure out: it's just not worth it to try to force a child to eat. The best way to deal with that often infuriating subspecies of children known as the picky eater is to simply refuse to let her push your buttons. Serve whatever it is you're serving and let your child decide whether or not she's willing to eat it.

Does this mean that you should cater to the every whim of a child who wants to call the nutritional shots in your family? *Au contraire!* You're still the one in charge of making the family's nutritional decisions. You get to decide what types of foods show up on the family dinner table. Your child simply gets to decide whether or not that food ends up in her mouth.

Rest assured, if you're dealing with a card-carrying picky eater, there will be nights when your child refuses to eat whatever it is that the rest of the family is eating. That's her choice. You only lose this particular battle if you feel a compelling need to make a substitute dinner for her because you're worried about what may happen if she goes to bed hungry. If you tend to fall into this particular camp, you may want to heed these reassuring words from Maria, a 34-year-old mother of three: "A child will not starve overnight if they choose not to eat supper. Many nights, I have put my kids to bed with very little in their tummies because they have either said they are not hungry, or they have refused to eat what I have prepared. I never make something different for my kids than what I am preparing for my husband and me, with a few exceptions. If I am making veggie burgers, it's easy to make beef burgers, too. And if we're having pasta, I simply don't put sauce on my children's servings. But I make sure that my kids understand that I am not a short-order cook. I make one meal, and that is what we all eat."

Rita, a 38-year-old mother of two, takes a similarly low-maintenance approach to dealing with the picky eaters in her house at dinnertime, but, in her case, she allows the reluctant diners to have a healthy post-dinner snack after the rest of the family is finished eating: "I cook one meal for dinner. I provide several types of foods, when possible, and put a little of everything on their plate. All I ask is that they try everything. If they don't like what I'm serving, they don't have to eat it. Sometimes, they don't eat much, but I still do not cook anything else. If, after dinner, they are still hungry, they can have something healthy like grapes or cereal. I think if you constantly cater to your kids' food whims by cooking them separate meals, you are setting yourself up for years of headaches. Kids need to realize that dinner is the same for everyone, except on nights when you're eating in a restaurant."

MOM'S THE WORD

"After weeks of picking lima beans out of the frozen vegetable mix and calling them 'yucky,' my four-year-old son decided the other day that he actually likes them. He ended up stealing everyone else's off of their plates!"

—*Elouise, 33, mother of two*

Here are some additional points to keep in mind when you're dealing with a picky eater:

- **Encourage your picky eater to try new foods.** You'll increase your odds of getting your child to give new foods a chance if you stick to introducing one new food at a time and you make a point of introducing the new food alongside other more familiar foods. Although you'll want to encourage your child to try the new food, you shouldn't force the issue. If your child tries the food and announces that she hates it, accept the verdict calmly and try reintroducing the food again in a few weeks' time. Studies have shown that it sometimes takes up to 15 exposures to a new food for a child to finally accept it.

- **Be prepared to practice what you preach.** You can hardly expect your child to sign up for the Veggie of the Month club if it's been years since you tried anything more adventurous than mashed potatoes. Nor can you expect your daughter to dutifully pack a piece of fruit in her lunchbox if she can't remember the last time she saw you holding a piece of fruit in your hands. Whether you feel worthy of the position or not, you're your child's number one nutritional role model!

- **Don't force your child to try new foods if she's not ready.** According to dietitian and author Ellyn Satter, this strategy can backfire big-time by convincing your child that there must be something wrong with the food in question if you have to oversell it.

- **Accept the fact that we all have our own personal tastes when it comes to food.** Just as there are probably foods that you aren't overly fond of, there are likely foods that your child simply isn't overly eager to dive into either. Don't sweat it.

- **Strike up an alliance with your child's inner control freak.** If your picky eater has control freak tendencies, make that fact work to your advantage. Allow her as much choice as possible when it comes to planning her own meals. (Of course, if you present your picky eater with a couple of different food choices, you want to make sure that each food choice is acceptable to you. That way, you can't lose—literally.)

You can find out about the ins and outs of feeding a vegetarian child or preteen by visiting the Food and Nutrition Information Center Web site at www.nal.usda.gov/fnic/.

 NO KIDDING!

Unclear about the difference between a food allergy and a food intolerance?

A *food allergy* is an immune system reaction (an allergic reaction) that is triggered by eating a particular food or food additive. Food allergy symptoms may include wheezing, hives, eczema, vomiting, and diarrhea, and can be triggered by a small amount of food. These symptoms can be serious or even life-threatening. In this case, a child is said to be experiencing anaphylactic shock or anaphylaxis. Children under the age of five are most susceptible to food allergies because their digestive systems are not yet mature. Common trigger foods include cow's milk, nuts, eggs, peanut butter, fish, and shellfish. Although children tend to outgrow most food allergies, some—including nut and fish allergies—are usually permanent.

A *food intolerance*, on the other hand, is an adverse reaction to food that does not involve the immune system. If your child experiences such symptoms as bloating, loose stools, and gas after eating a particular food, she may have a food intolerance. Because it's easy to mistake some of the symptoms of a food intolerance with those of a food allergy, it's important to have food intolerances properly diagnosed. Lactose intolerance is a common example of a food intolerance. A person with lactose intolerance lacks an enzyme needed to digest milk sugar. When she eats milk products, symptoms such as gas, bloating, and abdominal pain may occur.

If your child is diagnosed with a food allergy, you'll need to take steps to avoid the offending food. This may be relatively easy when you're cooking meals from scratch at home, but it can be a lot more challenging when you're buying packaged foods or eating out. You'll probably want to ask your doctor or public health nutritionist for a list of ingredients that could cause problems for your child: for example, not every product that contains wheat identifies it as such (wheat is sometimes identified as gluten). Note: If your child has a serious allergy such as a peanut allergy, you'll need to ensure that she carries injectable epinephrine. It could literally save her life in the event of an allergic reaction.

Don't try to diagnose food allergies on your own, or you may place unnecessary restrictions on your child's diet—something that could deprive her of much-needed nutrients.

MOTHER WISDOM

Don't encourage your child to overeat by insisting that she "clean her plate" when she clearly doesn't want any more food. You'll only be teaching her to ignore her body's natural signals of hunger and fullness—something that could lead to weight problems down the road.

- **Get your picky eater on your side of the food battle.** Try to win over your picky eater by involving her in various aspects of food preparation: everything from shopping for groceries to growing her own vegetables and herbs to whipping up meals and snacks in the kitchen. She'll be more inclined to try a new food if she played a role in getting it to the dinner table.

- **Don't overdo it when it comes to portion size.** Remind yourself that it's unrealistic to expect a young child to eat adult-sized portions. A preschooler's stomach is roughly the size of her fist, so if you serve her any more food than that, she's unlikely to be able to get through it all.

- **Trust your child to eat the amount of food that's right for her.** Your child is the best judge of how much food she needs. You'll probably find that she eats more at some meals than others. She's simply adjusting her food intake to match her energy needs—a skill many adults have lost along the way.

Walking the Talk: Fun Ways to Stay Active as a Family

Gone are the days when children filled their leisure time by playing tag or basketball with the other neighborhood kids. According to a recent article in *American Family Physician*, the most popular physical activities for today's generation of kids are watching television and playing video games. Is it any wonder that kids today are three times as likely to be overweight than kids were a generation ago?

Parents have an important role to play in encouraging kids to make physical activity part of their lives from early childhood onward. If your child isn't already physically active on a regular basis, the best way to encourage her to get more active is to "walk the talk" of physical fitness yourself. Here are some pointers on making physical activity a regular part of your family's routines:

- **Give the gift of activity.** Buy birthday and holiday presents that promote physical activity: a set of rollerblades, a basketball, or a softball and glove.

- **Find ways to make physical activity fun.** As with any-thing else in life, variety is the key to making your family fitness program enjoyable. Exercising to the same aerobics tape day after day isn't likely to hold your daughter's atten-tion, but weekly trips to the local swimming pool, rollerblading arena, indoor baseball diamond, and other points of interest likely will.

- **Work additional physical activity into your family's daily and weekly schedule.** Walk your kids to school in the morning. Play hide and go seek as a family after dinner. Get in the habit of going on a hike at a nearby conservation area every Saturday morning.

- **Head for the park.** What do you get when you combine a park and a van full of people? A terrific workout, that's what! Who says fitness has to be boring–or super-serious? Throw around a Frisbee (yes, even in January!). Play a game of tag. As long as you're moving your bodies vigorously enough to get your hearts beating faster, you're exercising.

- **Go for a walk indoors.** Don't skip your walk just because the weather's bad outside. Take your family fitness program indoors! You can either walk around your local mall or head for some spot that's a little more inspiring: even strolling through a museum can be a fitness activity. It doesn't matter what you're doing while you're walking, as long as you're mov-ing quickly enough to get some benefits out of your workout.

- **Hit the pool.** Few exercises will give you as good a work-out as swimming, and water adds a dimension of fun to a workout that can't be found on dry land.

- **Come up with creative ways of keeping your kids active during the winter months.** Resist the temptation to hibernate. Instead, help your kids to build a snow fort or go hiking as a family—anything to beat the February blahs.

- **Get involved in planning physical activity at your child's school.** Volunteer to help organize a sporting event at your daughter's school—unless, of course, she's made it perfectly clear that having you there would cramp her style and would be decidedly uncool. (You can offer to pretend to be some kindly stranger from the neighborhood who offered to help with track and field day, but there's always the chance that one of your kid's friends will blow your cover.)

- **Work fitness into your family vacation.** Stay at a hotel with a pool or bring your bicycles along when you go camping so that you can explore the bike trails in the campground where you're staying.

- **Get a dog**. Or—if you're not up for full-time pet ownership—offer to walk your neighbor's instead. You and the kids will have a reason to hit the pavement in all kinds of weather if Fido is counting on your family to get outdoors so that he can get a walk around the block.

MOM'S THE WORD

"Don't force your child to play football just because you like it. It's important to avoid living vicariously through your child. If your child hates football, let them try something else—something else that they want to try. The point is to help nurture their interests or at least to help them to find and cultivate their own niche."

—*Anne, 45, mother of one*

Of course, your best bet is to find a fitness activity that you and your child will enjoy doing together year in and year out.

Here's the kind of activity to look for when you're shopping for a family-friendly fitness activity:

- **An activity that will appeal to both children and adults:** Swimming, cross-country skiing, walking, biking, and rollerblading are activities that appeal to both young and old. They're a better bet than activities that are more suited to members of one age group, but not the other. Remember, the name of the game is to choose an activity that each member of the family can enjoy together, regardless of age, fitness level, or ability.

- **An activity that's convenient to do:** The easier you make it for everyone to exercise, the more likely you are to make the effort. It's one thing to get a family membership at the swimming pool down the street; it's quite another to purchase one at the pool across town. Be honest with yourself: how often are you going to want to pile everyone into the van to make that trek to the pool? Probably not often enough to make that pool membership worthwhile.

- **An activity that's budget-friendly:** There are already enough demands on your paycheck. Why put more pressure on your budget when there are so many inexpensive–even free!–ways to stay fit? That's not to say that you shouldn't be prepared to invest some money in your family's fitness activities. Just don't make the mistake of assuming that you have to spend a fortune in order to reap the benefits of physical fitness.

- **An activity that can be enjoyed in a family-friendly environment:** There's no point purchasing a family membership at your local gym if children and preteens aren't particularly welcome there. Remember: There can be a world of difference between what the fitness facility's brochure says and how the staff members and other clients *actually feel* about having kids at the gym.

Promoting a Healthy Body Image

Parents also have an important role to play in promoting healthy body image in kids. Here are the key points to keep in mind:

- **Encourage your child to think about her body's abilities rather than her physical appearance.** "We try to focus on all the great things Meagan can do, such as playing hop-scotch, jumping rope, and climbing," explains Judy, a 34-year-old mother of one. "That way, when she makes a comment about her looks, we remind her that what's really important is how her body works."

- **Make sure that you're modeling healthy body image yourself.** "If your kids see you happy with yourself the way you are—or improving yourself because you want to be healthy, then that's great," says Mary, a 36-year-old mother of three. "Just don't berate yourself or go around putting yourself down. And if you're trying to make improvements, make sure that they're getting the message that you're trying to be a healthier person, not a skinnier one."

- **Be conscious of the food messages that come out of your own mouth.** "Talk about food as a means to stay healthy and strong, not as a means to stay thin," advises Lisa, a 41-year-old mother of one. "Don't say, 'I can't have that. It's fattening.' Say, 'That's not really healthy, so I try not to eat too much of it.'"

- **Remind your child about the ebb and flow.** Make sure that your child understands that it's perfectly normal for children to go through periods when they're slightly chubby as well as periods when they are slightly thinner. This is because children's bodies don't increase in both height and weight at the same time. A child will likely become slightly chubbier just before an increase in height; and she may become skinnier if she's experiencing a particularly sudden increase in height without a corresponding weight gain.

- **Limit the amount of time that your kids spend watching TV.** Studies have shown that media messages that equate thinness with beauty can contribute to the development of a negative body image. When your kids are tuned into their favorite shows, sit down and talk with them about what they're seeing. Giving them the tools to think critically about media messages can help them to challenge rather than accept what appears on the screen. (See *Body Talk: The Straight Facts on Nutrition, Fitness, and Feeling Great About Yourself*—the body image book for preteen girls that I cowrote with my then preteen daughter Julie—for more on this subject.)

- **Realize that your feelings about your child's weight can help to determine whether or not she starts dieting.** A study at the Harvard University Medical School found that a parent's concern about a child's weight can impact on a girl's self-esteem from age five onward.

 NO KIDDING!

Both sexes take a self-esteem hit around adolescence. Although 67 percent of elementary school boys and 60 percent of elementary school girls report being happy with themselves "all of the time," by the time they reach high school, only 46 percent of boys and 29 percent of girls report being similarly satisfied with themselves.

- **Be on the lookout for signs that your child may be dieting.** Studies have shown that between 20 and 40 percent of girls have dieted at least once by age 10. If your child is a picky eater, those "picky eating" behaviors could actually be an attempt to restrict her food intake and control her weight. It's also important to familiarize yourself with the early warning signs of both anorexia and bulimia (see Table 12.2) so that you can seek help for your child as early on as possible if she appears to be developing an eating disorder. Although eating disorders can be extremely challenging to treat, the prognosis is generally better if the eating disorder is diagnosed promptly, and treatment begins as soon as possible.

- **If your child has a weight problem, deal with it head-on.** If you are concerned that your child may have a weight problem, get advice from a qualified health professional such as a dietitian or your family doctor on dealing with the problem. Children who are overweight need to be encouraged to make healthy food choices, become physically active, and feel good about themselves. (Note: See www.cdc.gov/growthcharts/ for growth charts for children ages 2 through 20.)

TABLE 12.2

Does Your Child Have an Eating Disorder?

Type of Eating Disorder	Incidence	Warning Signs	Treatment/Prognosis
Anorexia (self-induced such as starvation)	Approximately 1 percent of teenagers and young adults suffer from anorexia, but anorexia is 10 times as common in girls as it is in boys. Anorexia can show up in girls as young as 7 or 8 years of age. Certain groups are at particular risk: dancers, long-distance runners, skaters, models, actors, gymnasts, and others for whom thinness is emphasized and rewarded.	Dieting; preoccupation with weight; significant weight loss; feeling fat even when the number on the scale indicates otherwise; fear of weight gain; obsession with food, calories, nutrition, and/ or cooking; visiting pro-eating-disorder Web sites; preferring to eat alone; compulsive exercise and/or laxative, diuretic, or diet pill abuse in an effort to lose weight; binge eating and purging; lack of menstrual periods; insomnia; brittle hair or nails; feeling cold all the time; and/or depression with social withdrawal.	Anorexia can cause physical damage to the body such as heart and kidney damage and damage to the immune system. Although the mortality rate for this illness is high (10 to 20 percent), 50 percent of anorexics will make a complete recovery. Treatment generally consists of medication, nutritional counseling, and therapy (both individual and family counseling).

continued

Does Your Child Have an Eating Disorder? (continued)

Type of Eating Disorder	Incidence	Warning Signs	Treatment/Prognosis
Bulimia	The lifetime incidence of bulimia is 1 to 3 percent of women and 0.1 percent of men. This illness is most common in adolescents and young adults, but it can occur in younger children, too.	Uncontrollable eating; purging through strict dieting, fasting, over-exercising, or self-induced vomiting, or the abuse of laxatives, diuretics, and/or diet pills in an effort to lose weight; going to the bathroom right after meals; reddened fingers from self-induced vomiting (she may use her fingers or objects such as a toothbrush or a spoon); swollen cheeks or glands (from self-induced vomiting); weight preoccupation; visiting pro-eating-disorder Web sites; irregular	The mortality rate for bulimia is much lower than that of anorexia. While up to 3 percent of women with the disease eventually die from complications resulting from bulimia, about 50 to 66 percent f bulimics respond to treatment, which generally consists of a combination of medication, nutritional counsel-ing, and therapy (both individual and family counseling). The relapse rate is about 30 percent.

menstrual periods; dental problems such as tooth decay and gum problems; heartburn and/or bloating; depression or mood swings; and/or problems with drugs, alcohol, sexual activity, or other risky behaviors. Can lead to kidney damage as well as damage to the esophagus, tooth enamel, and gums.

CHAPTER 13

The Changeling: The Joys and Perils of Parenting a Preteen

*"By accident one day I knocked one of Marissa's school books off the
table and a piece of paper fell out. I picked up the paper and
decided I would just put it in any page of the book. I flipped open
the book to a page with pictures of both the male and female reproductive systems, the words 'penis' and 'vagina' everywhere on the
pages, and a question-and-answer section with questions like 'What
causes a boy to have wet dreams?' to which my innocent, 10-year-
old little girl had written 'Sexy thoughts.' I started to get dizzy. I
thought I was going to pass out. It seemed like every page I turned
to, there was another picture of a penis and I thought to myself,
'Marissa is too young for this. I'm too young for this. This can't be
happening.' I think it took me two weeks to get over the incident."*
—Ed, 36, father of two

The preteen years have a way of sneaking up on you and
catching you unaware. One moment, you're raising a
nine-year-old who barely even notices members of the
opposite sex and who considers soap the enemy; the next, you're
being asked to chauffeur that same child to video dances and to
ensure that the family bathroom is amply stocked with hair gel.

It's enough to make you want to demand ID to verify that this kid is actually the same person. ("You look familiar, but there's something different about your hair. Oh, yeah: it's clean!")

Of course, adjusting to the fact your child is suddenly fighting you for the shower rather than fighting the mere idea of *having* a shower is the *easy* part of parenting a preteen. The tough part is dealing with the yo-yo-like mood swings that are so characteristic of the preteen years and figuring out how to relate to your preteen as he embarks on that precarious tightrope walk from childhood to adulthood. Add to that the fact that the preteen years are increasingly becoming a time of experimentation with sex and drugs (kids today don't always save that stuff for the teen years anymore, Moms and Dads), and you can see why these years can be tough on kids (and, some would argue, even tougher on parents!).

This chapter is designed to arm you with the facts you need to survive your tour of duty in the preteen trenches. I talk about what puberty is like for boys and for girls; I offer tips on talking to your kids about the really big issues; I suggest some strategies for dealing with the small (clothes and hairdos) and not-quite-so-small (piercings!) stuff; and I discuss what you can do to increase the odds that your child will come through the preteen and teen years relatively unscathed. Then I wrap up the chapter (and the book) by talking about how having a child enriches your life in ways you couldn't have even imagined when the pregnancy test came back positive a gazillion years ago.

Puberty: What It Feels Like for a Girl (and a Boy)

Can't quite remember what you learned about puberty back in your sixth-grade health class? Here's a quick refresher course on the physical changes associated with puberty.

What puberty is like for girls

Puberty occurs earlier in girls than it does in boys.

The first sign of puberty in girls—breast budding—typically occurs around age 10. There can be wide variation in terms of the timing, however, so don't be alarmed if your daughter is an early or late bloomer: some girls experience breast budding as early as 8 or as late as 13.

Around the same time that this initial breast development occurs, your daughter is likely to start developing pubic hair, and she may develop a body odor. Approximately one year after the breast budding begins, girls go through a growth spurt in which they gain weight and shoot up in height. Then, about two years after the initial breast budding, most girls get their periods.

MOTHER WISDOM

Some young girls who detect some initial budding on one breast but not the other worry needlessly that there is something wrong with them (for example, they think may have developed breast cancer), so it's important to let your daughter know up front that breasts don't always develop completely in synch; and that, if this occurs, over time, the other breast will catch up.

Most girls' concerns about puberty relate to that milestone event—the first menstrual period. It's important for a young girl to understand what to expect prior to and during her early menstrual periods. She may experience an increased vaginal discharge (physiologic leukorrhea) during the months leading up to her first period, and her periods may be irregular at first as her body adapts to the dramatic physiological changes of puberty. She also needs to know how to practice proper hygiene (she needs to change her pad or her tampon several times a day, and she should not wear a tampon overnight) and what to do if her cramps become severe (she may want to exercise or take some sort of medication to help ease her discomfort). Note: It's important to let your daughter know that it's perfectly safe to engage in her normal activities during her period. There's still a surprising amount of misinformation about menstruation making the rounds.

What puberty is like for boys

Puberty typically occurs in boys at around age 11, but it can happen at any time between ages 9 and 14 years. The first sign that a boy is entering puberty is an enlargement of the testes and a thinning and reddening of the scrotum. Boys typically experience a growth spurt around two years after entering puberty.

MOM'S THE WORD

"The biggest challenge in dealing with preteens is the moodiness. It is unbelievable. My 12-year-old will be happy one moment and ticked off the next. She'll be talking on the phone to her friend in the most joyous, bubbly voice ever; then I'll try to talk to her when she gets off the phone and she'll whine at me like a baby, or snap at me like a bear. Until you get there, you can't imagine what it's going to be like. I keep warning some of my friends who have daughters two years younger than mine. They talk about *their* daughters being hormonal. I tell them, 'Just wait!'"

—Christine, 39, mother of four

Boys' puberty-related worries typically center around voice changes, wet dreams, involuntary erections, breast enlargement, and having uneven testicles. Your son will be reassured to find out that the voice changes that he's experiencing are temporary (they're caused by his growing vocal cords); his wet dreams are caused by ejaculation, not urination, and that these nocturnal emissions are not a sign that he's had a sexual dream (something he may find too embarrassing for words); his involuntary erections are perfectly normal, not in any way linked to sexual thoughts, and a limited time phenomenon, to boot! (He won't have to deal with this embarrassing problem for the rest of his life, even though it may feel that way!) The breast enlargement or tenderness he may be experiencing should disappear after a couple of months; and that it's not at all unusual for boys and men to have uneven testicles.

The Big Talk(s)

Keeping the lines of communication open is one of the major challenges you'll face as your child heads into the preteen years. If you ask too many questions, your child will clam up entirely; but if you don't show an interest in his life by asking the occasional question, he may not volunteer any information at all. It can be quite the balancing act. But over time, you'll start to figure out when your preteen is most willing to talk and to make a point of being available at those times. Of course, you'll want to take advantage of those opportunities to initiate discussions on such all-important topics as smoking, alcohol, drugs, and sexuality.

Getting a dialogue going about smoking, alcohol, and drugs

Although it may feel strange to be talking to a 9- or 10-year-old about the importance of steering clear of cigarettes, drugs, and alcohol, you can't start the dialog on these particular issues too soon. Consider the facts for yourself:

- According to a 2003 study by researchers at the University of Michigan, 10 percent of eighth graders and 17 percent of tenth graders have smoked at least once in the previous 30 days; and 5 percent of eighth graders and 9 percent of tenth-graders smoke on a daily basis.

- According to the Centers for Disease Control and Prevention, 24.2 percent of female students and 34.2 percent of male students surveyed in 2001 admitted to having consumed their first alcoholic beverage before age 13.

- According to the U.S. Department of Health and Human Services, in 2002, 11.6 percent of 12- to 17-year-olds admitted to being current users of illicit drugs, and 20.6 percent admitted to having used illicit drugs on at least one occasion.

If you suspect that your child is smoking, drinking, or using drugs, you'll want to have a frank discussion with him about your suspicions. Although you may be tempted to hit the roof or to launch into a lengthy lecture on the potential health costs and other long-term consequences of these particular activities, neither reaction is particularly effective with preteens. Your best bet is to try to find out what's motivating the behavior and how often it's occurring (that is, was it a one-time experiment, or is your child smoking pot on a regular basis?), and then to use this opportunity to communicate your thoughts and feelings about smoking, alcohol, and drug use—what you consider to be right and wrong, healthy and unhealthy, safe and unsafe.

If the problem recurs or it appears that your child has been smoking, drinking, or using marijuana for some time, you will want to talk to your family doctor or some other health or mental health professional about the situation. Not only are these habits worrisome in and of themselves, but also children who engage in these types of activities at an early age are at risk of becoming involved in other risky behaviors, such as early sexual activity, dropping out of school, and getting into trouble with the law. Of course, that's not to say that every child who gets caught lighting up a cigarette behind the local elementary school is necessarily destined to make an express trip to juvenile detention. It's simply worthwhile paying attention to this particular behavioral red flag and to see whether your child would benefit from any additional treatment or support before he heads into the potentially stormier teen years.

MOM'S THE WORD

"Make sure your preteens have a haven—a safe place where they can go to get away from it all: maybe to their room, the basement recreation room, a youth center, a friend's house. And make sure they have an outlet for their feelings—someone to talk to, a journal in which to write, a band where they can write and play music, sports activities—something to channel those emotions in positive rather than negative pursuits."

—*Jennifer, 35, mother of two*

Talking to your kids about sex

While you're in "big talk mode," you'll also want to make sure that your preteen has the facts on sex. According to the Centers for Disease Control and Prevention, almost half of teens will have had sex at least once by the time they finish high school, and approximately one in seven high school students will have had four or more sex partners. So, clearly this is one conversation you can't afford to postpone for too long.

Because the sexuality of preteens has not been studied in any great detail, there are far more questions than answers about the sexual habits of preteens. However, a lot of anecdotal evidence backed up by reports from adolescent health professionals indicates that there's been a major shift in attitude in so far as oral sex is concerned. Although previous generations may have considered oral sex to be an act that is as intimate or perhaps even more intimate than vaginal intercourse, preteens and teens today don't necessarily categorize oral sex as sexual behavior; in fact, some news stories have indicated that preteens are engaging in oral sex as a means of postponing intercourse (something that they may view as a more risky activity, due to the risk of pregnancy). Unfortunately, these preteens and teens tend to lose sight of the fact that sexually transmitted diseases can be transmitted via oral sex—a very dangerous blind spot in their sexual decision-making.

Clearly we parents owe it to our kids to have "the big talk" about sex and sexuality at an early age. In fact, most sexuality experts say that we should start the dialogue back at the toddler and preschool stage by answering children's questions about bodies and sexuality in a matter-of-fact way. Here are the key points to keep in mind if you're unsure about how to get the conversation started or what types of sex-related issues you should be discussing with your preteen:

 NO KIDDING!

Teens tend to ignore the risks posed by sexually transmitted diseases. A study conducted by the Centers for Disease Control and Prevention found that 42 percent of sexually active high school students did not use a condom the last time they had sexual intercourse.

- **Be up front about your own feelings.** Don't be afraid to let your child know that you feel a bit awkward having this discussion if, in fact, you do. (Hey, not every parent breaks into a cold sweat at the thought of explaining sexual intercourse to a nine-year-old!) If you're feeling awkward, your child may be feeling awkward, too. You may want to point out that people weren't quite as frank and open about sexual matters in generations past as they are today. In fact, you may find it's a good icebreaker to let your kids know how you learned about sex (or didn't learn about sex!) from your own parents.

- **Start out with the basics.** Make sure that your preteen has a solid grasp of the physical and emotional changes that he can expect to experience as he passes through puberty, as well as a handle on the fundamentals of reproductive biology—the infamous "plumbing lessons" from generations past. (There's nothing wrong with the plumbing lessons, of course. The problem is that the discussion about sex circa

1970 generally consisted of little more than a crash course on the reproductive functions of the penis and the vagina!)

MOM'S THE WORD

"My mother dealt with sex education by handing me a set of four books called *The Life Cycle Library* when I was 10 years old, telling me to read them, and to come to her if I had any questions. I had one question, which she answered, and we never discussed it again. Ever. I think she was proud of herself for handling it so well. She later gave those books to a neighbor and asked me a couple of years ago if I'd like her to get them back so that I can give them to my kids. No thanks. Not only are the books 30-plus years out of date, I remember them as being very dry and sanitized and loaded with a sort-of prude Western morality. It's a wonder I wasn't scarred for life after reading them!"

—*Anita, 40, mother of four*

- **Move on to the more complex issues.** Don't stop talking once you've covered the basic mechanics of sex and reproduction. Your job isn't finished quite yet. You'll also want to touch upon such related issues as:

  - *gender identity* (the average gay teen comes out at age 13 or 14, so you'll want to make sure that your preteen understands that some people are attracted to members of the same sex, just in case he's struggling with gender identity issues himself or has a friend who is trying to sort out his or her sexual orientation)

  - *masturbation* (the fact that it's healthy and normal, but something that should be done in private)

  - *dating and relationships* (including date rape, dating violence, and the importance of both being clear about your own sexual boundaries and respecting the other person's boundaries)

- *sexually transmitted diseases* (how such diseases are transmitted and what you can do to reduce the risk)

- *pregnancy* (how pregnancy occurs and why those schoolyard myths about it not being possible to get pregnant the first time you have sex, if you have sex while you're standing up, if you douche right after having sex, and so on are just that—*myths!*)

- **Round out the conversation by talking about the non-physical aspects of sex.** You want your child to understand that sex is much more than a physical experience (or at least it should be). He'll find it easier to hold out for "the right person" and "the right time" if he has a sense that losing his virginity should be something special, not something done on a whim or because everyone else is "doing it."

- **Don't be afraid to "fess up" if you don't know the answer to one of your child's sex questions.** No one's expecting you to be a walking, talking sex encyclopedia. (In fact, your child may be secretly relieved if you're not! I mean there are some things you would rather your Mom and Dad not know too much about, right?) If your child asks you something you don't know the answer to, promise him you'll do some research and get back to him. Then make a point of following up. Nothing slams the door on communication faster than unanswered questions and dropped conversational threads.

- **Remind yourself that Rome wasn't built in a day.** It's unlikely that you're going to be able to cover every sex-related topic in a single sitting (nor would you want to: this is heavy duty stuff for you and your kid!), so you'll want to make sure your preteen knows that this is just the start of a dialogue that you expect to continue for many years to come, and that he's welcome to come and ask you questions about any sex-related matter and to talk to you about his

worries or concerns anytime. Hint: You may want to reini-
tiate conversations about sex from time to time when the
opportunity presents itself naturally, for example, if you're
watching a movie with your preteen and the story raises a
key issue related to sex. If you wait for your child to initiate discussions about sex on his own, those discussions may
never happen.

• **Accept the fact that your child is the one who is going to
be making the key decisions in so far as his own sexuality is concerned.** You're not going to be there peering over
the backseat of the family minivan the first time things start
getting hot and heavy between him and his date, so there's
no point "forbidding" him to have sex until he's 18—or
35!—no matter how much you would like to. The situation
is out of your hands. What you *can* do is educate him on the
downside to becoming sexually active too soon (a message
that sometimes gets lost in our sex-crazed culture!) and help
him to develop strategies for postponing sex for as long as
possible—for example, talking with his partner about his
desire to go slow on the sexual front and/or avoiding situations where it would be easy for him to have sex.

MOM'S THE WORD

"My oldest daughter got pregnant at the age of 16. Does this make
me a failure? I thought so for a while, but, no, it doesn't. I would have been a
failure as a parent if I had given up on her, but I didn't. We weathered the
storm, worked through it, prayed through it, talked through it, and survived."

—*Lillian, 39, mother of three and grandmother of four*

• **Get the message out that no topic's off limits.** Make sure
that your preteen knows that he can come to you if he finds
himself dealing with some sort of sexual health problem
down the road—perhaps a partner's unplanned pregnancy

or some sort of sexually transmitted disease. You don't want your child to feel that he has to turn to total strangers for information and support in times of crisis; you want him to know that he can come to you no matter what.

The Smaller Stuff

If you're breaking out in a cold sweat at this point and assuming that every conversation you ever have with your preteen is going to focus on some major life-and-death issue, relax: I've got good news for you. The bulk of your conversations are going to be much more mundane—things like what types of fashions meet the family dress code, how late a curfew you're prepared to give your kid, and how you feel about extreme hairdos and even more extreme hair colors.

It generally works best to decide early on which issues you're willing to take a firm stand on (certain types of piercings, for example) and which issues you're willing to be much more laid back about (your preteen's desire to use spray-in hair color before he heads off to a video dance). You'll probably find that you handle certain issues differently, depending on the circumstances; the preteen dress code that you can live with 364 days of the year may not work on the 365th day when your child's aging (and ultra-conservative) great-grandmother is in town!

MOM'S THE WORD

"Boundaries should be flexible enough to accommodate modern tastes, but firm enough to ensure that family and personal values are not compromised. I realize low jeans and high shirts are in style right now, but that does not make them appropriate for an eight-year-old, nor are these the only styles in town. There are other fashions that are not as revealing, but equally stylish."

—Jennifer, 35, mother of two

Most parents find that it works well to take a relatively *laissez-faire* approach to clothing choices because many preteens choose to express their individuality through what they wear. Unless the outfit in question is morally outrageous or likely to result in a severe case of frostbite, it's best to simply ignore the bizarre outfit that your child has assembled in the name of fashion or, alternatively, to offer your opinion in a frank but low-key manner: "My 10-year-old son and I have an ongoing disagreement about his clothing choices, but I don't allow it to become a battle," explains Mandy, a 27-year-old mother of two. "I simply tell him I really don't think his clothing choices are appropriate, but ultimately he has to be the one to decide what is going to be comfortable to wear and what will make him feel good about himself. And if wearing hiking boots, dress pants, and a Hawaiian shirt at the same time is his thing, I have to respect that, even if I secretly think it looks ridiculous. I don't want my children to ever think that expressing their individuality is not okay. We are all individuals, and there's nothing wrong with that."

Turf Wars

Remember the battles of wills that occasionally erupted between your toddler—how he used to fold his arms across his chest, give you a fierce scowl, and utter a thundering "No"? Well, you're about to experience a reprisal of that parent-child tug of war now that your child is entering the preteen years.

At the root of the problem is the fact that you have to decide how much power to relinquish to your preteen. If you hand over too much power too soon (that is, the amount of power he would like you to relinquish!), your child may end up making foolish—even dangerous—choices. If you try to hold on to the reins of power too tightly or for too long, however, you risk triggering a full-blown rebellion. "You have to love them and care for them and watch over them and definitely have rules—but you also have to ensure that there's a balance so that they don't feel like they are in a cage and have to escape," explains Lillian, a 39-year-old mother of three.

MOTHER WISDOM

As much as your child may complain about having to be home by 10 P.M. when everyone else in his circle of friends is allowed to wander the streets as late as they would like (or so he claims!), he's probably secretly glad that you have some rules. Your rules give him an easy out with his friends if he's ready to come home.

But even if he's not exactly ecstatic to have you cramping his social style, frankly, that's not your problem. I mean, who ever said it was the parent's job to make their kid *like* the rules?

Just don't necessarily assume that you're being too controlling if your preteen complains about your rules. Most preteens would prefer to live in a rule-free universe—even though it would obviously not be in their best interests to do so—simply because they like to be the ones calling the shots. Unluckily for them, that's not how this parenting thing works!

Winning at Teen Roulette

If you have friends with older kids—you know, those brave souls who've already done their time in the teen trenches!—you've no doubt heard your fair share of teen horror stories by now: hair-raising tales of wild parties thrown while the unsuspecting parents were out of town; newly purchased family cars coming back looking like world-weary farm trucks; cheery, sweet-faced pre-pubescents morphing into snarly, mega-pierced adolescents overnight; and worse. Much worse.

You may be wondering what you can do to keep your kid on the straight-and-narrow (or at least the *relatively* straight-and-narrow) as he makes it through the teen years. Although there are no guarantees when it comes to parenting—you can do everything right and still end up with a kid who strays from the beaten path or, worse, deliberately tosses his compass and roadmap away—there are certain things you can do to increase your odds that your child will weather the journey through adolescence, with minimal wear and tear to him or to you.

Here are some strategies that promise to tilt the teen roulette wheel in your favor, however slightly:

- **Be prepared to rewrite the parenting playbook on an on-going basis.** Smart parents understand that the rules of the parenting game change dramatically between middle childhood and the teen years and make a point of adjusting their parenting styles accordingly.

- **Work at finding ways to bridge the generation gap.** Just don't kid yourself: staying truly connected to your kid takes work, and you need to be laying the groundwork for a strong parent-teen connection right now. You'll find it easier to keep the dialogue going as your child heads into the teen years if you hold your chat sessions on neutral turf (say a bagel shop) where no one has a clear psychological advantage. Just make sure you find the time and the place on a regular basis; kids who feel a powerful bond with their parents are less likely to run into difficulty during the teen years.

- **Make sure that your parent radar is fully operational.** Although little kids secretly wonder if parents have eyes on the back of their head, big kids know that parents have an even more powerful tool at their disposal—a highly tuned sixth sense that tells them if something about their child's just not right: the much-feared parent radar! Although you'll want to resist the temptation to engage in a lot of heavy-duty snooping, which can take a toll on the parent-child relationship, there's nothing wrong with being tuned in to what's going on in your child's life—paying attention to whispered telephone conversations or other suspicious behaviors. That's what being a caring and attentive parent is all about.

- **Give top grades to success both in and out of school.** Doing well in school and being involved in extracurricular activities decreases the likelihood that your child will run into trouble during the teen years. So make sure that you do whatever you can to support your child's achievements, both in the classroom and in other areas of his life. You want him to feel like a winner through-and-through. After all, self-esteem can help to inoculate kids against a smorgasbord of risky teen-year behaviors.

- **Help your child spread his wings socially.** If your child is more of a social caterpillar than a social butterfly, you may want to provide him with a little coaching from the sidelines so that he can experience some early successes on the social front. Socially awkward kids tend to take a rockier road through adolescence than other kids. So, encourage your preteen to invite a friend along when you're heading off to the movies or the amusement park as a family; he'll find the role of host much less demanding if there's some sort of activity involved.

- **Become the poster child for resilience yourself.** Sending your child into the teen years without a certain amount of resilience is like sending him off for a canoe ride without a life jacket—something no responsible parent would do. Because kids are more likely to learn the art of resilience if they see this particular skill modeled at home, you'll want to show your child that you can handle whatever curveballs life tosses your way and that you don't need to abuse alcohol and drugs just to get through the day.

- **Make sure you have a solid handle on what adolescence is all about.** You'll find it easier to weather the highs and lows of the teen years if you understand that pulling away from Mom and Dad and becoming your own person is both normal and healthy, and that a bit of rebellion is to be expected. You may even find it helpful to reflect back on your own growing-up years—unless, of course, that's pretty much guaranteed to give you a decade-long case of insomnia!

- **Vow to steer clear of the ultimate parent trap—failing to be the parent.** We all know parents who are so desperate to be their kids' "buddies" that they forget to be their parents. While your child may be getting older and more self-sufficient by the day, he needs you to be his parent. Don't kid yourself into believing otherwise.

The Gift of Parenthood

One of the amazing things about being a parent is that you get to learn and grow right alongside your child. At the same time that you're busy teaching your child about the universe around him, he's busy challenging you to look at that same universe through a new set of eyes: his eyes. "Everything that we take for granted is new and amazing to our children," notes Tammy, a 33-year-old mother of two. "I think they give us the gift of reflection."

 MOM'S THE WORD

"There are a million hidden treasures in life and all it takes is one child to show them to you."

—*Anne, 45, mother of one*

Kerri, a 37-year-old mother of six, agrees: "Having children has taught me to stop and take the time to notice and enjoy the small things like the inchworm that seemed one day to hang from the clouds in the sky and stop right in front of my son's eyes. How amazing it was to watch the inchworm so intently as it used its silk to move about in the air and then land gently on a blade of grass."

Jacqueline, a 35-year-old mother of four, has also learned to take pleasure in the simple things in life, thanks to lessons learned from her children: "My children have taught me about the value of innocence," she explains. "Whatever they do, most of the time it is done so innocently, so purely, and done with love. Like when Hope tapes two pieces of paper together and calls it a butterfly and says, 'Here, Mama, this is for you because I love you.'"

 MOM'S THE WORD

"My children teach me to slow down. They remind me that time does not belong to me or to them, and that when each moment is gone, I have that much less left to enjoy. They make me notice the little things and to enjoy all aspects of life."

—*Mandy, 27, mother of two*

 MOM'S THE WORD

"I took a day off work last week and took Marissa and Jessica to the beach for the day. At one point, I was watching the two of them playing together in the water. They were both wearing swim masks and diving for 'pearls' and other secret treasures. They were having so much fun and the sky was blue, the water was warm, and the sunlight was shimmering on the water. It was one of those moments that made me realize how much I love my two little girls and how much I miss my youth. I don't think I will ever forget that day at the beach."

—*Ed, 36, father of two*

Some parents feel that they have become better people, by virtue of having had children: "I'm more patient and more out-going," says Jennifer, a 35-year-old mother of two. "I'm also calmer, less judgmental, more optimistic, and more enthusiastic about life."

The kind of shift in perspective that can occur when you have children can be nothing short of life-altering, according to Anita, a 40-year-old mother of four. "The greatest gift of parenthood for me is a new and profound appreciation of life. I used to think that if I was terminally ill, I'd want no heroic measures taken to keep me alive; that I'd want to be made comfortable and pain-free so that I could just slip away. Now I think I would not go so gently into that good night. I'd fight it tooth and nail just to spend one more minute—one more second—with my children. I love them beyond measure."

Judy, a 32-year-old mother of two, feels that being a parent has given her a greater understanding of her place in the tapestry that weaves one generation to the next: "Becoming a parent has really taught me the truth about the circle of life," she explains. "When we are young, we think that we are invincible. When I was six months pregnant with Eli, I lost my mother after a lengthy illness. It would have been very easy for me to fall apart, but I still had my children who needed me as much as—or even more than—I needed my mother. I had to continue to take care of myself to keep my unborn baby healthy and to be there for my four-year-old to help him to adjust to life without his beloved Nanny. Through it all, I came to realize that our children look to us the same way I looked to my parents when I was little, and that we are the ones who mold their lives more than anyone else ever will. We are the grown-ups now, and childhood is fleeting."

"Becoming a parent has taught me a lot about what made my own parents tick," adds Christine, a 39-year-old mother of four. "I don't think I would be as understanding of their ways and what frustrated them when I was growing up if it weren't for finding myself in similar 'shoes' with my own children. As a teenager, I thought everything my parents did was wrong. But now that I have children of my own, there are times when I open my mouth and my mother's voice flies out. I am much more forgiving of my parents now. I also know without a doubt that my kids will have many complaints about me as they grow into adults, and that this or that will be my fault, but I know in my heart that some day they will understand why I acted the way I did. It goes full circle."

MOM'S THE WORD

"Becoming a parent allows you to nurture and witness growth that might be so incremental as to be invisible to a casual observer, but that will live in your memory forever."

—*Anne, 45, mother of one*

Index

CPSIA information can be obtained at www.ICGtesting.com
Printed in the USA
LVOW01s1348061213

364218LV00009BA/42/P